Feminism in the Worlds
of Neil Gaiman

Feminism in the Worlds of Neil Gaiman

Essays on the Comics, Poetry and Prose

Edited by TARA PRESCOTT *and* AARON DRUCKER

McFarland & Company, Inc., Publishers
Jefferson, North Carolina, and London

Library of Congress Cataloguing-in-Publication Data

Feminism in the worlds of Neil Gaiman : essays on the comics, poetry and prose / edited by Tara Prescott and Aaron Drucker.
    p.   cm.
Includes bibliographical references and index.

ISBN 978-0-7864-6636-8
softcover : acid free paper ∞

1. Gaiman, Neil — Criticism and interpretation.
2. Feminism in literature.   I. Prescott, Tara 1976–
II. Drucker, Aaron, 1975–
PR6057.A319Z63 2012
823'.914 — dc23   2012035678

British Library cataloguing data are available

Front cover image courtesy of Alvin Booth; background image © 2012 Shutterstock

Manufactured in the United States of America

McFarland & Company, Inc., Publishers
Box 611, Jefferson, North Carolina 28640
www.mcfarlandpub.com

For Gisele and William, still dreaming...

Acknowledgments

I would like to thank Dr. Molly Ierulli, first and foremost. She shepherded my initial essay, which then formed the basis of this collection, while being supremely understanding of my horrific Latin and peculiar readings of classical mythology. Though it may seem to go without saying, Tara Prescott has been a fabulous, insightful, and ridiculously committed partner in this project, and I can't think of anyone with whom I'd rather be working. I also want to thank Farah Mendlesohn, whose omniscience continues to baffle me. (Seriously, how can one person be so right about so much so often?) Conversations with Amanda Palmer and Roz Kaveney provided valuable insight into the project's potential, and I can't help but continue to admire these extraordinary women. I want to thank Ms. Pardee (my high school religion instructor) and Tori Amos, both of whom brought me to Neil Gaiman in their own ways. The latter brought my attention to the fact that one could, in fact, be hangin' out with the Dream King, and the former taught the class I was cutting when I first discovered "Season of Mists" at the local 7–11, which looked like a reasonable equivalent of the religion curriculum and subsequently set the course of my career. I want to thank all of the contributors for their patience and the nonstop hurry-up-and-wait that inevitably occurs during this kind of project. To Robert G. Weiner, yes, I took your suggestion and here it is. Thanks for the encouragement. Alvin Booth, an extraordinarily talented artist and photographer, was very generous in allowing us to use the image on the cover. And lastly, Gisele and William, my wife and son, to whom this work is dedicated.

AJD
Los Angeles

I would never have imagined that I'd meet Neil Gaiman and Amanda Palmer on Halloween night, on a wide stage in front of hundreds of fans, after a raucous introduction by Margaret Cho, dressed head to foot in Puritan costume. As Gaiman approached me, bathed in the reflected red glow of the LEDs embroidered to my chest, my first thought was *This isn't happening.* My second thought was *Well, of course I'm meeting Neil Gaiman while dressed as Hester Prynne. This makes total sense.*

Welcome to the world of Neil Gaiman.

There are many people who helped make this project possible. I would like to thank Aaron Drucker, my partner in crime, for many long discussions about why Gaiman matters to us. I would also like to thank Seth Anderson, doctoral candidate in history at Claremont Graduate University, for offering excellent feedback at any hour of the night. Jennifer Osorio, librarian for English and American literature at UCLA, helped me to track down some of the more slippery Gaiman sources that are no longer available in print or online. I am also grateful to Sadie MacFarlane, who graciously provided PDFs of the *Magian Line* (anagram for "Neil Gaiman") newsletter.

Finally, I would like to thank Bob Borden, owner of Fantasy Books and Games in Livermore, California. I first stumbled into Bob's comic book store when I was a teenager, unsure of what comics to read, but knowing that I wanted more than *Betty and Veronica*. Bob introduced me to it all: *Sandman, Strangers in Paradise, Barry Ween, Watchmen, The Books of Magic, Preacher, Zero Girl, A Child's Life and Other Stories, Blankets, Fun Home*. In an era where bookselling is experiencing unparalleled challenges, I feel fortunate to be able to continue to support Fantasy Books and Games. Thanks for all the great reads, Bob.

TP

Los Angeles

Finally, we all would like to thank Neil Gaiman, for all of the obvious reasons. We hope he receives our thoughts, reflections, and sporadic criticisms in the vein they are meant, with respect and proper deference ... and the hopes of eventually reading that once-mentioned historical fantasy set in restoration London. Truly, we do this out of dedication to and fascination with the material. Thank you for letting us in, if only for a moment. It was a lovely time, and now we're talking about it in our own, peculiar way.

Table of Contents

Preface

There is, to our knowledge, no collection on this topic published before this one, which we still find startling. Neil Gaiman's reputation as a writer of strong, independent female characters is common knowledge in our circles (admittedly of comic book and science fiction/fantasy aficionados). But little academic writing has been done on his work in this area, though there is the occasional essay available here or there. We suspect this is because his work is relatively new. His most famous body of work, DC Comics' *The Sandman* comic book series, wrapped a mere 16 years ago, which is long enough for a generation of comic readers to rediscover it but (like geological time) mere moments in literary history. On the other hand, what Gaiman has brought to female readers of comic books has rarely been paralleled since the unlikely run of the Dream King and was unprecedented in its time.

Previous readings of Gaiman's work were almost entirely limited to his important comic series, but altogether remiss in his other graphic and literary work. This collection seeks to remedy that (or at least begin the process). In constructing the call for contributors, we intentionally cast an unusually wide net: any work the author completed to the date of composition. A still-living author, Mr. Gaiman is inconveniently adding to his corpus, but it's so awfully good that we'll forgive him this literary transgression. In any case, it turns out that as we researched the available topics, his work spread to all corners of the literary world. Simply to list his published work would take a number of pages, and that's without accounting for his extensive online presence and incidental contributions to public commentary (personal, social, and political). From these hundreds of sources, we chose 16 essays covering a variety of Gaiman's work. Of course, we addressed aspects of *The Sandman*, in large part because we knew that this would be the topic most familiar to our interested audience, but we also included his other major comic work, the sorely overlooked *Black Orchid* (and even managed an essay on *1602*). Even as roughly half of the essays chosen address Gaiman's graphic work, we didn't get the opportunity to address his occasional contributions to comics, like *Swamp Thing Annual #5* or *What Ever Happened to the Caped Crusader?* We tried to address the range of his prose, some poetry, and brilliant oddities like

Who Killed Amanda Palmer? And we overlooked some things, too. Most particularly, and much to our regret, his novels are not well represented in this collection. That's for next time.

We wanted to get a broad overview of Gaiman's sensibility, his approach to feminism, the feminine, and (perhaps) the "feminist." We'd like to think we managed to say some interesting things on the topic and offer some occasional insight into the complex negotiations in the discourse of gender studies. There are some obvious complications for the topic, to be sure. The fact that Gaiman is male proffers a clear would-be obstacle for obvious feminist credentials in his work. The list of "feminist" male authors is startlingly short, and there is some dispute about whether Gaiman is, in fact, a "feminist author" at all. While appropriately lauded for a variety of extraordinary female characters and powerful feminist depictions, several of Gaiman's works are written from a decidedly male, occasionally chauvinistic perspective. Several depict sadistic misogynists and willing victims of patriarchy. Many of the works we cover are not kind to women in their representation. Even so, through most of Gaiman's work there remains a surprisingly strong strain of will and agency in the women he creates. Some are categorically reflections of people in his experience (it's hard not to see a bit of Tori Amos in the character and design of Delirium, who was once Delight). Some are Freudian nightmares of his own reflection. And many are inventions of his experience and imagination, blossoming in the occult light of fiction enhanced by a superlative imagination.

In the end, we found a balance in evaluating the author and his work against the ever-shifting criteria of a "feminist" author. Gaiman's goal is not to be proactively feminist. He is a teller of stories, and he remains in the service of the narratives he explores. His language is that of the traditions he inhabits, and this is something we tried to address throughout our analysis. But as he works his way through science fiction, fantasy, horror, comic books, and children's literature, he consistently manages to upset the traditional expectations in ways that are consistently against genre type. Perhaps that is why his ability appears so fluid (how many authors can rightfully say they succeeded in such a range of genres?). More likely, it's just a sensibility, reflected and refracted through the contrasting needs of a decent bloke trying to make a dime telling stories in this queer, troubled modern world. Yes, it seems there's another book in that last sentence, too. We'll see.

Introduction

AARON DRUCKER
and TARA PRESCOTT

This collection of essays opens a door into the worlds of Neil Gaiman, specifically into the ways that he illustrates, narrates, and complicates feminist concerns. The two editors have selected sixteen essays and grouped them roughly by genre. Because of the overwhelming preference of readers to his original (and originary) *Sandman* title for Vertigo Comics, we chose to begin there, followed by examinations of his other comics, screenplays, children's stories, short stories, novels, and assorted difficult-to-categorize creations. Collectively, these essays offer a rich exploration of Gaiman's worlds. But even so, there is so much more to examine. Gaiman's explorations of feminism deserve an ongoing conversation and this collection represents only the beginning, an offering to the elder gods and goddesses of literature.

In her talk for the 2012 Bradshaw women's studies conference, writer Sandra Gilbert, co-author of *Madwoman in the Attic,* describes collaborative writing as a feminist act. "In collaboration, you form a single writer who is different from either writer," Gilbert states. The "sacrificial merging" that Gilbert describes in collaborative writing is a trope that reappears in many of Gaiman's interviews. For example, when Gaiman is asked how much of the co-authored novel *Good Omens* is his, and how much Terry Pratchett's, he refuses to definitively answer. The collaborative nature of comics (and, in truth, fiction generally) is often overlooked in terms of its feminist possibilities, simply because the world of comics has been almost exclusively masculine. However, as more and more female artists, writers, publishers, and readers enter the genre, the face of comics is changing dramatically. And in many ways, Gaiman is at the forefront of this change.

The sixteen essays in this collection take a look at Gaiman's work through the broad lens of feminism. As there are many personal, political, and literary ways to define this term, we kept our parameters purposely open, selecting essays that emphasize female agency in Gaiman's narratives. Rather than con-strain the definition, we encouraged our contributing scholars to define what "feminism" means for them. The results are as varied and inspiring as one might expect, much to our great delight.

The collection begins with an essay by Rachel R. Martin that discusses "feminist" language and the traps of communicating feminist ideas in Anglophone discourse, which was mainly created and mediated by men. In this "phallocentric" discourse, Gaiman's work negotiates a particular sensibility. Martin argues that Gaiman tries to transgress the limitations of language, but with limited success. After establishing how Gaiman resists the limitations and boundaries of language, our contributors next turn to arguably his most important contribution to the genre, and certainly the creative masterpiece that cemented his reputation.

The Sandman ran for seventy-five issues over seven years and had relatively modest origins. The Sandman was originally a character created and published by DC Comics, a noir crime fighter and crusader who fit the mold of several traditional comic book heroes of the early pulp days like The Shadow or The Phantom. He was not particularly popular or successful as a character, yet Gaiman chose him as the focal point of a broad reinvention of the DC Universe, an industry-polarizing and fan-energizing offshoot called Vertigo Comics. Perhaps unintentionally, he would reinvent DC (notably the most prominent adherent to the strict self-censoring rules of the Comics Code Authority). Taking the nebulous notion that DC's characters were more like gods than men (Superman, Aquaman, Wonder Woman, to name a few), Gaiman transformed the cartoonish Sandman into the elegant and enigmatic Lord of the Dreaming, also known as Morpheus or Dream. Rather than a constructed icon of nobility with near infinite ability and little or no dramatic plausibility or a mere anthropomorphized idea of some Jungian subject, Gaiman's Lord of the Dreaming was a literalization of the idea of dreams in all of their flawed, troubled, complex, symbolic, frustrating humanity.

In *The Sandman*, Gaiman re-envisioned a character whose sustainability was marginal in the comic book marketplace and created a new mythology that led to an industry revolution on the heels of such important and groundbreaking work as Frank Miller's *Dark Knight Returns* and Alan Moore's *Watchmen*. He broadened and deepened the narrative and the DC Universe by creating Dream's brothers and sisters, collectively known as The Endless: Death, Delirium (who was once Delight), Despair, Desire, Destiny, and Destruction. The rich narratives of these seven god-like characters continue to captivate new generations of readers and inspire and expand the imaginations of current writers and artists throughout the industry.

In order to appreciate the extent of Gaiman's craft, and to enjoy the essays in this collection, it is helpful to briefly cover the traditions and conventions within which Gaiman writes. A comic book universe frequently relies upon its own internal world-logic and is governed by a set of basic, if intrinsic, rules. Writers who enter "the continuity" of a "house" (like DC) or a "title" (like Superman) are expected to create new narrative threads, but they are limited by the established storylines for their characters, participating in and perpetuating the overarching storyline. Gaiman wrote *The Sandman* within the DC Universe continuity, focusing largely on the "magic" and "supernatural" storylines that run continuously throughout the history of the publishing company.

Most readers will be familiar with the pantheon of the DC Universe, comprised of several iconic (and many relatively unknown) superheroes who live on an Earth comparable to our own, with a few critical differences. In this universe, major fictional cities like Metropolis and Gotham exist alongside familiar surroundings such as Washington, D.C., and Los Angeles, and the inhabitants of these cities are cultural icons of our own landscape: Superman, Wonder Woman, The Flash, Batman, and many others. Still, the world is inhabited by everyday people like ourselves, but also supernatural heroes such as Doctor Fate or extraordinary gifted figures such as John Constantine. *The Sandman* series takes place in a world between the standard DC Universe and an alternate realm of Gaiman's own invention, "The Dreaming," a liminal space where consciousnesses drift when people are asleep, and where dreams literally occur.

Gaiman creates elisions between The Dreaming and the waking world, between fantasy and sleep. In The Dreaming a dream is as real as a waking experience, though often without the physical consequences (thus falling off a cliff in The Dreaming elicits awakening rather than death). Hence, it is possible to inhabit The Dreaming physically (as it does exist), though it is much less common than the normal, temporary visit that we all make while asleep. Morpheus and the other mythological or magical entities in the stories can influence events in both worlds. The internal logic of The Dreaming can be initially difficult for readers, as indeed it is for some of Gaiman's own characters. In The Dreaming, once a thing is conceived in the mind, it literally exists — from a library filled with unwritten books to the Biblical battle between Cain and Abel, two brothers locked in an endless, over-determined battle for impossible supremacy. Gaiman constructs his narratives from this world of the impossible and infinitely possible. We selected several essays that focused on this highly wrought and complex mythology, highlighting several of the issues we felt were both germane and important. Time and length are never on an editor's side, and inevitably we had to limit our selection with full knowledge that there is much more that can be explored within this masterwork of the genre.

Lanette Cadle privileges the character Death, *Sandman's* most popular and enduring female character, and addresses the manifold concepts of a complex and appealing character whose appeal is both feminist and something that is more difficult to define and categorize. Justin Mellette offers an overview of the discordant sister Delirium, examining the limits of feminine agency and influence within the text. Tara Prescott then focuses on a single issue from the series, "Calliope," exploring Gaiman's metacritical dialogue with his audience and his representation of myth, narrative, and sexual violence. Aaron Drucker takes a wider look at the sprawling nature of the series, pondering Gaiman's critique of second wave emblematics. The four *Sandman* essays in this collection explore the issues that attract and problematize the relationship between the author and his audience, between the narrative and the moral, and between the commercial, the philosophical, and even the mythological.

After exploring feminist issues in Gaiman's comic literature, the collection turns to somewhat lesser-known but equally accomplished works. Gaiman's early works about relatively minor DC characters reveal a sea change in how comics can be perceived and the audience they can attract. Gaiman's comic series *Black Orchid* is an early revisioning of another minor character in the DC Universe. In her essay on *Black Orchid,* Sarah Cantrell looks at the importance of Gaiman's transformative interpretation of this little-considered figure. Unlike the overwhelming majority of comics, Gaiman's books attract significant numbers of female readers, making a target and subject for feminist interpretations and critiques. Even his more commercial ventures, like the historically revisionist series *Marvel 1602,* reimagine and renegotiate the histories of long-established characters, breaking with tradition. In this series, Gaiman subverts continuity by presenting an infamous playboy as a gay man and depicting a notorious beauty as an androgynous boy. Renata Dalmaso explicates the impact of these changes, focusing on how, by retelling a tale and resetting the past, Gaiman addresses issues of sexuality and identity that impart complexity to familiar characters, resist expectations, and deny easy answers. Rounding out the discussion of feminism in Gaiman's comics, Coralline Dupuy examines *The Dream Hunters,* delving into the Japanese-inspired fairy tale world which features a mythopoetic Orpheus, an alterative Dream, and a mediated and hybridized text.

As Gaiman moves away from comic books to greater opportunities in prose (and occasionally poetry), his peculiar ability to revise with an errant comment does not fail him. He writes one episode of *Doctor Who* and revises a thirty-year canonical history with a feminine twist and a single word (bettering The Doctor by three). Emily Capettini's essay on Gaiman and the good Doctor looks at the fraught nature of this casual and cataclysmic emendation. Gaiman moves from one medium to another, with equal felicity, imparting messages to little boys and girls, to grown men and women about agency and ability, about transgression and the improbably bizarre world right in front of them. He whispers in his reader's mind of death and life and life in death, of the living (in spite of the odds), and of the pleasant haunting of those never quite gone. Our contributors selected a few examples from his dozens of stories and several novels, focusing on prevalent themes that recur throughout his work. Themes emerged, as they often do, and recurrent motifs are emphasized in several essays. What we thought would be a clear example of Gaiman's feminist tendencies is well explored in Danielle Russell's essay on *Coraline* and *MirrorMask*, which examines the questions raised by Gaiman's interrogation of third wave motherhood. The representation of "mother" and the issue of female agency is natural and recognizable fare for feminist critique, but Gaiman's approach is often at odd angles to the traditional take on either.

Continuing the exploration of motherhood, children's literature, and genre expectations, Elizabeth Law looks at what it really means to have skin as white as snow and lips as red as blood in Gaiman's short story, "Snow, Glass, Apples." The departures from traditional Romance and fairy tale traditions is also the subject of Jennifer McStotts's essay about the short story "Chivalry." Moving away from individual short stories, Monica Miller discusses the collaborative (and rather difficult to locate) *Who Killed Amanda Palmer?*, a coffee table book Gaiman co-created with Amanda Palmer — lead singer of The Dresden Dolls, ukulele aficionado, Gaiman's wife, and all-around cool cat. She observes the multifaceted approaches to the fairy tale in Gaiman's re-visions as he works traditional (and somewhat less traditional) narratives to complement the evocative images of Ms. Palmer. The Princess, it turns out, sometimes lands face down in the gutter, burbling her last breath as treacle that drains into a sewer. In fact, fairy tales don't always happen in a land far, far away or necessarily end happily ever after.

Moving away from the theme of fairy tales, Agata Zarzycka looks at Gaiman's exploration of domesticity in another short story, "Queen of Knives," as well as the depiction of older women and their own types of empowerment in her reading of "Chivalry." The expectations of fairytale witches and the power of older women takes a stranger turn in Gaiman's comic novel, *Good Omens*. Jessica Walker explores what it means to be a witch in this novel (hint: weight relative to a duck is irrelevant) and the influence of the classical notion of female "secret writing" in English literary tradition. Finally, in the last essay of the collection, Kristine Larsen illustrates Gaiman's progression from fairy tale to mythology as she explores the physics of Gaiman's universes, offering a fresh, multidisciplinary approach to understanding his texts.

This collection of essays started with a fairly simple proposition: what is the relationship between Gaiman's work and feminism? All too quickly, one question led to more: is Neil Gaiman a feminist? Is his writing feminist? What does it mean to be a feminist writer or to create a feminist work? The essays in this collection do not offer a definitive answer to these questions because we can only speculate on the nature of Gaiman's own feminist convictions. However, we do have some tentative propositions, relationships that show a clear trail of affective narrative as an author revises one genre and the next, finding ways to reach the marginalized, the questioning, the curious, and those that speak for the ones who can't.

What is left is the next conversation, which must necessarily take place in two parts. First, there is the conversation we begin here: the reactions to and revisions of the claims we make in the essays in this book. We hope they are fruitful. We know reading each essay that we were constantly driven to add a note in our own "to do" library of essays yet to be written. The second is to address the many things we necessarily missed because of space and time constraints. There is certainly a book-length engagement on *The Sandman* series and its dialogues with feminism still awaiting, as there are myriad commentaries on the novels, teleplays, and social media that we are looking forward to reading. There is a long and productive future discussion to be had, both in conversation and in print, and we believe that this is a fine way to get it started. With that in mind, let's begin.

@AaronDrucker
@DrTaraPrescott
#gaimanandfeminism

A Note on Citation

Comic books and graphic novels have the unique privilege of being relatively new to literary scholarship. As scholars integrate this new medium into our scholarly vocabulary, there is some disagreement about how to formalize the citation process. We adopted a slight variation on Allen Ellis's citation guidelines for the Popular Culture Association. He argues, rightly, that comics are a multi-contributor medium, and while we will often discuss one primary aspect of the work (the writer or the illustrator, for example), it is appropriate to list the significant artistic contributors to the work. As such, we have followed his bibliographic citation system:

> Author (w), Illustrator/Artist (a), Inker (i). "Story Arc/Issue Title." *Series* # (month year), Location: Publisher. Media.

Thus, a standard citation for an issue of *The Sandman* looks like this:

> Gaiman, Neil (w), Chris Bachalo (a), Malcolm Jones III (i). "The Doll's House: Part 3." *The Sandman* #12 (Jan. 1990), New York: DC Comics. Print.

And a complete arc, including multiple artists and inkers, is referenced:

> Gaiman, Neil (w), Chris Bachalo, et al. (a), Malcolm Jones III, et al. (i). "The Doll's House." *The Sandman* #10–16. (Nov. 1989–June 1990), New York: DC Comics. Print.

Within a given title, comics are listed first by author, then in chronological order (so Sandman #1 will come before Sandman #19). When the artist and inkers are the same person, we use the notation (a, i). If there are multiple writers, artists, or illustrators in a series, then we list them by frequency (so if Mark Hempel illustrates the majority of a run, his name is first, then additional contributors by sequence).

There is no agreement on in-text citation, so we chose to use an issue:page structure. Subsequently, a quote is followed by (Gaiman 42:10) for *The Sandman*, issue 42, page 10. If the discussion requires panel sequencing, we append a frame number: (Gaiman 42:10 fr. 2). While Ellis adopts a slash (42:10/2) for the frame, we think that this becomes distracting when referencing multiple sequential frames. So, multiple frame reference is noted by (fr. #). Consequently, when we discuss panels in issue 42 on page 10, the notation sequence reads: (Gaiman 42:10 fr. 1) then (fr. 3), (fr. 5), (fr. 6). Names are omitted if the writer is clear, but all in-text citations utilize the issue:page annotation for clarity.

For a more thorough explanation of the bibliographic reference system we are using, please see Allen Ellis's article at: http://www.comicsresearch. org/CAC/cite.html.

Speaking the Cacophony of Angels

Gaiman's Women and the Fracturing of Phallocentric Discourse

Rachel R. Martin

"Becoming a woman really does not seem to be an easy business."
— Luce Irigaray

Comic books and graphic novels are often criticized as being solely a male genre: by men, about men, and for men. Critics attack comics for depicting women as two-dimensional stereotypes, whose limited role in the stories is only to further the masculine narratives. When Neil Gaiman began working with DC Comics on the 1989 series *Black Orchid,* he asked if they thought anyone would buy this story, and their response echoes the idea that comics are the realm of men: "[The main character's] a female character, and nobody buys books about female characters. So, no, we don't think it's going to sell" (qtd. in Wagner, et al. 201). Gaiman challenged this notion and wrote (and continues to write) for and about women. His narrative women resonate with male and female readers alike to considerable achievement. When discussing Gaiman's most popular series, *The Sandman,* Hank Wagner and colleagues in *Prince of Stories: The Many Worlds of Neil Gaiman* write:

> In addition to the typical comic book readership — mostly male — the series developed a passionately loyal female readership. At the time, sales to female readers were a small fraction of the overall business of comic book retailers. Other series had appealed to that small group of female readers prior to *The Sandman,* but Gaiman's flagship series was able to do so without alienating the existing male readership [30].

Gaiman's writing entices and draws in female readers through his inclusion of feminine lead characters. However, Gaiman's inclusion of women as subjects and readers highlights the extent of the masculine discourse at work. Gaiman operates within and utilizes the phallocentric discourse in his creation and depiction of women, even to the extent that he evokes some of his strongest, most popular female characters through the voices of his male characters and through dominant narrative structures, utilizing the dominant discourse to critique and problematize its own assumptive frameworks. Writing about women or writing women into comic narratives does not legitimate the subject of woman[1] within comics or within society completely because these narratives still deploy a phallocentric discourse and construct women via this discourse. As Beaugrand observes in his "Search for Feminist Discourse": "Each solution eventually becomes another part of the problem" (255). The language of Gaiman's narratives strives for a critical self-awareness within a discourse he is unable (and perhaps unwilling) to fully transgress, but in the attempt, he motions towards a fuller understanding of the limits the language we use.

Neil Gaiman writes tales, comics, and novels, which many (including Gaiman himself) consider feminine narratives. For Gaiman, "books have sexes; or to be more precise, books have genders. They do in my head, anyway. Or at least, the ones I write do" ("All Books Have Genders") and many critics agree with Sarah Jaffe's observation that "Gaiman is far better at writing women and getting into their heads than most other male writers, comic or otherwise" (para. 5). He crafts tales about characters other than men, stories with fully developed female protagonists, and narratives showing those not fitting into a simplified gender binary. He depicts girls conquering worlds and saving adults (*Coraline, Mirror Mask,* and *The Wolves in the Walls*), women acting as superheros or antiheros (*Black Orchid,* Death, and Lyta Hall in *Sandman*), and beings who occupy spaces as both/neither man and/or women (Desire, Delirium, and the angels in "Changes"). The women in much of Gaiman's work draw readers in as recognizable and identifiable, but why are they read as such? What is it about Gaiman's writing and the women he creates that speak to his readers?

Drawing from the theories of feminist scholar Luce Irigaray and French philosopher Jacques Derrida, language and discourse are not an "essentially neutral conceptual apparatus" but a "violent hierarchy in which one of the two terms governs the other" (Beaugrande 256–7). In the case of Gaiman's writing, as feminist readers of Gaiman's works, we clearly see men assigning, creating, and governing the identity of woman, and whether or not the writer or speaker appears to be cognizant of the hierarchical discourse does not matter, as he is bound to it and by it:

Thought, reality, the self or subject ... [are] determined by, if not created by, language.... We cannot deny that language influences our vision of the world at large and that its problematics spill over into many areas of human situation. Language subjects the world to a barely resistible power to posit, designate, signify and organize [Beaugrande 257].

Whether aware of his placement within phallocentric discourse, Gaiman's words and narrative structures demonstrate the masculine/feminine binary at work therein. His depictions exemplify for us the ways women are always "already dominated by an intent, a meaning, a thought; by the laws of a language" (Irigaray *Speculum* 230).

The Doll's House (1995), Neil Gaiman's second arc in his ground-breaking *Sandman* series, begins with an origin narrative of an unnamed indigenous people. The speaker, an elder of the tribe, frames the story by acknowledging that *this* story, like all the stories he knows and has heard, is man's version, not one of the "tales the women tell, in the private tongue men-children are never taught and older men are too wise to learn" (9:1). Gaiman here recognizes the differences in languages and stories spoken by men and spoken by women: even the best male storytellers, telling stories about women in the most effective ways, utilize a masculine language. In this (albeit brief) section, Gaiman appears to echo Luce Irigaray's notion of the absence of a language to describe women due to the fact that we abide within phallocentric discourse. The elder continues in the tradition of man to tell his grandson the story of their tribe's origin in his masculine language. Through the weaving of his narrative, the elder creates the first queen of their tribe. Each of the tribe's generations repeat this story and recreate this queen in the masculine, phallocentric discourse, whereby "women are trapped in a system of meaning" (Irigaray *This Sex Is Not One* 122f). Society never hears woman's voice, her language, her discourse. Woman never enters the story that creates and defines her. She is always created within the elder's (read: father's) words, through his tongue. Gaiman, through this elder in *The Doll's House*, recognizes that "woman's language might articulate experiences that are devalued or not permitted by the dominant discourse," according to Carolyn Burke (290). Using Gaiman's naming of women's "private tongue" and Irigaray's call for a deconstruction of phallocentric discourse, even some of Gaiman's most lauded feminine characters (Black Orchid, Death, Helena Campbell, and Coraline), his lesser known ones (Lyta Hall and Lucy), as well as his androgynous characters (Desire and the angels), when critically examined, show how their identities, their personal and familial narratives, and our understanding thereof continues to come solely from the masculine representation of woman.

As part of Gaiman's acclaimed *Sandman* series, *The Doll's House* volume draws upon the idea that the mortals are the playthings or the dolls of the Immortals (specifically The Endless). Through this theme and the volume's title, Gaiman directly draws from Henrik Ibsen's *A Doll's House,* in which the main character realizes that she and her entire life are lived as a doll in a doll house, performing perfectly for first her father and then her husband, where "femininity is a role, an image, a value imposed upon [her] by male systems of representation" (Irigaray *Sex* 84). In Part Three, "Playing House," Lyta Hall perfectly embodies this image of femininity: "she has all the dresses she can wear, and a husband who has very important job.... In her dream house, in her pretty dresses, Lyta doesn't think about anything much any more" (12:1). The rouge Immortals, Brute and Glob, trap Lyta and her husband Hector in a pocket realm of The Dreaming, limiting her to the isolated and static role of domestic housewife. As she sits and examines her own image, brushing her long hair in a mirror, her thoughts drift over her own existence, questioning:

> Is this what she wants? Is this what she wants? She always wanted to be with Hector ... but she must have wanted more than that. Mustn't she? But Hector's dreams came first. They always did.... Why did she do that? Become a cheap copy of her vanished mother? ... And, after the wedding, she came to live in this house. And she was very happy. They were all so very, very happy [12:9].

Lyta's life is frozen in the Dream Dome with her husband, very literally, "frozen in a showcase": like many women, she has been "misinterpreted, forgotten, variously frozen in show-cases, rolled up in metaphors, buried beneath carefully stylized figures, raised up in different idealities" (Irigaray *Speculum* 144). Having sealed both Lyta and her husband's soul in their alternate dream world, Brute and Glob play with Lyta like a doll in a dream house. Lyta's value and role is imposed upon her by her husband, her life is held secure by Brute and Glob, and she has no other narrative options.

Upon entering the Dream Dome, Lyta is six months pregnant. Her pregnant body mirrors the societal stereotypical representation of femininity, and because she exists in the Dream Dome outside of time, she is perpetually with child. Lyta thus in her frozen prenatal state embodies the patriarchal notion that "better than *a* mother, then is the working out of the *idea of the mother*, or the *maternal ideal*. Better to transform the real 'natural' mother into an ideal of the maternal function which no on can ever take away from you" (Irigaray *Speculum* 81). Lyta represents the patriarchal fantasy of the mother "as a volume ... as 'the support of (re)production.' ... But man needs to represent her as a closed volume, a container; his desire is to immobilize her, keep her under his control, in his possession, even in his house. He needs to believe that the container belongs to him" (Whitford 28). By keeping Lyta frozen in time, Brute and Glob keep her as an image or ideal of motherhood without ever allowing her to actually become the mother: for as long as she is in the Dream Dome, she will remain six months pregnant. These immortals keep Lyta as a "closed volume," completely immobilized in their frozen showcase of "her" home. Lyta looks the part of (re)production without the means to ever actual (re)produce. She remains cut off from every means of production and (re)production as the plaything of the Immortals.

Despite the vague recollection that she at one time wanted something more, Lyta cannot remember exactly what that was and can barely hold on to much of a thought of her own. She briefly recollects at one point wanting to be a superhero like Hector,[2] but she reminds the reader that Hector's dreams came first, so now she exists solely in the role as pregnant housewife, the ultimate dominant fantasy of motherhood, completely cut off from any other identity, unable to access even her own body through birthing a child. Through his depictions in *The Doll's House*, Gaiman offers the reader an image of woman existing as the plaything of men while being defined and created by men despite woman's efforts to be otherwise. It exists as an explicit critique of the male hegemony, but Gaiman offers little hope of a newly integrated normative language.

The construction of woman in masculine language and voice repeats in Gaiman's 1989 comic *Black Orchid*, in which we see an identity-less protagonist searching to find who or what she is. In the opening scene of *Black Orchid*, the superhero and comic's namesake is captured and immediately killed. In the comic book realm and the superhero story arc, the bad guy wins in the first few pages, a hazard of Black Orchid's *modus operandi*: "infiltrating and working for criminal organizations in human guise and, once inside, taking them out as Black Orchid, [who] is capable of flight, feats of superhuman strength, apparent invulnerability to bullets, and more" (Wagner et al. 196–7). But this death is not the end of Black Orchid: she is reborn. "Sylvian [develops] a plant human hybrid capable of surviving the planetary environmental apocalypse he considered inevitable in his creation of the Black Orchid" (Wagner et al. 200). The birth of this Susan actually constitutes her second rebirth. Originally, Susan Linden, a childhood friend of Phillip Sylvian, dies at the hand of her gangster ex-husband, Carl Thorne. However, Dr. Sylvian takes Susan's DNA and uses it to create a hybrid human life out of an orchid, birthing a second, fully grown and developed Susan with all of original Susan's memories and the addition of superhuman strength and power. This second Susan becomes the superhero Black Orchid, who dies in opening sequence of Gaiman's comic. The third iteration of Susan awakens upon the death of Black Orchid. Second Black Orchid's rebirth arrives prematurely, so she lacks the completed memories of the original and second Susan. This third Susan, the central character of Gaiman's narrative, bears the physical resemblance to Susan, but lacks any semblance of cohesive identity.[3] This woman does not know who she is and the narrative consists of her identity quest. Throughout this quest, she learns of her former selves, being defined thereby and answering her continual question, "Who or what am I?"

Many of the other characters in *Black Orchid* work as the voices through which Gaiman defines and shapes the constructed identity of this latest Susan. She begins her quest for the meaning of self in the place of her rebirth by asking Dr. Sylvian very plainly, "Who am I?" (1:25). Sylvian "begins to explain the riddle of her origins and being, and mentions his former classmates [Alec Holland and Pamela Isley, both superpowered individuals in the DC Universe]" (Wagner et al. 200). After listening to his story of her previous incarnation, Susan asks to call Sylvian "father," and he agrees because he attributes himself as her creator.[4] He is literally the scientist who "grew" her body and, perhaps prematurely, figuratively through his identity delimiting conversations. Through their conversations, Black Orchid tries furtively to formulate an understanding of who he says she is. She is a stranger to her own identity construction process: she neither understands nor has access to tools to aid in her own identity creation. In one sense, her identity already exists before her: the man merely needs to tell her what it is. She is literally defined by the father and his language: "The woman neither is able to give herself some meaning by speech nor means to be able to speak in such a way that she is assigned some concept" (Irigaray *Speculum* 229). Black Orchid remains a blank slate upon which the masculine characters pencil in the details of her being.

Another voice the reader and third Susan hear answering her identity inquiries is that of original Susan's father who appears to her in a dream: "He just sits me down. And he talks to me. He explains everything. Who I am. Where I'm going. The whole thing. The meaning of it all" (2:3). Even in her dreams, Susan's self-awareness pieces together through a masculine voice. Susan's own thoughts "are monopolized by men" due partly to the fact that "all thought, all language ... all discourse is masculine" (Irigaray *Sex* 121). Transgressing the masculine discourse and identity creation appears beyond woman's reach. Gaiman highlights this process, forcing Black Orchid to define herself for or against a type and identity defined and controlled by men who pre-exist her awareness, and yet she continues to resist their definitions as complete and fails to maintain her complicity in the structure of their narratives.

In her identity quest, Black Orchid must then seek others to tell her who she is, including Sylvian's former classmates: Poison Ivy and Swamp Thing.[5] Black Orchid speaks with Pamela Isley, also known as Poison Ivy, in Arkam Insane Asylum. Black Orchid questions Poison Ivy: "I came to you because I need answers. What am I? Who am I? Are there more like me? ... Do you really know what I am? Will you help me?" (2:39). But Isley provides no help. Her sentences and words make no sense to Black Orchid. Although readers are familiar with Ivy's character from the DC Universe, to Black Orchid, Ivy's words are fragmented and appear as ramblings disconnected with her uninitiated reality. Ultimately Poison Ivy kicks Black Orchid out of her cell, leaving her to continue her search elsewhere. The only woman that Black Orchid speaks with does not help her and appears to refuse aid in her identity search. The information that the readers garner from Poison Ivy bypasses Black Orchid: Black Orchid is unable to access the information Ivy is trying to convey. The failure of communication is due to Black Orchid's inability to access the language: "woman does not have access to language except through recourse to 'masculine' systems of representation which disappropriate her from her relation to herself and to *other women*" (my italics added for emphasis — Irigaray *Sex* 85). Ivy's discourse appears chaotic and irrational to Black Orchid precisely because it exists liminally, on the margins of comprehension because it perpetually attempts to deconstruct the frameworks of the dominant masculine language, and interpreting it requires both a comprehensive understanding of that discourse and the project to which it is subjected. Of itself, the phallocentric discourse disallows true dialogue between women: one woman cannot help another woman because the discourse or language necessary to construct their own identities remains not only inaccessible to them but as yet undeveloped in any extant discourse. Black Orchid's identity resides within the voices of men because she is trapped within the language limits of the question itself. She can ask only "Who am I?" within the phallocentric discourse because the reconstructed framework of a genuinely feminine language exists only in its most rudimentary form: the discoordinated rambling of a feminist icon whose existence has been relegated to the basement of a madhouse.

   Shut out from viable alternatives, Susan seeks out the remaining voice to aid her quest, Alec Holland, otherwise known as the Swamp Thing. Out of options, he is "the only one who could help" (3:3). In the form of Swamp Thing, Holland helps Black Orchid. She calls him a "god" as he delineates the story of her creation and assigns her one complete origin narrative. Swamp Thing weaves a story for Black Orchid, completing the cycle in which every aspect of her creation and identity is "assigned meaning through auto-representation of the male" (Irigaray *Speculum* 233). This final masculine voice fills in the missing pieces of third Susan's identity by inscribing her identity upon/within her. Then, he "completes" her in yet another way by which patriarchy defines woman: he impregnates her (3:9). Seemingly out of nowhere, Swamp Thing knows exactly what Black Orchid "really wants" and he gives her babies in the form of seeds to sow. Nowhere in the text prior to this moment does Black Orchid mention wanting babies, though Dr. Sylvian foreshadows this problematic resolution by defining the original project as a kind of ecological restitution project; she only mentions needing to discover her

true identity. Peculiarly, sexuality never enters the narrative. In this phallocentric discourse, the female libido or sexuality never explicitly enters the
conversation. It simply never occurs to the men involved that this is an issue
of sexuality, though Holland's wife, Abigail, recognizes this fault as Black
Orchid departs.

> "Alec?" Abby intrudes at the bottom of the page. "**Who** was **that**?"
>
> "She was ... **is** ... an old friend ... of an old friend. I was ... giving her ... **babies**,"
> he states in paused, broken response.
>
> She looks at him: "Uh. **Right**. Y'know, Alex. I, uh, I **think** we're going to have
> a **talk** about this" [3:9 fr. 6–8].

Clearly Alec's wife understands the implications and potential violations of
his act, and though she is understanding (given the context of her husband's
existence) she implies that certain boundaries are not his to transgress. Gaiman
intentionally abides within the phallocentric discourse by creating a female
hero who needs to reproduce as a part of her identity quest without ever mentioning her sexuality and makes apparent the dissociative break that discourse
creates. The phallocentric language disallows for feminine sexuality and merely
represents reproduction of the male within the female form. Ultimately, Black
Orchid, like all women according to Irigaray, "must inscribe herself in the
masculine, phallic way of relating to origin that involves repetition, representation, *reproduction*" (my italics added for emphasis—*Speculum* 78). The act
of mothering will re-subjugate woman within hegemonic norms and "again
she will be inscribed or will inscribe herself in this way, in an in-finite
genealogical process/trial, an open count of the discount of origin ... *with no
closure of the circle or the spiral of identity*" (Irigaray *Speculum* 76). Thus Gaiman
weaves Black Orchid's identity through the phallocentric, hegemonic, dominate voice, placing her in a predetermined role that according to patriarchy
satisfies her deepest desire (desires defined and assigned by patriarchy). As
Christine Holmlund points out, for Irigaray, "time and time again, ... phallocentric discourse equates female identity with motherhood.... Because phallocentric discourse emphasizes motherhood and reproduction, the mother is
deprived of her identity as a woman" (Holmlund 290). As the Swamp Thing
provides Black Orchid with the details of "who she is," he assigns her the role
of motherhood, depriving and limiting her identity as anything else.

Through the act of reproduction, Black Orchid's identity forms and
solidifies. Thereby, through (re)production, Black Orchid becomes her own
origin, or at least "the place where origin is repeated, re-produced and reproduced" (Irigaray *Speculum* 41). By bringing forth a child, woman becomes the
place of origin where (re)production and (re)iteration take place. For her identity to be counted, it must be repeated: repetition must take place for a sign
to be a sign, for identity to be formed. Black Orchid, like all the Susans before

her, must reproduce or be reproduced for her identity to be validated. For Black Orchid to truly be Black Orchid she must "divide her own identity *a priori*" (Derrida *Limited Inc* 53). Likewise, for Black Orchid to become the sign, she "*must be able* to function in the absence of the sender," and she shows she can function without her creator after Sylvian's death, because "this possibility is always inscribed" (Derrida *Limited Inc* 54), and the trace of her discourse, now lost, is nonetheless iterated in her being. Because she is always already Black Orchid, the possibility of her functioning without her creator and reproducing or reiterating her identity always already exist. In spite of the differences between herself and original Susan or other Black Orchids, all of these women add up to one sign, one identity: Black Orchid. Their differences constitute simply "the ever-changing 'life' of signs" (Halion 3). Hence, "a woman becoming a mother will be *the Mother*" (Irigaray *Speculum* 76). The identity of the sign, thereby the identity of Black Orchid, depends on two things: the similarities to the sign, despite the differences, and the repetition, (re)production, or iteration of the sign.

In *Black Orchid*, Gaiman creates for his readers, men and women alike, a feminine hero who observes the terms of her own narrative, but whose story and identity comes from the mouths of his male characters and a patriarchal, phallocentric language, which limits and confines her within the constructs of this limited, already existing identity. Despite having super-human powers, Black Orchid remains limited and narrowly defined, repeating this identity through reproduction and fulfills the narrative of the phallocentric discourse, at which point she dismisses it. After delivering and defending her young, she decides to leave her role as mother. Admitting to the knowledge of her past, she says: "I have too many of Susan's memories to be truly happy here ... and it isn't paradise any longer. If it ever was" (3:45). She departs, returning to the world but in her own language: "The flight will be long, and tiring; but I can caress the updrafts of the wind with my form. I am alive in the colors of the leaves, and in the sunset, and in the moist tropical air. I have never been more alive" (3:46). In this comic, as in all phallocentric discourse, no room abides for a language for women to speak, no room for women to create themselves until the framework of the discourses is fulfilled or dismantled, so woman's identity and her deepest desires are assigned to her until she can deconstruct, deny, or erase the structures of language that imprison her potential. Finally, a woman can speak for herself when she transcends the expectations and possibilities defined by her male progenitors, those who would define and limit her to the expectant and identifiable roles of mother and caretaker.

Gaiman repeats this similar sort of masculine narrative in creating other characters beyond those in *Black Orchid* and *The Doll's House*. In *Death: The*

High Cost of Living (1993), Gaiman gives his readers a closer look at the hugely popular character of Death. As Dream's older sister and mentor, the female character of Death first appears in the coda of the first arc of the *Sandman* series in the story "The Sound of Her Wings." In *Death: The High Cost of Living,* the beautifully simple premise is that "once a century Death spends a day as a mortal, simply living life, to better understand the nature of mortality" (Wagner et al. 151). In her single day as mortal this century, Death interacts primarily with a suicidal teenage boy, Sexton Furnival. Like Susan in *Black Orchid*, the reader of *Death: The High Cost of Living* sees and learns more about Death through the thoughts and words of Sexton's narrative.

The structure Gaiman creates around the dialogue comes from Sexton's point of view. His voice very literally narrates Death. He constructs her for the reader: the male voice defines this woman. At the points in the text where Death defines herself, explaining who she is, the male narrator repudiates her claims upon her identity. Even though the reader knows Death to be telling the truth about who she is, Gaiman still shows the way the male voice continually attempts to put woman into a role of his own understanding, defining her by his own terms, those accessible to him through the masculine discourse. When Death, in the form of Didi, reveals her true identity to Sexton, he tells her she is crazy and storms out of the scene. His narrative refutes her claims to self-identify through a discourse of rational logic and cultural types: "First, there's no such person as Death. Second, Death's this tall guy with a bone face, like a skeletal monk.... Third, he doesn't exist either. Fourth, I'd say ... you're nuts.... You're temporarily unhinged" (*Death: HCL* 1:24). From a suicidal boy, the accusation of being unhinged rests on questionable authority, as does the rest of his denial in the face of the reality presented. In the realm of the phallocentric discourse, Sexton reclaims and renames Death, by designating her as something he understands. He disallows her the ability to name herself utilizing the discourse of reason and logic, which does not allow the impossible (in this case, an anthropomorphized representation of Death, who is alive and breathing and standing in front of him. He states that this is an impossible state of being, much like the sentence "I am dead" is impossible to say truthfully in the hegemonic discourse). In this way, woman (here Death) "does not enter a discourse whose systematicity is based on her reduction into sameness" (Irigaray *Sex* 152). Gaiman displays how the phallocentric discourse traps all women, including the character of Death, and for Sexton to hear Death's voice and her truth, he "would have to listen with another ear, as if hearing an 'other meaning' always in the process of weaving itself, of embracing itself with words, but also of getting rid of words in order not to become fixed, congealed in them" (Irigaray *Sex* 29), denying the framework of logic and reason that carefully traps him away from the possibility of the reality before him. Thwarting Death's attempts to enter into the discourse of identity construction, Sexton reduces her to a reproduction of the sameness — the self-representative of a masculine subject. The dominant, masculine, phallocentric discourse of society cannot hear her and therefore disavows her identity, reassigning her a meaning he understands — "nuts."[6]

At the end of this comic miniseries, the male narrator again relates that Death is not truly someone; she is not even a person. Sexton Furnival reveals that "it *would* be really neat if Death *was* somebody, and not just nothing, or pain, or blackness. And it would be really good if Death could be somebody like Didi. Somebody funny, and friendly, and nice, and maybe just a tiny bit crazy" (*Death: HCL* 3:22). For all their experiences together and all his wishing, Sexton still cannot deconstruct the claim that Death is who or what she claims to be because, as part of the male dominated hierarchy, phallocentric language defines what constitutes reality and not the other way around. Sexton decides, although it would be nice if Death was a person, she certainly is not a person, let alone a woman, and her words exist merely the mutterings of madness.

Sexton's discourse has no words and no room for Death: she is beyond his narrative capacity, beyond description in his discourse. Because of his limitations, he cannot process or acknowledge her existence, much less recognize her true identity, and so he reduces and limits her to an identity he understands. Sexton and, in this narrative, the masculine discourse he uses, still operate as if man is the center of all things; however, Death's very existence, beyond description by Sexton's narrative powers, disrupts the center of Sexton's discourse. Derrida's notion of free play applies here. Between Death's presence and the absence of discourse to define her, her very being alters or completely removes the fixed origin of Sexton's discourse. Sexton himself continues on unaware of this disruption: "in the beginning was the end of her story, and that from now on she will have one dictated to her: by the man" (Irigaray *Speculum* 43). The masculine discourse operates despite the disruption of its center: it operates regardless of the existence of woman, who is ultimately beyond its definition, and reduces her to merely the m/other of man, literalizing the originary definition, "from man," as a stabilizing buttress of the dialogic discourse.

One way of maintaining the subjugation of women, the masculine discourse disallows two women means of communicating in productive ways with one another. Positing two women against one another reoccurs thematically in several other Gaiman's works, particularly where the one is a mother and the other is her daughter. Irigaray and other feminist scholars say a great deal about the relationships of women or rather the inaccessibility of female-to-female relationships due to the limitations of the phallocentric discourse in which society operates. Gaiman's works exemplify the way phallocentric discourse places women at odds with one another in ways that readers see as natural relationship strains by (re)iterating relationships in doubled binaries that fracture the phallocentric discourses of his female protagonists. The Other Mother in his 2002 novel *Coraline* is the most clear formation this iteration in Gaiman's works. Brought into the world through the door (reminiscent of Alice's Rabbit Hole), the titular protagonist, Coraline, momentarily confuses Other Mother as being her mother and briefly succumbs to the seduction of the phallocentrically circumscribed mother-type. Upon first meeting Other Mother, Coraline admits that Other Mother's voice "sounded like her mother" and she even looked mostly like her mother (*Coraline* 27). Coraline also notes the difference in Other Mother: "She looked a little like Coraline's mother. Only ... only her skin was white as paper. Only she was taller and thinner. Only her fingers were too long, and they never stopped moving.... Her eyes were big black buttons" (28). Upon confessing that she never knew she had another mother, Coraline learns that "everyone does" (29). Coraline's Other Mother and Other Father have been waiting for Coraline: they are attentive to her and fawn over her in ways that her first parents do not. All of the attention leads Coraline to think, "*This is more like it*" (30), and she acquiesces to the seduction of Other Mother: "at first that reality seems to be perfect, complete with attentive parents and delicious food. But Coraline soon comes to realize that horror hides behind the façade of that world, and she struggles to return home" (Wagner et al. 365).

Repeating his own pattern of young girl heroines like Coraline, Gaiman depicts Lucy in his 2003 children's book *The Wolves in the Walls*. Lucy hears wolves living in the walls of her house. She tries futilely to warn her family, who dismiss her warnings. The inability of Lucy (or the inability of all girls) to garner her family's attention with her words is because "the 'reasonable' words — to which in any case she has access only through mimicry — are powerless to translate all that pulses, clamors, and hangs hazily in the cryptic passages" (Irigaray *Speculum* 142). The wolves in the walls become louder and louder with each passing day, but still "Lucy alone recognizes the initial threat; silenced, ridiculed, and ignored, she is unable to protect her family from the disaster she alone sees coming" (Wagner et al. 371). Lucy first attempts to talk about the wolves with her mother. Her mother is the picture of domestic work, busy making preserves and jams: "Lucy's mother embodies domestic order" (Wagner et al. 371). Without even looking up from her jams, Lucy's mother rebuffs her daughter's warnings, telling her, "There are no wolves in the walls. You must be hearing mice, I suppose" (*Wolves* 5). When Lucy insists, her mother retorts, "I'm sure it's not wolves, ... For you know what they say ... if the wolves come out of the walls, then it's all over" (*Wolves* 5). The underlying phallocentric discourse at work excludes the little girl from any real relationship with her mother (Irigaray *Speculum* 77), so no matter how hard Lucy tries, communication fails between the mother and daughter, in a similar fashion to Helena and her mother in *MirrorMask*.

Because her conversation with mother leaves her lacking, Lucy attempts to talk to her father about the impeding dangers. When the discourse disallows true communication between the mother and the daughter, "the girl turns towards her father ... because she turns away from her mother in disillusion" (Irigaray *Speculum* 62). In Lucy's case, conversation goes no better than the one with her mother: "I don't think there are [wolves in the walls], poppet.... You have an overactive imagination. Perhaps the noises you heard come from rats. Sometimes you get rats in big old houses like this" (*Wolves* 9). Lucy's warnings continue to fall on deaf ears as she then tries to warn her brother. Even once the wolves come out of the walls, proving Lucy's assertions of their existence, the family does not listen to this little girl. "At its core, *The Wolves in the Walls* is about a child's [a girl child's] frustration with a family's fragmentation and lack of communication" (Wagner 371). Lucy is bound by the masculine discourse, which strips her warnings of any potency.

After single handedly mobilizing her family and reclaiming their home, at the end of this story, the reader finds Lucy hearing larger things in the walls: "she heard rustlings and scratchings and squeezings and creakings in the old house, and then, one night ... she heard a noise that sounded exactly like an elephant trying not to sneeze" (*Wolves* 49). Instead of being confident that her family will believe her warnings this time around, Lucy seems to recognize her powerless place in the phallocentric society and decides not to tell her family, accepting that "they'll find out soon enough" (*Wolves* 51). Like many of Gaiman's strongest heroines, who save their parents or the world and restore order to their homes, Lucy is ultimately still mute within the phallocentric discourse. Women and young girls have no access to the language they need to find their voice.

In his 2005 script *MirrorMask*, Gaiman depicts just such a relationship between the protagonist Helena Campbell and her binary relationships with her true mother (the Queen of Light) and the Queen of Shadows, her mother's narrative counterpart. Reiterating themes from other children's works, including C.S. Lewis' *Narnia*, Gaiman's own *Coraline*, Stephen King's *The Talisman* and Catherine Storr's *Marianne Dreams*, *MirrorMask* tells the story of a girl, 15 years old and on the cusp of womanhood, who must save the world, or at least save an imaginary world of her own creating by "escap[ing] the control of the Queen of Shadow, find[ing] the MirrorMask, figure[ing] out how it works, and revers[ing] the magic that the anti–Helena has worked so she can return her and her twin back to their own lands before the Lands of Light and Shadow are forever destroyed" (Wagner et al. 468). All the destruction that Helena must undo correlates directly with a fight she and her mother have at the very beginning of the movie (mirrored in the fight between anti–Helena and her mother the Queen of Shadows), which sets the plot in motion.

According to Wagner, in this movie Gaiman "plays upon the common childhood fear that our parents (particularly mothers) will turn out to be something else entirely, either secretly evil or not our parents at all" (Wagner et al. 469), but Gaiman's depiction more accurately shows the struggle between mothers and daughters, specifically a daughter's rebellion against the mother, due to their enclosure within the phallocentric discourse. Although mother and daughter love each other, they constantly clash and communication fails them time and time again. The first instance of this failure appears at the beginning of the movie when Helena and her mother fight. "You'll be the death of me," says her mother, and Helena retorts, "I wish I was" (*Mirror-Mask*). Later we see the fracture and failure of true communication when Helena attempts to apologize and then confesses to her father that despite her attempt, she has not "been able to say I'm sorry — not so that she really believes me" (*MirrorMask*). Gaiman shows perfectly what Irigaray means by the absence of genuine dialogue between mother and daughter. Because of this absence of genuine dialog, "love borders on hate" (Holmlund 291). The inability to "speak" to one another limits, stunts or destroys the mother/daughter relationship and this is due to the dominant discourse: "The domination excludes the little girl from any discovery of the economy of her relationship with her mother" (Irigaray *Speculum* 77). Gaiman's depiction of the mother/daughter relationship represents this void created by the phallocentric discourse.

Accurately enough, Helena directs her rebellious words and attitude towards her mother and not at her father.[7] Even when Helena's father directly asks her what she has been saying to her mother, giving her the perfect opportunity to lash out at him as she just has her mother, Helena responds, "Nothing" (*MirrorMask*). Helena's respect for her father stems from the fact that "woman's rebellions are never aimed at the paternal function — which is sacred and divine — but at that powerful and then castrated mother" (Irigaray *Speculum* 106). Western culture, aided by the terms of Freudian discourse, often talks of the struggle between mothers and daughters and notes the reverence little girls have for their daddies, and Gaiman gives us just such a family dynamic in *MirrorMask*.

Both the theme Wagner describes of the childhood fear of the mother turning out to be something "either secretly evil or not our parent at all" and the positing of mother against daughter also appear in Gaiman's *Coraline*. The story centers on a young girl, Coraline, and her adventures in another reality, "a distorted version of the world she already knows" (Wagner et al. 365). Coraline spends a great deal of time wandering around by herself because her mother and father pay little attention to this little girl: "they treat her with a sort of benign neglect" (Wagner et al. 366). When Coraline talks to her parents, they either kindly tell her to "go away" (Gaiman *Coraline* 18) or ignore her words complete. At one point, Coraline shops with her mother and even though her mother asks her questions, when Coraline answers, "her mother ignored her" (23). Like Helena's relationship with her mother, Coraline's relationship with her mother leaves her lacking and bored: "she is left with a void, a lack of all representation, re-presentation, and even strictly speaking of all mimesis of her desire for origin" (Irigaray *Speculum* 42). To fill this void, like Helena, Coraline finds a second mother figure, attempting to seduce her with the attention and affection she lacks in her original maternal relationship.

While Coraline and Helena's second mothers appear to be bad copies of the protagonists' mothers (both Coraline and Helena ultimately abscond from the seduction and see the other mothers as evil, as Lucy recognizes the wolf family as a doubling of her own family, including their faults and vulnerabilities), the other mothers are a repetition of the sign (mother) nonetheless. These other mothers "will be 'like' her mother but not in the same 'place,' not corresponding to the same point on the number line. She will be her mother and yet not her mother" (Irigaray *Speculum* 76). Coraline's mother and Other Mother, Helena's White and Shadow Queens, and Lucy's binary families constitute parts of the same sign/word-type: mother. Even as these young women grow to recognize the differences, they accept the binary as part of the discursive term:

> For the structure of iteration implies *both* identity *and* difference. Iteration in its "purest" form — and it is always impure — contains *in itself* the discrepancy of a difference that constitutes it as iteration. The iterability of an element divides its own identity a priori, even without taking into account the fact that this identity can only determine or delimit itself through differential relations to other elements and that it hence bears the mark of this difference [Derrida *Limited* 53].

The differences in Other Mother, those things that make her and her narrative parallels the Other in Gaiman's work, are inherent to the iteration of the mother. In other words, "when something is repeated, another instance of that something comes into existence. Thus repetition is tied to alterity, i.e. otherness. In the case of signs, what counts as a repetition may appear quite different" (Halion 4). Without the mother, there could be no Other Mother and thereby Coraline knows her mother is her mother because of the existence of her Other Mother, Helena validates the significance of her matrilineal bond because of the Queen of Shadows, and Lucy inverts the hierarchy of domestication by recognizing its unviability in the failures of the substitution. The sign becomes an event, becomes a sign, through its repetition.

Even when Gaiman pens characters who supposedly breach the gender binary, these characters still act out and are acted upon in very gender specific ways: despite their attempts to transcend the hegemonic roles of masculine *or* feminine, the discourse labels, defines, and limits them nonetheless. When Gaiman fans think of androgyny in his work, they immediate think of *Sandman*'s Desire. First appearing in *The Doll's House*, Dream's[8] younger sibling, Desire, takes the form of whatever or whoever it is that humans desire, male and female — both/and, either/or. Twin of Despair, Desire is the third youngest Endless, whose siblings refer to as "sister-brother." At first glance, Gaiman has written Desire to abscond the gender binary and in many s/he does: s/he plays with gender, embodying every little whim the mortal heart wants — man, woman, and anyone or anything in between. Desire looks and sounds much like Derrida's description of the copy: "mimicry imitating nothing" as "a ghost that is a phantom of no flesh, wandering about without a past, without a death, birth, or presence" (*Dissemination* 206). Desire, by taking on the forms of all human desires, represents the ghost of a character without a true identifiable self. With this understanding of Desire, Dream makes sense when he tells Desire that the Endless are the servants of mortals, evoking a hierarchy with the mortals at the top: "we do not manipulate them. If anything, they manipulate us. We are their toys. Their dolls, if you will" (*Sandman* 16:23). However, Desire disagrees with Morpheus' proposed hierarchy and the reader through this text has seen why.

Despite Gaiman's claims at universality and androgyny in the form of Desire, the reader experiences "what claims to be universal is actually the equivalent of a male idiolect, of a male imaginary of a sexed world — and not neuter" (Irigaray *Speak* 250). Upon first read, Desire may be viewed as represented gender in the form as a continuum; however, being able to take on any form of gender allows Desire to fully embody all that defines man and demonstrate the full extent of masculine power embedded within the phallocentric system. At the conclusion of *The Doll's House*, in a confrontation with sibling Dream, Desire confesses to impregnating a *sleeping* Unity Kincaid — in other words, Desire confesses to the rape of an unconscious woman. Desire rapes and impregnates Unity in a plan to trap the Sandman by having him unknowingly kill a blood relative. When Desire needs power to meddle in the life of her/his brother (Dream), Desire enacts a violent act against womankind. Desire performs masculinity in a way that removes woman's voice and choice, and in fact acts in a counterintuitive manner to his/her own dialectic. Through Desire, Gaiman demonstrates how even his androgynous characters operate within the phallocentric discourse and when in need of power their "neutrality" becomes "masculinity" when the need to exert dominant control overrides the strictures of

Gaiman's language around this act of violence is also troubling: Dream never uses the word "rape," but instead issues a euphemism: "fathered her mother on sleeping Unity" (*Sandman* 16:22). However, Gaiman's initial description tells the reader: "[1939] Unity Kinkaid was **raped** seven years ago. She gave **birth** to a baby **girl**. The **scandal** was **hushed** up" (1:18). Gaiman reminds the careful reader that Morpheus is softening the accusation; the feminist reader acknowledges this rape. Unity cannot consent because she is asleep, exhibiting one way in which the phallocentric discourse disallows for feminine sexuality and solely represents reproduction of the male. For although Desire can embody all forms of gender, in this context, s/he dons the sexual agency of man and utilizes that power to force reproduction upon woman. When desire is forced rather than mutual, Desire is defined by the misogyny of phallocentric dominance. Desire not only eliminates woman's sexuality, but also her choice to reproduce in motherhood. While sidestepping the crime, Dream emphasizes the violation, telling his sister-brother that "the endless are the servants of the living — we are NOT their masters" and threatening more serious (possibly lethal) action if such a violation is repeated; however, the actions of the other characters speak in stark contrast, and their actions speak louder than his words as the threat carries no penance for the act (16:23). Desire shows the reader how the mortals, particularly women, are in reality pawns in the games of the Immortals they create, and to transform his/her creators into pawns, Desire simply taps into the power available to "him" inherent in the dominant discourse.

Gaiman demonstrates yet again how "neutrality is impossible where hierarchical thinking prevails" (Homans 387) in his short story "Changes" from his collection *Smoke and Mirrors* (1998). Presenting the reader with other characters who, at first glance, challenge the gender binary, Gaiman displays the ways in which phallocentric discourse dominates and defines androgynous characters, rendering them unable to break free of the gender binary. This story commences with a cure for cancer. That cure, which operates by "rebooting" the patient's genetic code and "fixes it," produces an interesting side effect: it changes the person's sexual identity. Rajit, the creator of Reboot, spends the days after the first successful test wondering at the result: "[A]s the autopsy demonstrates beyond a doubt, the [female] patient now has a penis and is, in every respect, functionally and chromosomally male" (133). Twenty years after the creation of Reboot, people take this cancer drug recreationally to change sexes and genders at will. One character, Jo/e takes a dose to change into a female/woman for a night out, donning "the bustle, the petticoat, the bodice, and the gown, new breasts (high and conical) pushed together" (134). After the weekend, Jo/e takes another dose before going to bed because "Jo/e's job identity during the week is strictly male" (134). The drug makes "gender reassignment surgery obsolete" and people take it for "reasons of desire or curiosity or escape" (135). Due to this drug, changing one's sex and gender becomes fluid and a choice a person can make on their own and at whim.

Unfortunately, the dominant phallocentric discourse abides and in this story, Gaiman shows his readers how it operates still to oppress those who are still not considered men. Taking advantage of the changes Reboot brings, patriarchy utilizes the drug to maintain its tight grasp and subjugate women:

> Boys (in Thailand and Mongolia) were being forcibly rebooted into girls to increase their worth as prostitutes. In China newborn girls were rebooted to boys: families would save all they had for one single dose.... In several of the Pan-Arabic countries men who could not easily demonstrate that they had been born male and were not, in fact, women escaping the veil were being imprisoned and, in many cases, raped and killed [135–6].

Instead of providing a sense of freedom from the dominant discourse, sectors of the patriarchy initially use this drug as a means of oppression, perpetuating the oppression of the gender binary. The hegemonic hierarchy shifts slightly, but still remains, as it segregates between the "changed" and the "unchanged." Being born man still prevails as the top of the food chain as the possibility of making gender irrelevant enters the diaspora. Gaiman shows here not how the dominant discourse allows for more varying voices, but how it perpetuates itself by recognizing the new voices as still Other. These new men, these "changed" men, while now literally possessing a penis, are still devalued for being "changed": they are not natural men and despite their penises still do not possess the phallus/power.

The story ends, however, with Gaiman painting a picture of a future society that moves beyond phallocentric discourse, moving beyond the gender binary, and evidences a perspective and discourse that is propagated on truth rather than convenient fictions. A generation later, the creator of Reboot, Rajit is now a very old man and as he dies upon the beach, he is "surrounded by the golden people, who were not men, who were not women" (Gaiman "Changes" 140). Everyone is changed. Rajit calls them "Angels" (140), and these "angels" reiterate Rajit's story emphasizing the true events rather than the fictionalized version generated by the current discourse (starring recognizable actors in lead roles and directed by the man responsible for *Back to the Future* and Gaiman's own revision of *Beowulf*). Much like his admission by the elder in the beginning of *The Doll's House*, Gaiman echoes Luce Irigaray, except this time it is her notion of angels: "Through the angel (or rather angels, for Irigaray conceives them most brilliantly and suggestively in a couple), Irigaray gestures to the as-yet-unimagined, perhaps unimaginable flourishing of identity that might occur with the advent of true sexual difference" (Ugrina 13). For Irigaray, these angels operate as higher forms of femininity and masculinity, simultaneously different and alike, beyond the understanding of the phallocentric discourse. "Between them the flesh holds back and flows forth before any mastery can be exercised over it, or after a fort-da far more sophisticated than the real, a fort-da of the possibility of presence and of sharing in something divine that cannot be seen but can be felt, underlying all incarnation" (Irigaray "Belief Itself" 45). In the form of these angels, Gaiman and Irigaray imagine gender and sex differences as fluid and flowing, but only in the realm beyond the phallocentric discourse. Unfortunately, this "unimaginable" realm exists only in the worlds of speculative science fiction.

Neil Gaiman posits his female and androgynous characters into the already established masculine discourse and thereby creates comic narratives that "[substitute] feminine power for masculine power," yet remain circumscribed "because this reversal would still be caught up in the economy of the same ... a phallic seizure of power" (Irigaray *Sex* 129). Still, despite the repetition of sameness (or possibly because of the repetition of sameness), the pervasiveness of male voices, and the limited identities and voices of even his highly lauded female characters, Gaiman's gender discourses resonate with the women who read his comics, and can legitimately be called "feminist" within the operating discourse of Anglophone culture. We identify with Gaiman's women and with the phallocentric discourse because we too abide therein, and this discourse functions in creating our own identities and limiting our relationships with other women, including our mothers. We identify with Gaiman's female characters because they feel "true" and the desire for truth determines "the order, the hierarchy, the subordination of the interventions by which differences are regulated and declinable as more or less 'good' copies of the same" (Irigaray *Speculum* 262). But they are, of course, not exact copies. Their dissonance begins to deconstruct the anticipated frameworks of the phallocentric narrative. The good and the bad copies of women and mothers in Gaiman's works operate together in the iteration of each of these signs, slightly modifying the graphé of the iterative subject. In this way we see and understand Gaiman's characters as we see and understand ourselves, retroactively defined by the discourse and always already at a dissonance with it. For Gaiman there is "no longer is any truth value attributed to [purely phallocentric discourses]" due to the limiting nature of the framework they operate within, and his readers face a "readiness to abandon them, if necessary, should other instruments appear more useful" (Derrida *Structure* 201). Without the appearance of a more useful instrument, without any other language or discourse readily available with which writers can create and become "angels," creative minds like Gaiman's critique the existing discourse and employ it "to destroy the old machinery to which they themselves [we ourselves] are pieces. This is how the language [of Gaiman] criticizes itself" (Derrida *Structure* 201). Like the indigenous grandfatherly elder, all the stories told no longer utilize the language of women, if they ever did. Gaiman's work points to a need to rediscover what he calls "tales the women tell, in the private tongue men-children are never taught and older men are too wise to learn" (*Sandman* 10:1), moving to a new, and perhaps divine, way of thinking the world.

NOTES

1. Another issue this raises for me is the question of the universality of "female identity" and the way in which I and other critics use the term "women." In this work, I recognize that I use "female identity" and "women" narrowly, particularly with regards to race. However, a discussion of the universal assumptions of terms such as "female identity," "women," and "feminine" with regards to race is not part of the purview and scope of this paper, but better served by a lengthy analysis.

2. Brute and Glob have convinced Hector that he is the Sandman, protecting the dreams of the world's children.

3. There is yet a fourth "Susan" introduced in Gaiman's narrative. She is neither fully grown nor fully cognizant of her identity. Naming herself "Suzy," she is the infantilized and undernourished Susan, utilized in the narrative as a pawn for the plot and as a foil to Susan's growing self-awareness (both as a catalyst and an alternative).

4. Sylvain not only imprints Black Orchid's identity upon her verbally, but he also literally creates her in his greenhouse through his scientific breakthrough. Like many earlier comics, the theme of man "messing with" nature leaves characters who do not seem to belong within society, displaying nature (which is always referred to in the feminine pronoun) as enslaved to man's "arrogant claim to sovereign discretion over everything" (Irigaray *Speculum* 204).

5. Black Orchid originally appears in other earlier DC comics, but without any origin narrative or background. Gaiman includes in his origins narrative of Black Orchid other DC comic characters and settings, including Swamp Thing, Poison Ivy, Batman, Lex Luthor, and Arkham Insane Asylum: "coaxing an origin from both the Mayer/DeZuniga originals and a story from the first narrative arc of the Alan Moore/Stephen Bissette/John Totleben *Saga of the Swamp Thing*, Gaiman ingeniously linked the various DC vegetable characters via a singular backstory" (Wagner et al. 197).

6. And the double entendre, of course, reinforces the phallocentric language of the discourse, though perhaps this only a bit of supplemental play.

7. We do see anti–Helena fighting with Helena's dad, but we are told time and time again that she is *not* Helena: Helena says, "She looks like me, but she isn't me" (*Mirror-Mask*). The reader could interpret anti–Helena as another example of iteration in this film.

8. Dream is known by many names: Dream, the Sandman, and Morpheus.

WORKS CITED

Burke, Carolyn. "Irigaray Through the Looking Glass." *Feminist Studies*. v. 7 no. 2, Summer 1981. 288–306. Print.

de Beaugrande, Robert. "In Search of Feminist Discourse: The 'Difficult' Case of Luce Irigaray." *College English*. v. 50 n. 3, March 1988. 253–272. Print.

Derrida, Jacques. *Dissemination.* Barbara Johnson, tr. Chicago: University of Chicago Press, 1981. Print.

_____. *Limited Inc.* Samuel Weber, tr. Evanston, IL: Northwestern University Press, 1977. Print.

_____. "Structure, Sign and Play in the Discourse of the Human Sciences." Alan Bass, tr. *Writing and Difference,* 1966: 278–95. Print.

Gaiman, Neil. "All Books Have Genders." Web. 13 March 2011.

_____. "Changes." *Smoke and Mirrors: Short Fictions and Illusions.* New York: Harper Perennial, 1998. Print.

_____. *Coraline.* New York: HarperCollins, 2002. Print.

_____. *MirrorMask.* Dir. Anthony Shearn. Perf. Jason Berry, Rob Bryson, Stephanie Leonidas, and Gina McKee. Sony Pictures, 2005. Film.

Gaiman, Neil (w), Dave McKean (a, p). *Black Orchid* #1–3 (Dec. 1988–Feb. 1989), New York: DC Comics. Print.

_____ (w), Chris Bachalo, Dave McKean (a), Dave McKean, Marck Buckingham (i). *Death: The High Cost of Living* #1–3 (March–May 1993), New York: DC Comics. Print.

_____ (w), Mike Dringenberg (a), Malcolm Jones III (i). "Tales in the Sand." *The Sandman* #9 (Sept. 1989), New York: DC Comics. Print.

_____ (w), Chris Bachalo (a), Malcolm Jones III (i). "Playing House." *The Sandman* #12 (Jan. 1990), New York: DC Comics. Print.

_____ (w), Mike Dringenberg (a), Malcolm Jones III (i). "Los Hearts." *The Sandman* #16 (June 1990), New York: DC Comics. Print.

Gaiman, Neil (w), Dave McKean (p). *The Wolves in the Walls.* New York: HarperCollins Children's, 2003. Print.

Halion, Kevin. "Parasitic Speech Acts: Austin, Searle, Derrida." *Deconstruction and Speech Act Theory.* Web. 18 March 2002.

Holmlund, Christine. "The Lesbian, the Mother, the Heterosexual Love: Irigaray's Recoding of Difference." *Feminist Studies.* v. 17 no. 2, Summer 1991. 283–308. Print.

Homans, Margaret. "The Woman in the Cave: Recent Feminist Fictions and the Classical Underworld." *Contemporary Literature.* v. 29 no. 3, Autumn 1988. 369–402. Print.

Irigaray, Luce. "Belief Itself." *Sexes and Genealogies.* New York: Columbia Universtiy Press, 1993. 25–26 Print.

_____. *Speculum of the Other Woman.* Ithaca: Cornell University Press, 1985. Print.

_____. *This Sex Is Not One.* Ithaca: Cornell University Press, 1985. Print.

_____. *To Speak Is Never Neutral.* New York: Continuum, 2002. Print.

Jaffe, Sarah. "Neverwhere and Neil Gaiman's Female Characters." Web. 1 January 2009.

Ugrina, Luciana. "Redeeming Sexual Difference: *Stigmata, The Messenger* and Luce Irigaray's *Bleeding Woman.*" *Journal of Religion and Popular Culture.* v. 21 n. 1, Spring 2009. Print.

Wagner, Hank et al. *Prince of Stories: The Many Worlds of Neil Gaiman.* New York: St. Martin's Press, 2009. Print.

Whitford, Margaret, ed. *The Irigaray Reader.* Cambridge: Blackwell, 1995. Print.

The Power of the Perky

The Feminist Rhetoric of Death

BY LANETTE CADLE

Death is just a girl, after all. Just a perky, Goth-clad, ankh-wearing girl, or at least in the world of Neil Gaiman she is. Gaiman's Death defies expectations while adhering to the letter of the folkloric law. She does have a thing for black, but to rephrase Jessica Rabbit, she could claim, *I'm not depressed, I'm just drawn that way.* The visual rhetoric of black clothes, pale skin, and Egyptian Book of the Dead-style makeup paired with a positive feminist outlook makes for an unlikely personification of Death, but one so effective that the old hooded guy may as well set down the scythe and head to the archetype employment office. With the opposing visual rhetoric of black clothes and makeup on pale white skin combined with Death's incessant, calm cheerfulness, she could be viewed as an embodiment of millennial feminism. Seen that way, her outward appearance — the nod to the past — honors the role Death plays in the cycle of life. The irrepressible perkiness, especially when faced with those who are depressed or unaccepting of their fate, is the source of her power and an expression of the feminist rhetorical move towards consensus over conflict, with *consensus* being in the original meaning of agreement within the body developed by the sophists rather than in the later, more bloodless Aristotelian sense. Gaiman's Death takes the iconic character and gives it her own, joyful twist, making her far more than the dull, sinister wraith found in legend. The change is greater than a shift from male to female or from morose to upbeat. With her embodied rhetoric, Death invokes the power of the perky — a confident acceptance of femininity and its performance — and in doing so, gives a possible answer to how feminist rhetoric works.

In appearance, her style is distinctive, yet easily recognizable to anyone who has a teenager — or has been a teenager — who embraced the fashion outlook called "Goth." She varies her look a bit within the genre. In "Façade" she goes for a shredded top with a deep-v neckline, the better to show cleavage;

in *Death: The High Cost of Living* she shows less skin in a camisole covered by a blazer, but what skin shows is still ultra-white, soft, and rounded. When shown in a historical context, as in "Men of Good Fortune," she matches the era while remaining stylish, feminine, and far from demure (1:1–4), but the ankh necklace, top, skin-tight pants, and adventurer's boots (like pirates wear) all in black is her standard current-day look. In chapter three of *Death: The High Cost of Living* she accessorizes with a smiley face button (the yellow is her one splash of color) and a top hat (1:17). Her face, usually smiling, is accentuated by deep red, almost-black lipstick and heavy, cat-eyed eye makeup that would fit equally well at a rock concert or in an Egyptian tomb. All of this is of a piece and expected; it is definitely a power look, not that of a demure young miss. However, like some of the teens who take up this look, she smiles too much to be defined by it. She is not sad. On the contrary, she is young in appearance and irrepressibly perky, as only a young, healthy woman with good, common sense can be. Roland Barthes speculates that "rhetorics inevitably vary by their substance (here articulated sound, there image, gesture, or whatever) but not necessarily by their form; it is even probable that there exists a single rhetorical form, common for instance to dream, literature, and image" (161). Barthes's point about image is well made; the representation of Death is indeed embodied rhetoric on all those levels. In other words, the image of Death is consensual, an embodied act of consensus, not something off to the side or something superficial which is not to be considered.

As far as her body is concerned, it is obvious that Death is gendered female, and not half-heartedly female at that. In her first visual appearance in the *Sandman* series, "The Sound of Her Wings" (she is mentioned several times in issue one but not seen), she mimics her brother Dream's body language but not his facial expression and begins the conversation with a joke about pigeons. She is bubbling over with life, albeit a stark, white-skinned black-wearing form of life, but lively she is, wearing a spaghetti-strap camisole and, at one point, shades, the better to soak up the sun and enjoy the day (8:4–5). Granted, Dream has earned his morose mood this time, having just escaped "three score years and ten" (1:22) of imprisonment in a bubble, but in opposition to the traditional role played by the folkloric death, Gaiman's Death is bent on turning Dream's view away from the past and towards life and the simple joy found in the folly and foibles of being human, despite the fact that the two of them are, of course, not human. It could be argued that by creating a female Death character, especially one that embraces such positive feminine and feminist energy, Gaiman is practicing feminist reclaiming in the same way the Cheryl Glenn did in *Rhetoric Retold: Regendering the Tradition from Antiquity Through the Renaissance*. Outside of scholarly circles, feminism might be considered a joyless pursuit; as a counterpoint, Death is female, all-powerful, and joyful. Clearly, there are feminists who are comfortable in their skin and clearly, there are ones who celebrate life with all its folly, but the contemporary stereotype can be a dour one, thus the need for a reclaiming of feminine values into the feminist picture. In *Rhetoric Retold*, Glenn does a similar reclaiming by taking the rhetorical canon and weaving back existing female rhetors. She writes about how they were previously silenced:

> Even though *gender* is merely a concept borrowed from grammar, it nevertheless continues to have far-reaching effects on cultural notions of the relation between the sexed body and its behavior. Gendered experiences continue to be difficult, if not impossible to separate from human ones. And for that reason alone, the masculine gender, just like every male experience or display, has come to represent the universal. Men have appropriated many public social practices, particularly prestigious practices like rhetoric, as universally masculine; the feminine experience (that of bodies sexed female) has come to represent exceptions, or the particular [173].

Since mythology is very much a place of constructed being (and we are definitely talking about restructured mythology when discussing Gaiman's Endless family), and since myth is a place where the telling and retelling fabricates reality, who are we to say that Gaiman does not tell the truth when he offers a vision of Death that is female ... and perky? By taking an archetypal figure and regendering, Gaiman moves Death out of historical patriarchy into a mythos where women are just as likely to hold power, and not merely by re-inscribing old practices. This iteration of Death is new, and all woman.

In her book, Glenn also points out that "the project of regendering rhetorical history is a feminist performative act, a commitment to the future of women, a promise that rhetorical histories and theories will eventually (and naturally) include women" (174). She adds that "it is regendering that unsettles stable gender categories" (174), an idea that transfers well to the regendering and retelling of myth. Gaiman's mythology is remarkably gender-inclusive, and can also be seen as a "feminist performative act."

Of course, when the term *performative* is used, one has to turn to its source, Judith Butler's concept of gender as performative in *Gender Trouble*. She writes, "That the gendered body is performative suggests that it has no ontological status apart from the various acts which constitute its reality" (185). Death, then, is female and clearly marked as feminine not because her body has breasts and hips, but because Death chooses to be feminine: her performance is her reality. Going one step further, a feminist performative act, such as Gaiman's creation of Death, is not just for show; the very act itself is saturated feminism, not a surface gesture. Whether or not Gaiman intended Death to be a feminist performative act, she exists, and through her existence, she unsettles staid gender tropes in a genre (comics, graphic novels) that at times relies on bulbous breasts and heavy-handed gender stereotypes that are easy for readers to decode.

Death is a less predictable representation and joyfully smashes the female stereotype when needed. In "A Night to Remember" (Gaiman *Death: HCL* 2) she breaks out of what could be seen as stereotypical, nurturing femininity to show her badass side when she chastises Sexton for being overly superficial in making a judgment about a fellow human being. She asserts, "I don't want to hear that stuff, Sexton. This is a real person you're talking about, and he's not breathing properly, and I'm sure he's done a lot worse than saying **not**, but I'm telling you, sometimes you **really** piss me off, and right now that last smart-aleck shit is the **last** thing I need to hear, right?" (2:23). Feminism operates in a similar, slippery way. Just when you think you have it defined, it shows another layer, another way to celebrate its performance, whether by female, male, or an all-powerful iconic Death archetype who chooses to show an egalitarian, feminist side. After all, complete predictability is simply another way to describe a stereotype, and even though stereotypes serve a function, seen up close and in the flesh, real people, real feminists, are more complicated. Part of the embodiment for Death is her character, using the term in the sophistic sense, that of *ethos*.

The stylistic choices made by Death become more complex when viewed as an aspect of *ethos*, a concept that is part of Aristotle's Trivium of *ethos*, *logos*, and *pathos*, but also a concept widely used by others, most notably the sophists. Her ethos, in other words, her intrinsic character or what qualities she has that makes her worth listening to, contributes to that complex rhetoric which is Death; her words, actions, intentions, and motives embody more than the clothes on her body. Beginning with that appearance though, one assumes that Death could appear in any form she pleases, so this one must please her and either assists in her job or runs contrary to occupational function while lending a sort of ironic, comic pleasure by its incongruity. One thing it could never be is random. The beauty of visual rhetoric involving the body is that the rhetor makes choices even when she (or he) denies making a choice. That too is a choice and one that adds to the allure of visual rhetoric, in this case a constructed identity. Since Death could choose any appearance, it is interesting to consider how she reacts to her own: is she pleased, is she indifferent, does she think her hips are too big? There is no direct evidence for how she thinks of her appearance. She doesn't check herself in mirrors; she also never makes that scrunched-up face many women make when they look at themselves and are unsatisfied. On the contrary, she oozes self-satisfaction and is happily amused by the male reaction to her as Didi in "The High Cost of Living." When she is on her once-a-century vacation, she gets to have skin and she is comfortable in it. In other words, once she is in the flesh, she takes on the pleasure of bodily senses while she has them, giving her body memory for when the embodied vacation ends. Even better, this means that others are comfortable talking with her, which results in a heightened ability to use her allure to romance them into a sensual (through the senses), consensual agreement. For example, in *The Sandman: Three Septembers and a January* (*Sandman* 31), Death comes for the Emperor of the United States, a beloved historical figure who lived in San Francisco during the latter half of the nineteenth century. In this retelling, Dream ultimately wins a bet with Desire by giving the man Joshua Norton a dream that gives Norton a new identity: an Emperor who has nothing yet desires nothing more than to serve others. When Death comes for him, Norton has already defeated Desire and Despair, and is standing, grey-toned, next to his body in the rain. Even then, he thinks of others first, and tips his hat at Death, for after all, this Death is a lady. She empathizes with him and celebrates the selflessness of his life as Emperor by pointing him towards a possible role in the afterlife that he would find as equally alluring as the life he had once led. She notes his Jewish past and tells him of the "36 Tzaddikim": "They say that the world rests on the backs of 36 living saints — 36 unselfish men and women. Because of **them** the world continues to exist. They are the secret kings and queens of this world.... I've met a lot of kings and emperors and heads of state in my time, Joshua. **I've** met them all. And you **know** something? I think I liked **you** best" (31:24). He thanks her for her kindness and they walk off arm in arm, his top hat on her head. She loves him, and that love is a reflection of the man's love for all humanity. In this case, consensus was easy. The Emperor Norton is an exceptional example in that he allows Death to fully be that softer self. He is practicing the same feminist, even sophistic, approach to *ethos* in persuasion by letting what is highest and best in him speak to what is highest and best in her.

With those less noble, Death does not seek to dominate, but still aims to persuade in the feminist sense of an embodied argument that embraces both writer and audience. There is no doubt that she could dominate. Volume 4 of Gaiman's *The Books of Magic* has Death appear at the end of time to wrap things up, end the universe, and send her eldest brother, Destiny, to his end as well. She has no girlish hesitancy in completing these most final acts; instead, she notes, "it's my job to put it all in order, now, and lock the place behind me as I leave" (4:40). Rather than the domination-mode familiar to viewers of Sunday morning press debate shows or the manipulative words that are commonly referred to as "just rhetoric," Gaiman's Death constructs an embodied, feminist rhetoric, seeking consensus and actively mentoring (in the feminist, not the classical sense) rather than merely imposing her will, as of course, she could. It could be argued that, in this end-of-universe scene Death imposes her will by making the villainous Erik walk back to his own time (4:41). At the same time, her decision to send him back to his own time is a compassionate one; she could have let him stay and be destroyed. Instead, she gives him time and a possibility — the possibility that sometime through that billions of years journey back, he might reclaim his humanity. Talk would not have worked; instead, Death creates a situation, a piece of embodied rhetoric that forms an argument for change that each step of Erik's body would understand and use to convince him. Yes, it was a power move, but one tailored to the situation, one that uses *kairos*. After all, she's Death. She is comfortable talking to everyone, she goes out of her way to be engaging, and she knows fully what each rhetorical situation is and uses that knowledge for the good of all concerned.

Clearly, communicating effectively to one and all in their final moments is her job, and it is a tricky one. To do it well, she takes the contrast between her appearance and demeanor and uses it to appeal to and engage others to act in ways that aim towards the general good (as well as the specific, i.e., their lives and deaths). That is why Death is a natural for the public service comic, "Death Talks About Life." In it, she details safe sex practices, including how and why to use condoms, noting, "there's **another** side effect to unsafe sex. I mentioned it in the beginning. It's called **life**." Her demeanor is calm, but with a bountiful sense of humor waiting to emerge, as it does with the requisite banana jokes. There's no preaching involved, just a calm detailing of the consequences of unsafe sex (AIDS, gonorrhea, Chlamydia, herpes) and the obvious one that young people nonetheless may not consider: a new life, a baby. Her persuasion is born of identity, the ultimate ethos, rather than technique. She's there, she knows, and her audience knows it.

This cellular-level knowledge of Death's ethos means that Gaiman doesn't need to include the character sketch that he gives for the other immortals in "The Season of Mist: Prologue" (*Sandman* 21). For example, "Desire smells almost subliminally of summer peaches, and casts two shadows, one black and sharp-edged, the other translucent and forever wavering, like heat haze" and is "never a possession, always the possessor, with skin as pale as smoke, and eyes tawny and sharp as yellow wine: Desire is everything you have ever wanted. Whoever you are. Whatever you are" (21:9). Delirium is also described, her (and his, for s/he is also dual) scent that of "sweat, sour wines, late nights, old leather. Her realm is close, and can be visited; however, human minds were not made to comprehend her domain, and those few who have made the journey have been incapable of reporting back more than the tiniest fragments" (21:10). Each of the Endless get a turn in the spotlight, but for Death Gaiman only notes, "And there is Death" (21:11). To know more about who Death is when she's at home, one has to turn to the woman that Gaiman chose to give that inside view. Tori Amos writes a visually patchworked, somewhat stream-of-consciousness introduction to *Death: The High Cost of Living*. It was reworked into an afterword for the edited collection of short stories, *The Sandman: Book of Dreams* while still retaining the stream-of-consciousness flow and Amos's distinctive reasoning. In it Amos writes:

> She told me once that there is a part of her in everyone though Neil believes I'm more Delirium than Tori, and Death taught me to accept that, you know, wear your butterflies with pride. And when I do accept that, I know Death is somewhere inside of me. She was the kind of girl all the girls wanted to be, I believe, because of her acceptance of "what is." She keeps reminding me that there is change in the "what is" but change cannot be made till you accept the "what is" [394].

This insider view of Death acknowledges the surface contradiction between the girlish performance and the all-knowing all-powerful self. Death uses this acceptance of "what is" to help others do the same. For example, in "The Sound of Her Wings" (*Sandman* 8) she holds a baby gently in her arms, and when the infant asks, "But is that all ***there was***? Is that all I get?" she acknowledges the validity of that last plea when she replies, "Yes, I'm afraid so" (8:18). Of course, being gentle to a baby is no stretch, but Death is also kind to those who may appear to deserve it less. For example, she offers solace to the lowlife character Theo in "The High Cost of Living" (*Death: HCL* 3:16–23). Death can be a badass to the core when needed, but she never stops being a soft, pretty girl who would prefer to deal with those she faces in her role as Death as equals. In this case, even though Theo intends to lead her to robbery and her death, she treats him with kindness, even seeking medical attention for him, up to the moment of his death. The reason why is given in "Death: A Winter's Tale." In this story, she muses about her existence, her job, and the sadness she felt in the beginning when "the only people who greeted me with relief did so as an escape from something bad or intolerable. The rest of them just wished I'd go away, as if dying were some kind of admission of failure" (222). Her reaction was "walking out," in other words, removing death, the result being a world where life did not end, a place where "the chaos and the pain got bad, and they got worse" until a young man came to her and "pleaded and I went and looked at what I'd done" (223). Even so, she later found herself becoming "hard and cold and brittle inside" until as an answer to another plea, this time from a young girl, she decided to take on flesh and live the human viewpoint for one day a century (224), a physical and very persuasive form of consensus. After all, a meeting of the minds, a consensual joining, is far more abstract when one of the entities involved is abstract, i.e., not alive. The embodied Death is capable on the cellular level of deep knowledge about what it means to be human, which means she has essentially joined the body human, an ultimate and complete version of putting oneself in another's place, the root of consensus. The result is a Death with compassion and a greater understanding of the balance between her world and the human one.

This ability is what sets her apart from her Endless siblings, Destiny, Dream, Desire, Despair, Delirium, and yes, even Destruction, who walked away from his realm and in part 7 of "Brief Lives" (*Sandman* 47) ineffectively tries his hand at creation as human, making bad art (47:1–2) and better cooking (47:28). To rephrase Plato's claim about rhetoric, it is all cookery for Destruction, thus his success with cooking and not with poetry or art. In contrast, Death is not trying to be human. She is trying to be her best possible self, and that means knowing humanity intimately while retaining her own features and functions. This yearning for community, for communing with humans, is the emotional force behind her consensual persuasion.

The idea of consensus as a persuasive method is not new, of course, but it is one that is greatly valued in feminist rhetorics because of its egalitarian nature and its embodiedness. In consensus-based argumentation, the audience is not passive; in fact, by being consensual, this form not only includes the audience, it needs the audience and what they bring to the argument in order to be complete. The goal is not to subvert the audience's will or to attack a viewpoint and come out victorious; the audience is a larger part of the process in that the goal is to have most of the audience agree that the viewpoint being proposed is reasonable. This is done through a call to *ethos* and *pathos*, with a comparison of alternatives rather than an attack on an alternate point-of-view. Death does this well when faced with Hob Gadling, the man who in "Men of Good Fortune" (*Sandman* 13) cheerfully calls death a "mug's game" (13:1). Not knowing who he is speaking to, Hob gives an energetic argument for his plan of simply not choosing death in order to live forever. Death listens actively and weighs the man's *ethos*, meaning who he is and how much his character is wrapped up in his argument, and his *pathos*, the emotional weight he gives the argument. Since his argument appeals to her, she does not bother trying to talk him out of his idea by revealing her identity and her authority over life and death, thus not using the agonistic method that attacks head-on and conquers. Instead, she listens, acknowledges, and then gives him a gift — immortality until he calls for her — that will persuade him through his future experiences, choosing actual persuasion over abstract persuasion. ·

This method is especially good for situations that are too complex for the traditional reliance on *logos*, situations with multiple yes and no possibilities. Classical rhetors who were proponents of consensus include the sophists and later Aristotle, who introduces the idea of common knowledge, although his vision of this form centered on abstract ideas rather than the people behind the ideas or audience. A contemporary theorist who deals with consensus and what he calls *rational-critical debate* is Jürgen Habermas with his concept of the *public sphere*, the physical or intellectual space where ideas are exchanged. Applying his view of the public sphere to the egalitarian, webbed media typical of social media such as Twitter, blogs, or forums, Matthew Barton in "The Future of Rational-critical Debate in Online Public Spheres" points out that the equality proclaimed for the French salon or the English coffee house was of a particular, limited sort, beginning with Habermas's claim for equal opportunity for expression within these societies:

> In principle, anyone with reason and the willingness to learn was "able to participate" in these societies (p. 37). Of course, in practice there were many people altogether excluded, yet the idea of universal access and equality was highly influential in bourgeois thinking of this time. The public's use of its reason was only an influential concept as long as that reason was generally considered free from prejudice; the truths arrived at through reason were true for all.

Barton goes on to propose that online writing venues such as forums, wikis, and blogs form a more inclusive, egalitarian public sphere, a view that Habermas himself famously does not share since he does not view the internet as a potential public sphere, but Barton's view is one that has been gaining ground in technical and writing scholarship since he introduced it in 2005. What is important about Barton's view of the public sphere in terms of how Death persuades others is how Barton sees the need for more inclusion and less of a top-down, mass media/consumer binary. This webbed rhetoric is far closer to the feminist representation of Death and how she consensually deals with those who face her.

In fact, a good example of a parody of rational-critical debate is the "family dinner" scene in "Season of Mist: Prologue" (*Sandman* 21). In it, Destiny is prompted by the Fates to refer to his book and then call all of his siblings (*sans* Destruction) for a face-to-face meeting. Given the wildly differing personalities involved, there is little hope for any rationality and plenty for the wrong kind of critical talk. All the same, it is predestined in his book, so he must do it. The first to arrive is Death, dressed in blue jeans and a black sleeveless top. She quickly changes, after being prompted by Destiny, to a more formal black dress, which is tight on top blossoming into a tutu below with coral beaded accents and a deep coral fob (21:5), reminiscent of Dolce and Gabbana or a shredded update of eighteenth-century elegance. Next is Dream, morose and elegant in a tricorn, a gold-trimmed driving coat, and skin-fitted trousers to rival any Regency buck (21:6). He is quickly followed by Desire and Despair, and at last, Delirium is summoned (21:7). Once they are seated around a seven-sided table, the scene quickly deteriorates into the kind of awkward silences and infighting that family does best (21:12–18).

Finally Dream rises to Desire's bait and storms out of the room, quickly followed by Death (21:19–20). The dinner table "debate," interspersed with Delirium's odd stream-of-consciousness narrative and Desire's practiced taunting is far from rational and eerily like most current public political debates: petty, avoids anything of substance, and aims to hurt. In lieu of the travesty of a dinner party inside, one without dinner and without polite small talk, the conversation between Dream and Death in the garden is direct and goes straight to the point; Death considers Dream's feelings, but also considers him enough of an adult to face facts; Dream needs to right a past wrong and Death unflinchingly states it. Dream replies, "Is this how you feel? Truly? That I have been unjust?" Death simply answers, "Yes," leading Dream to state, "Very well, then. My course is clear" (21:22). His decision is emotional, but emotion based on his knowledge of his sister and her ethos. He trusts her judgment, leading to an easier meeting of the minds than through any family council, especially for a family like this, which has had centuries to disagree. Traditional debate with assumed opposing positions is a poor fit for human interaction where concerns are far less likely to be abstract and "sides" less clear. Death's appeal to Dream's sense of justice using his knowledge of her ethos was much more likely to succeed. Death's reclaimed sophistic rhetoric works well while also allowing her to incorporate her feminine, feminist, emotional self.

Another reclaimed rhetoric that connects well to the character Death appears in Patricia Bizzell's "Praising Folly: Constructing a Postmodern Rhetorical Authority as a Woman." In it, Bizzell uses an analysis of the 1515 Hans Holbein pen and ink drawing of Folly in Desiderius Erasmus's *The Praise of Folly* to reclaim what could be viewed as a negative stereotype of women in order to construct a postmodern rhetorical authority. She begins by pointing out that Folly is in academic garb teaching a group of men who are also in academic regalia (27), a renaissance situation just as unlikely as Gaiman's Death being young, female, perky, and in full goth regalia.

Next, Bizzell points out the postmodern connection and the reason why this is a good female figure to reclaim. She writes that the fool "is allowed to wander over boundaries supposedly held inviolable; and again, insofar as we watch without preventing the violation, we become complicit in it" (34). The fool speaks truth and wanders freely, speaking forthrightly to emperors and sycophants alike. The pastiche of millennial times means many overlapping communities or discourse groups, many overlapping borders; Death speaks effectively to all by letting her appearance and good humor romance them and her intimate knowledge of what it means to be human allure them. Like Bizzell's careful construction of a female rhetorical authority through the reclaimed female figure, Folly, the character Death is necessarily a creature of the borderlands, a term often associated with the work of Gloria Anzaldua and her *new mestiza* and *mestiza consciousness*. For Anzaldua, being Indian, Mexican, and living as an academic in a white world makes her declare the following about what that borderland would be like:

> So, don't give me your tenets and your laws. Don't give me your lukewarm gods. What I want is an accounting with all three cultures — white, Mexican, Indian. I want the freedom to carve and chisel my own face, to staunch the bleeding with ashes, to fashion my own gods out of my entrails. And if going home is denied me then I will have to stand and claim my space, making a new culture —*una cultura mestiza*—with my own lumber, my own bricks, and mortar and my own feminist architecture [44].

Death's metaphoric borderland, which is not inhabited by any "lukewarm gods," is no small space; instead, it is a dimensional layer, overlapping all space and time. This eternal border is physically defined in "The Sound of Her Wings" (*Sandman* 8) when she walks the streets that are not the streets with her brother Dream. He muses:

> Soundlessly we travel.
> No heads turn to mark
> our passing.
>
> The churning crowd
> parts as we walk
> through it looking
> everywhere else
> but not at us.
>
> In the world of the
> waking, of the living,
> we move silent as a
> breath of cool wind [8:11].

The haiku-like speech gives the context for their borderlands, their meta–Earth. She must walk in the spaces between heaven and Earth, must communicate with humans in the moment when communication seems beside the point but is in fact, of the utmost importance. Gaiman's Death seeks understanding for those about to pass over and does it by performing consensus, by channeling her audience-of-one's emotions into a more peaceful acceptance of the inevitable. As she tells Raine in "Façade" (*Sandman* 20):

> Anyway, I'm not blessed, or merciful ... I'm just **me**. I've got a **job** to do and I do it. Listen, even as we're talking, I'm there for old and young, innocent and guilty, those who die together and those who die alone. I'm in cars and boats and planes, in hospitals and forests and abattoirs. For some people death is a **release**, and for others death is an **abomination**, a **terrible** thing. But in the **end**, I'm there for **all** of them.

This speech can be seen as simple declaration, but how it declares shows the feminist and consensual nature of Gaiman's version of the character Death. She chooses existence and performance over manipulation. The empathic witness, in the end, is valued more than the most carefully chosen words.

To show the reasons behind the declaration, when enacting her role, Death takes pains to be egalitarian; she aims for the commonalities rather than the supernatural differences between herself and humans. For instance, her iconic role is a "job," not divine appointment, and her function is to be there, humbly, for all, an apt description for feminist mentoring, a form of persuasion which only works between equals. It also shows that to this Death, how her audience feels matters, and even though in the end her argument is the one that no human can win, she approaches it as a calm appeal to shared reason rather than an agonistic battle to be won. In this speech, Death reaches for consensus, even consubstantiation through her femininity, her calm "I'm just me," and that stance is her feminist strength.

Part of that strength is accepting rather than fighting the views of others. Bizzell states that through the voice of Folly, Erasmus "proceeds to demonstrate how to argue all sides of a question and to force the reader who attempts to make sense of her varying tones to see all sides of a question too" (37). The personified Folly in *The Praise of Folly* is female and historically a figure of ridicule rather than an icon of wisdom. The act of perceived folly is to show enough feminine weakness to acknowledge all alternate points of view and by doing so, let the reader make sense of the complete rhetorical situation. In Death's case, or in the case of the mortals who face her when at the point of death, seeing multiple points of view rather than the bodily "I hurt" or "Why me" is the only path to acceptance, the way to bypass despair. By using consensus and the egalitarian stance of a feminist, the character Death exemplifies *kairos*— using the best persuasive tools at hand for her situation, a move any classical or contemporary rhetor would approve, but one especially valued by feminist rhetors such as Bizzell or Anzaldua. Finally, Bizzell describes acting the fool when persuading, or "the woman who adopts a mock-innocent rhetorical stance is thus enabled to break taboos about what may be spoken of," with the caveat that even so, she may not be believed (40). Bizzell's "hope is that the widespread hunger for compassion and for an expression of compassion in a more just social order will allow this speaker to be heard" (40–41). There is no situation more immediate, more pressing, than the moment of death. If Gaiman's Death to the uninitiated (the living readers) seems a bit frivolous, even foolish in her perkiness and tattered folderols, it is only so she can use all the means at hand, even her living or not-so-living flesh, to ease one more spark of humanity to their natural and inevitable end. The living have no other mentor available in that moment than Death, and a compassionate Death is much more effective and uses *kairos* better that the tradition-ally dispassionate characterization.

In terms of mentoring, the times when Death walks the Earth as human are the best examples of her feminist mentoring. This mentoring could be viewed as on-on-one consensus, a leading that is both sensual and consensual. The three-volume *Death: The High Cost of Living* is an extended mentoring piece, one where she shakes a young man named Sexton out of his precocious ennui and shows him not only what it is to live, but what its value is. Even the character's name makes a point about his role: a *sexton* is the church official in charge of church property, usually the graveyard, and the name employs the obvious pun on "sex," which is, of course, the ultimate consensus. It makes sense that Death would spend her one day on Earth in a century helping a Sexton.

And she does help him, but as a mentor rather than an authority. In fact, the very word *mentor* may mislead with its lexical roots in "man." How-ever, it is the term still used even within feminist studies, despite being less top-down hierarchical and lacking the assumption of an all-male *polis*. In order to practice feminist mentoring, one must avoid an unequal power con-struct where the relationship is a simple sending and receiving from mentor to mentee. In other words, this is not the business school form of mentoring where a powerful vice president takes an up-and-comer under his wing; this form of mentoring demands a letting loose of power, a setting aside, so that the mentor can fully understand the mentee's needs as an equal. Using the mentoring situations typical of graduate school, Janice Lauer, well known for her feminist scholarship, states that "this process of mentoring and graduate student professional development contributes to an ethic of care" (234). This *ethic of care*, a now common term originated by Lauer that is used to describe the feminist approach to mentoring, means that even though the mentor has knowledge the mentee does not, the mentor approaches the mentee as an equal and does not co-opt her cognitive processes; instead the mentor gives what knowledge is needed, but treats the mentee as equal by letting the mentee work out her or his own way to the answer. In other words, *care*, an emotional and ethical point-of-view, is part of the mentorship role. Instead of acting as the superior giving instructions, the feminist approach to mentoring reposi-tions the mentor as a co-equal, one ready to assist but not impose. Just like in the best poetry, the trick is to show, not tell. Death in the human form of Didi cares about Sexton and wants him to enjoy the tremendous gift he has, that of being alive. Her best persuasion, aside from the example she gives through her actions of living each moment to the utmost and accepting it all — good and bad — is when they walk in Central Park. She listens to Sexton, letting him share his own troubles in more words and more reflectively than he has spoken before (3:15). Her response, after a few attempts at metaphor, is to answer directly his question about whether she enjoyed bad things along with the good: "No, I **didn't** like that. But ... it's part of the whole thing and there **is** a whole thing out there. And it's all part of living. The good bits and the bad bits and the dull bits and the painful bits" (3:16). Through her mentoring, Death exhibits an "ethic of care" in order to show Sexton how to live, not just exist — even through the bad bits.

Through the countless years, the emotions, the deaths, and the temporary experiences of living, Death constructs her own gender, her own feminism, and does it through a sequence of performative acts, as do we all. She earns her perkiness. Laboring through the centuries, through the initial sadness, the rejection of her role, her reborn acceptance, and through her continuing return to a temporary humanity, she has earned an irrepressible joy. That perkiness, which after all, is just joy with a thin layer of mockery given to it by those who think they are better than the young and female, that perkiness is a most persuasive and engaging emotion, one that allows Death to approach mortals with sincerity and a sense of equality, even though she literally holds their fate in her hands. She chooses consensus, she chooses to mentor, and that choice is of a piece with her femininity and yes, her feminism. After all, death is bad enough without adding the agony of agonistic persuasion on top of it. What could be viewed as perkiness and disparaged as silly female emotion is really a positive, consensual approach to persuasion, one that uses *kairos*, the available means, and allows those near the embodied Death to embrace a consensual decision and have peace.

WORKS CITED

Amos, Tori. "Afterword: Death." Eds. Neil Gaiman and Ed Kramer. New York: Harper-Torch, 1996. 393–395. Print.

Anzaldua, Gloria. *Borderlands: La Frontera: the New Mestiza.* 3d ed. San Francisco: Aunt Lute Books, 2007. Print.

Aristotle. *On Rhetoric: A Theory of Civic Discourse.* Trans. George A. Kennedy. Oxford: Oxford University Press, 1991.

Barthes, Roland. "Rhetoric of the Image." *Visual Rhetoric in a Digital World: A Critical Sourcebook.* Ed. Carolyn Handa. Boston: Bedford/St. Martin's, 2004. 152–163. Print.

Barton, Matthew D. "The Future of Rational-critical Debate in Online Public Spheres." *Computers and Composition.* 22 (2005): 177–190. Print.

Bizzell, Patricia. "Praising Folly: Constructing a Postmodern Rhetorical Authority as a Woman." *Feminine Principles and Women's Experience in American Compostion and Rhetoric.* Eds. Louise Wetherbee Phelps and Janet Emig. Pittsburgh: University of Pittsburgh Press, 1995. 27–42. Print.

Butler, Judith. *Gender Trouble.* New York: Routledge, 2008. Print.

Erasmus, Desiderius. *The Praise of Folly.* London: Hamilton, Adams and Co., 1887. Print.

Gaiman, Neil (w), John Bolton (p). "The Road to Nowhere." *Books of Magic* #4 (Feb. 1991), New York: DC Comics. Print.

_____ (w), Dave McKean (i). *Death Talks about Life*. New York: Vertigo-DC Comics, 1994. Print.

_____ (w), Chris Bachalo, Mark Buckingham, and Dave McKean (a, i). "A Night to Remember." *Death: The High Cost of Living* (March — May 1993), New York: DC Comics. Print.

_____ (w), Sean Phillips (a), Kent Williams (i). "Death: A Winter's Tale." *The Absolute Death*. New York: DC Comics, 2009. 220–225. Print.

_____ (w), Mike Dringenberg (a), Malcolm Jones III (i). "The Sound of Her Wings." *The Sandman* #8 (Aug. 1989), New York: DC Comics. Print.

_____ (w), Michael Zulli (a), Steve Parkhouse (i). "Men of Good Fortune." *The Sandman* #13 (Feb. 1990), New York: DC Comics. Print.

_____ (w), Colleen Doran (a), Malcolm Jones III (i). "Façade." *The Sandman* #20 (Oct. 1990), New York: DC Comics. Print.

_____ (w), Mike Dringenberg (a), Malcolm Jones III (i). "Season of Mists: Prologue." *The Sandman* #21 (Dec. 1990), New York: DC Comics. Print.

_____ (w), Shawn McManus (a), Pepe Moreno (i). "Three Septembers and a January." *The Sandman* #31 (Oct. 1991), New York: DC Comics. Print.

Glenn, Cheryl. *Rhetoric Retold: Regendering the Tradition from Antiquity Through the Renaissance*. Carbondale: Southern Illinois University Press, 1997. Print.

Habermas, Jürgen. *The Structural Transformation of the Public Sphere*. Trans. Thomas Burger. Cambridge: MIT University Press, 1998. Print.

Lauer, Janice M. "Graduate Students as Active Members of the Profession: Some Questions for Mentoring." *Publishing in Rhetoric and Composition*. Eds. Gary A. Olson and Todd W. Taylor. Albany: SUNY, 1997. 229–235. Print.

Agency Through Fragmentation?
The Problem of Delirium in The Sandman

BY JUSTIN MELLETTE

Over the course of its 75-issue run, Neil Gaiman's *The Sandman* presents myriad characters who rebuke the gendered criticism often leveled against comics and graphic novels. From Rose Walker in the "Doll's House" story arc to Barbie in "A Game of You," *The Sandman* presents female characters that acquire a sense of agency that has generally been denied to them in comics. Instead of presenting the damsel in distress and fetishistic heroine archetypes commonly associated with the medium, Gaiman creates characters grounded in a reality that acknowledges women as more than victims or objects of sexual objectification. The Sandman, also known as Dream, is a member of the Endless, seven siblings who serve as anthropomorphic embodiments of fundamental ideas. Death, the Sandman's older sister, has become one of the most popular comics characters in decades, with Gaiman himself admitting that the issue introducing Death (#8, "The Sound of Her Wings") was the "first story in the sequence I felt was truly mine" (*Absolute Sandman Volume I* 609). Considering the prominence of the series' female characters, proclaiming Gaiman as a "feminist" author who complicates normative stereotypes regarding women in comics certainly appears warranted.

Delirium, the youngest member of the Endless and originally known as Delight, stands in stark contrast to the slew of independent and unique heroines in the series. Unlike the majority of Gaiman's other female characters, Delirium appears to hearken back to the weak, feeble women of past comics with the added elements of neuroticism and madness. Often unable to sustain a prolonged idea in her mind, and with a physical appearance that constantly varies, sometimes several times on a single page, Delirium is a stark contrast to the other women in *The Sandman*. Her narrative role also seems ambiguous; in the limited issues she appears in she often acts as comic relief with her array of colorful fish and endless non-sequiturs, such as discussing "chicken and telephone ice cream" (48:15).[1] At first glance, her chief purpose in the series seems to be as the initiator of the "Brief Lives" story arc, where she accompanies Dream on a quest to locate their prodigal brother. While it would be easy to read Delirium chiefly as a victim to be pitied and nurtured, doing so privileges the patriarchal structure and reading practices that have long plagued comics. Though Delirium appears to be the most unstable member of the Endless and a modern representation of the madwoman trope, I argue that Gaiman's portrayal of a character haunted and scarred by an unseen psychological trauma problematizes the way in which readers and critics have treated depictions of female victims and presents a unique examination of new possibilities regarding women in comics.

Damsels in Distress and Men with Tits: Women in Comics

"The world of comics is unquestionably male-dominated because on the one hand society at large is unquestionably male-dominated, and on the other hand the public of the comics is unquestionably male-dominated," writes Maurice Horn in a useful summary of one of comics' oldest stereotypes (12). The earliest female characters in the late nineteenth and early twentieth century were little more than matronly archetypes, always performing domestic tasks such as cleaning, washing, and child-raising. Rudolph Dirks's Mamma Katzenjammer, the first recurring female character in a comic strip, had little personality beyond what was required to watch over her children. Young girls, in comics such as *The Yellow Kid*, were seldom more than "stupidly grinning child-shrews," subordinate to their male counterparts (Horn 17). As the industry slowly matured, giving rise to more fleshed-out characters, women retained their second-class status, with characters sharing "an acceptance for their social role as the weaker sex" (Horn 18). While more assertive women, such as Positive Polly in *Polly and Her Pals,* achieved popularity before and during the Jazz Age, comics almost universally reflected a male-dominated society.

Depictions of flappers and working girls in 1920s comics were certainly a positive step in comics equality, but the modern perception of women in comics derives largely from the (disproportionately) buxom heroines of superhero comics. Wonder Woman, who first appeared in 1941, was drawn as something far more than a female vigilante; her creator, psychologist William Moulton Marston, endowed her with a skin-tight outfit and exaggerated feminine shape to explore themes of sexual dominance and submission.[2] Indeed, her two primary weapons, a golden lasso and the bracelets of submission, allowed for numerous stories with "scenes of men or women tied up, chained, manacled, or otherwise trapped in fetishistic paraphernalia"

(Hajdu 78). Interestingly, reading Wonder Woman comics reveals that the heroine herself, rather than the villains, is the general victim of bondage. The sexual implication — that women were fit to be submissive and tied down by more aggressive men — helped fuel criticisms leveled against comics at the time by the Catholic church, sociologists, and, eventually the U.S. government.

Romance comics, which began appearing in abundance in the late 1940s, also added to the stereotypical representation of women as sexually submissive and passive recipients of male attention.[3] The protagonists in the comics, with titles such as *My Love Story, My Love Life, My Love Affair, My Love Secret,* and *My Secret Affair,* were generally presented with little more than a choice between two suitors, one rugged and disreputable, the other dull and secure. As one of the few genres written with a female audience in mind, the tales were often platitudinous and attempted to reinforce societal constraints of the postwar era. The Comics Code, released by the CMAA (Comics Magazine Association of America) in 1954, included amongst its requirements a promulgation of the stereotype: "the treatment of love-romance stories shall emphasize the value of the home and the sanctity of marriage" (Hajdu 292). Later comics also fed into the stereotypes surrounding a women's supposed domesticity. Spider-Man, for example, "is a superhero who's always fretting because he needs money, money to take his girl out before she ditches him for a more generous escort" (Glicksohn 8). The image of the self-centered, greedy girlfriend, not privy to her boyfriend's alter-ego, sets a line of demarcation that proliferates in superhero comics: women are, at best, passive and in need of rescue and, at worst, shrewish, fickle, and insensitive.

By the time Neil Gaiman first published *The Sandman* in 1989, comics were just beginning to address women's liberation and feminism through characters such as Ms. Marvel. There was no reason to know that the characters in Gaiman's new series would offer anything different from decades of sexist portrayals. B. Keith Murphy suggests that, being raised in England rather than America, Gaiman had an easier time breaking the "mold" of American comics because his "exposure to the books and their generic expectations/restrictions was limited, whereas American children who were inclined to become comic-book creators had been inundated with the powerful imagery and storytelling of the Silver Age of American Comics" (Murphy 10). Gaiman himself notes the typical sexist disparity regarding women in comics, claiming "the really progressive thing" about *Sandman* was its ability to "represent *any* sort of woman, regardless of sexual orientation, as nice, cool, and sensible, when the tradition in comics was to portray a woman as either a damsel in distress or a man with tits" (Gaiman 124).[4] Though Gaiman was not the first comics writer to treat women as more than one-dimensional over-sexualized heroines or meek damsels in distress, *The Sandman's* complexity allows for a more nuanced and mature discussion regarding feminism in comics.

Delirium, Who Was Once Delight

Considering the well-known male demographic of the comics industry at the time, Gaiman's willingness to spend a great deal of time with female characters in *The Sandman* is both surprising and potentially problematic, if Marston's fetishistic tastes are kept in mind. Still, Gaiman's characters generally veer away from the demeaning stereotypes of earlier heroines. While Rose and Barbie, each protagonists of an entire story arc, ultimately require the Sandman's aid, neither is drawn nor represented in an overtly stereotypical manner. Barbie, in defiance of her namesake, covers her traditionally good looks with checkerboard face paint early in the "A Game of You" storyline. Later, to the disgust of her transvestite friend Wanda's elder family members, Barbie draws on a veil, masking her looks with a tribute for her deceased friend. Claiming that "*Sandman* was always designed to move from male stories to female stories," Gaiman reveals a desire to combat a male-dominated narrative (117). He notes that "A Game of You" "deals with girl versus boy fantasies, and the idea of gender versus the reality of gender" (118). Barbie's final act in the storyline, crossing out the name "Alvin" and replacing it with "Wanda" in vibrant pink lipstick, shows that, in spite of a namesake suggestive of heteronormativity, Barbie is willing to acknowledge the complexities of gender and celebrates her departed friend's individuality.

Enter Delirium. Her first appearance, in the prologue to "Season of Mists," is a visually jarring moment. Destiny's hall contains portraits of each of the Endless, each depicted in formal garb. As befitting his stoic, unchanging personality, he retains a portrait of Delirium's earlier incarnation, Delight. Also, unlike several of the other members of his family, he refuses to call her by name, referring to her as "youngest of the Endless," revealing his unwillingness or perhaps inability to accept his sister's altered state (21:7). Also, by referring to her as the youngest, he positions her as inherently inferior in relation to their family. At a family meeting called by Destiny at the beginning of the "Season of Mists" story arc, Delirium wears ripped and tattered leggings, a stark contrast to the formal attire worn by the rest of the family. Her appearance is also markedly different from her own portrait, where, as Delight, she wears a light blue dress and bonnet, standing before rolling hills of green. Her first lines, "Yesterday I did some really bad stuff. I mean real bad. You know. But today I did some good things. I don't know. You know" reveal a disparate, fragmented personality, marred by self-consciousness (21:8). Throughout the meeting, Delirium struggles to maintain her composure; she absent-mindedly creates butterflies before Desire coldly and cruelly uses her influence to send them into a candle. Desire, who appears male or female depending on the situation and an individual's perception, frequently utilizes her powers to influence or goad others into uncomfortable and difficult situations.[5] She continuously needles Delirium, calling her by her former name. "Delight was a long time ago," Delirium quietly responds, followed by an impassioned outburst: "Don't laugh at me, Desire. Don't make fun of me. I know what you think about me" (21:17). In the frame where Desire calls her Delight, Delirium is cloaked in shadow, accentuating the tragic fall from her original form. While Desire frequently shows malice towards Dream, who responds to her with derision of his own, her treatment of her sister exacerbates Delirium's condition.

In contrast to the forceful, independent-minded members of the Endless, Delirium appears as a fragmented, neurotic, young woman. The other female members of the Endless are assertive and strong-willed; Death, in ironic opposition to her title, is free-spirited, exuberant, and energetic, Despair appears to handle her often unseemly duties competently and Desire is aggressive enough to plot Dream's downfall.[6] Delirium, on the other hand, appears to be a character with little influence, constantly pitied, patronized, and at the mercy of stronger-willed characters such as Desire. Considering the lack of voice for women in comics for decades, why would Gaiman make his most overtly troubled and seemingly voiceless representative of many aspects of the victimized, helpless female archetype? Though calling them male or female is somewhat misleading since the Endless are embodiments of ideas, the gendered appearance of the various members often correlates to their personas. That Destruction is male comes as no surprise, and Desire's dual sexuality / gender also makes sense considering the need to appeal to either men or women, depending on the situation. Making Death feminine and cheerful, as opposed to the gloomy Grim Reaper stereotype, is a surprising though welcome approach to the character. Making Delirium female, however, could imply to readers that the mental instability and neuroticism she represents is somehow more applicable to a female rather than male character. In keeping with his references to the madwoman trope throughout *Sandman* (through characters such as Chantal and Zelda in "A Doll's House"), Gaiman gestures towards stereotypes against women and mental instability with the character of Delirium. His treatment of her, however, is more complex than merely classifying her as a victim of mental unbalance. Over the course of the series, Delirium comes to stand as a vessel for reader identification, open to numerous interpretations of her bizarre mental state.

Though she frames her discussion in terms of autobiographical graphic narratives, Hillary Chute's examination of the feminist concerns can also be used to better understand Gaiman's use of a problematic character such as Delirium. Claiming that "some of today's most riveting feminist cultural production is in the form of accessible yet edgy graphic narratives," Chute examines authors such as Marjane Satrapi and Alison Bechdel that have chosen stories that require both showing *and* telling (2). This of course is hardly unique to the nonfiction narratives Chute focuses on and applies equally well to a comic like *The Sandman*; Delirium's fragmented, chaotic appearance, coupled with her loopy, psychedelic word balloons adds an indispensable visual aid to her internal struggles. Like the women in the narratives Chute discusses, Gaiman presents Delirium as both a "looking and looked-at subject" (2): in addition to following her narrative function in the story, readers are free to project their own insecurities and concerns onto her unnamed and unexplained transition from Delight. Delirium's youthful appearance and more approachable nature make her an enticing vessel for reader identification in comparison with the stolid, unflappable Dream.

The most notable aspect of Delirium's supposed victimhood is that readers are never privy to the knowledge of why Delirium, who was once Delight, altered her self-identification. While much of *The Sandman's* plot is ambiguous, such as Dream's complex plan in the "Kindly Ones" arc that ultimately results in his own death, Delirium's alteration is one of the few mysteries that remain deliberately unanswered. Inviting readers to hypothesize as to her condition is hardly a novel element in comics. As Scott McCloud points out, comics universally make use of closure, which he defines as the "phenomenon of observing the parts but perceiving the whole" (McCloud 63). Though McCloud is referring to the way in which the brain processes the juxtaposed images of comics and what occurs between panels (the gutter), the elements of reader-response take on a new meaning when applied to comics. As McCloud describes it, "every act committed to paper by the comics artist is aided and abetted by a silent accomplice. An equal partner in crime knows as the reader" (68). The reader, then, not the artist, determines how hard an axe falls or other such grisly details that occur between panels, to use McCloud's example. In Delirium's case, readers must imagine the violence or tragedy that befell her and led to her transformation from Delight since it is left deliberately ambiguous.

By intentionally leaving Delirium's tragedy unresolved, Gaiman invites readers to assign their own rationale for her fragmented status and prevents pigeonholing Delirium's transformation into one form of trauma. Such an approach invites individual interpretation, hearkening back to the hallmarks of reader-response criticism. In Stanley Fish's words, "it is the structure of the reader's experience rather than any structures available on the page that should be the object of description" (152). Thus, in the case of Delirium, *why* she has changed in the *Sandman* universe is not as important as how readers approach her condition. Wolfgang Iser also points to the importance of the reader's reaction to a text, maintaining a work is "composed of a variety of perspectives, which outline the author's view and also provide access to what the reader is meant to visualize" (35). Rather than depicting Delirium as, say, the victim of a spurned lover or a family catastrophe, her tragedy is universal, all-encompassing and open for readers to see her or his own experiences in her character. In the opening description of Delirium, the narrator posits that "some say the tragedy of Delirium is her knowledge that, despite being older than suns, older than gods, she is forever the youngest of the Endless," but this explanation is merely one possibility (21:10). What makes her unique in comics is that her tragedy is unseen by the audience; as Fish points out, a reader's own experience can color his or her reaction to the character. The closing line of her opening description forces the reader to consider her state of existence: "Who knows what Delirium sees, through her mismatched eyes?" (21:10). For all of her seeming inadequacy in comparison to her siblings, Delirium represents a universal tragedy in which readers can project their own anxieties and societal concerns.

Even when Delirium herself discusses her change, Gaiman leaves room for interpretation. In "The Song of Orpheus" special issue, she briefly mentions nearly getting married, adding "but that was a long time ago. It never happened. Maybe that was my fault. I don't know. Shit happens" (*Sandman Special* 1:5). While heartbreak remains a possible explanation for her transformation, the idea is not brought up again in the series and ultimately feels too inconsequential to account for such a drastic change of identity. Her most direct comments on the matter reveal the universality of her experience. After witnessing her eldest brother Destiny upset Dream, she attempts an explanation: "Do you know why I stopped being Delight, my brother? I do. There are things not in your book. There are paths outside this garden. You would do well to remember that" (47:11). Earlier, during her outburst towards Desire, Delirium proclaims, "I know lots of things. Things about us. Things not even [Destiny] knows" (21:17). Her determination and confidence that all of existence is *not* at the mercy of the fate delineated and contained in Destiny's book reveals that, unlike the scores of voiceless women in comics past, Delirium has a measure of agency both unexpected and welcome in the medium. Rather than just an insignificant pawn, Delirium is an agent of a constructive, theoretical approach to existence. Her use of the active verb "stopped" suggests that her transformation was self-induced, perhaps out of her own realization that a permanent embodiment of Delight was impossible to sustain in the universe. In spite of the patronizing attitude other characters show towards her, Delirium reveals insight into the nature of the Endless that marks her as more independent and wiser than her siblings, and potentially readers, give her credit for.

The most powerful and stirring representation of Delirium's tragedy comes during her flashback near the beginning of the "Brief Lives" arc. While waiting for Dream to decide whether or not he will accompany her on her journey, she reflects on her days as Delight: "The moment she realized what was happening, that the universe was changing, that she was growing up or at least growing older she was no longer Delight; and the blossoms had already begun to fall in her domain, becoming smudged and formless colors, and she had no one to talk to" (42:20). The contrast in the artwork between Delirium and Delight on this page is striking. No gutter separates the images; Delirium is hunched over, looking concerned and apprehensive, with a dull gray shirt over her tattered stocking in front of a drab background. Delight, on the other half of the page, is stunningly beautiful, with flowing blond hair, dotted with flowers, standing on a vibrant patch of land in front of a cliff. Delirium's memory also includes a visit from Destruction, who calmly tells her "things are changing" (42:20). The narrator's implication, that growing up or growing older, led to Delight's change, while ambiguous, provides more rationale for Delirium's fragmented state. Her fall is emblematic of a general fall from innocence, an awakening of an undefined nature. Potentially a metaphor for blossoming sexuality, Adam and Eve's expulsion from the Garden of Eden, or just recognition of the cruelty of the world itself, Delirium's state is a mirror of society at large and a reflection of injustices leveled against women, the specifics of which can be applied by the individual reader. That Delirium had "no one to talk to" suggests that as time goes on, fewer and fewer people live lives completely unmarred by sadness or tragedy. Eventually, nobody can remain in Delight's realm because pure happiness is impossible. While some, such as Destiny and Death, continue with their responsibilities in the face of such injustice without hesitation, other members of the Endless, including Dream and Destruction, struggle with them. Delirium, on the other hand, who has clearly suffered the most for her awareness of her family's complex nature, endures in spite of her unbalanced state. Whether or not gender is a key factor in her change is unclear, though it bears remembering that the only member of the Endless to show mental instability is indeed female. As Julie Goodspeed-Chadwick points out, "depictions of traumatized female bodies are fraught with political implications related to gendered identity. Gender matters in representations of trauma" (9–10). Reader response to a male Delirium would be decidedly different; certainly less patronizing and less fraught with sexist implications. Nevertheless, examining Delirium's narrative purpose in the series dispels any notions that she bears anything more than a superficial resemblance to women in comics past and reveals a complex and nuanced character that undergoes vast changes of her own, in spite of her psychological affliction.

A Journey of Her Own

While Delirium's complex personality rises above normative stereotypes of female victimhood, her narrative purpose also marks a shift in traditional attitudes towards women in comics. As an emotionally fragile individual, the general assumption of both *The Sandman* character as well as the readers raised on traditional comics is that Delirium requires male assistance and "rescue." At first glance, however, much of her personality seems derivative of comics' sexist history. Women are frequently depicted in ways that "undermine their own strength and power," and it might appear that Delirium is no exception (Knight x). When compared to Dream, with his forceful, intransigent manner, Delirium seems unhinged and devoid of control. Her madness, though certainly powerful and even horrific in its unpredictability, suggests a lack of competence in relation to her more stable siblings. Throughout the series, readers see less of Delirium's abilities than her siblings. One of her few actions towards mortals is cursing some unassuming policemen with invisible insects for the rest of their lives, a far cry from her siblings' powers, though the act does result in the cops losing their sanity (45:5). Delirium also appears to share many of the normative traits of women in action genres: "Men epitomized physical power, emotional control, and brawn, and women were deemed to be their polar opposites" with traits such as "emotionalism, physical weakness, dependency, gullibility, ability to nurture, and a lesser intelligence than men" (Knight xv). The near universal negativity of these traits paints an alarming picture for Gaiman's representation of her; the "Brief Lives" story arc, encompassing the search for the prodigal member of the Endless, Destruction, is brought about by Delirium's own pain at missing her brother. At a nightclub, after mistaking a Goth woman for her sister Death, Delirium breaks down, screaming and afraid. Shortly thereafter, in Desire's realm, she acknowledges that she is "finding it harder to hold on" (41:13). When Desire tells her to pull herself together, Delirium explodes into a swarm of multicolored butterflies, and, after reassembling anthropomorphically, sadly remarks, "I'm together. Aren't I? I know I used to be" (41:13–14). Afraid to look for her brother alone, she seeks Dream's help and appears to be at best a voiceless accomplice and at worse a needy nuisance during the journey. As the story progresses, however, Delirium comes to take a more active role, belying her early appearances of being weak and helpless.

While Delirium is the chief instigator of the "Brief Lives" story, whether or not this in itself serves as any sort of feminist representation or agency has been questioned. In "Illusory Adversaries?: Image of Female Power in *Sandman: Kindly Ones*," K.A. Laity argues against overzealous praise of Gaiman's treatment of female characters. Though acknowledging a "profusion of well-rounded characters," Laity maintains that *The Sandman*'s circular, complex structure "undercuts the power and menace of the supposed adversaries of Morpheus" (66). Because Dream brought about his own destruction over the course of the series, Laity argues "all these female characters serve only as instruments for Dream's death-wish and creator Gaiman's narrative completion.... Apparent female power turns out to be merely a tool for male composition" (66). Though Laity focuses almost entirely on the "Kindly Ones" arc, a similar claim could be made concerning Delirium. While undeniably true that the ancillary characters act to assist Dream throughout the series, that does not necessarily preclude that the women themselves lack a story or narrative of their own, particularly Delirium. While the quest to find the prodigal brother Destruction ends with Dream fulfilling his son's wish to die, Delirium's role is more than supplementary; she is the essential driving force of the narrative.

Dream, ostensibly in charge of their journey, nevertheless falters when Destiny confronts him about his son Morpheus. Being reminded about the son he has forsaken greatly upsets Dream, who shows what could be considered a stereotypically feminine emotive response for the comics medium. Delirium, on the other hand, makes a decidedly masculine appraisal of the situation, urging Dream on and chastising Destiny for being narrow-minded: "There are paths outside this garden. You would do well to remember that" (47:11). During this sequence, Delirium's eyes are a matching shade of blue rather than their traditionally mismatched representation. She also speaks with less sporadic, chaotic word balloons. When Dream comments on her appearance, she calmly explains, "If you're going to fall apart, then one of us has to keep this thing going. Please get up. I don't know how much longer I can be like this. It hurts very muchly" (47:12). While recognizing her own limitations, Delirium pushes herself, for the first time in the series, to a more intact, together state. While Laity would likely argue that the scene merely shows Delirium fulfilling Gaiman's narrative purpose which, admittedly, it does, such a view ignores the fact that the scene reveals Delirium to be far more complex and stable than her normally neurotic personality suggests.

Though she is unable to convince Destruction to return to his duties, Delirium, unlike her siblings, shows an understanding as to why he abandoned them in the first place. After relating the story of her journey with Dream in her typical, roundabout manner, complete with references to airplanes and chocolate lovers, she acknowledges having to put herself together. Once again, her eyes are the same color (green, as opposed to blue in the scene with Destiny) as she cries and quietly tells Destruction that "it hurt" (48:6). Dream, on the succeeding panel, is looking down, a pained expression on his face as he reflects on his own complicity in the matter. As Destruction and Dream debate about the nature of personal responsibility and the Endless' roles in the universe, Delirium calmly follows along, stating her brother left "because there's no such thing as a one-sided coin" (48:17). Dream, who sees the universe predominantly in how it relates to his realm, the Dreaming, is less willing to accept his brother's departure. Destruction continues, mentioning a conversation with Death where he was told, "everyone can know everything Destiny knows. And more than that. She said we all not only could know everything, we do. We just tell ourselves we don't to make it all bearable" (48:17–8). Dream is skeptical and Destruction maintains that he, too, is puzzled by the quote, but Delirium, who has often referenced knowing matters that the rest of the Endless do not, claims "she is. Um. Right. Kind of. Not knowing everything is all that makes it okay, sometimes" (48:18). Delirium, who has suffered far more than the rest of the Endless, is the only character able to comprehend the price that an abundance of knowledge places on a psyche. If we read her transformation in part as a fall (or Fall) from innocence, then it becomes clear that only by pretending that painful, traumatic aspects of life do not exist can we continue living in the universe mentally unscathed. Doing so, however, is living a shadow life, devoid of reality and responsibility.

While the quest ostensibly ends with the pair finding Destruction and his subsequent departure, Dream's journey is not over until he grants his forsaken son Orpheus the reprieve of death. Delirium, however, appears to be finished and, for all intents and purposes, only a marginal character for the remainder of the series. Viewing her as nothing but Dream's accomplice and the progenitor of the quest undermines her own adaptability and character growth. While Dream exhibits far more traits of the traditional hero, following many of Joseph Campbell's stages of the monomyth. He answers Delirium's "Call to Adventure" and acquires the necessary knowledge from Destruction to become "Master of Two Worlds," his Dreamworld and the mortal world embodied by Orpheus and others. Delirium, however, also shows traits of a narrative hero, even if they are less visibly heroic. In this interpretation, the "Brief Lives" arc serves as the precursor to Delirium's solo quest in the "Kindly Ones" story; the recovery of her dog Barnabas. While she tells Dream at the conclusion of their quest, "I don't think I could have done it on my own," the truth remains that Dream also could not have done it on his own (49:8). Now, with a restored sense of confidence and relative stability, Delirium embarks on an individual quest in the climactic story arc of *The Sandman*.

Compared to the tragic overtones of Dream's battle with the Furies, the ultimate consequence of his granting Orpheus the release of death, a search for a lost dog seems trivial and inconsequential. Both characters' actions, however, are a direct result of their reactions to the circumstances of their earlier quest. Dream is ultimately unable to cope with the loss of his son and, rather than abandon his domain as Destruction does, he constructs an elaborate narrative in which he is the tragic victim of events supposedly beyond his control. While his devotion to his responsibilities is in many ways admirable, it also reveals the limitations of his character. Throughout the series, various characters comment upon their perceptions of his new personality, from his former wife Calliope to his past lover Nada, whom he frees from Hell after acknowledging that his ten-thousand-year-old grudge may have been unjust. Dream constantly denies changing, however, and appears uncomfortable regarding any inclination that he has. Ultimately, Dream accepts the reality that he can no longer perform his duties and allows a new embodiment of Dream, the child Daniel, to replace him, presumably with a more humanist outlook. Delirium, on the other hand, also shows newfound resilience and a more expansive growth than would normally be associated with a victimized female in comics.

Delirium's first appearance in this story arc is intentionally misleading, apparent belying any belief that she has changed since her previous appearance in "Brief Lives." The narrator matter-of-factly notes, "It was then Delirium noticed that she had absent-mindedly transformed into a hundred and eleven perfect, tiny multicolored fish. Each fish sang a different song" (59:12). On the next page, a now anthropomorphic Delirium, with a somewhat pensive look on her face, muses about wanting a dog before recalling "there had been a dog around at some point, hadn't there?" (59:13). Though humorous, as her appearances often are, the scene is effectively the start of a quest that will showcase her newfound sense of order and control. Considering the lack of female characters, especially victimized ones, who undertake worthwhile adventures of their own, Delirium's journey is uncommon and refreshing. She mirrors some of her steps with Dream by visiting their elder brother Destiny, whom she reminds "last time I had a quest to find someone I did really well" (63:9). Destiny, rather than repeat his previous admonition to abandon her quest, advises Delirium that the choice is hers whether or not to attempt to aid Dream, showing a slight change in his attitude towards his youngest sister. Instead of his patronizing treatment in "Brief Lives," he shows a respect for her competence and tells her to continue her journey.

Though Dream refuses to accompany her on her search for Barnabas, Delirium's encounter with him showcases more of her incisive understanding of the Endless' duties. As a mild chastisement of her brother talking about his "responsibilities," Delirium reminds him, "Our existence deforms the universe. That's responsibility" (64:8). Her illustration of the maxim, that a member of the Endless admiring a bolt of lightning would leave a lingering effect on the people who encounter the same spot manifests itself in the "reality storm" of the "Worlds' End" story line, where the funeral procession for Dream reveals how much of an impact his demise has on the universe. Dream voices no response to her, and the narrator tells us "if he was shaken inside, or disturbed in any way by this meeting, he gave no evidence of this" (64:9), though, like Destiny, he at least treats Delirium with more respect than in previous encounters.

As her quest winds down, Delirium encounters Nuala of Faerie, who assists with some advice, and finally encounters Lucifer, moonlighting as a nightclub pianist. During their conversation, Delirium shows more control and restraint than nearly any previous appearance. In a panel where she says, "I want my doggie back. And I want my brother all right. I don't want him hurt or anything," her appearance is strikingly *normal* (68:13). In spite of the multicolored hair and eyes, Delirium's face is earnest, sincere, and controlled. She is also grasping her hands together in a pleading fashion, showing a human element that many of the Endless struggle to reveal. Lucifer sends her along to find Barnabas, but not without being moved. Her appearance causes him to reflect on his own talk with Dream on the nature of abandoning one's kingdom and acquiring "the ultimate freedom. The freedom to leave" (68:14). He also recalls his first encounter with Dream in *The Sandman,* and, rather than harbor resentment at Dream's embarrassment of him in front of the legions of Hell, he pities him: "You know, I swore to destroy him. Your brother ... he embarrassed me ... now I feel almost sorry for him" (68:13). Just as with Destiny and Dream, Delirium elicits a complex response from a more stereotypically strong and powerful character.

Dream's death, the climactic moment of the entire series, occurs over several visually striking panels, culminating in Death and Dream's fingers meeting in a manner reminiscent of Michelangelo's *Creation of Adam* segment of the Sistine Chapel (69:10–1). Merely a few pages later, in a grand reversal of the high tragedy of Dream's demise, Delirium and Barnabas are reunited, with the dog knocking her over, licking her face ebulliently. The juxtaposition of the end of the two quests provides an emphatic statement on Delirium's resilience. In place of her static ancestors in comics, women forced to wait for their savior to arrive, Delirium embarked on a quest that, in spite of its seeming inconsequentiality, revealed her ability to endure despite her fragmented condition. Delirium also meets the homeless man who had been watching Barnabas and offers a gift, mentioning "palaces and golden touches and Oh! Never dying and things?" (69:15). The man declines, however, stating that though he is "kind of yours anyway," he realizes the implications of asking a boon of Delirium could have potentially drastic results (69:15). Still, Delirium offering a boon reveals a parallel between her and Dream. Two of his boons — granting Orpheus his death and leaving the Dreaming to visit Nuala — play a major role in his destruction. By ultimately not granting the man a boon, Delirium is free from the rigid constraints that come back to haunt Dream. As she and Barnabas walk off into Delirium's realm, which is bright and colorful, another contrast to the overwhelming blacks and blues of the Dreaming, Barnabas tries to comfort Delirium about her brother, stating, "I'm sure he can take care of himself" to which she responds, "I ... I don't think so..." (69:15). The use of ellipses intensifies her level of concentration and introspection here; for all of Dream's officious, perspicacious nature, the story arc ends with Delirium, thought by so many to be weak and enfeebled, doubting her brother's ability to look after himself.

In the final *Sandman* story arc, "The Wake," Delirium continues to be an active participant, showing her ability to maintain composure in times of necessity. Joining the rest of her family to make preparations for Dream's funeral, her behavior is relatively reserved, as she comments upon her sorrow and her desire that Destruction would have come (70:4–5). She is also the first member of the family to begin building the Envoy out of mud and grants him his name, Eblis O'Shaughnessy. Throughout the story, she wears a pink dress, with wings attached to the back, resembling a young girl. Though her leggings are tattered and the wings seem out of place for the formal occasion, the outfit still stands in stark contrast to her typical multicolored clothes. During the funeral ceremony, Delirium reveals the depths of her pain, including yelling at Desire for mocking Destiny's manner of speaking at the funeral (72:5). Before she begins her own speech, Barnabas offers to comfort her to get her through it. "He was my big brother. He really was. I was always a bit scared of him. But I'm not scared of him anymore. I'm a bit sad of him instead. Okay. That's all," she says amidst a small field of flowers and lawn decorations (including an octopus) that she has created (72:12). Though brief, her words reveal the pain she feels at his loss. In a brief panel below her talk she is shown walking off with her head bowed. With the exception of Death, Delirium spends the most time with Dream than any other member of the Endless throughout the series, and her words speaks volumes to the grief she feels, in spite of her initial fear of her daunting, brooding older brother.

Conclusion: "I am hope"

When asked to summarize *The Sandman* in twenty-five words or less, Neil Gaiman remarked, "The Lord of Dreams learns one must change or die, and makes his decision" (Intro. *EN*). The nature of change and one's ability to cope with its repercussions is the dominant theme of the entire *Sandman* series. While the Sandman's subtle changes after his decades-long imprisonment do ultimately open his eyes to realize that a new, kinder, more humane facet of Dream is necessary moving forward, his death comes as a result of his inability to reconcile himself with the world around him. Delirium, on the other hand, who, through unnamed and unidentified trauma and hardship, had change forced upon her, is one of the series' strongest survivors. As Hy Bender points out, Dream in many ways is the opposite of Delirium, a being "who's forgotten the wonders of childhood, who's become so stuffy that he's lost his sense of play" (208). While "neither of the extremes represented by these two Endless is a practical way to live," "Delirium had the wisdom to reach out for a balancing influence, first via Destruction and then via Barnabas" (208).

In one of the most memorable sequences of the early issues, Dream engages in a battle with the demon Choronzon. Playing "the oldest game," the pair announces identities that must be countered. When Choronzon moves beyond animals and announces he is anthrax, Dream announces he is "a world, space-floating, life nurturing." Choronzon counters with a planet destroying nova, before Dream counters with another burst of optimism: "I am the Universe — all things encompassing, all life embracing." Choronzon's final play, "anti-life ... the end of universes, gods, worlds," is defeated by Dream's simple statement "I am hope" (4:18–9). The sequence is remarkable in its affirmative qualities, which in retrospect seem somewhat surprising for the normally steadfast and morose Dream. By the end of the series, Dream is no longer able to proclaim himself as hope, and must die in order for a new aspect of Dream that can. Delirium, however, a character who so often seems utterly helpless and hopeless, resides in optimism. From her first appearance in "Brief Lives," where she dances in place chanting "change change change" (41:9), the narrative has hinted that her identity as Delirium may not be permanent. Gaiman himself makes this point: "She's been one thing, she's become something else, and eventually she'll change into something else again" (Bender 241). Shortly before departing, Destruction tells her, "I trust that when your next change comes, it proves easy on you" (48:17).

In her earlier incarnation of Delight, she was arguably the only wholly positive aspect of the Endless; while Destruction allows for new creation and Death is a reprieve for many, Delight is in stark contrast to Despair, eternally hopeful, optimistic and joyous. Her transformation comes in part due to the realization that untarnished delight and happiness is impossible in the universe, and her inability to maintain that state is part of why she becomes Delirium, fractured and lacking unity. Though this change seemingly removes any positives from the Endless entirely, Delirium does reveal an inner strength and resiliency that is necessary for survival in the world. In stark contrast to stereotypical female victims in comics, the series ends on an optimistic note for the character. While her future remains uncertain, *The Sandman* ends with the contention that her ability to endure will lead her out of her fractured state of Delirium into a brighter, more stable future.

NOTES

1. All references will be made to the issue number followed by the page number.

2. Marston wrote under the pen name Charles Moulton, which combined his and All American Publications founder Max Gaines's middle names.

3. According to David Hajdu, romance comics accounted for "nearly a fifth of the more than 650 comics published" in 1950 (157).

4. Quoted in *The Sandman Companion*. Interestingly, before *Sandman*, Gaiman was working on *Black Orchid*, and ultimately stopped because his editor Karen Berger told him "Black Orchid is female, and female characters don't sell" (Bender 22–3).

5. I will refer to Desire with the feminine pronoun throughout for continuity, though this does not encompass her various range of genders and bodily forms.

6. It is worth noting that, due to Desire's ambiguous, shifting gender, the Endless are equally divided with three and a half males and females.

WORKS CITED

Bender, Hy. *The Sandman Companion.* New York: Vertigo, 1999. Print.

Campbell, Joseph. *The Hero With a Thousand Faces.* Princeton: Princeton University Press, 1949. Print.

Chute, Hillary L. *Graphic Women: Life Narrative and Contemporary Comics.* New York: Columbia University Press, 2010. Print.

Fish, Stanley. *Is There a Text in This Class?* Cambridge: Harvard University Press, 1980. Print.

Gaiman, Neil. *The Absolute Sandman Volume I.* New York: DC Comics, 2006. Print.

_____. Quoted in *The Sandman Companion.* Print.

_____ (w), Sam Kieth (a), Mike Dringenberg (i). "A Hope in Hell." *The Sandman* #4 (April 1989), New York: DC Comics. Print.

_____ (w), Mike Dringenberg (a), Malcolm Jones III (i). "The Sound of Her Wings." *The Sandman* #8 (Aug. 1989), New York: DC Comics. Print.

_____ (w), Mike Dringenberg (a), Malcolm Jones III (i). "Season of Mists: Prologue." *The Sandman* #21 (Dec. 1990), New York: DC Comics. Print.

_____ (w), Jill Thompson (a), Vince Locke (i). "Brief Lives." *The Sandman* #41–49 (Sept. 1992 — May 1993), New York: DC Comics. Print.

_____ (w), Mark Hempel, D'Israeli, Mark Estes, Glyn Dillon, Charles Vess, Tim Truman, John Muth, Richard Case (a, i). "The Kindly Ones." *The Sandman* #57–69 (Feb. 1994 — July 1995), New York: DC Comics. Print.

_____ (w), Dave McKean, Michael Zulli (a, i). "The Wake: Chapter Three." *The Sandman* #72 (Nov. 1995), New York: DC Comics. Print.

_____ (w), Bryan Talbot (a), Marck Buckingham (i). "The Song of Orpheus." *The Sandman Special* #1 (1991), New York: DC Comics. Print.

_____ (w), Craig Russell, et al. (a, i). *The Sandman: Endless Nights* #1–4. New York: DC Comics, 2003. Print.

Glicksohn, Susan Wood. *The Poison Maiden and the Great Bitch: Female Stereotypes in Marvel Superhero Comics*. Baltimore: T-K Graphics, 1974. Print.

Goodspeed-Chadwick, Julie. *Modernist Women Writers and War*. Baton Rouge: Louisiana State University Press, 2011. Print.

Hajdu, David. *The Ten-Cent Plague: The Great Comic-Book Scare and How It Changed America*. New York: Picador, 2008. Print.

Horn, Maurice. *Women in the Comics. Vol. 1–3*. Philadelphia: Chelsea House Publishers, 2001. Print.

Iser, Wolfgang. *Prospecting: From Reader Response to Literary Anthropology*. Baltimore: The Johns Hopkins University Press, 1989. Print.

Knight, Gladys L. *Female Action Heroes: A Guide to Women in Comics, Video Games, Film, and Television*. Santa Barbara: Greenwood, 2010. Print.

Laity, K.A. "Illusory Adversaries? Images of Female Power in *Sandman: Kindly Ones*," in *The Sandman Papers*. Ed. Joe Sanders. Seattle: WA: Fantagraphics, 2006. Print.

McCloud, Scott. *Understanding Comics*. New York: HarperCollins, 1993. Print.

Murphy, B. Keith. "The Origins of *The Sandman*," in *The Sandman Papers*. Ed. Joe Sanders. Seattle: Fantagraphics, 2006. Print.

It's Pretty Graphic

Sexual Violence and the Issue of "Calliope"

BY TARA PRESCOTT

> "Actually, I *do* tend to regard myself as a feminist writer."
> — Ric Madoc, "Calliope"

Calliope truly is a writer's goddess. Her Greek name, *Καλλιόπη,* means "beautiful-voiced," and not only is she the source of eloquent speech herself, but she also has the power of inspiring poetry in others (*OED*). Like any dedicated writer, Calliope is almost never seen without a tablet to jot down ideas, and her beautiful words, either written or spoken, define her as the muse of heroic poetry. She comes from a beautiful tradition as well—but also a terrifically violent one. In "The Myth of the Heroic Rapist," Susan Brownmiller catalogues several rape narratives that appear in Greek mythology. "People often ask what the classic Greek myths reveal about rape," she adds, but "it is far too easy to retell a Greek myth to fit any interpretation one chooses" (283). While male gods "raped with zest, trickery, and frequency" their (often) mortal victims "rarely suffered serious consequences" (283). But what if the tale of a god raping a mortal was told in reverse? The result is Neil Gaiman's "Calliope."

Gaiman insists on telling the stories of people who are traditionally marginalized, missing, or silenced in literature in general and in comics in particular. He acknowledges his conscious decision to include women's narratives, noting that story arcs within the *Sandman* series were written "about women, and men's attitudes to women" (Bender 41). The disturbing 17th issue of *Sandman,* "Calliope," continues to force us to question our role as readers, our assumptions about women and romanticized concepts, and the degree to which we are responsible for those around us.

Although *Sandman*'s female characters sometimes follow a more traditional or narrow view of feminine beauty (tiny facial features, large breasts, tight-fitting or skimpy clothes, unnaturally thin bodies), they are far closer to looking like "real" women than their freakish superhero contemporaries. Gaiman's female characters that have depth and range are too numerous to fully list here. It is particularly hard for female *Sandman* characters to receive their due attention while in the shadow of the series' most popular character, Death. One way of approaching Gaiman's feminism is by focusing closely on a single character, a single story, and tracing the ramifications. A self-contained issue, *Sandman* #17 ("Calliope"), from early in the series, offers a glimpse into a specific part of Gaiman's feminist oeuvre, as well as his broader connections to women's voices and women's experiences.

In his introduction to the stories collected in the *Dream Country* trade paperback, novelist and critic Steve Erickson writes, "In 'Calliope,' a once successful novelist who's become so impotent in his art he can no longer write makes a bargain to enslave a muse, devouring her for his inspiration when he isn't ravaging her for his pleasure." Erickson's word choice — "impotent," "enslave," "devouring," "ravaging," and "pleasure" — emphasizes the dual tension in the story that takes the common clichés and metaphors of writing and literalizes them. "Calliope" is a story of sexual and creative energy, enslavement and release, consumption and violence.

The story begins in May 1986, with Richard Madoc in profile, stating, "I don't have any idea" (*Sandman* 17:1). This seemingly casual declaration at the start of the story eventually repeats at the end, bookending Madoc's terrible life story. In the opening scene, Madoc is in the middle of purchasing an item for someone else. He doesn't "have any idea" what the object is or what it is for. In addition, Madoc is a frustrated writer, so he doesn't "have any idea" of what to write. He is clueless in all aspects of his life and does not realize what he is getting into when he purchases an imprisoned muse for his own inspiration.

The market economy of "Calliope" presents several questionable financial, social, and spiritual transactions. The first exchange involves a trichnobezoar, or calcified ball of hair. What makes this object particularly interesting and gruesome is that it was procured from the stomach of a "young woman" with "lovely long hair" (17:1). This gross currency is Madoc's means to a very specific end: purchasing artistic inspiration. By the third panel of the story, Gaiman establishes that this is a world where a woman's body is a source of unparalleled wealth to men, particularly at the woman's expense. The surgeon Felix Garrison procured the bezoar by cutting it out of the host's stomach and offered it to Madoc in exchange for a signed copy of Madoc's novel, *The Cabaret of Dr. Caligari*. The source of the bezoar was a woman who suffered from the aptly-named "Rapunzel syndrome," and as the reader will soon learn, Calliope also suffers from an amalgam of fairy tale syndromes. Calliope is a flaxen-haired beauty trapped in a tower, spinning the thoughts of straw-men into gold.

The repugnant token transferred, Garrison next asks Madoc the inevitable fan question: "Where do writers get [their] crazy ideas?" (17:2). "It's research, really," Madoc responds with false modesty. "Calliope" is the tale of Madoc's twisted "research." In true Wordsworthian fashion, "Our meddling intellect / Mis-shapes the beauteous forms of things," but rather than murdering to dissect, Madoc is raping to write (136).

The business transaction completed, Madoc fields a call from his agent, checking on a manuscript that is nearly nine months late. This is a novel that, Madoc admits to the reader, he has yet to even begin. The pressure mounting, Madoc takes his hairy treasure to the successful writer, Erasus Fry. Fry is crippled with age, haphazardly dressed in a green smoking jacket creepily reminiscent of Hugh Hefner. From his first few lines, Fry establishes and builds a sexual undercurrent to his conversation with Madoc. The senior writer jokes that he doesn't "give a toss" about what others think and inquires if Madoc has written anything "stirring" recently (17:3–4). In these examples, Gaiman not only draws the reader's attention to the already sexually-charged metaphors commonly used to describe writing, but he also capitalizes on them by turning the metaphors into literal description. "Calliope" takes the sexual power implied by descriptions of artistic creation and literalizes them. In this story, Gaiman erases the analogy between artistic creation and procreation and draws a direct correlation between the physical act of sex and the physical act of writing. In the case of Madoc, then, he aligns writer's block with sexual frustration; tortured Madoc hasn't "written a *word* in a *year—nothing*" and agonizes, "Do you *know* what that's *like?*" (17:4).

As Madoc wallows in self-pity and frustration, the reader notices what Madoc cannot: that he is standing directly in front of a great potential source of ideas and creation. Fry is a pun-dropping philologist ("Rapunzel, let down your hairball") who discusses the etymology of "bezoar" and spins lustrous tales, but Madoc is too self-involved to hear or interpret the clues as anything other than prattle. Not only does Madoc miss a potential muse, but he also misses clear signs of danger. Fry's crazed greed should be an obvious warning that to follow him is to follow madness. Clueless Madoc, however, does not pay attention to the warnings that are obvious to the reader.

After accepting his hairy "present," Fry reveals his secret: in 1927 he captured the Greek muse Calliope. "They say one ought to **woo** her kind, but I must say I found **force** most efficacious," Fry reveals, foreshadowing the terrible methods Madoc will also enact upon Calliope (17:5). Fry emphasizes her difference as an immortal by using the phrase "her kind." Yet there is a double tension in this phrase, as it also calls attention to another difference:

in her human aspect, Calliope is a woman. At the bottom panel of page 5, Fry is poised to open the door to Calliope's chamber. He holds the key with his right hand and pushes against the door with his left. The last speech bubble on the page announces, "Here she is." The door in the image, like the page in the comic, is hinged on the left, and in preventing the reader from seeing Calliope until the next page, Gaiman constructs a situation where the reader momentarily becomes Fry, on the verge of turning the page and opening the door.[1] The escalating tension and anticipation make the reader, like Madoc, yearn to see what lies behind that door, behind that page. It forces the reader to participate in an act which is both innocent and complicit.

With the turn of the page, the reader suddenly encounters a single, full-page, shocking and terrible image: a naked and skeletal woman, kneeling, with arms and hands braced at unnatural angles in a desperate attempt to simultaneously shield her eyes from the light and her body from view. Because the reader now shares Madoc's and Fry's point of view, Calliope also cowers from the reader's gaze. The image is stark and terrifying — thrown in relief against a black background, Calliope's yellow mane and hints of pale flesh are the only color on the page. She is figured in profile, mostly in shadow, with countable ribs, the underside of one (disproportionately full) breast swelling under her arm, long fingernails, and a mane of lush, lively hair that emphasizes how dead the rest of her body appears.

Remarkably, this is a toned-down version of the art. According to Gaiman, "Kelley [Jones] drew Calliope as really, *really* skinny, with horribly protruding ribs. [Editor Karen Berger] felt that this was too extreme, and when Malcolm [Jones III] inked it he made her a little less skinny" (*Dream Country*, "Episode 17," 10). "Calliope" was penciller Kelley Jones's *Sandman* debut, and his background in horror (*Action Comics'* "Deadman," *Deadman: Love After Death*, and later *Batman* and *The Last Train to Deadsville*) clearly informs his terrible depictions of the captured muse. In interpreting Gaiman's script, it is easy to see why Jones's depiction of Calliope is so horrifying:

> A thin, fifteen-year or possible just sixteen-[year] old girl. She has a beautiful face, with deep cheekbones — she's a goddess after all — and a thin body: she looks as if she's been starved for a couple of weeks. [...] She looks very vulnerable — this is the vulnerability of nakedness; if you've ever seen photos of famine victims, or concentration camp victims, there's a point at which nakedness totally ceases to titillate, instead just arouses feelings of pity [...] The key here is vulnerability — This shouldn't look titillating, it's not a hubba hubba kind of naked woman shot; it's one that it almost hurts to look at. Tear their hearts out, Kelley ["Original Script of Calliope" 10].

Jones's artwork does indeed tear out the reader's heart, as this is an incredibly difficult page to look at. Although the final printed version of Calliope looks mercifully older than sixteen, and her ribcage goes against Gaiman's suggestion that we can "not quite count her ribs," nearly every other direction from the script is evident. Calliope's extreme vulnerability arouses the "feelings of pity" which the script called for. The script shows Gaiman's awareness that a naked, beautiful woman would be titillating, and that he consciously strove to avoid exploiting this moment, of at all sexualizing or romanticizing Calliope's rape. In his handwritten marginalia, Jones reiterates, "Shocking — not sexual" (19). The degree to which this intent is successful or not, of course, depends on the individual reader. Part of what makes reading "Calliope" so unnerving are the moments when the artwork seems to veer towards titillating, especially in the depictions of Calliope's full breasts and nipples. She is an odd mixture of terrible and beautiful.

After the splash page, the story resumes. Resigned to the rape to come, Calliope notices the unfamiliar figure of Madoc and bitterly asks, "Is this man to be our audience?" (17:7). By having Calliope raise the issue of audience, Gaiman forces the readers to realize their own role in the comic, a role that becomes increasingly more difficult to neutrally maintain as the level of graphic violence increases. Calliope is horrifying to look at; her bare ribs and penetrating eyes are at odds with the way she is sexualized in the art. It feels almost shameful to look at her on the page, to derive pleasure from reading her story. Jones's art frequently highlights her pert, erect nipples and rich Barbie doll mane. It is uncomfortable for the reader to see the mixture of sexuality and violence, to gaze upon a woman who is depicted as both beautiful and violated.

Fry soon announces that he isn't the first writer to pimp out Calliope; he is the most recent successor in a long line dating back to Homer. "Calliope, I'm giving you to Richard. You're *his* now," he announces, with the lettering emphasizing the possessive pronoun (17:7). Calliope is a prized possession, and in emphasizing ownership, Fry begins Madoc's thought process of de-deifying, de-humanizing, and finally objectifying Calliope, which allows him to justify his horrific treatment of her.

Fry's language continues the thread of sexuality and misogyny established early in the story; he cautions Calliope not to get "all worked up," he introduces Madoc to her as someone "unable" to write, and he calls the skeletal woman a "little cow" (17:7). There is no doubt in the reader's mind that Fry is lascivious and evil, but Madoc's position is still undetermined. When Madoc first appears in the comic, he is young, handsome, naive, and sympathetic to a degree, especially when he wraps a coat around Calliope before ushering her from Fry's home. The gesture could be chivalrous or self-serving, and juxtaposed against Fry's horrible parting words, "Take the little cow *away*," the panel offers some small hope that Madoc might in fact do the right thing in rescuing her from Fry's grasp.

Once the reader turns the page, however, Madoc's intentions become all too horrifyingly clear. At the top of a page 8, a lovingly rendered horizontal panel shows Calliope lying on her side, facing away from the viewer, an odalisque with full round buttocks and loose, tousled locks. Once again, it is her rib cage and the dark, crosshatched shadows that indicate there's something horrifically wrong with this image. A closer look reveals a barred window framed by decadent, sashed curtains: a domestic prison fit for Charlotte Perkins Gilman.

The next panel, however, is the most jarring image in the story, and the one that many readers recall after reading "Calliope." The text box starkly and coldly announces, "His first action was to rape her, nervously, on the musty old camp bed" (17:8). The narrator focuses on Madoc rather than Calliope, offering an adverb that emphasizes *his* emotional state during *his* action, and adjectives that focus on the mundane aspects of the scene of the crime. The details are extrinsic to Calliope herself. Yet the text, like the image of Calliope's body that it accompanies, is blunt, naked, stark, and horrifying. It feels invasive to view this panel, to gaze at Calliope in this moment of violence. The image presents a faceless Madoc with muscular forearms, his hand enclosed like a manacle around Calliope's wrist. She is depicted as a smooth, pale, prostrate body, again with that odd erect nipple thrown in relief against black, head fully extended at a painful, inhuman angle, eyes open and empty, her face a skull-like mask. Calliope is resigned rather than fighting, a living corpse. In this image, Gaiman references a sensation that many survivors of trauma describe: a complete sense of numbness, the sense of being disembodied or dead.

In his pivotal work, *Understanding Comics,* Scott McCloud writes:

> Closure in comics is far from continuous and anything but involuntary. Every act committed to paper by the comics artist is aided and abetted by a silent accomplice. An equal partner in crime known as the reader. I may have drawn an axe being raised in this example, but I'm not the one who let it drop or decided how hard the blow, or who screamed, or why. That, dear reader, was your special crime, each of you committing it in your own style [68].

McCloud's point that reading comics necessitates a specific kind of reader participation is poignant when examining why the experience of reading "Calliope" is so particularly disturbing. Just as the reader must supply the plot for what happens between panels, to fill in the gap in the gutter, the reader of "Calliope" is "an equal partner in crime," and it is we who decide how long Calliope is raped, what sounds Madoc makes as he forces himself upon her, and how much she resists him. The medium forces us to use our imaginations to "commit" Madoc's crime. Just as we earlier became Fry, mimicking the action of opening the door and exposing Calliope by turning a page, we also become Madoc, and we also feel Calliope's pain. "Calliope" is a story in which the reader does not want to identify with any of the main characters, and yet, by nature of the medium, must.

In addition, Madoc's resolve briefly wavers, making the reader consider the thought process that people must, at some level, come to believe in order to commit atrocities such as rape or murder. The text box reads:

> **She's not even human**, he told himself. **She's thousands of years old.** But her flesh was warm, and her breath was sweet, and she choked back tears like a child whenever he hurt her [17:8].

There is abundant evidence that Calliope is a being capable of feelings, but Madoc wills himself into believing otherwise. For a *Sandman* reader antici-pating a new installment about dreams, this panel is particularly unsettling because it forces the reader to become a witness of rape and slavery. The act could have been described purely in text, or inferred through art; but instead, "Calliope" depicts rape staged against rich folds of cloth. The text tells us the scene includes a "musty camp bed," but the art offers Calliope prostrate as if she were a still life. The scene draws upon familiar romanticized tropes of women — the damsel in distress, the imprisoned princess, the passive odal-isque, the tease who "secretly wants it" — and presents them as horror. By doing so, Gaiman forces us to question the typical representations of women in art, folk tales, love stories, and even in romanticized rape narratives. In *Against Our Will,* Susan Brownmiller notes, "Permissible rape as an act of manhood infused the theories of courtly love propounded by the social arbiters of the Middle Ages" (290). If a knight were to win a damsel in combat with another knight, then he had the right to "have" her (Brownmiller 291). In Madoc's mind, and according to the rules of romantic fairy tales, because Madoc has "rescued" Calliope from Fry, then she is his. In this scene, Gaiman draws upon the tropes of romanticized violence in order to subvert them. When viewing the right half of the middle image on page 8, it could be mis-taken for a romantic love scene. When viewing the left half of the image, however, the scene is sickeningly violent. The reader cannot look away in order to continue reading, and this forces the reader to participate in a terrible voyeurism, to confront the hideous reality behind the rape fantasy.

After this gut-wrenching panel, Madoc's postcoital retirement to his study is a visual relief. Once again, his niggling conscience rises, and in con-sidering his actions, Madoc mirrors a system of denial and justification that is unfortunately recognizable. He questions for a moment whether or not Calliope is a "real girl" and whether "he, Rick Madoc, might possibly have done something wrong, even criminal" (17:8). Madoc acknowledges that rape can be "wrong" or "criminal" in certain circumstances, but since he has convinced himself that Calliope is not a real person, he does not believe his act is technically rape. And once this justification occurs, there is no turning back.

In Jones's art, Calliope is alternatively fragile, beautiful, terrifying, and pitiable. The reader's response to Calliope's gaunt body connects it to the body of images we have that are similar, the most terrible of which being the bodies from the Holocaust.[2] Calliope's skeletal frame should completely repulse, but instead the reader's reaction is complicated by the detailed beauty in her long lashes, delicate limbs, and long, lush hair. In some ways, Calliope's gaunt, tortured, sexualized figure is all-too-familiar to contemporary readers inured to anorexic models and photoshopped bodies in advertising. In *The Beauty Myth,* Naomi Wolf notes that one of the terrible consequences of living in "the Surgical Age" is that "the average fashion model now is even thinner than were the Amazons of the eighties and nineties" (7). In the most recent iteration of her famous *Killing Us Softly* series, Jean Kilbourne connects the objectification of models in advertising and the growing trend of violence against women:

> We all grow up in a culture in which women's bodies are constantly turned into things, into objects. [...] Of course this affects female self-esteem. It also does something even more insidious. It creates a climate in which there is wide-spread violence against women. [...] Turning a human being into a thing is almost always the first step toward justifying violence against that person [Kilbourne].

It isn't just Madoc's process of turning Calliope "into a thing" that horrifies the reader. It is Calliope's representation as beautiful-and-emaciated that adds another layer to the reader's repulsion and horror. The reader experiences the uncanny, a combination of recognition and revulsion — recognizing that Calliope is beautiful, even the parts of her that are meant to be repulsive, because of the cult of beauty that we currently live in. We have been trained to find emaciated women alluring without questioning the methods that lead to their emaciation or the cultural expectations that keep them that way.

In Madoc's decision to secure inspiration, the reader also recognizes the appeal of the easy fix — if only writing were that easy! Rather than laboring over drafts and revisions for weeks on end, it is so much more romantic to think of artistic inspiration as a gift from the divine. But just as quickly as this thought occurs, its opposite arrives in full force: a series of seemingly harmless concessions, small allowances, and minor justifications can nonetheless become a slippery slope to a terrible crime. A cascading series of decisions leads Madoc to trade in his humanity in exchange for the power of writing. The result is a special kind of abject horror for the reader, because as remote as the situation is, the reader can empathize with and imagine being Madoc.

As Vladimir Nabokov no doubt knew, anyone can make a saint look sympathetic, but it takes great skill to make readers side with a rapist. The character Madoc takes a shortcut to become the type of writer that his creator, Gaiman, had to become the hard way. As Humbert Humbert famously remarks in *Lolita*, "You can always count on a murderer for a fancy prose style" (Nabokov 9).

Madoc's "fancy prose style" clearly improves once he has Calliope in his power. But what of his victim? Up until this part of the story, Calliope has barely spoken. When she does finally speak, the power of her entreaty is striking. Not surprisingly, the muse of epic poetry has great rhetorical power. The "beautiful voice" prays for help with eloquent, effective speech (17:9). She turns to the three Fates to intercede, and although they cannot or will not help her, they do hint at someone who can: Oneiros (from Homer's *Iliad*), also known as the Sandman, Morpheus, or Dream. In this scene, Gaiman also reveals that Calliope is Dream's former lover and mother to his son Orpheus. However, Dream's record with his past loves is problematic at best.[3] As Hy Bender notes, "It's not a stretch to guess that the way Rick Madoc perpetually uses Calliope and then returns to his obsession with his career is an exaggerated echo of the way the Sandman himself used to treat Calliope when they were lovers" (66).

Because Dream has recently escaped 70 years of naked, solitary confinement, the famously dour paramour with little capacity for forgiveness is now in a unique position to sympathize with Calliope. Interestingly, several aspects of "Calliope" are in fact prefigured by *Sandman*'s first issue, "Sleep of the Just," which in some ways reads as Dream's captivity narrative. When Alex Burgess pleads for Dream's forgiveness for his capture and imprisonment, Dream simply states, "There are offenses that are *unpardonable*. Can *you* have any idea what it was *like*? Can you have *any idea*?" (1:36). The emphasis on "unpardonable" offenses sets the stage for the rapes in "Calliope," and the phrasing of "have any idea" echoes in Madoc's "I have no idea." Indeed, Dream's response to Burgess (damning him with "eternal waking") prefigures his response to Madoc (damning him with neverending ideas).

But before Dream comes to Calliope's rescue, the story flashes back to her capture at the hands of Fry. This allows Calliope to "narrat[e] the dark side of being treated as a beautiful object" (Wolf 285). "It had been her own fault," Calliope recalls, echoing the common rhetoric of blaming the rape victim and the victim in turn internalizing that blame. She describes the events in the third person, as if they were happening to someone else (17:11). This has the effect of reminding the reader of the ways in which rape is typically described in news accounts and popular media, as if the type of clothing a woman wore (in Calliope's case, a Grecian toga) or the type of behavior she exhibited (in Calliope's case, bathing in a stream and accepting a flower) in some way made her consent to sexual violence. The reader clearly sees that

Calliope had done no wrong and certainly never asked to be enslaved. There is no ambiguity.

The young Fry, like a suitor, woos the goddess with flowers — more specifically, moly flowers which "had power over her kind" (17:11). In doing so, Fry performs a sick mockery of the courtship ritual, paying a call on a young woman and bringing her flowers. Next, Fry picks up Calliope's Grecian scroll and burns it, commanding her to call him "master."[4] The connection between Calliope's freedom and a piece of paper, combined with the "master" term, draws a direct comparison between this moment and the history of American slavery. And the enslavement of another human being is never permissible, as Dream earlier in the series tells his friend Hob Gadling (13:20). In Calliope's brief recollection, Gaiman is able to create a situation where the reader sees parallels between romantic idealization and courtship practices, the harmful rhetoric of rape, and the false justification of slavery.

Calliope's meditations are interrupted by a disrobing Madoc, celebrating his latest literary success. He is no longer the nervous, doubting man from the initial panels of the story, but rather a self-assured, violent villain who cracks jokes about making "two and a half minutes of squelching noises" with his captive (17:11). "You're my ***personal*** muse, sweetheart," he tells Calliope, "Now. Let's party" (17:11). If the reader had any remaining sympathy for Madoc by this point, it is now gone. Curiously, as he becomes more and more an object of loathing, the details of Madoc's literary success align him with another celebrated, multi-talented writer who transcends genres: Neil Gaiman. Madoc is a cautionary tale against hubris, the embodiment of what writers fear they must give up in order to be successful, a "sell-out" on a hideous new scale. As Justine Gieni notes in her essay about the rhetoric of rape in "Calliope," "Fry is Madoc's monstrous double, who mirrors his ambition, perversion, and malevolence." Yet in addition to the two fictional fiction-writers being doubles for one another, they are also doubles for the *non*fictional fiction writer behind the entire tale.

"I had a lot of trouble getting it to work," Gaiman says about "Calliope" (Bender 68). The issue's artist, Jones, recalls Gaiman's own struggles with writer's block during the genesis of the story:

> I sat down and read over what Neil had sent, the initial thing he threw out. It was something that was supposed to be called "Sex and Violets," but he never did that. [...] Neil said, "No, it was terrible, dreadful, forget about it. I'll get something to you." I waited and waited and finally it came. He kept apologizing. He had had writer's block, and then "Calliope" came [McCabe 87].

Perhaps it is not too much of a stretch to imagine that Gaiman's writer's block during "Sex and Violets" fed into the sex and violence in "Calliope." "Calliope" emerged out of Gaiman's own battles with writer's block. The parallels between

Gaiman and his horrible reflection are present in the artwork as well. For example, Gaiman sent Jones "a bunch of reference photos" of his own office, which then became the basis of Madoc's office in "Calliope" (Bender 69). Madoc's rise to fame also follows a trajectory very like the one Gaiman experienced. He does the talk show circuits, cuts movie deals, attends packed book release parties, and earns critical accolades. He mimics the same meteoric rise to commercial fame that Gaiman was just beginning to experience in the early 1990s.[5]

In many ways, Madoc faces a familiar dilemma that resurfaces in many genres, from Dorian Gray selling his soul in order to stay young to the villagers of Ursula Le Guin's Omelas attaining great happiness at the expense of one terribly suffering individual. Each scenario asks: What would you be willing to sacrifice in order to achieve your dream? Would you sell your humanity? "Calliope" dramatizes the author's typical fear of "selling out" or compromising principles in the pursuit of success.

By May 1987, Madoc is a roaring success, which the comic presents through a depiction of the launch party for his new novel. Ironically, the title of Madoc's rape-generated book (*My Love, She Gave Me Light*), like Fry's before him (*Here Comes a Candle*), references knowledge given to the author from a female source. It is the romanticized title of what the reader now knows should actually be *My Victim, I Stole Her Life*. The oblivious, besotted fans at the party, however, have no reason to see the dark inspiration behind Madoc's success. Gaiman heightens the irony by depicting a scene between a fawning female fan and Madoc. "I loved your characterization of Aileen. There aren't enough strong women in fiction," notes the young blonde (17:12). "Actually, I *do* tend to regard myself as a feminist writer," Madoc boasts in return (17:12).

In this exchange, Gaiman presciently describes one of the very qualities that his work also became known for: the characterization of strong women. Yet we cannot know for certain if Madoc's female characters truly are feminist, or whether his own elaborate façade merely translates onto his characters. Madoc is so removed from reality, so cynical and self-serving, that he doesn't see the hypocrisy of the situation — that he must rape a female deity in order to write strong female characters. Is this scene an example of how strong Calliope's power is — that through her rape, even the most loathsome and misogynist of writers can nonetheless create feminist characters? Or is it perhaps that Calliope expresses herself in some way through Madoc's characters, and the gradual increase in their strength aligns with Calliope's own resistance? As the readers observe a scene of other readers, it forces them to ascertain their own ethical position. If the real-world readers had access to *My Love, She Gave Me Light*, would they also be struck by how wonderfully strong Aileen is? And does it matter how vile the author is, if the work is good? At the very least, Gaiman asks readers to more actively question which authors and works they read as "feminist"—including his own.

In a roundtable session on Gaiman and feminism at the 2012 National Popular Culture and American Culture Association joint conference, several scholars and Gaiman fans hotly debated this very issue.[6] One of the most obvious shortfalls in Gaiman's work is the lack of racial diversity—most of his heroines, like Calliope, are white women. Another common concern raised the possible disconnect between what Gaiman intends as the author and what the reader takes away from his work. For example, in the case of "Calliope," Gaiman clearly intended for the naked drawings to inspire pity and horror rather than lust, but when a fourteen-year-old boy reads the issue, what is his reaction? Writers cannot control the reception of their works, of course, but intent and reception are considerations when thinking about feminism and literary production. It is important when considering Gaiman as a feminist to place his work in its cultural context and time—when *Sandman* was first published, there were hardly any mainstream comic depictions of women as anything other than sexy villains, virginal damsels in distress, and balloon-breasted heroines. Curiously Gaiman's very success in the 1990s is partly what led to his female characters sometimes falling short of our expectations two decades later. Today's comic readers are the lucky inheritors of a graphic novel and comic book renaissance largely made possible by authors like Gaiman. He knew that comics had a great untapped potential as a medium for telling women's stories and the success of his stories contributed to women artists and writers breaking through Wonder Woman's invisible glass ceiling. Ultimately, the launch party scene from "Calliope" indicates that readers should be critical of works and authors that we claim as "feminist," but more importantly, that we should make the determination for ourselves.

The disconnect between the feminist elements of Madoc's book and the misogyny of his character brings Roland Barthes to mind, except in "Calliope," the "death of the author" becomes quite literal—Erasmus Fry commits suicide after he can no longer publish without Calliope and idea-frenzied Madoc is writing himself to death. Gaiman repeatedly aligns Madoc with himself, perhaps even anticipating his inclusion in a book like the one you are holding right now. He cautions us to question whether or not his work has earned the title of "feminist." It's a fascinating moment where Gaiman creates a character like himself only to tear him down. If we are already wondering whether or not we should read this story as feminist, Gaiman, through Madoc, is warning us not to. Yet inviting critique in the interest of continuing discussion is an important feminist goal.

Through the foil of Madoc, Gaiman also embeds his own warning about the perils and prices of success. Fry and Madoc wrote "huge, towering romances," but the true source of their work is locked in a tower, and there is nothing romantic about rape (17:14). Madoc has adopted the trendy moniker "Ric" and the overweening attitude to match. By presenting Madoc's hypocrisy, Gaiman not only cautions against self-aggrandizing, but also offers a critique of using feminism as a selling point, or at least, hints that as readers, we should look deeper into the works we view as feminist. Following so closely to Madoc's "feminist writer" statement that her speech bubble actually touches his, the young woman at the party poses that tell-tale question, "Where do you get your ideas?" (17:12).

This is a question that continually dogs Gaiman himself. He discusses it in several interviews, and even created a short comic with Bryan Talbot entitled "An Honest Answer: 'Where Do You Get Your Ideas?'" The comic features a caricature of the author, in his trademark black sunglasses and leather jacket, stating, "It's a question writers are asked all the time. And we don't tell any of you how we get our ideas because it's a secret — deeply, inextricably linked with the entire creative process" (McCabe 144). Gaiman's character then carries a candelabra and ascends a narrow staircase to an attic room to ask "the infinite" for "an idea for a four-page comic strip." The existence of the strip itself shows that the infinite obliged.

Madoc, of course, doesn't need to ask "the infinite" for inspiration; he simply takes it. Finally, as Madoc's accolades reach a crescendo and Calliope nearly withers away into nothingness, Dream arrives. He is the first character to clearly acknowledge Calliope as a living, feeling being. "You are keeping a woman imprisoned here, Richard Madoc. Keeping her against her will. I have come to request that you set her free," he states (17:16). Dream's white-text words may technically be a request; his glowing red eyes, folded arms, imposing stature, and blue-black leather jacket imply otherwise. "There's no woman here," Madoc denies (17:16). In this moment, Madoc pathetically attempts to uphold the farce he has established throughout the story, to deny Calliope's selfhood in order to justify his actions. But while he may be able to fool himself, and to fool others, he doesn't have a shot at fooling Dream. For once, Madoc is in the passive, powerless position, and his attempts to fight it are comically useless. "There's a *law* against people like you!" he self-righteously shrieks (17:17).

Up until this point in the story, Gaiman relies on the images rather than the text to deliver the most devastating messages. Once Dream arrives, however, the terrible horrors are described in verbal terms. Dream lays out in language what the earlier panels illustrated in visuals: "She has been held captive for more than sixty years. Stripped of all possessions. Demeaned, abused, and hurt. I ... know how she must feel" (17:17). Dream identifies with Calliope, something Madoc has worked hard to avoid. Disgusted by Madoc's denials, which continue even up until the end, Dream finally gives Madoc what he's always wanted: "IDEAS IN ABUNDANCE" (17:17). Madoc then realizes the horror of getting what you wish for: Dream gives him an endless, overwhelming, maddening supply of ideas.

Madoc awakes, wondering if his encounter with Dream was merely a "weird dream" from Calliope. She informs him that he has been visited by her former lover, then, for the first time in the story, brutally and graphically phrases her experience for him: "I am real, Richard. I am more than a receptacle for your seed, or an inspiration for your tales" (17:18). As Madoc's rhetorical abilities plummet, Calliope's return in full, devastating force.

Not until Madoc goes completely mad, scribbling his incoherent stories with the blood of his finger-stumps, does he finally acknowledge for the first time that Calliope is a person. "At the top of the house, there's a room. There's a woman in there. Let her out," he begs a friend (17:21). She is no longer a thing, no longer "his most valuable possession," but a woman (17:13). Madoc's friend goes to the house and heads to the bedroom where Calliope was kept in order to free her. However, he discovers only an empty room — and a copy of Erasmus Fry's out-of-print favorite novel, *Here Comes a Candle*, lying in the center of light on the floor. It is the first time in "Calliope" that the reader sees the book's cover, which depicts a woman in profile with impossibly long, light hair, carrying a candle. The corny pulp novel subtitle reads, "She was his muse — and the slave of his lust!" In this self-reflexive moment, Gaiman takes the plot of his own comic, summarizes it in ten words, and places it on a story-within-a-story.

Finally, Calliope is free, restored to her former glory, clothed in Grecian robes with coiffed hair and long tight curls. She has been rescued, but she does not follow her prince from the tower. Dream respectfully keeps his distance from his former lover, the mother of his child, and they go their separate ways. With Calliope released and Dream departed, Madoc finally reverts to where he started, bereft of creative inspiration. "It's gone. I've got no idea any more. No idea at all," he states in the last panel of the story (17:24).

It sounds paradoxical to say that a story with rape as a key plot device, that depicts a woman as helpless and features a knight in shining armor (or a Dream in shining night), is feminist. But the act of putting on the page the horrible logic of rape is part of what makes this work feminist. Gaiman uses everyday tropes and situations and extends them to horrific conclusions. He draws to the surface issues that are normally erased in order to force us to see them and question them. He invites us to turn this same introspection and critique against *him,* even demands that we do so. "Calliope" is not comfortable to read, but it is immensely powerful. This experience has been described by one close Gaiman friend and unlikely "Calliope" fan — Tori Amos.

When asked in 1994, "What piece of Neil's work has had the most resonance for you, specifically?" Amos answered, "Calliope" (Hibbs). Given that Amos is a rape survivor and that she co-founded the Rape, Abuse, and Incest National Network (RAINN), is it hard to imagine what the experience of first reading "Calliope" was like for her. One would expect Amos would identify solely with the title heroine. But in her interviews, Amos highlights the connection not with Calliope as the victim of rape, but with Madoc as the victim of ambition. "It's not like he's a bad guy," she states, "He just bought into something, like I have, like we all have. And it's understanding what these choices cost, and then are we willing to take responsibility when we do something to somebody else?" (Hibbs). She continues, "I understood what it was like for the guy, not being able to write. And how he would do anything to be able to write again." Curiously, Amos also credits Gaiman as one of her "male muses" (McCabe 204).

Amos first encountered Gaiman's work through a friend who was staying with her. He brought several *Sandman* comics, including the first work of Gaiman's that Amos had ever read: "Calliope." In an interview published in the fan zine *The Magian Line,* Amos states that she relates to Gaiman's female characters because "he has a lot of respect for women" (Hibbs). She was powerfully changed by her first encounters with *Sandman,* so much so that they bled into the album that she was working on at the time: *Little Earthquakes.* Inspired by *Sandman,* Amos famously wrote Gaiman into the lyrics for one of her songs even though she had yet to meet him.[7] The friend who introduced Amos to Gaiman's comics took a demo tape of her songs to the San Diego Comic-Con and gave the tape to Gaiman.[8] The rest is history.[9]

When recommending "Calliope" to new readers, one feels compelled to warn them: "It's pretty graphic." The depictions of sexual violence in *The Sandman* are "pretty" graphic, in multiple senses: the issues are considerably violent and visually appealing. The acts of sexual violence in Gaiman's graphic novels are particularly unsettling to the reader, as they should be. And yet we read them and reread them. Even Amos says, "the 'Calliope' piece, I reread it a lot, and it makes me remember about where I stand with myself, and why I do certain things" (Hibbs). Through works like "Calliope," Gaiman continues to challenge the perceptions of what comics can be, what they can do, and how they are a site of untapped potential for revolutionary female characters and explorations. Although some issues came closer to feminist ideals than others, feminist readings of *Sandman* continue to reveal new possibilities of this earth-shattering series.

NOTES

1. "Calliope" maintains this page placement in its original single issue format, in the 1995 DC Comics / Vertigo trade paperback, and in the 1997 "Essential Vertigo" reprint. When it was published in 2006's *Absolute Sandman,* the page placement unfortunately

changed, shifting the door-opening scene from the right page to the left. In this edition, the connection between turning a page and opening the door is still there visually and metaphorically, if not physically.

2. Gaiman clearly meant for the specter of the Holocaust to be present, as his script notes specify concentration camp victims and at the end of the comic, Madoc raves about "a holocaust of some kind" (17:19). The text references the Holocaust as a reminder that an examination of one person's abuse is a study in understanding much larger atrocities. In this move, Gaiman ties his story about one individual's act of violence to violence on a large scale. The story implies that the same dissociation and self-justification that allow a person to commit rape and other acts of sexual violence are the same mental gymnastics that eventually allowed "ordinary men" to kill in devastating numbers.

3. "Well, you ***don't*** exactly have trouble-free relationships, do you?" Desire later goads her brother at a family reunion. "Let's see ... there was that little one in Greece, ***what*** was her name? ***Carousel?*** Something like that" (21:18).

4. Because Calliope is the muse of epic poetry, she is frequently depicted holding a tablet or scroll. Therefore, Fry's theft of the scroll could be seen as stealing her writing. It gives him complete power over her.

5. Madoc also appears on the television show *The Book Nook,* whose host, curiously enough, was physically modeled on writer and *Sandman* contributor Kim Newman.

6. Another sign of Gaiman's self-awareness in terms of his writing and the character of Madoc comes in the form of poking fun at literary conferences and fan conventions. In issue 14, he presents a "cereal convention" with a panel discussion on "Women in Serial Killing." The panelist named Dog Soup offers her twisted feminist manifesto: "I tell you, I'm sick and tired of women in our line being stereotyped as black widows or killer nurses. I'm a serial killer, and a woman, and I'm proud of it" (14:26). This issue is also notable for several instances of sexual violence, including an assault on the character Rose and a terrible rape joke told by the emcee Nimrod.

7. In "Tear In My Hand" Amos sings, "If you need me, me and Neil'll be hanging out with the Dream King."

8. It is worth noting that the album that features Amos's "wink" to Gaiman also features the devastating autobiographical song, "Me and a Gun," which chronicles the night in 1985 when Amos was raped after a concert.

9. Gaiman and Amos later collaborated on several projects. In terms of thinking about Gaiman and feminism, his contribution to Amos's 2001 album *Strange Little Girls* is particularly interesting. Gaiman wrote short prose pieces to accompany Cindy Sherman-esque photographs of Amos. Excerpts from these pieces were published in the album's liner notes and the full text was published in the Strange Days concert tour book and reprinted in Gaiman's *Fragile Things* collection.

WORKS CITED

Bender, Hy. *The Sandman Companion.* New York: Vertigo, 1999. Print.

Brownmiller, Susan. *Against Our Will: Men, Women, and Rape.* New York: Fawcett, 1975. Print.

Erickson, Steve. "Introduction." *The Sandman: Dream Country.* Vol. 3. New York: Vertigo / DC Comics, 1995. Print.

Gaiman, Neil et al. *The Sandman: Dream Country.* Vol. 3. New York: Vertigo / DC Comics, 1995. Print.

_____. "Original Script of Calliope." *The Sandman: Dream Country.* Vol. 3. New York: Vertigo / DC Comics, 1995. Print.

_____ (w), Sam Kieth (p), and Mike Dringenberg (i). "Sleep of the Just." *The Sandman* #1 (January 1989), New York: DC Comics. Print.

_____ (w), Michael Zulli (p), and Steve Parkhouse (i). "Men of Good Fortune." *The Sand-man* #13 (February 1990), New York: DC Comics. Print.

_____ (w), Kelley Jones (p), and Malcolm Jones III (i). "Calliope." *The Sandman* #17 (June 1990), New York: DC Comics. Print.

_____ (w), Mike Dringenberg (p), and Malcolm Jones III (i). "Season of Mists: Prologue." *The Sandman* #21 (April 1989), New York: DC Comics. Print.

Gieni, Justine. "Rape and Revenge in Graphic Detail: Neil Gaiman's 'Calliope,' in *The Sandman* Comic Series." *Forum.* 13. Web. 3 March 2012.

Hibbs, Brian. "Interview with Tori Amos." *Magian Line.* 1.3 (1993). Web. 1 March 2012.

Kilbourne, Jean. "Killing Us Softly 4: Advertising's Image of Women." Media Education Foundation, 2010. DVD.

McCabe, Joseph. *Hanging Out with the Dream King.* Seattle: Fantagraphics, 2004. Print.

McCloud, Scott. *Understanding Comics.* New York: Harper Perennial, 1993. Print.

Nabokov, Vladimir. *Lolita.* New York: Vintage, 1997. Print.

Wolf, Naomi. *The Beauty Myth.* New York: Harper Perennial, 2002. Print.

Wordsworth, William. "The Tables Turned." *The Norton Anthology of English Literature.* Vol. 2. Ed. M. H. Abrams. New York: W.W. Norton, 1993.

Empowering Voice and Refiguring Retribution

Neil Gaiman's Anti-Feminism Feminist Parable in The Sandman

BY AARON DRUCKER

In medias res, Lyta Hall is expecting. For two years she has lived with her husband in the "Dream Dome," seeming to assist him in saving the world's children from nightmares and only dreamed of terrors. In this liminal place, she survives with her husband (who was fatally wounded in the real world but whose being is caught just before passing over, not yet dead) and her unborn child, awaiting a future that cannot come, for it is "in maternity that she must be transfigured and enslaved" (de Beauvoir 171). Brought into the (false, barren) Dreaming by her desire, her potency is static; she is unable to generate — thought, control, movement, life. She is surrounded by the world constructed by the dreams of lesser men, the trophy companion without purpose or function. Her acquiescence to the patriarchal renders her barren. She believes she follows her heart, her love, her femininity. In fact, she is submitting to the role of perpetual wife-not-yet-mother, the subservient place to the ghost of her husband, as frozen in time as the Ghost of Hamlet's father, whose command solicits stultifying ambivalence. We are introduced to Lyta Hall in the midst of metaphor quickly turned to allegory during the story arc aptly named "The Doll's House" in *The Sandman* series by Neil Gaiman. From her first appearance to the climax of her narrative arc, Lyta serves as a figure for feminist tropes in Gaiman's fantasy, constructed to ironically critique the second-wave feminist archetypes of empowerment in a male-constructed narrative of the feminine in the world of dreams.

The story opens on a woman looking in a mirror, the panel shaded in a monochromatic pale blue. The reader sees her name as she looks into the mirror, seeing her as a reflection, brushing her hair, staring blankly through the doubled image and towards the reader (12:1). We see her through her female gaze,[1] doubling the apparent androcentric production of the work. Gaiman is transparently aware of his gender perspective: a male author in a male dominated environment constructing a female character. From the beginning, he clearly understands the male-orientated perspective of the comic book medium. Since young men are the target demographic of most comics, it is unusual in that — according to his editor, Karen Berger — roughly half of *The Sandman*'s readers are female (Goodyear para. 27). Many are ardent fans (Bender 186). When the author then appropriates a female figure from the larger world of the comic oeuvre, he immediately opens with the trope of the gaze, openly doubled through the mirror image of the issue's protagonist. The frame is followed by her staring blankly, outside her bedroom door, lost and resigned to her oblivion, appealing to the apparent male authority: "He'll know. Hector knows everything" (12:1). Betty Friedan remarks in *The Feminine Mystique*:

> The apathetic, dependent, infantile, purposeless being, who seems so shockingly nonhuman ... is ... the familiar "feminine" personality. Aren't the chief characteristics of femininity ... passivity; a weak ego or sense of self; a weak superego or human conscience; renunciation of active aims, ambitions, interests of one's own to live through others; incapacity for abstract thought; retreat from activity directed outward to the world, in favor of activity directed inward or phantasy? [286].

Her identity has been completely absorbed by her husband, so much so that she is (ineptly, inappropriately) referred to as "Mrs. Sandman" by him, the man for whom she has abandoned her godhood. Lyta Hall was The Fury, daughter of Diana of the Amazons and the human Steve Trevor, granddaughter of Hippolyta, Queen of the Amazons.[2] Gifted with superhuman strength, speed, endurance, and near invulnerability, and trained in multiple forms of combat, she falls in love with Hector Hall, a teammate from the superhero alliance Infinity, Inc., and marries him. Soon, she becomes pregnant with his child and voluntarily gives up her costume, opting instead to raise their child and perform the role of homemaker. When Hector is killed in battle, she becomes despondent and, when offered the chance to join him in a between-realm called the "Dream Dome," she readily accepts, giving up not only her powers, but her place in the "real" world as well. She is the heir to Wonder Woman, but in her husband's home, she is "babycakes" (Gaiman 12:4). Lyta begins her story as an intentional stereotype, a self-reflexive trope of the sexist vision of femininity. Her entrance to the Dreaming is through Hector's dream, that of the "superhero" Sandman and his Dream Dome, supposedly protecting children (though in fact he's contributing to an abused child's psychosis). Lyta Hall is the fool's dream of a man's woman: barefoot and pregnant, constantly tending her hair, the literal representation of the iconic stereotype.

But she is more than merely a characterization pulled from the masculine repertoire of feminine tropes. She is Echo, too, following Hector's relentless Narcissus into self-inflicted nothingness, "in the extremity of her alienation from ordinary fleshly life, this ... angel-woman becomes not just a momento of otherness but actually a *momento mori* or ... an 'Angel of Death'" (Gilbert and Gubar 24). Her life is the daily reminder of his death, and her subjugation to his vision of her place — static, unchanging, unknowing, disabled — is the necessary condition that predicates his survival. By accepting his offer, she engages in the patriarchal construct of the Universe, more literally so than in "real life," since her world is a literalized dream. This raises the question, of course, whose dream? In the context of the story, the Dream Dome resides within a "fold" in the larger Dreaming, inside the mind of a young boy who has been found and co-opted by two nightmare creatures (the literal "Brute and Glob," who are doubled again in his abusive uncle and aunt). However, to create this haven, the monsters of the Dreaming require a "bozo" to believe in the construct, to fill out its edges and solidify its reality (Gaiman 12:10). Hector is the second such entity, just desperate enough to desire his existence and just narcissistic enough to believe in his importance. He is the man, the savior, the hero. Hector Hall builds a world in his own image, a technological marvel inside a boy's mind. The Dream Dome reflects all of Hector's desires for himself: the everlasting, never failing hero with his wife and child-to-be. He is insulated from failure and responsibility. He is, as the title of the issue suggests, "Playing House," and it is in his house that Lyta searches for her own being. But this is a man-made womb: a cave within a cave within a cave. The boy's imagination folds a space upon itself, making a cavernous space of his own ego-construction, into which Hector has inserted his "Dream Dome," which contains his representation of his life. Each shell harboring the frozen embryo of that which created it, finally culminating in Lyta's stalled womb. "Darling," she asks her husband, "how long have we been living in the Dream Dome?" He responds, "Must be a couple of years by now, Hon. Why?" "Well, it just seemed to me like, maybe I ought to have *had* a *baby* by now. I *was* about six months pregnant when we got here..." Lyta sadly muses (Gaiman 12:4). And then Hector dismisses her with an infantile response:

> You know, Precious, I'll bet that the *Stork* doesn't know how to get to the Dream Dome. He's probably got our little bundle of joy in its white cotton diaper, right *now*. [...] I'll tell Brute and Glob about it. *They'll* know how to get a message to that ol' Stork. *You'll* see [12:4].

She is an adult woman, in her third trimester, beyond the age where the story-time myth of birthing produces its comforting magic, but she is stripped of her womanhood, reduced to passivity. Lost in Hector's deluded trope of her, she is rendered into nothingness: a receptacle, full but unable to ripen. Her body, the real object trapped inside the construct, doubled and then doubled again, is left *in medias res*, without end. In her present nothingness, her identity is beyond her reach.

Her instinct is to explore her self, but in Hector's world, she can only see her reflection in his mind. "Lyta lives in a pretty house, with her husband, their two servants, and a thousand thousand screens" (12:4); Hector's world proliferates with her own reflection, and she can only see what is reflected from the patriarchal construct in which she resides. "Is this what she wants? Is this what she wanted?" (12:9 fr.1). She sees herself again reflected in the mirror: Hector's pregnant wife. Then, her image shifts. She is a happy child, though she still desires her heteronormative life: "She always wanted to be with Hector. Even when they were children" (fr. 2). Her reflection brushes her hair, the trappings of adulthood (hairspray, makeup) are replaced by a teddy bear and some unread books. She smiles, as if the brush can solve any problem, and the listless days are far into the future. A child Lyta imagines herself with her knight, with her "hero brat" still out there to rescue her. The scene shifts, and now Hector stands behind her adolescent self, staring at her reflection, admiring her beauty. She sees herself through his eyes, and finds joy in her second place. Together, they live their lives, "but Hector's dreams came first. They always did" (fr. 3). She is now The Fury, "a cheap copy of her vanished mother" (fr. 4). Absently stroking her hair, getting ready to fight alongside her man. In costumes, in alter-egos, she has taken on the identity of her mother's form and function. She is Hector's; she is her mother's. And as the smile recedes into the blank stare of the conformed, the scene shifts again. Lyta's reflection continues to sit and stare, lost in the "nightmare times when she thought Hector was dead" (fr. 5), but the real Lyta stands and turns to go. "And, after the wedding, she came to live in this house. And she was happy. They were all so very, very happy" (fr. 6), she poses to the tear-stained reflection left behind in the callous reality of the mirror. In the corrupted world of the Dream Dome, the mirror is reality. Gaiman inverts the traditional depiction of the imprisoned woman. As Gilbert and Gubar observe:

> Dramatizations of imprisonment and escape are so all-pervasive in ... literature by women that we believe they represent a uniquely female tradition.... Interestingly, though works in this tradition generally begin by using houses as primary symbols of female imprisonment, they also use much of the other paraphernalia of "woman's place" to enact their central symbolic drama of enclosure and escape. Ladylike veils and costumes, mirrors, paintings, statues, locked cabinets, drawers, trunks, strong-boxes, and other domestic furnishing appear and reappear in female novels ... to signify the woman writer's sense that, as Emily Dickinson put it, her "life" has been "shaven and fitted to a frame," a confinement she can only tolerate by believing that "the soul has moments of escape / When bursting all the doors / She dances like a bomb abroad" [85].

Lyta's life is the protected, but deathly, static dream of a patriarch's woman. When the bomb explodes, bursting all the doors (perhaps more literally than Dickinson had proposed), Lyta is not let into a world of ecstatic freedom (12:19). She neither dances nor escapes. Rather, she is paradoxically imprisoned by her release. In the construction of Hector's projection, Lyta can walk away from the aberrant and assaulting reality of her lived experience. The loss, the fear, the terror, and ultimately the future are bound and separated by the static vision of the ordered patriarchy in the Dream Dome. But when Dream interferes, reabsorbing Hector Hall's world into the natural order of things, he reveals Lyta's world for what it is. Gaiman's construction runs the risk of advocating the patriarchal at this point. At first reading, it appears that Lyta prefers the Dream Dome's inverted reality, a place in which she appears happier and better off than in the real world, at least in the immediate aftermath of her exposure. She resists, and even openly defies, the reality imposed upon her by her restoration to reality. But Gaiman's construction is careful to frame the imposition of Dream's interference. Brute and Glob, resolutely male characters and attributes of the worst of masculine tendencies, are abusive, vile creatures whose purpose is to use and abuse others to their own satisfaction, even without an apparent purpose. "I am waiting for an explanation," Morpheus asks of them. Glob responds weakly, "Well ... we thought ... we could maybe make our *own* Dream King. One *we'd* be running..." (12:20 fr. 2–3). Beyond nonspecific mischief and a diversion of limited scope, Brute and Glob abuse one man to the point of suicide (fr.4) and then turn to Hector Hall, who could not be lost through death (as he was already dead) but whose wife would become a static and hollow shell of herself. Remorseless, they abuse without purpose, for little reason other than to exercise some minimal sense of power. When faced with accountability, they fold immediately and acquiesce to the most restrained prodding of authority. Brute and Glob are the overt attributes of Hector Hall's vision of patriarchal structure. While he covers his misogyny with awkward acts of kindness and contrition, his apparent sadism inserts itself into his marriage when he seeks and accepts the static tragedy of Lyta's condition, denying her both her sex and her identity in his abusive fiction. Even as Lyta denies the reality of her situation, as she walks away from the tragic mirror-of-the-real, as she turns from the pronouncement of Dream's observation of Hector's "unseemly" state (12:21), Lyta's preference for the trappings of her imprisonment betrays the complex relationship with reality that feminist independence demands. Through Lyta, Gaiman postulates that sometimes the static entrapment of being the "second sex" seems preferable to the uncompromising and bitter realities of independence, and yet he cannot — and he will not — allow the protected subject of the patriarchal construction continue unabated. Like feminists before him, Dream issues the ultimatum of freedom. Released from Hector's tower/prison, Lyta asks Morpheus, "So, what are you going to do to me?"

"Nothing," he replies.

"Nothing? You killed Hector. You destroyed our home. You've ruined my life. You call that nothing?"

"Exactly. Nothing," he continues. "You are free to go. Build yourself a new life..." [12:23].

In that moment, Gaiman leaves Lyta with the choice after Feminism: does the empowered woman return to her old life, her old ways, the old patriarchy, or does she build something new? Dream does not help her shape the new possibilities (the story does take place in the modern world, after all, and Lyta was once a hero with the powers of a goddess). Whether or not this is a sinister act, a final act of cruelty, or just the bitter reality the newly freed woman faces is ambiguous in Gaiman's presentation. Dream acts with certainty and fairness, setting aright what has been abused and degraded. However, he is also pictured as dark and shadowed, with an imposing glint in his eye that betrays a threatening aspect to his masculine intrusion. His act is not of compassion or of kindness but of necessity. If, through Dream, Gaiman speaks for the freedom imposed by Feminism, of the complex and often bitter realities faced by the newly independent woman, it is a terrifying freedom, potentially overwhelming, positioned upon her and leaving her in the spotlight (figured literally in the final frame of the issue), left only to react to the last tropes of patriarchy.

In an image uncannily reminiscent of the Virgin Mary, Lyta turns from Dream, waking into the nightmare of the real world (12:21 fr.4). The child she now carries is a child of the Dreaming, and the Lord of the Realm will return to claim him. Dream, in an overtly creepy and threatening rendition of the Annunciation, predicts, "The child — the child you have carried so long in dreams. That child is mine. Take good care of it. One day I will come for it" (12:23 fr. 5). Splayed in the spotlight, head down, eyes shadowed, Lyta swears, "You take my child over my dead body, you spooky bastard.... Over my dead body" (fr. 7). Unlike Gabriel's pronouncement to Mary, Morpheus's prediction is not taken as tidings of wonder and joy, though it remains a distinctly male action. The woman's labor is taken for the man's use. Like Jesus's mother, Lyta will carry, bear, and raise a child that is not truly hers. She will be responsible for the safety of the male God's progeny, under implicit threat should the child come to harm. The Bible fails to explore what might happen to Mary should Jesus have taken an unfortunate fall in his early years, but Dream is explicit by his bearing, if not by his words. His admonition carries with it a threat of harm, should something go amiss with Lyta's son. Daniel's safety is Lyta's responsibility, but this is to satisfy Morpheus's command rather than the natural inclinations of motherhood, should something go amiss with Lyta's son. The reader encounters Daniel for the first time some 10 issues later, in *The Sandman* #22. "Have you got a name for him yet?" Lyta's friend asks (22:12). "Not one I *like*," she responds. "He doesn't *look* like a Steve. Or a Hector, does he?" She plays with the nameless child and discusses her future:

"Had any other ideas about what you're going to be doing?"
"You mean like bringing up 'Hey You' Hall isn't going to keep my busy *enough?*"
"No. No ideas yet. But I will do something when he's a bit bigger. Maybe go back to school. I don't think the *costume* stuff, now ... not with Hector gone. It wouldn't be the same..." [fr. 4–5].

Perhaps a year after her first encounter with Dream, Lyta Hall has adopted the role of "mother." While she plays the role of guardian and protector, she has not built a new life for her son or herself. True, she is not encumbered by the necessities of practical living ("Money's not a problem," she explains [fr. 7]), but her life is a facile continuation of the proscribed roles of the feminine she refuses to release.

When Morpheus visits Lyta Hall's son in the "Season of Mists" story arc, Lyta fears he has come to take her child and she reacts violently: "**You**— you get **away** from *my child*—you—don't *touch him*—I'm *warning* you" (22:13). Her impassioned expression, emphasized by striking force lines[3] in the static frame, underscores that she is the Mother/Goddess fiercely protecting her young. While she may not be ready to go back to the "costume thing," she is nonetheless in possession of a formidable arsenal for defending herself and her young son. Dream responds, telling her that this is just a visit and that avoiding a violent conflict that Lyta would surely lose, but her ire is misdirected. The threats continue, even as Morpheus reminds Lyta that her child is special — not because he is the biological product of two supernaturally endowed parents, but because "it is unusual for a child to gestate in dreams.... A child formed in my realm..." (22:13), and he tapers off without a hint of how the story ends. Simone de Beauvoir expresses Lyta Hall's situation eloquently: "Every mother entertains the idea that her child will be a hero, thus showing her wonderment at the thought of engendering a being with consciousness and freedom; but she is also in dread of giving birth to a defective or a monster, because she is aware to what a frightening extent the welfare of the flesh is contingent upon circumstances" (de Beauvoir 497). Lyta has reproscribed her identity through the birth of her child: she is "mother." But she only wears the costume of a mother. She cannot act; she cannot exist independently from patriarchal control. While she may, in her role, defend and protect her progeny, as a mother is supposed to do, she cannot engage the responsibility for his being. He is the object of her production but not a person to her until she is repatriated by the patriarchy. It is Dream who announces the baby's name: Daniel (22:14).[4] Her initial reaction to Morpheus's pronouncement is anger, but it quickly turns to consideration and acceptance. She continues to be, as she was with Hector, bound by the social ideologies of the patriarchal order: what the man says, is so. Morpheus is now figured as the "father": the absent, distant, and abusive male who makes the decisions and defines the reality of Lyta's existence. Once the reality is stated, she can embrace it, literally holding and smiling comfortingly at her son for the first time in the series. In positioning Dream as the male figurehead, she can now complete her subjective position. For her, motherhood is a role, like the "costume thing" or life with Hector. It is dictated by a director whose control she outwardly resists but receptively capitulates in order to constitute her identity. She can now be "Daniel's mother," greater than the woman who is merely keeping busy "bringing up 'Hey You' Hall." She is secured by the reinforcement of her deferred role in the act of identifying and is defined by the object of her production. "But this is only an illusion. For she does not really make the baby, it makes itself within her" (de Beauvoir 496).

In an interlude some eighteen issues later, Daniel takes a nap. Lyta is again talking to a friend,[5] this time on the phone, and she has put her son to sleep. He lays in his crib and silently, happily goes to sleep. His willingness to nod off would seem a boon to any single mother, but his desire to dream takes literal form quickly enough, as Lyta inadvertently admits: "Daniel just gets everywhere.... It won't be long before he figures out how to get out of his crib" (40:2). And in Daniel's dream, he is able to do just that: leave the confines of his crib, his room, and his world. The issue's main action focuses around Daniel entering The Dreaming, the realm of Morpheus, and hearing stories from Cain, Abel, and Eve.[6] While the stories these avatars of the Dreaming relate to the toddler are interesting, Daniel's brief adventure recalls de Beauvoir's admonition of a mother's fears, for Daniel is, on the surface and in every physical way, a perfect child. Blonde haired and blue eyed, he is sweetly tempered, alert, healthy, and receptive — if a bit precocious. But he is also unnatural. He moves consciously and deliberately between veils of reality, crawling from his crib into the dreaming world with wanton intent. Inasmuch as it is curious exploration, he is innocent in the engagement, but he is nonetheless tainted as supernatural, defective in the sense that he is beyond the normal expectations. While in the world of comic books it is normal for the children of super-powered couples to have extraordinary gifts, Daniel's abilities go beyond the limits of what Hector and Lyta Hall's abilities should produce. His gestation in The Dreaming has left him different, altered. While Lyta talks on the phone, her son transcends the human boundaries of reality and crawls into another universe of his own volition. In ignorance, she wakes him after his return from the Dream Lord's realm only to discover a black feather in his bed. Its origins never occur to Lyta. It is tempting to read this story as "just a dream" of Daniel's, if an extraordinary one, but Gaiman forces his readers to resist this at several points: Daniel's movement from reality to The Dreaming is deliberate (he gets out of his crib and crawls through the boundary (40:3); the characters and stories told to Daniel are known to the reader but unknown to him, so it is not invention but experience in which he is engaged; and finally, the story is punctuated by Matthew's[7] feather brought back into the real world when Daniel returns. Lyta discovers it, pronouncing it "a dirty old feather" and wonders, "Where on Earth did you get this from?" (40:24). While Lyta is caretaker to her son, the connection that she assumes to him is only an appearance, as illusory as a dream. She has no sense at all of who her son is, what he can truly do, or the contents of his reality. As in de Beauvoir's reflection, Daniel is not the being of Lyta Hall, and as she defines herself through him, her definition is ultimately as hollow as her existence with Hector. Again, she does not acknowledge her reality. While with Hector, she was living in the static limits of the old patriarchy, the dutiful wife: barefoot and pregnant. She could not acknowledge the monotonous trance of her bound world. After her release from the dream prison (the thousand thousand screens of Bentham's panopticon), she enters the nightmare of the real world. Her illusion disintegrates, leaving her with only her independence. With the birth of her son and Dream's naming, she is circumscribed by the "mother" trope. She lives for her son exclusively, without boundaries. Her motherhood is her defining characteristic, imposed upon her by the patriarchal figures that foreground her. Hector's dreams always came first, and now Dream's constant presence, through his original admonition, defines her actions. Lyta's only purpose is to confound Morpheus from his promised purpose. Without understanding whether Morpheus's intent is malicious or benign (or even heroic), she would stand in his way, and thus she structures her identity as mother/protector. When she returns to the series in "The Kindly Ones," she continues to be confounded by the evidence of Daniel's excursions into the Dreaming: "SAND! There's sand all **over** the bed. Why, you, you little.... So, Daniel was sleeping in my bed. I put him down for his nap, there. Next thing you know, the sheets are *covered* with sand" (57:4). In the intervening two years, she has not recognized Daniel's connection to his father figure's realm. While he continues to sleep and return with foreign articles upon his awakening, she has only become suspicious of Dream, assuming that it is his interference (and not Daniel's own initiation) that causes these anomalies. To that end, she has never left his side, giving up all outside endeavors from socializing to "the costume thing." She has become overprotective of him, to the point of assaulting a homeless man for his kindness.[8] And yet, Gaiman does not allow the limitations of Lyta's circumscribed identity to wallow in her paranoia. When she steps away for just one evening out (and granted, it is engineered by Lucifer and engaged by Loki and Puck), Daniel is taken. Constructing Lyta's identity through pre-feminist configurations of feminine patriarchal identities, those original female roles so hard-fought against by the second wave feminists of the late 20th century, Gaiman sets the ground for the argument in "The Kindly Ones." He literalizes the woman bound by hearth and home and umbilical cord as a hollow shell of herself: static and immobile, her depth and independence curtailed utterly by her externally defined identities. The image of woman de Beauvoir and her contemporaries sought so hard to reform is carefully represented in the figure of Lyta Hall as Gaiman builds the narrative towards Daniel's kidnapping. When the child is taken, Lyta is not merely devastated; she is un-defined. Seeking definition, Lyta turns to the empowerment methodologies of the 20th century feminist movement by seeking to engage and acquire the tropes of feminine mythological power.

However, as Lyta descends into her mythological exploration of feminine power, Gaiman asserts two significant narrative arguments about her direction. Lost, she seeks to regain her son by killing Morpheus. To do so, she begins a Dantesque journey through a reality that is both real and beyond real. But before she begins, she encounters three women divining over a cauldron. Awakened in a dream, she descends a steep stairwell into a dark, cave-like room, where she encounters the women focused on a divining ritual (58:14–17). They are unknown to Lyta Hall but instantly recognizable too the reader. They are the Triple-Goddess in their tripartite role. They wear the guises of the Hecate, the Fates, and the Furies, and the reader has been warned before: "Be satisfied with the trinity you have. F'r example, you wouldn't want to meet us as the Kindly Ones. We can only caution you, Sister. We can't protect you" (10:19). To Lyta Hall, they are instantly recognizable as the Weird Sisters, the three witches of Shakespeare's *Macbeth*. Their appearance in *Sandman* echoes Banquo's description of the Weird Sisters:

> ... What are these
> So wither'd and so wild in their attire,
> That look not like th' inhabitants o' th' earth...
> You greet with present grace and great prediction...
> If you can look into the seeds of times
> And say which grain will grow, and which will not,
> Speak then to me, who neither beg nor fear
> Your favors nor your hate [I.iii ll.39–41, 55, 58–61].

From these "so wild" women, Lyta, gathers a prediction of what is to come, what path she should follow to gain her ends. The Crone promises: "Of course we're going to hurt you. Everybody gets hurt" (Gaiman 58:15 fr. 3). The

Mother confirms for her: "Your babbie *has* been stolen from you, after all....
They're going to put him in the fire, my little diddly-pout" (fr. 4; 58:16 fr.
4). The Daughter informs: "You've met already those who took him" (58:16
fr. 3). The Triple Goddess provides the future but not the answers Lyta seeks,
as Macbeth is told of his rise to glory and its ultimate futility. But it is not
Lord Macbeth but Lady Macbeth who is told of fate, and like Lady Macbeth,
Lyta concludes that to attain the goal she seeks, she must acquire power
through means available only to her. And like Lady Macbeth, following that
path ends in folly and pathology. The final stroke of Gaiman's narrative arc
begins when the first "clear" prophecy of the Weird Sisters appears to come
to fruition. In the guise of police officers, the kidnappers (Loki and Puck)
show Lyta a photograph of Daniel's immolated corpse. She remembers
Dream's annunciation; she reiterates Dream's perceived abrogation of her happiness; and she goes mad. From its inception, Lyta's journey is an act of
(im)potent madness, and her consciousness splits into two worlds, walking
both through city streets and the world of mythology. She meets a cyclops
who waits for the "seventh son of a seventh son comes by, carrying a white
rose and a golden whistle" to grant her release (60:9). The cyclops metaphor
remains the classic representation of the monocular vision, the tunnel vision
of those who cannot attain perspective. The cyclops waiting at the crossroads
is the woman who cannot see the absurdity of her position. She awaits the
impossible (or at least, highly improbable), and yet she continues to carry the
identity defined by her "seven poor sons, and my faithless husband, the king"
(60:9). At her first stop, Lyta meets a warning about her journey: focused
only on one outcome, her perspective lost, she is destined to be bound by the
impossibility of success. External validation will never come, though the
cyclops is only a vision, an anthropomorphic hallucination of a stoplight, and
Lyta continues on her journey when the light changes. She then encounters
Bast, the Egyptian cat-goddess, a sympathetic ear but equally locked in her
own story. Again, Gaiman echoes a warning: "But ... don't they ever learn?"
Lyta asks her companion (60:10). "They can't. They're part of the story, just
as I am," she replies (fr. 5). Lyta is again reminded that she falls into the cycle
of her own narratives: wife, then mother, invested in form by the patriarchal
hierarchy. She is defined by what she has been told to be, and she is about to
return to her narrative pattern. Bast gives her the truth by which she may
break the pattern and restore her sanity. But she does not. She seeks something
more than simply undoing her limiting narrative, and in so reaching, she dismisses the warnings granted to her by negative example: females trapped in
roles of power and persuasion, but as trapped as the prototypical feminine
roles that these new tropes violate. She does not learn from the old stories of
women bound and beguiled by patriarchal narratives, instead seeking another

path than the traditional feminine traits of obedience, false hope, and guile. Fully rejecting the patriarchal expectations of femininity as ineffective exercises in power, she descends into the appropriation of modern feminist tropes of empowerment. Gaiman's allegory has reached its first apotheosis with the wholesale rejection of the pre-feminist ideal of womanhood. In Lyta Hall's breakdown, Gaiman frees her to choose her own path to independence, released of the patriarchal demands and strictures imposed upon her by the men who would define her. But without that definition, she again becomes un-defined, and she must make a choice.

She begins her journey alone, discovering herself through the contemporary tropes of illicit knowledge. She encounters first the three-headed snake, who Gaiman notes in *The Sandman Companion* is Geryon, killed by Hercules during his twelve labors (197), but he also doubles as Eden's tempter. Offered to join the sisterhood by two veiled women, Stheno and Euryale, she sits in their garden and eats of the golden apple, "more like the other tree ... the tree of life" (60:18). He encourages her to take all she wants. But he warns her, "Ladies who *sent* you down here.... Sleep in their house — eat this food.... Well, wouldn't recommend it, that's all" (60:19). But like Eve before her, she eats. The veiled ladies are gorgons themselves, inviting Lyta to join them, but again, this visage "whether she is beautiful or hideous, the veiled woman reflects male dread of women" (Gilbert and Gubar 472). While potentially figures of empowerment for the contemporary feminist, becoming Medusa's successor embraces the misogyny of patriarchal empowerment. Perhaps she would have remained there, stuck in the garden (or even ultimately expelled), and accepted the gorgon's gift ("Life until death" (61:15)), but as she requires the attributes of the gorgon, as her hair begins to transform into snakes (61:3), she recognizes the futility of their offer. They are liminal creatures whose purpose is to create the indefinite stasis that is cast in the patriarchal figuring of the powerful woman. She must move on. As she wanders, she encounters the reflection of herself, but it turns into mere confusion: "But which one of us am I?" she asks herself. "It doesn't matter," she responds (61:21). She remains unable to define herself without assistance, and for the first time in her narrative, it is a woman, Larissa (previously called Thessaly), who finds her. Once Dream's lover, Thessaly is a witch: independent, outspoken, knowledgeable. She is a modern woman, and she protects Lyta so the journey can continue. She appears to Lyta as a white bird, the signifier of an oracular presence (as the dove descends to announce the Holy Spirit's word (John 3.15), and when she is secure in Larissa's protection, she faces her mirror for the second time.

Lyta's journey is not easy. She struggles, literally and metaphorically, up a cliff side only to encounter a vanity, a replica of her mirror in The Dream

Dome. She sits and she converses with herself. The last conversation Lyta held with her mirror-self, the figure in the mirror was also the reality as she sat in The Dreaming. This time, her conversation offers her a decision: continue on her journey or "open your eyes, climb off this bed, walk out the door, put your life back together again" (63:17). It is the choice offered her by Hector, Brute, and Glob in The Dream Dome. It is the choice offered her by Morpheus after her release. The third time, she answers clearly for herself—"Sometimes there just aren't any choices at all..."—and she smashes the mirror, forfeiting her last connection to her real self (63:18). Here, she meets the Furies. Gaiman has carefully crafted a feminist narrative for Lyta Hall. He begins by characterizing her as the classical woman whose security is ripped away by a forced, patriarchal independence as she is invested by the external hierarchy to assert her individual (feminine) identity. Thus freed and left to her own devices, she flounders until given a direction, focusing on an external identity that was wholly dependent on the randomness of chance, and ultimately limited by the inevitable separation of mother and child. When stripped of the name of mother and protector, she is lost in anger and vengeance; she cannot see another direction. While Gaiman is careful to represent the masculine tropes of feminine power, he necessarily has Lyta reject them. All that remains in Lyta's narrative is the choice between independence and another hierarchical system. What follows is certainly a critique of contemporary feminism, and is answered twice in a single word. There is a sense that Gaiman attributes this drive for power from a deep well of misplaced resentment, for Lyta's ire is directed towards Morpheus, who has not wronged her. In fact, as the story unfolds, it is other malevolent characters who frame Dream for Daniel's kidnapping and still others, like Larissa, who assist Lyta in furtherance of their own agendas. In a metaphor for the modern feminist movement, Gaiman seems to be asserting that the anger, the force of destruction that Lyta Hall represents when she becomes The Fury is ultimately misplaced. The mode of myth appropriation that fuels the misandrist ire from the feminist left falls short of genuine empowerment.

Feminist criticism in the face of three thousand years of male-dominated literary composition asserts that the feminine embrace and embody the monstrous representation of her, the madwoman: "What this means, however, is that the madwoman in literature by women is not merely, as she might be in male literature, an antagonist or foil to the heroine. Rather, she is usually in some sense the *author's* double, an image of her own anxiety and rage" (Gilbert and Gubar 78). The critical bedrock of this theory is, of course, *The Madwoman in the Attic* by Sandra M. Gilbert and Susan Gubar. Their thesis is, in essence, that women writers (directly; implicitly all women) must appropriate both the positive and negative tropes of femininity in order to understand, overcome, and revise them into their own unique form of gendered generation. Gaiman disagrees. To understand what he finds problematic and to address his solution, however, the reader must continue the story of Lyta Hall to its conclusion. The Eumenides are a curious choice for Gaiman to use as the tropes of feminist empowerment. "The Kindly Ones" is named for its principle actors, the Eumenides, who have been figured previously in the series as the Weird Sisters (10:19), the Hecate, and the Fates (57:1). Once the super-heroine "The Fury," Lyta Hall calls to her namesakes: "There's a ... man. I want to do **more** than bother him. I want to destroy him ... he killed my son. He **stole** and **killed** my **son**" (63:22, 23). But the oldest rule of the Furies requires that they exact revenge for the killing of kindred blood (Aeschylus ll.210–213), and Lyta Hall's call for personal vengeance is not enough. As fate (or machinations, such as it is) would have it, however, Morpheus has killed his own son in an act of mercy. This warrants the Furies' ire. They will hound the Dream King, destroy his kingdom, and before they are done, they will have ensured the death of Lyta Hall's son (and Dream's heir), Daniel. The mythological "Furies" appear a few times in various guises, and while some situations in which they are depicted (Athena's court case in *The Oresteia*, for example) are sociologically significant, of themselves they are incidental: road blocks to the greater message of the story. While they don't even merit their own chapter in Robert Graves's compendium, *The Greek Myths*, they are still respected powers in the Greek pantheon. A single paragraph, though, suffices to capture them. "It is unwise," Graves writes, "to mention them by name ... hence they are usually styled the Eumenides ... 'The Kindly Ones'" (122). They are the "personification of curses pronounced upon a guilty criminal" (Peck, par. 1), euphemized by Orestes after his acquittal (par. 1). Three women, born of Night, along with their sisters the Fates (Hesiod 9). They are the Erinyes: Tisiphone, Alecto, and Megaera, and in English, they are called the Furies (Peck, par. 1). Like many of the ancient Gods, the origin of the Furies multiplies with the sources available. In the oldest, they are the daughters of Earth, born of blood wrought from the Genitals of the Great Heaven (Hesiod 8). Yet within a few moments, their identity is confused with those daughters of Night, "who prosecute the transgressions of men and gods — never do the goddesses cease from their terrible wrath until they have paid the sinner his due" (Hesiod 9). Their identity begins in question, but their function never wavers. In Homer's *Illiad,* the Furies curse Phoenix with infertility for transgressing his father's will (266, ll.554–558). Iris soothes Poseidon, reminding him that "the Furies always stand by older brothers" (394, ll.239–244). Agamemnon invokes their name, swearing to his honor:

... and Furies stalking the world below
to wreak revenge on the dead who broke their oaths —
I swear I never laid a hand on the girl...
Briseis remained untouched within my tents [498–499, ll.305–307, 310].

They enforce order by punishing transgression. In fear of them, Telemachus refuses Antinous's demand to expel Penelope from her home:

and some dark god would hurt me even more
when mother, leaving her own house behind,
calls down her withering Furies on my head,
and our people's cries of shame would hound my heels.
I would never issue that ultimatum to my mother [*Odyssey* 97 ll.150–155].

The threat of their retribution forestalls the abandonment of the mother and Queen. And they do not reserve their power for the favored alone (*Odyssey* 368 l.525). They are the vengeance of the lost, the hounders of the damned, and the embodiment of retribution. They are the enforcers of family honor. Given voice in Aeschylus's *The Eumenides*, they appear as the "women who serve [Clytemnestra]'s house, they come like gorgons, they wear robes of black, and they are wreathed in a tangle of snakes ... the bloodhounds of [Orestes'] mother's hate" (Aeschylus *LB* l.1048–1050, 1054). When Orestes is found by Apollo, he is surrounded by their hideous, sleeping forms (*Eum* ll.46–59), and they are soon awakened by the ghost of Clytemnestra (ll.94–130). In the consequent conversation, Aeschylus states what Gaiman will later refer to as "the oldest rule" (XII 23): The Furies hound those who are guilty of "shedding of kindred blood" (Aes *Eum* l.213), for "motherblood drives [The Furies], and I go to win my right upon [Orestes] and hunt him down" (ll.230–231). But they are not just. Protected by Apollo, Athena, law, and judgment, The Furies still pine for the punishment of Orestes (ll.778–792). The murder of Clytemnestra and her husband is demanded by Apollo as retribution for her murder of Orestes's father, but for The Furies, it is irrelevant. They condemn the blood-transgression. The rest of the story is white noise (ll.582–613). Ancient, powerful, feared, and unjust, The Furies are the embodiment of the feminine mother-voice in Greek mythology. As the religion fell into the tropes of mythology, the fearsome revenging Furies ceased to function. Their ability to drive men mad with their whispers, their hideous shapes, and their vicious revelations become the nag, the hag, the mother-in-law. By the Romantic period, Shelley's Prometheus knows "Thy words are like a cloud of winged snakes / And yet, I pity those they torture not" (Shelley I.632–633). Unable to fulfill their proscribed function, they depart with a flourish: "Thou pitiest them? I speak no more!" (634). The old gods no longer serve their function; they are, without any irony, impotent, unable to rise to their function. The

Eumenides, denuded by Athena, dismissed by Shelley, lost in the list of near-forgotten "Classics," their fearsome countenance is only a shadow, a faded memory, an echo of a power able to drive men mad. By the age of the Romantics, the Eumenidies could be well-described as the most annoying Gods, able to drive men to distraction with their incessant harping. They were caricatures of themselves. Gaiman's revision imbues them with their old power, focused through the once-heroic super-heroine, The Fury. She owns both the light and dark of her genetic identity, as Gilbert and Gubar suggest.

> In projecting their anger and dis-ease into dreadful figures, creating dark doubles for themselves and their heroines, women writers are both identifying with and revising the self-definitions patriarchal culture has imposed on them. All the nineteenth- and twentieth-century women who evoke the female monster in their novels and poems alter her meaning by virtue of their own identification with her. For it is usually because she is in some sense imbued with interiority that the witch-monster-mad-woman becomes so crucial an avatar of the writer's own self [79].

Lyta Hall becomes the "witch-monster-mad-woman" literalized and set upon the masculine patriarchy of the creative endeavor. The Furies, for all their power and prowess, are the most potent critics of males in the history of literature, and Dream is nothing if not the anthropomorphic figuration of the facility of (masculine) imagination. The purpose, one hopes, of the feminist formulation is to empower women and deny force to the misanthropic troping of the female in literature, thus allowing women to be freely creative without the overwhelming confinement of patriarchal imposition. But Gaiman proposes, through Lyta's narrative, that this approach may be flawed. To appropriate the basest and most disfiguring tropes of male literature as a reactionary stance, born of anger, frustration, and desperation is — in sequence — destructive, self-defeating, and ineffective.

Lyta is inhabited by the Eumenides, and she enters the Dreaming. Her arc is always drawn from the first-person perspective, she is the Triple Goddess and she is herself, The Fury and the Furies. When she is encountered, her victims address her in the singular. And they are all victims: Lucien, Marv, Cain, Abel, Eve, and the rest of Dream's avatars. They are injured or killed or worse: erased from memory. It is the greatest literary death, simply to be forgotten without another copy. Lyta Hall's swath of destruction leaves little to the allegorical imagination: her appropriation of feminine tropes as a means of empowerment destroys the figures, archetypes, and storehouses of imagination, whether or not they are of patriarchal construction. That is the purpose and always the intent of that power, and it is a sword — once drawn — that remains unsheathed, wielding itself wantonly on every possible subject, and ultimately unabated by its supposed goal. Gaiman seems to assert that even while the intent of appropriating misogynist types is to disarm them from their derogatory generation and empower their revisionists, they never stray from their original function. They are destructive and divisive by nature. When Lyta Hall discovers that Daniel is not dead, and in fact it was Morpheus who saved him from the kidnappers who would have destroyed him, she pleads for the Furies to call off their assault on the Dreaming. She cries, "We have to rescue Daniel. Bring him back. We don't have to hurt *anyone* anymore." The Furies reply, "We do not rescue, my little smelfungus. What do you think we are? After all, he killed his son. And we hated his son[9] ... he made us weep. He made the ladies weep with his songs and his things that never were and never shall be. Stories. Made-up rubbishy stories. Makes you sick" (67:21). Once unleashed, the Furies serve their own purpose: not merely to carve a space but to undo all that has been done. It is likely overstating things to say that Gaiman is anti-feminist. He is certainly not. However, his critique of the literary feminist agenda ends with Lyta's realization that, for all she has gained (power, identity, destruction, vengeance), she has lost the issue of her endeavor. She returns to her existence an exile, knowing what she's done, and in Larissa's words, "As I understand it, your actions have ensured that you will never see Daniel again ... I'd take a shower, and then start running, if I were you. Lots of people are going to want to hurt or kill you for what you've done. Including me" (69:20). Of course, there is some potent literary license here if one is to read this as a comment on feminist appropriations as a means to a positive identity, however it does speak to a more general sentiment that this approach, while clearly empowering, has unintended negative consequences. The effects of choosing this path to empowerment may be inherently flawed, since the tools for its inception are rooted firmly in an existing system of misogynist, or at least highly limiting, myths, stories, tropes, and types. Again, Lyta's failure is defined by her self-imposed limitations by choosing to appropriate the figurations of feminine power created in the patriarchal hierarchy and only realigned by a feminist hierarchy that serves no more constructive purpose than to tear down. In her act of vengeance, she fails to transgress the socially constructed roles she desires to fulfill. Thus it is with ease that Death dismisses Lyta's Furies.

Simone de Beauvoir imagines Lady Death as a figure from the French literary tradition: "Thus the Woman-Mother has a face of shadows: she is the chaos whence all have come and whither all must one day return; she is Nothingness" (147). The alternate face of "mother," she is the negatively constructed antidote of the masculine rising sun. With his usual penchant for the unexpected, and since he comes from the post-modern British tradition that figures Ingmar Bergman's Death whose black robe, white face, and scythe are more representative of imminent demise than de Beauvoir's matron, Gaiman offers a very different form of the empowered female in Death. She is poised as Gaiman's contrapuntal figure to Lyta Hall. Graphically, he illustrates the dichotomy through contrasting images: Lyta, joining the Furies, is drawn in shadow, her red eyes glowing and silhouette backlit by the moon (63:22). Death stands behind a mosaic figure of the sun, fully visible wearing a black jacket, a slightly bemused expression, and her ever-present ankh pendant. Gaiman's response to the feminist problematic is an ungendered solution. Like his Death, Gaiman's perspective seems to resonate with the matter-of-fact individuality that demarcates his most potent characters. As Mary Borsellino notes:

> [Gaiman writes:] "God gives you a body, it's your duty to do well by it. He makes you a boy, you dress in blue, he makes you a girl, you dress in pink."
> This quote from chapter six in *A Game of You* represents a way of thinking and a set of attitudes that Gaiman's work breaks down — not through contradiction or subversion, but through simple disregard [51].

Death does not need to be anything but what she already is, fulfilled in her complex and demanding role, she lives, empowered by her own knowledge of her self. She is the choice that Lyta denied. Gaiman introduces this practical, sensible, caring figure at the end of his first story arc, in an interlude. Dream sits feeding the pigeons, and Death joins him. She is soon excoriating him for not seeking her out and confiding in her: "You are utterly the stupidest, most self-centered, appallingest excuse for an anthropomorphic personification on this or any other plane! ... Didn't it occur to you that I'd be worried silly about you?" (8:8–9). She leads Morpheus through a few hours of her job, escorting the anticipating and the surprised through the transition between life and death, all to the sound of wings. She is, like Dream, just an idea (though in fiction, this is a marginal limitation), but she is free from the gendered types of the patriarchy, unlike Morpheus or Lyta. She has accepted the "person" she is, terrible, beautiful, finite, inevitable. She is feminine, certainly, but it does not define her: such definitions are incidental. So when the story ends, and Morpheus sits with Death upon the top of a craggy rock, awaiting the end, the Furies' vengeance in full force, they demand: "Dream-King, we are destroying the Dreaming. Can you not feel it? What will you do to stop us? What can you do?" It is not Dream who answers, but his sister. She ends it with a word: "Enough!" (69:9). And they are dismissed. When faced with the certainty of being, they have no power. Like Prometheus, who pities the Furies flying by him, their encounter with Death ends ineffectually. True empowerment is immune to the slings and arrows of mere fortune, and so she can dismiss what Dream cannot, what Lyta cannot bear, and what the Furies continue to be. The story ends with a return to the Furies, now the Fates, as they cut one string and begin another.

"There. For good or bad. It's done" (72:24). They remain unchanged, as critical perspectives often do, waiting to be unleashed again, for better or worse. But they are what they always were, a tool for the angry, the vengeful, the lost, and the insecure. Death continues on her way, being who she is, aware of and embracing the feminine that assists her, the self that defines her, and the knowledge that empowers her. From the beginning, she is the expectation fulfilled.

Notes

1. Comics are constructed as a cooperative medium. The writer manages both the dialogue and sequence of the art, thus Gaiman probably dictated much of the composition of the drawing. However, the artist, Chris Bachalo and later Marc Hempel in *The Kindly Ones*, may have also contributed considerably to the structure and certainly set the artistic tone of the illustrations in this issue. Throughout the references to the comic, I will make note of the illustrator. However, without the original script (which is not publicly available), it is impossible to tell how much of these sequences are uniquely Gaiman's and which are collaborative products. Scholars of film, another collaborative medium, have tackled the same problem by attributing decisions to the director. Therefore, I will follow this convention and attribute decisions to the "director" of the comic, which in this case is Gaiman.

2. Though, like most characters in the DC Universe, Lyta Hall has multiple "origin stories" due to a complex "reset" of the continuity called *A Crisis on Infinite Earths*, her career as "The Fury" and her namesake remain consistent. In the second revision, she is the daughter of The Fury, who was a founding member of the Justice Society and also the daughter of Hyppolita of the Amazons. The summary of her origin and life to the point of *Sandman #11* is taken from the D.C. Database (http://dc.wikia.com/wiki/Fury_(L yta_Hall)) and "Who's Who in the D.C. Universe" (http://dc.wikia.com/wiki/Hippolyta_-Trevor-Hall_(New_Earth)).

3. In comics books, a radiated series of straight, abstract lines that lead from, or follow from, a character's figure are called "force lines" and are traditionally used to express fast or violent motion.

4. While not directly relevant to this argument, the choice of "Daniel" as the name for Lyta's son is actually very clever in terms of the mythological typologies Gaiman is juggling. While Morpheus is Dreaming, his figured derived from the Greek God of Dreams, Daniel becomes the Dream of the Judeo-Christian age. As the pantheons of the Greeks and Romans (and other "pagan" religions) have been passed by as "mythology," the weaver of dreams, whose role as interpreter of dreams, maker of kings, and eventually king himself, in the contemporary pantheon is sensibly a figuration of the Bible's Daniel, whose book is a series of dreams told, dreams interpreted, and dreams yet to be. While Daniel's ascension does not come until late in the series (Issue 72), the naming concisely foreshadows the progress of events as they unfold to their ultimate reconciliation.

5. In a somewhat eerie echo of Issue 12, Lyta tells Daniel, "Now, you know what's going to happen now? **You** got it, babycakes. Time for your nap." She reassigns Hector's demeaning nickname for her to her son. While this is now an appropriate use of an affectionate term, it also echoes past abuse with disturbing implications of the user's own denial. Like Hector, Lyta does not see the real situation of her charge.

6. This, again, reinforces the general Judeo-Christian re-mythologizing Gaiman engages in his invention of Daniel's character.

7. An avatar of Dream, Matthew is a talking raven who was once a man and is now page (or counsel or jester) to Morpheus. He was one of the characters who attended Daniel on his excursion to Abel's home, the House of Secrets in The Dreaming.

8. While a "normal" mother might avoid a homeless man's gift, the reader always keeps in mind that Lyta Hall has nothing to fear from normal men and women, as her gifts make her extraordinarily able to defend Daniel and herself in "average" situations. When the homeless man attempts to engage her and her son with a flower in an effort to be charming, her violent reaction and forceful threat are disproportionate to any reasonable reaction to the situation.

9. According to the chronicles of The Sandman continuity, Orpheus was the son of Dream.

Works Cited

Aeschylus. The Eumenedies. Trans. Richard Lattimore. Chicago: University of Chicago Press, 1953: 133–171. Print.

_____. The Libation Bearers. Trans. Richard Lattimore. Chicago: University of Chicago Press, 1953: 91–132. Print.

Bender, Hy. The Sandman Companion. New York: D.C. Comics, 1999. Print.

Borsellino, Mary. "Blue and Pink: Gender in Neil Gaiman's Work." The Neil Gaiman Reader. Ed. Darrell Schweitzer. New York: Wildside Press, 2007. Print.

de Beauvoir, Simone. The Second Sex. Trans. H.M. Parshley. New York: Random House, 1989. Print.

Friedan, Betty. The Feminine Mystique. New York: W.W. Norton, 1963. Print.

Gaiman, Neil (w), Mike Dringenberg (a), Malcolm Jones III (i). "The Sound of Her Wings." The Sandman #8 (Aug. 1989), New York: DC Comics. Print.

_____ (w), Mike Dringenberg (a), Dave McKean (p), Malcolm Jones III (i). "The Doll's House." The Sandman #10 (Nov. 1989), New York: DC Comics. Print.

_____ (w), Chris Bachalo (a), Malcolm Jones III (i). "Playing House." The Sandman #12 (Jan. 1990), New York: DC Comics. Print.

_____ (w), Kelley Jones (a), Malcolm Jones III (i). "Season of Mists: Chapter One." The Sandman #22 (Jan. 1991), New York: DC Comics. Print.

_____ (w), Jill Thompson (a), Vince Locke (i). "Convergence: The Parliament of Rooks." The Sandman #40 (Aug. 1992), New York: DC Comics. Print.

_____ (w), Mark Hempel, et al. (a, i). "The Kindly Ones." The Sandman #57–69 (Feb. 1994 – July 1995), New York: DC Comics. Print.

_____ (w), Dave McKean, Michael Zulli (a, i). "The Wake: Chapter Three." The Sandman #72 (Nov. 1995), New York: DC Comics. Print.

Gilbert, Sandra M., and Susan Gubar. The Madwoman in the Attic, 2d Ed. New Haven:Yale University Press, 2000. Print.

Goodyear, Dana. "Kid Goth." The New Yorker (25 January 2010). Web. 29 April 2012.

Graves, Robert. The Greek Myths: Volume 1. Baltimore: Penguin, 1955. Print.

Hesiod. Theogony & Works and Days. Trans. M.L. West. Oxford: Oxford University Press, 1988. Print.

Homer. The Illiad. Trans. Robert Fagles. New York: Penguin, 1996. Print.

_____. The Odyssey. Trans. Robert Fagles. New York: Penguin, 1990. Print.

McGee, Arthur. "Macbeth and the Furies." Shakespeare Survey: An Annual Survey of Shakespeare Studies and Production. (1966): 55–67. Print.

Murphy, Patrick D. "The High and Low Fantasies of Feminist (Re)Mythopoeia." Mythlore. (Winter 1989): 26–31. Print.

Ovid. The Metamorphoses. Trans. Allen Mandelbaum. New York: Harcourt Brace, 1993. Print.

Peck, Harry Thurston. "Eumenides." *Harper's Dictionary of Classical Antiquities.* 1898. From *Project Perseus Archives.* Boston: Tufts University, 2005. Web. 20 April 2012.

Shakespeare, William. *Macbeth. The Riverside Shakespeare*, 2d ed. Ed. Evans, G. Evans. Boston: Houghton Mifflin, 1997. Print.

Shelley, Percy. *Prometheus Unbound. Shelley's Poetry and Prose,* 2d ed. Eds. Neil Fraistat and Donald Reiman. New York: W.W. Norton, 2002: 206–286. Print.

Virgil. *The Aeneid.* Trans. Allen Mandelbaum. Berkeley: University of California Press, 1971. Print.

Feminist Subjectivity in Neil Gaiman's *Black Orchid*

BY SARAH CANTRELL

In 1988, Neil Gaiman and illustrator Dave McKean took an obscure DC comic book hero, Black Orchid, and reworked the character for eponymous publication by Vertigo (a DC imprint specializing in slightly smaller-circulation, slightly less mainstream titles). Although Gaiman preserved a few of Orchid's basic characteristics, he completely revamped the feel of the comic and radically changed the degree to which *Black Orchid* emphasizes Orchid's consciousness. In so doing, Gaiman created a text especially rich for feminist study, particularly because its focus on a female superhero is housed in a first-person narrative. This type of narrative simulates autobiography. Both filter the text to some extent through a focal character's internal consciousness. The end result of both first-person narrative and autobiography is the privileging of interiority.

The narration in *Black Orchid* blurs the boundaries between first- and third-person, and in so doing functionally creates two separate Black Orchids — the Orchid who *thinks* and the Orchid who *speaks* in the text. Narratologists have explored a distinction between several types of first-person narration in a way that explains how this split self is produced. Monica Fludernik's handbook for narrative scholars explains that in fictional first-person narratives, "the focus can be either on the so-called *narrating self* or the *experiencing self*" (90). A narrating self reports events "from the perspective of a now older and wiser narrator" and often "indulges in retrospection, evaluation and the drawing of moral conclusions." An experiencing self, on the other hand, reports events as they take place and usually differs from a narrating self by relying more heavily on the present tense. The narrator of Gaiman's *Black Orchid* is clearly an experiencing self, occupying the same time frame as the actions being depicted in the story. The unity of time frame created by an experiencing-self narrator, however, does not in this case result in a corresponding unity of identity between the self as narrator and as character in the story. Fludernik suggests that an experiencing-self narrator, like that in *Black Orchid*, creates some tension between the part of the consciousness that narrates the action and the part of the consciousness that experiences the action. When in these narratives "the emphasis is on the protagonist's consciousness," Fludernik assigns them to the figural narrative situation (90). In making this claim, she utilizes the earlier work of narrative scholar Franz Karl Stanzel and his chart of the "typological circle." Stanzel's chart uses the term "figural narrative situation" to indicate third-person narrative, and it makes a distinction between that type of narrative and a first-person narrative with an experiencing narrator. By categorizing the experiencing-self narrative as a type of figural narrative, Fludernik shows that these narratives somehow function as both first-person and third-person, or at least that the experiencing-self narrator functions separately as narrator and as character. This is the case with Orchid. In Orchid, we see an attempt to negotiate between two selves, between the self as defined as an internal consciousness that narrates one's own story and the self as defined as an agent acting in the world. Ultimately, the self that is constituted by her internal consciousness is the focus of the Gaiman text.

The first-person narrative style in *Black Orchid* is paired with a plotline that is centered on Orchid's search for identity. Black Orchid, of course, is a fictional character, and she is not a character who literally writes. Nevertheless, in a metatextual sense, Orchid attempts to find and ultimately create an identity for herself, and in that sense she is writing her identity. This mirrors the characteristics of women writers of the nineteenth century as theorized by Sandra Gilbert and Susan Gubar. The parallel between nineteenth-century and twentieth-century comics literary history is more natural than it may seem at first. The struggle for acceptance of women in the comics industry of the twentieth century is not greatly different from nineteenth-century women novelists' struggle for acceptance in the broader literary scene. Orchid's struggle equally parallels the attempts of women to find a place in the comics industry, both as writers and as characters. That *Black Orchid* seems to echo two such temporally distant cultures reveals the extent to which superhero comics lagged behind other genres that more progressively broke away from gender stereotypes.

There is a great deal of scholarship on autobiography and fictional first-person narrative of the kind that *Black Orchid* utilizes, particularly over the past few decades, thanks in large part to the work done by narratologists on subjectivity and its representation. Since the 1980s, these genres have also become a locus of study for feminist scholars exploring the depiction (or construction) of gendered subjectivity. These genres are explicitly concerned with metaphysical selfhood, so they provide a glimpse into the ways in which women created and were created as selves.

In comics, autobiography and fictional first-person narrative were slow to find wide popularity with audiences and even with critics. In recent years, they have become an immensely popular comics genre. Marjane Satrapi's 2000 *Persepolis* was successful enough that it was adapted for film in 2007. In 2006, *Time Magazine* and *The Times* (London) both listed Alison Bechdel's *Fun Home* as a top entry in their list of the ten best books of the year. Earlier works like Art Spiegelman's *Maus* (which won a Pulitzer Prize in 1992), along with the work of largely autobiographical comic writers like Harvey Pekar and Robert Crumb, have seen a huge resurgence in popularity. Pekar was even the subject of the biopic *American Splendor*, released in 2003. Autobiography and fictional first-person narrative in comics, though, began with the underground comics movement.

Historically, autobiographical and autobiographically tinged comics have been published in limited numbers by small publishing houses. Justin Green's 1972 work *Binky Brown Meets the Holy Virgin Mary*, considered by some the first autobiographical comic, became highly influential on writers like Spiegelman and Crumb but was published by the obscure Last Gasp Eco Funnies and quickly went out of print (although a new edition was finally released by McSweeney's in 2009.) *Maus* began in 1972 as a three-page strip in *Funny Aminals*, an obscure underground comic published by Apex Novelties. Crumb and Pekar allied themselves from the start with the underground "comix" movement rather than big comics publishers like DC and Marvel. These authors and their groundbreaking work in autobiographical comics have until fairly recently been wholly separate from mainstream comics, which in America have traditionally been dominated by superhero stories that rely on action and dialogue and occasional third-person narration. If one can posit an opposition in style or approach between any two comics genres, that opposition historically lay between autobiographical and superhero comics.

The barrier between superhero comics (with their external focus) and autobiographical and fictional first-person narrative comics (with their internal focus) wasn't broken until the early 1980s, when Alan Moore took over as writer for DC's *Swamp Thing* superhero comic. This was the first superhero comic to present a sustained glimpse of the inner consciousness of a superhero. Other autobiographically styled superhero comics soon followed, including Alan Moore's *Watchmen*, also published by DC starting in 1986. These titles incorporated autobiographical style into mainstream superhero comics and for a brief period helped DC win readers away from Marvel, which was slower to incorporate the more subjective style. However, female superhero titles had yet to demonstrate an almost entirely first-person narrative style. The first comic to incorporate a first-person narrative style into a female superhero title was Gaiman's *Black Orchid* in 1988.

With *Black Orchid*, Gaiman and McKean created a new approach to female superhero comics. This radical reworking of Detective Comics' 1973 *Black Orchid* replaces the traditional superhero power narrative, which hinges on physical solutions, with an emphasis on subjectivity that borders on fictional autobiography. Gaiman's *Black Orchid* is about mind, not body.

With *Black Orchid*, Gaiman followed hard on Moore's heels in taking this more subjective approach and used it to rework the comic superheroine. Lillian Robinson, in her 2004 book *Wonder Women: Feminisms and Superheroes*, claims that "the female superhero originates in an act of criticism — a challenge to the masculinist world of superhero adventures" (7). Robinson presents superhero comics as more exclusively gendered than most genres. Superhero comics, according to Robinson and to the general consensus, are traditionally masculine, featuring male (even hypermasculine) characters. Robinson claims that any female superhero must contend with the masculine history of the genre. If a superhero is traditionally defined as masculine, a text that introduces a female superhero must then redefine the genre to allow for femininity. In traditional superhero comics, female superheroes behave much like male superheroes. The power sets are often similar (flight, super strength, speed). The plots center on the protagonists overcoming villains with physical combat in much the same way that male superheroes do. The femininity of these characters is mostly a matter of appearance — they have hyper-feminized or sexualized bodies, with tiny waists and large breasts. They're often drawn with costumes that emphasize their bodies. In other words, the traditional approach to female superheroes is to couch a male superhero's actions in an overtly sexualized female body. The gender of these characters is coincidental except as a matter of objectification. The engagement of Gaiman's *Orchid* in feminist conversation is perhaps inevitable. But Gaiman's *Black Orchid* grapples with gender and genre in a way that makes it strikingly different from the same title as originally handled in a more traditional way by Sheldon Mayer and illustrator Tony DeZuniga in 1973.

The first page of Mayer's original 1973 *Black Orchid* is dominated by the image of the titular figure in full costume, splashed full-length across the page, looking directly at the viewer. Her vivid purple costume stands out against the backdrop of an abandoned house, painted in greyscale. The only other bright color on the page comes from the golden moon in the background, which is partially obscured by the house and skeletal trees, and the title, which is partially hidden behind Black Orchid's lower legs. The impression in this panel is that Black Orchid, as a physical presence, is central to the text. That impression is strengthened by the final panel of Mayer's *Black Orchid*, a slightly larger than half-page panel that is nearly filled with another full-length image of Orchid, spread-eagled in flight against the backdrop of a house and distant lawn.

The opening page of Gaiman's *Black Orchid* takes a very different visual approach. It begins with a three-panel image series of an orchid flanked above and below in each panel by thought bubbles that express Black Orchid's consciousness. Where the reader's attention in the 1973 version was drawn inexorably to Orchid's body, the attention is here drawn to her mind. What's more, these thought bubbles express not a narration of action but rather what Orchid feels and desires: "Winter is coming. I feel it in the warm autumnal air. I scent it at sunset. I want to see the colors of the leaves before they fall, to caress the updrafts of the wind with my form" (1:3). This style of narration is wildly different from the third-person narration in the opening of classic superhero comics. The original *Black Orchid* begins:

> It was midnight ... a man ... a good man ... was in trouble ... and she appeared! It was as simple as that! She showed a strength that was impossible to believe ... removed the man from danger ... and then **vanished!** — Nothing more was known about her, except that everyone who saw her agreed that she looked like a huge flower — -an orchid — a — Black Orchid [AC 428:1].

This opening, more typical of traditional superhero comics, is full of action, both in what it narrates and in the use of exclamation marks and bold font. Not only does Mayer make no attempt here to convey Black Orchid's inner consciousness, he privileges corporeality over consciousness by placing emphasis on what "everyone who saw her agreed that she looked like."

The initial reveal of the protagonist Orchid in the Gaiman comic also makes her the visual center of the scene. Up to that point, and in fact throughout the comic, all the characters have been painted in extremely desaturated colors. Orchid, here and throughout the work, is painted in striking shades of purple. Gaiman's dialogue, though, pairs with the art in this scene to caution against the objectification of the heroine. The man who removes her disguise remarks solely on her appearance in a manner that immediately objectifies her: "Oh, nice. Verry pretty. You got one of those **costumes** under there too? Ohhh **Yesss**. Pretty in **purple!**" (1:7). This man goes on to kill Orchid. In this scene, the first scene where we see any version of Orchid, the only person who comments on her appearance is a villain, and he does so as a verbal slap in the face. In fact, throughout the Gaiman and McKean version, no one but the antagonists ever comment on Orchid's appearance.

By contrast, in the 1973 version, Orchid's appearance is a frequent subject of commentary by characters on both sides of the law and even by the narrator. In the second issue, the narrator even introduces her in a manner that places equal emphasis on her superpowers and her looks: "She has the strength of a regiment, flies through the air like a bird of prey ... and has the beauty and compassion of a young girl!" The narrator of Gaiman's *Black Orchid*, Orchid herself, only comments on her appearance once. This aspect of the text demonstrates the extreme to which Gaiman and McKean's version deviates from the original.

The final issue of Gaiman's *Black Orchid* closes much as Gaiman's first issue began, with an emphasis on Orchid's consciousness. Another triptych closes the final issue, this time a three-panel image series of Black Orchid silhouetted against a setting sun. The first of these panels flanks the image with thought bubbles, just as in the first panel of the first issue. However, while the series' opening displays an orchid icon, a stand-in for the actual Orchid, in the final panel, Orchid has shrunk into the upper distance, barely discernible against the light of the sun, and a thought bubble appears in the center instead. If the beginning of the series drew attention to Orchid's mind, the final image makes her consciousness inescapably central.

Just as in the first three panels of the entire series, the dialogue in the last three again emphasizes feeling and desire rather than action: "The flight will be long, and tiring, but I can caress the updrafts of the wind with my form. I am alive in the colors of the leaves, and in the sunset, and in the moist tropical air" (3:48). Orchid's final words leave her plan of action ambiguous: "I have never been more alive. And together we soar, we climb, we ascend. Together. Into the **sun**" (3:48). This ending leaves the narration situated within Orchid's consciousness. This deviates from classic superhero comics, which typically end with the same third-person narration with which they begin. Gaiman's ending is especially striking in comparison to the original *Black Orchid*, in which each issue closes on a male character from that episode musing about Black Orchid and her identity. These endings intimate that Orchid's existence in her own right is secondary to her existence as an object in the thoughts of even minor male characters. Gaiman's use of first-person narration radically increases the importance of Orchid's consciousness.

If the opening and closing of Gaiman's *Black Orchid* series emphasize Orchid's subjectivity, the plot makes her subjectivity absolutely essential. Her first spoken line is "Who am I?" (1:19). Finding the answer to this question becomes Orchid's guiding quest. Orchid, as rewritten by Gaiman, is not an action hero in the traditional sense. In fact, with her first-person narration and the extent to which the story is driven by her search for self, Orchid seems more like the protagonist of a fictional autobiography. If we view *Black Orchid* as ultimately a story about the search for self-knowledge, it mirrors characteristics of nineteenth-century women's autobiography as a text that is particularly concerned with parentage and parenting.

Soon after her initial awakening (which could perhaps better be described as a birth), Orchid encounters the man who helped create her, Phil Sylvian. Orchid directly asks, "Are you my father?" to which he replies, "Yes. **Yes**, I suppose I **am** ... in a way" (1:34). Sylvian is Orchid's first stop in her search for her identity. But ultimately, Sylvian, Orchid's "father," proves ineffectual in helping her establish a sense of self. He describes her history, or rather Susan Linden's history. He also explains some of the science behind her creation. However, he cannot satisfactorily explain her identity in her current incarnation except as a matter of DNA. He cannot explain who Orchid is in terms of her consciousness. After Sylvian is murdered, Orchid is even more lost in terms of her identity: "If I could be what Phil wanted me to be.... If I **knew** what he wanted.... If I knew what we **were**..." (2:23). Orchid's "father" dies, leaving her directionless.

Another type of ineffective father is present in the figure of Susan Linden's father, shown in flashbacks in *Black Orchid*. Mr. Linden runs to the opposite extreme from Phil Sylvian, but he proves no less ineffective. Linden attempts to tightly control Susan's identity. He sees her as "Daddy's little girl" and attempts to lock her into that version of herself. In short, he tries to keep Susan a child and reacts violently to anything that threatens that childhood. In this case, a prepubescent kiss between Phil and Susan drives her father into a rage and results in Susan running away from home. She reaches adulthood on her own, with no father for guidance. Where Sylvian proves inept and weak, unwilling or unable to direct Orchid, Mr. Linden proves too controlling, too determined to force Susan into an identity she is outgrowing.

Gaiman's text offers yet another father, less literal but no less symbolically potent. In terms of Orchid's identity as a superhero, Batman is one of her most prominent predecessors, and in a metatextual sense, he is another kind of father to Orchid. In the Gaiman story, Batman appears and leads Orchid to Pamela Isley, one of Sylvian's colleagues, who may have information to help Orchid decipher what or who she is. Once that avenue fails, Batman tells her how to find Alec Holland (the Swamp Thing), the last of Phil's surviving colleagues. On a metatextual level, however, Batman stands in for Orchid's fathers in the superhero genre. He gives her guidance in her own detective work, but he is unable to give her answers about her identity. Ultimately, Orchid leaves Batman behind much as Susan leaves Mr. Linden. On a metaphorical level, this is representative of the text, *Black Orchid*, leaving behind the traditional superhero comic tropes in search of a new space where a female hero like Black Orchid can establish her own identity.

The fact that Black Orchid's search for identity leads her to father figures who are ultimately unable to help ties to the "anxiety of authorship" theorized by Sandra Gilbert and Susan Gubar. In their seminal work *The Madwoman in the Attic*, Gilbert and Gubar rework Harold Bloom's theory of the "anxiety of influence" felt by authors, who are necessarily subject to the influence of their precursors in the field but who must also break away from that influence and strive for originality. In the hands of Gilbert and Gubar, the "anxiety of authorship" refers more specifically to the struggle of women writers to write themselves into a patriarchal literary tradition that includes few female precursors. Gilbert and Gubar make the case that even the few women who formed a part of the early literary canon were suspect, writing less with their own voices than they were with the voices of the patriarchal codes they were unable to overcome. A woman writer, particularly in the nineteenth century, which is the focus of much of *The Madwoman in the Attic*, had to invent not only a new literary tradition that included a space for women but also to invent herself, lacking, as she did, a literary "mother" in the canon.

Gilbert and Gubar's theory applies to women writers, not to characters, but in a sense, Gaiman's Orchid attempts to write herself, to give herself a story. To do so, she must grapple with the reality that, though a woman, she must model herself using only the limited definitions of woman available in the hegemonic patriarchal narrative tradition would "reduce her to extreme stereotypes (angel, monster) [which will] drastically conflict with her sense of self" (Gilbert and Gubar 48). These extreme archetypes of femininity, the Angel in the House and the prostitute, lingered longer in that most masculine of genres (superhero comics) than in many other literary genres of the twentieth century.

Like the nineteenth-century women writers that were the focus of Gilbert and Gubar's work, Gaiman's Black Orchid lacks a female precursor. The story of who the original Orchid was and why she became a superhero is fragmented and murky. The Gaiman text offers at least four separate plot-significant versions of Orchid. In addition to the incarnation of Orchid whose search for identity forms the majority of the story, there is Susan Linden, whose DNA was cloned to make the first Orchids. There is also the Orchid clone who dies in the first few pages of the text. Finally, there is "Suzy," the partially-matured Orchid clone who becomes a daughter/sister/sidekick to Orchid.

These multiple versions of Orchid call into question the boundaries between self and other. Each of these four share DNA, and to an extent Orchid sees these alternate versions as a possible clue to her own identity. She turns to the history of Susan Linden, but ultimately Linden's history can't satisfy Orchid as to her current identity. Orchid ultimately recognizes Linden as a separate individual, not as herself. The Orchid who dies in the beginning of the Gaiman text also provides few clues to the identity of the new version of Orchid. Orchid (and the reader) knows very little about that predecessor, except that she died and that, according to the best guess of Alec Holland, she "appointed herself to fight ... crime. Perhaps ... she sought revenge ... for Susan's death.... Perhaps ... that is too ... simple ... an explanation" (3:7). In other words, the history of Orchid's decision to become a superhero is left murky. The relationship between Orchid and Suzy is also slippery. Orchid most often refers to Suzy as "sister." However, near the end of the text, Suzy refers to Orchid as "Mom" (3:47). The identities and the relationship between the identities are fluid, blurred.

In fact, *Black Orchid* is a text full of multiplicities and eliding boundaries. Orchid's identity is the most uncertain, but other characters' identities are evasive and unreliable. Pamela Isley (Poison Ivy) appears in the text as a villain imprisoned in Arkham Asylum. Before we encounter Isley, we see the results of one of her cruel and gruesome experiments, a rat-eating cat-plant hybrid. The cat looks eerily like the result of a vivisection, with bleeding, fleshy tendons on top of its head. Isley rejects Orchid's desperate plea for help: "I never got any breaks, you know. I screwed up my life on my **own**, with no help on the way **down** from anybody else. You can damn well do the same" (2:40). Up to and including this point in the text, Isley acts as an antagonist, or at least a character designed to draw no sympathy from the reader. However, after Orchid leaves, Isley breaks down in tears, mourning the death of Phil Sylvian, revealing a complexity that blurs her identity as a villain in this text. The same blurring occurs with Carl Thorne, the man who murdered Susan Linden, the majority of her clones, and Phil Sylvian. As the primary villain in the story, Thorne seeks to murder the Orchid whose story guides the text. Nevertheless, his actions at the end of the story save Orchid's life, when he shoots the men who were sent to slaughter her. In an interesting confluence of events, Thorne's final line emphasizes the lack of boundaries to Orchid's identity: "You aren't Susan. You never were. You aren't anything..." (3:42). Orchid, of course, isn't "anything," in the sense that she is not any one thing in particular.

The blurring boundaries between Orchid and her other selves is also reflected in *Black Orchid*'s unusual art style. Most mainstream superhero comics up to the 1980s utilized bold linework, which gave objects and characters solid visual boundaries. McKean's art for *Black Orchid*, however, mostly uses very fluid washes of watercolor. Orchid's body, in particular, lacks finite and definitive boundaries. In almost every panel in which she appears, her hair and legs fade into the scenery. Julia Round, in her exploration of feminism in *Black Orchid*, claims that McKean "subverts the superheroic" with a "feminised aesthetic" (10, 3). Certainly, as she points out, "the Orchids are not costumed or linked to any specific logo," unlike nearly every other superhero in mainstream comics (10). Instead, after a short homage to the 1973 Orchid costume, McKean depicts Orchid in the nude. It may seem that Orchid's unclothed state emphasizes her body more than the skintight costumes worn by most superheroines. McKean, however, delays the depiction of Orchid's body and minimizes the detail in which her body is painted in order to de-emphasize her corporeality. His illustrations work hand in hand with Gaiman's writing to emphasize Orchid's consciousness rather than her body.

Orchid's lack of costume also seems appropriate to the unformed nature of her identity. The use of a costume is a kind of declaration of self that Orchid cannot participate in, since her selfhood is unformed. She does assert deliberate control over her appearance at one point in the text, but only to hide and not as a way of declaring her identity. In order to board a train, she takes on a human appearance. When someone comments on her violet eyes, she changes them to blue. She muses that "appearance is the simplest thing. Pigment and petal only" (2:25). But without a clear sense of the identity she wants to establish, a visual representation of that identity is meaningless.

McKean's softer, atmospheric renderings reverberate with third-wave feminist critiques of binaries. In her essay "Sorties," Hélène Cixous casts binary oppositions as characteristic of masculine writing and thinking. Feminine writing, she argues, must reject these firm and oppositional binaries and instead embody "the very possibility of change." She characterizes feminine writing as open and multiple, traits which Gaiman's *Black Orchid* certainly exhibits. This is not to say that such essentialist feminist thought is particularly convincing, or that Gaiman and McKean are men who are somehow writing an essentially female text. However, the openness and multiplicities within *Black Orchid* add to the ways in which this text attempts to establish a new way to approach feminine subjectivity in mainstream superhero comics.

If *Black Orchid* describes a complex relationship between Orchid and men as father figures, the relationship between Orchid and men as lovers is no less complex. Orchid's encounter with Alec Holland (the Swamp Thing) is in some ways the climax of this text, or at least of Orchid's search for a metaphysical selfhood. In this scene, Holland essentially impregnates Orchid, giving her the new identity and direction as mother. This placement of Orchid's moment of enlightenment is appropriate, given that Alan Moore's *Swamp Thing* was the superhero comic closest in narrative style to that used in *Black Orchid* and undoubtedly a strong influence on the Gaiman text.

When Orchid finally meets Holland, she kneels before him like a child, thinking, "I've never met a god before. He's **beautiful**" (3:9). Throughout the scene, she maintains a childish, slumped posture and diminutive height (compared to Holland). Her language breaks away from the fairly controlled, spare dialogue of the bulk of the text into emotionally-charged, rushed, over-long sentences: "And I thought you were **dead**, but the masked man said you were **here**. And I didn't know where else to **go** ... and I'm here and I don't know what's going on and I don't know what I am and I don't like it and, and, it's..." Holland hushes and comforts her. The "seeds" he gives her are literal ones, so although the fertilization here is technically sexual, requiring both a male and a female "plant," it is accomplished without sexual intercourse.

Nevertheless, this is the most sexually charged scene in the text. A brief exchange between Holland and his wife, Abigail Holland, points out the tension between the sexual and asexual natures of Orchid's encounter with Holland:

"Alec? **Who** was **that?**"

"She was ... **is** ... an old friend ... of an old friend. I was ... giving her ... **babies.**"

"Uh. **Right.** Y'know, Alec. I, uh, I **think** we're going to have to have a **talk** about this" [3:9].

Throughout the rest of *Black Orchid*, although Orchid is depicted in the nude, she is drawn without detailed postsecondary sexual characteristics. Nipples are absent, and pubic or any other body hair is never indicated specifically. In this scene with Holland, however, for the only instance in the entire story, Orchid's nipples appear (3:4). Orchid's more sexually complete appearance in this scene indicates the sexual awakening she experiences with Holland.

Ultimately, whether we read this scene as sexual or not, and whether we read Holland as a lover or a father or something entirely different, the aspects of the interaction most important to the story are the information and seeds that Orchid receives. In other words, this is ultimately a results-based encounter, and the results are both things that Orchid can take and use for herself as tools in forming her own identity. As Holland asserts, "How the story ends...? That is **your** affair" (3:8). The sexual awakening implied in this encounter requires that Orchid have a lover, but ultimately he merely acts as a necessary stage in her journey. The formation of her identity is still left to her.

Black Orchid presents motherhood as the most effective means for Orchid to establish an identity, although in the end even this is not entirely satisfying for Orchid. In the first portion of the text, Orchid meanders, directionless, except for the guiding question "Who am I?" Once she is in possession of the seeds, or what Holland calls "babies," Orchid takes on a more protective role toward Suzy, her partially-matured clone. She rescues Suzy from her kidnappers with the only feat of strength she exhibits in the story, ripping the door off an armored car. More importantly, Orchid establishes a concrete goal — to find a place where she and Suzy and the seeds can be safe. Orchid must create a home. It is important to note that the seeds Holland gives Orchid are taken from within Orchid's own chest.

The DNA linkage between Orchid, the "babies," and Suzy is significant. It produces a kind of self-mothering reminiscent of Gilbert and Gubar's take on women writers. Like the women writers of the nineteenth century who lacked satisfactory female predecessors, mainstream comic book female superheroes of the twentieth century lacked "mothers" as guides. Certainly, in their approach to Black Orchid, Gaiman and McKean were striking out from typical mainstream approaches to women in comics of that genre. Although Orchid is not self-aware in the title, in the sense that she recognizes her identity as a comic book heroine, the facts of her story and the style with which it is written and narrated suggest metatextual commentary on female superheroes. Orchid's search for identity is an attempt to write herself, or in Gilbert and Gubar's terms, to mother herself. For Gilbert and Gubar, the danger of self-mothering is that a woman's attempt to create her own story, without a female precursor to turn to, could "isolate or destroy her" (49). It could result in a text that will go unaccepted by mainstream literary culture. This isolation and destruction may even indicate a kind of loss of metaphysical self through the very attempt to assert one. In mothering herself, Orchid strikes a new path, one that certainly isolates her from the rest of humanity as depicted in the text.

Instead of opening the comic with an image of Orchid, as DeZuniga did in the original version, McKean uses the first three panels of the Gaiman series to depict Orchid as a series of thought bubbles and a representative icon, an actual orchid. Her first real appearance doesn't occur for thirteen pages, when the face of a nondescript secretary in the scene is revealed to be Black Orchid behind a rubber mask. In that scene, Orchid doesn't speak or even move — she remains captive while the action of the scene takes place around her. Once she finally escapes from the chair in which she is bound, she is all but totally obscured by flames, until a few panels later when she dies in an explosion. She appears three pages later, but in a completely different incarnation. We don't get a clear, unobstructed view of that version of Orchid, and she never reappears in that form again. Her first appearance as the incarnation of Black Orchid that serves as the protagonist of the text is on page 15, almost one third of the way through the first issue of the series. The end result of these delays and changes is to give an impression that Black Orchid's physical presence is secondary to her consciousness.

Gaiman and McKean further emphasize Orchid's consciousness by giving it a permanence that her corporeality lacks. Each of the Orchid incarnations in the text has a separate and unique appearance. Despite the fact that the Orchids are clones, their different circumstances result in widely different appearances. Susan Linden, the original source of the Orchid DNA, is wholly human. The Orchid who appears at the beginning of the Gaiman version has been operating in the world long enough to alter her physical appearance with clothing, specifically a Black Orchid costume (modeled by McKean after DeZuniga's concept for the original Black Orchid). The Orchid who serves as the protagonist is nude throughout the comic, so her floral features (the purple skin, the orchid-petal hair) are more prominent. The other remaining clone, who takes on the name Suzy, didn't fully mature before her "birth," so she takes the form of a little girl. These physical forms, though linked by a shared DNA, are unique, and when one of the Orchids dies, that physical form dies with her.

McKean also deemphasizes Orchid's corporeality by frequently hiding her body. The view of her is often partially obscured by plants, shadows, furniture and other objects. In the 1973 original, DeZuniga places Orchid on display with a combination of full-length views and placement of her in the center or top of most of the panels in which she appears. DeZuniga also poses Orchid in ways that make her curves, especially her breasts, particularly prominent. In the panels where she looms largest, she is invariably shown with back arched, in slight, sometimes three-quarter profile. Although his Orchid is drawn in a full bodysuit that even covers her hair, the suit fits like a second skin, so tight that it doesn't in any way obscure her shape. What's more, DeZuniga's Black Orchid is proportioned such that her breasts, eyes, and lips are enlarged, and her waist is unrealistically small.

This sort of gratuitous costuming, posing, and proportioning of female characters is still a topic of debate in mainstream superhero comics. The firestorm over a buxom and provocatively posed statuette of Mary Jane Watson doing Spiderman's laundry, released with Marvel's approval, grew heated enough that the story was picked up by both Fox News and the *New York Post*. Fans were outraged at what seemed to be a monumental backwards step in the depiction of women in popular culture, and the official description from the company that sold the statuette didn't help matters: "The consummate 'girl next door,' Mary Jane discovers that her superhero husband has slipped some of his laundry into the mix, but she's not looking too displeased about Peter's naughty little transgression" (Sideshow). More than one commentator, however, noted that "the way MJ is presented in this maquette is pretty much par for the course" in comics, especially pieces influenced by the Japanese anime style ("Why the MJ Kerfuffle Matters"). As recently as 2009, *Power Girl*, one of the DC superheroine titles, made the news for an issue in which Power Girl "actually appears to lecture readers for complaining about her costume" (Hudson). Power Girl is notorious for having possibly the largest breasts of any character in superhero comics, and for her spandex costume which features a large oval cutout that explicitly highlights her cleavage.

McKean's decision to recreate Black Orchid as an entirely naked superheroine would certainly have drawn similar criticism, except that the way he proportions and details her body strip it of the titillating factor so often present in comics. Her breasts are not especially large, and McKean draws them without the round shape and extreme cleavage used in the depictions of Mary Jane and Power Girl that drew fire. Her waist and hips are more realistically proportioned, and her buttocks, the scant handful of times they can even be seen in a panel, aren't particularly shapely. She is also drawn flat-footed, so her feet and calves lack the extreme curvature demonstrated in most superheroines, typically drawn in high-heeled boots or with bare but pointed feet.

As a whole, McKean's Orchid is drawn in realistic, ordinary proportions. McKean also leaves out any detail on Orchid's body. She is a collection of vague impressions, shading that forms seamlessly from and in the space of the frame. The only parts of Orchid that are drawn with any detail anywhere in the comic are her face and hands. Her body, more often than not, simply fades into the scenery in a wash of purple.

McKean's approach to depicting Orchid fits perfectly with the nearly autobiographical feel of the text. As Shirley Neuman posits, "Bodies rarely figure in autobiography" (1). Instead, "traditional autobiographies highlight a person's spiritual and cultural course. Women, however, are socially constructed as bodies and thus have to work doubly hard to be 'worthy' autobiographical subjects" (qtd. in Benstock 8). If women are constructed as bodies in society at large, they are even more so in the world of superhero comics. Gaiman's *Black Orchid* instead locates the female self in the consciousness, establishing a new model for including a woman's voice in a genre that has historically objectified women.

WORKS CITED

Benstock, Shari. "The Female Self Engendered: Autobiographical Writing and Theories of Selfhood." *Women and Autobiography*. Eds. Martine Watson Brownley and Allison B. Kimmich. *Worlds of Women* 5. Wilmington, DE: Scholarly Resources, 1999. Print.

Cixous, Hélène, and Catherine Clément. "Sorties: Out and Out: Attacks/Ways Out/Forays." *The Newly Born Woman*. London: I.B. Taurus, 1996. 63–134. Print.

Fludernik, Monika. *An Introduction to Narratology*. London: Routledge, 2006. Print.

Gaiman, Neil (w), Dave McKean (a, p). *Black Orchid* #1–3 (Dec. 1988 — Feb. 1989), New York: DC Comics. Print.

Gilbert, Sandra, and Susan Gubar. *The Madwoman in the Attic*. New Haven: Yale University Press, 1979. Print.

Graves, Neil. "Mary Jane is Spidey 'Sensuous.'" *New York Post*. 16 May 2007. Print.

Hudson, Laura. "Power Girl Lectures Women for Complaining about Her Costume." *Comics Alliance*. 23 November 2009. Accessed 31 December 2011. Web.

"Mary Jane's Assets Causing Stir in Spider-Man's World." Fox News. 16 May 2007. FoxNews.com. Accessed 31 December 2011. Web.

Mayer, Sheldon (w), Tony DeZuniga (a, p). "Black Orchid." *Adventure Comics* #428–430 (July — December 1973). New York: National Periodical.

Neuman, Shirley. "Autobiography and the Construction of the Feminine Body." *Signature: A Journal of Theory and Canadian Literature* 2 (1989): pp. 1–26. Print.

Robinson, Lillian S. *Wonder Women: Feminisms and Superheroes*. New York: Routledge, 2004. Print.

Round, Julia. "'Can I call you "Mommy"?' Myths of the Female and Superheroic in Neil Gaiman and Dave McKean's *Black Orchid*." *Debating the Difference: Gender Representation and Self-Representation*. Eds. Rachel Jones, Hamid van Koten, Chris Murray and Keith Williams. Dundee: Duncan of Jordanstone, University of Dundee, 2010. Print.

Sideshow Collectibles. "Mary Jane Comiquette." 2007. Accessed 31 December 2011. Web.

"Why the MJ Kerfuffle Matters: (Probably Not Why You Think)." Brown Betty. brownbetty-live-journal.com. 12 May 2007. Accessed 31 December 2011. Web.

When Superheroes Awaken

The Revisionist Trope in
Neil Gaiman's Marvel 1602

BY RENATA DALMASO

"[W]e are in a universe which favours stories. A universe in which no story can ever truly end; in which there can only be continuances," Dr. Reed Richards ponders in Neil Gaiman's *Marvel 1602* (7:19). This quote is particularly apt for thinking about re-writing as re-vision. For indeed we live in a universe filled with stories that are continuances of each other — Reed's meta-narrative commentary could even be perceived as being a continuance itself, an echo of Virginia Woolf's claim that "books continue each other," for example — and part of this continuance is done through the constant re-writing of stories (612). *1602*'s central premise is based on the dislocation of the Silver Age Marvel superheroes — most of them originating in the 1960s — to the 1600s. In other words, the series is a re-writing of the classic characters from the Marvel universe into the late–Elizabethan period. The act of re-writing is certainly not new, but is particularly popular within the postcolonial and feminist contexts, as theorists from those perspectives seek to undermine binary assumptions and naturalized oppressions, present everywhere and, specially, in the canon. Adrienne Rich, in "When We Dead Awaken: Writing as Re-vision," uses the term "re-vision" for this practice, defined as "the act of looking back, of seeing with fresh eyes, of entering an old text from a new critical direction" (18). Neil Gaiman's re-writing of the Marvel universe is in fact a re-visionist work.

By dislocating Marvel's classic superheroes through time, the series brings a new light to the old texts. Dear old characters — such as Scott Summers, Jean Grey, Professor Xavier, Peter Parker, Nick Fury, and the Fantastic Four, just to name a few — are recreated, redesigned, relocated, and reconnected in an Elizabethan setting. This revised context presents Doctor Stephen Strange as the court magician of Queen Elizabeth I and Sir Nicholas Fury as her head of intelligence. In this world, the rise of the mutant age occurs about 400 years early. The original ensemble of the X-Men (Iceman, Cyclops, Beast, Angel, and Marvel Girl) appears as the group of disciples (Roberto Trefusis, Scotius Summerisle, Hal McCoy, Werner, and Master "John" Grey, respectively) of Carlos Javier and his College for the Sons of Gentlefolk. The College serves as a haven for the "witchbreed," the seventeenth-century term for the "mutants." *1602* also recreates their classic foil, Magneto, as the Grand Inquisitor Enrique, head of the Spanish Inquisition, who, among other things, is in charge of persecuting the witchbreed with as much fervor as practitioners of witchcraft. The new frontier in this reality is represented by oceanic navigation, and, as such, the Fantastic Four are re-written as explorers that gained powers while sailing on board the Fantastik towards the New World.

In this sense, the series is a revisionist work, as it re-writes the entire Marvel world from a different perspective. Doubtlessly, the possibility of looking at this universe with fresh eyes is very welcomed, for within the comic industry the Marvel continuity is as canonical as some of the literary master narratives that have been re-vised. Rich's definition of re-vision, nevertheless, is very particular, it goes beyond the simple act of re-writing and emphasizes a specific kind of looking back: one that entails a "new *critical* direction" (18, my emphasis). But does Gaiman's re-vision of the Marvel universe lead into a new *critical* direction?

1602 not only appropriates the characters and traits of the Silver Age Marvel superheroes, but it also deals with the appropriation of historical events and the context of the early 1600s. The storylines — which range in location from Elizabeth's Court to the lost colony of Roanoke, Virginia — reference cultural anxieties connected to the Spanish Inquisition, the hopes for the New World, the tensions between Catholics and Protestants, and the growing interest in the natural sciences. The very title of the series chronologically situates the narrative and signals the importance of temporality in this historiographic metafictional version of the Marvel universe. The transposition of the Marvel superheroes to a Renaissance setting, however, does not work merely to mark the action within a specific timeframe, it also functions in a way as to intertwine what we understand as the historical facts of the time with the characters' continuity. The result is a blurring of the lines between the fictive personal and the historically political. Linda Hutcheon characterizes the use of historical events in postmodernist fictions as a way to call historical knowledge itself into question, which can then be seen as "unstable, contextual, relational, and provisional" (67). Therefore, in historical metafictions "events no longer speak for themselves, but are shown to be consciously composed into a narrative" (66).

The inherent "composition" of history is evidenced in the case of the

Gunpowder plot in *1602*. By "historical account," the failed attempt on King James I of England's life took place in 1605 and was orchestrated by a group of discontent English Catholics that were planning to blow up the House of Lords. The plot was discovered through an anonymous tip, leading to dozens of public executions and the further persecution of Catholics in England (Robinson). In *1602*, however, Gaiman appropriates and undermines this historical account. In its new incarnation, the conspiracy is in fact a means to guarantee public support for the future King and support his persecution of the witchbreed. Enrique, the Grand Inquisitor in Spain, reassures James that the latter will have no problems convincing the public of the righteousness of his persecution: "Easily done. Tell him that, when he is King, we shall endeavor to demonstrate that the Witchbreed are plotting against his throne — obviously they wish to blow up the Houses of Parliament in some sort of explosion" (1:20). Enrique's conspiracy with James of Scotland (later King James I) underscores the inherent fictional nature of all historical accounts. As Hutcheon emphasizes, this type of historical narrative has a doubleness that points at the same time to the events represented and to "the act of narration itself" that constitutes these "facts," something that is particularly dependent on "social and cultural context of the historian, as feminist theorists have shown with regard to women writers of history over the centuries" (76). Thus, by appropriating known historical events and subverting them, the historiographic narrative questions the notion of authenticity attached to history. This leads, then, going back to Rich's definition of the term, to a double kind of "re-vision," for in the case of *1602*, not only are the Silver Age Marvel superheroes seen through fresh eyes, but the accountability of history itself, and its intrinsically discursive feature, is also called into question.

The role-played by the colony of Roanoke in the series and its symbolic importance as an emblem for the New World is another example of the appropriation of historical narratives in *1602*. The actual fate of this early English settlement and its people remains a mystery. Historians know that the colonists disappeared into the continent about three years after the last supplies came from England, in 1587, never to be heard from again (Hoffer 112). *1602*'s appropriation of these historical events offers a different version for the account of the "Lost Colony." In the series, the colony is still active in 1602, in spite of a continuing struggle. The survival of the settlers in this reality is only due to the protection of the "Indian" Rojhaz, later revealed to be Captain America recently arrived from the future. In Gaiman's historiographic metafiction, it is only fitting that the responsibility of ensuring the maintenance and prosperity of Roanoke colony and, incidentally, of the first child born in America, Virginia Dare, befalls on the most overtly patriotic hero of the Marvel universe. Both Roanoke and Virginia Dare represent the nation's lost innocence, one that a superhero such as Captain America, created under the pretense of the wholeness of those innocent values, desperately seeks to salvage. As the character retells his story about arriving in the late sixteenth century from the future and coming across the early settlers of Roanoke, he expresses this desire:

> [...] And then the white people came across the great water, and I found them starving, and I fed them.
> And then there was *Virginia*...
> She was just a baby then. But I knew what she was. What she represented. What she *meant*. My America...
> I knew I had to protect her. To guard her. To fight for her, if I had to. I wasn't going to let **her** die.
> I failed before. I wasn't going to fail again.
> [...]
> We don't have to make the same mistakes again. We're here at the birth of a nation ... of a dream [8:4,26, original emphasis].

His tale becomes entangled, symbolically, with the birth of the nation he was chosen to protect, something that illustrates further the undermining of the clear distinction between private and public in *1602*'s historiographic metafiction.

As Hutcheon argues, the social and cultural contexts are also embedded in the historian's role in the narration of history, and, as such, they should also be taken into account in the *production* of these types of historical narratives. In the first scene of *1602*, the reader is transported to the Elizabethan Court, in the presence of the Queen herself, who takes counsel with two very memorable heroes: Doctor Stephen Strange and Sir Nicholas Fury. The problem is the unsettling weather (blood-red skies at noon, thunderstorms, and earthquakes across England and possibly Europe), which for some is a harbinger of the end of the world. This anxiety over the future of the planet and consequently of human kind, though ever constant in some way or another in our society, would be particularly familiar in the post–9/11 context in which *1602* was produced. As Julia Sanders points out, historiographic metafictions often appropriate particular events or lives for the "parallels and comparisons [they] evoke with more contemporary or topical concerns" (139).

The aftermath of the 2001 terrorist attacks in the United States clearly informed the creation of *1602*. According to Gaiman:

> The idea for the story came about in part because I was plotting it immediately after September the 11th. The first day planes were flying again, I had to go to a Sci-Fi/Comics thing in Triest, in Northern Italy, and I wound up with a day on my own in Venice just to sit and plot whatever it was I was going to do for Marvel. I decided that whatever I did, given the mood I was in at that point, it wasn't going to have skyscrapers, it wasn't going to have bombs and it probably wasn't going to have any guns or planes in it. That was simply what I felt like at the time. "I don't think this is stuff I want to put into my fiction right now" [Weiland].

The issues of political uncertainty, the risk of pending war, the rise in religious intolerance and the threat of terrorism, all present in the early 1600s of the series, have a clear resonance with the same issues faced in the post 9/11 world in which the narrative was produced and consumed. The fears associated with the consequences of a successful terrorist attack against a prominent political figure in a politically uncertain context are certainly evoked in the killing of the Queen. As Strange points out: "[t]here have been riots. Many people believe that the Queen's murder signals the end of the world. Given the strange manifestations we have been experiencing, I am no longer convinced that they are wrong" (4:4). Even though the population was well aware of the Queen's advanced years and approaching end, the actuality of her death was still "for most people [something] unimaginable" (Fraser xxii). This feeling was due to the fact that her rule had been particularly long, allied to the delicate problem of succession, or lack thereof, topped by the fact that to even discuss such a topic openly was a crime punishable by imprisonment — a problem which, incidentally, would also evoke contemporary concerns. The issue of legitimacy was also familiar to a readership that had recently seen the repercussions of a disputed election between George W. Bush and Al Gore (xxii). If the Queen's natural death was already something "unimaginable," her murder was an idea beyond the general population's grasp. It is understandable, thus, that the political assassination of the Queen could manage to stir fears akin to the dread of the apocalypse.

Consequently, the murder of Queen Elizabeth I marks a major turn of events in *1602*'s narrative. Carlos Javier and his witchbreed students are forced to leave the country while Fury and Strange are deemed traitors. In the climate of suspicion and paranoia characteristic of the post 9/11 context, filled with tensions and debate over the legitimacy of the Guantanamo Bay Detention Camp and the Homeland Security Act, the themes of xenophobia, unlawful persecution, and fear of terrorism dealt within *1602* carry the political undertone mentioned in Hutcheon's definition of the postmodernist fiction. The political aspect of Gaiman's re-writing is, thus, definitely associated with the idea of a re-visionist work.

The persecution of mutants is certainly spawned by paranoia and fear of the unknown, but the fact is that the world in *1602* is indeed coming to an end. Its very existence is an impossibility, a temporal anomaly that led to the rise of a mutant age 400 years too early. The inconsistency of these two realities, early modern England and the postmodern superhero age, is the cause of the apocalyptic weather in the beginning of the series. Thus, the paradox of the conflicting universes creates what Michel Foucault calls "heterotopia":

> There is a worse kind of disorder than that of the incongruous, the linking together of things that are inappropriate; I mean the disorder in which fragments of a large

number of possible orders glitter separately in the dimension, without law or geometry, of the heteroclite; ... in such a state, things are "laid," "placed," "arranged" in sites so very different from one another that it is impossible to find a place of residence for them, to define a common locus beneath them all.... Heterotopias are disturbing, probably because they secretly undermine language, because they make it impossible to name this and that, because they destroy "syntax" in advance, and not only the syntax with which we construct sentences but also the less apparent syntax which causes words and things (next to and also opposite to one another) to "hold together" [xix].

1602 can be seen, then, as a world without syntax, one in which fragments of each reality are tossed together without a common ground.

The reflection of this heterotopia within the narrative is not only perceived by the bizarre weather that foreshadows the end of the world, but also through various other incongruous details throughout the narrative, such as the presence of dinosaurs. The main symbol of this incongruity, though, is the figure of the Forerunner, later revealed to be Captain America, and his dislocation through time. Steve Rogers, a.k.a. Captain America, is known in the *1602* reality by a different alias: Rojhaz. He is the underlying cause of the destruction of syntax in this world. As the link that connects these irreconcilable realities and that, consequently, creates the heterotopia of a superhero age in the Renaissance period, his very existence is out of place. He is an anomaly, and the universe treats him as such. As the character Watcher explains in a vision to the mystic Stephen Strange: "the forerunner could be seen as an infection, which the universe must create antibodies for, which then destroy the host organism" (6:3).

If, as Sanders suggests, historiographic metafictions often work to evoke contemporary concerns, the analogy of an autoimmune disease afflicting the universe further establishes the parallels between the world of *1602* and the post 9/11 context in which the series was produced. A similar diagnosis, for instance, is used by Jacques Derrida when discussing the events that led to the terrorist attacks of September 11th. The attacks were, in his view,

a distant effect of the Cold War [that mutated into] an *autoimmunitary process* [...] [that is] that strange behavior where a living being, in quasi-*suicidal* fashion, "itself" works to destroy its own protection, to immunize itself *against* its "own" immunity [Borradori 92, 94, original emphasis].

Thus, working within this metaphor, in *1602*'s reality, Captain America, who was originally created to protect the country against a foreign enemy (the Nazis), mutates into the catalyzing element that brings forth the quasi-suicidal impulse of the universe "to destroy its own protection, to immunize itself *against* its "own" immunity" (94, original emphasis).

As the epitome of the paradoxical nature of *1602*'s universe, Captain America's recollection of his life before being sent back through time is perhaps the best example of the contrasting and contradictory features of both realities.

His autobiographical account is a composition of panels that show him as Rojhaz, in 1602 telling his story to the other characters on board the Virginia Maid, juxtaposed with others that show him as his alias from the future, twentieth-century Captain America. Contradictorily, the panels that show him from the future are drawn in the Silver Age comic era style, whereas his 1602 self is seen in the same style as the rest of the narrative, decisively more realistic and detailed. The result is that the panels that happen in the "future" have a vintage–Jack Kirby-looking style, while the ones that take place in the "past" look extremely contemporary, the outcome of Andy Kubert's penciling added to the technology of the digital painting done by Richard Isanove. The irony in this anachronism is precisely what confers it its postmodern quality, something that "takes the form of [a] self-conscious, self-contradictory, self-undermining statement," as Hutcheon puts it (1).

The anachronism in Rojhaz's account is a statement that challenges the categories of "past," "present," and "future." Accordingly, the ideals behind the persona of Captain America are also ultimately called into question. He professes them in one of the vintage–Jack Kirby-looking panels — one in which Captain America appears in the iconographic superhero pose: fist forward and charging body while dodging bullets — "I fought for America. My country. I protected America. Life, liberty and the pursuit of happiness. Democracy. Not something you people have seen much of yet. But it's worth fighting for..." (8:2). The idea of an America composed of democracy, liberty, and the pursuit of happiness appears almost naive here, and it is implicitly related to out-of-datedness of that Captain America in the panel. In a following contemporary-looking-panel, Rojhaz says that eventually, with the rise of "dark times," he "had to face facts. That [that] America wasn't [his] America any longer" (8:3). "That" America is an America where heroes are persecuted and the government abuses its powers through the figure of the President-For-Life. In the post–9/11 context in which 1602 was produced, Rojhaz's statement is particularly relevant, for it undermines the over-patriotic rhetoric seen just after the terrorist attacks and again reaffirms Hutcheon's claim that "[p]ostmodern art cannot but be political" (3).

This political facet of postmodernism, however, is embedded in the ambivalent discourse of being at the same time complicit with and critical of said discourse (Hutcheon 149). This is evidenced in Captain America's 1602 narrative. For example, the ideals of his character are validated by his earnestness while simultaneously undermined by an anachronistic juxtaposition of panels. This type of complicity is a point of discordance between postmodernism and feminism in relation to politics, as Hutcheon argues:

> there is a major difference of orientation between the two [...]: we have seen that
> postmodernism is politically ambivalent for it is doubly coded — both complicitous

with and contesting of the cultural dominants within which it operates; but on the other side, feminisms have distinct, unambiguous political agendas of resistance [142].

Seeing that feminism cannot afford that kind of ambivalence, Hutcheon questions the possibility of converging both the postmodernist and feminist strategies. She argues that

> [c]omplicity is perhaps necessary (or at least unavoidable) in deconstructive critique (you have to signal — and thereby install — that which you want to subvert), though it also inevitably conditions both the radicality of the kind of critique it can offer and the possibility of suggesting change. The feminist use of postmodern strategies, therefore, is a little problematic, but it may also be one of the only ways for feminist *visual* arts to exist [152, original emphasis].

In this sense, can the political tone of a postmodernist work such as *1602* be seen as feminist as well? Hutcheon's emphasis on the "visual" is particularly relevant in trying to answer that question, for the visual narrative element is fundamental in portraying the inherent paradoxes of the reality seen in the series. Although Hutcheon's definition refers more specifically to the deconstruction of the male gaze in the representation of the female subject through the visual arts, I would argue that the unsettling of the cross-discursive form of the comics genre could also allow for a more political, and eventually feminist, statement (156). Hillary Chute addresses this issue when referring to the possible feminist repercussions embedded in the comics genre. She claims that

> [w]hile foundational feminist criticism has detailed the problem of the passive female film spectator following and merging helplessly with the objectifying gaze of the camera, the reader of graphic narratives is not trapped in the dark space of the cinema (or even the voluntary, contingent space of spectatorship generated by her own television or computer). [...] Hence while the visual form of graphic narrative enables an *excess* of representation [...], it also offers a constant self-reflexive demystification of the project of representation. In graphic narrative the spectator is a necessarily generative "guest" (to borrow Mulvey's term), constructing meaning over and through the space of the gutter.
>
> We may note, then, that the form of comics even at its most basic is apposite to feminist cultural production [9, original emphasis].

Within this understanding, while *1602*, as a postmodernist work, can indeed be seen as complicitous with the discourse that it subverts, its potential as a feminist narrative is evidenced through a series of narrative elements that manage to undermine that very discourse.

Clea Strange's character is a good example of this sort of feminist potential in the series. Like Captain America, she is an outsider. While he is from the future, she is from another dimension altogether, one in which she used to be a Queen. By the end of the series, both Clea and Captain America leave this reality towards their respective places (or temporalities) of origin. In her case, she voluntarily leaves whereas his return home is forced (he is knocked out by Fury who then carries him through the portal that would send him back). Visually, the parallels between Clea Strange and Captain America go even further, since a similar discontinuity in the style of the panels appears in Clea's exit scene. As soon as she and the rest of the characters realize that the universe is safe from its impending destruction, Clea proceeds to open a portal to her home world. The visual style of the portal is remarkably different from the panels on the page and from the rest of the overall work, suggesting a rupture in the narrative similar to the one seen when Rojhaz recounts his life from the future as Captain America. Clea's portal shows a glimpse of her home dimension, a universe composed of nothing but abstract lines, colors, and shapes: possibly another heterotopia. Immediately after Stephen's death, Clea's first impulse is to return to her home dimension and leave the rest of the characters in this reality to face their impending doom on their own, but a promise to him and the subsequent knowledge that the fate of *this* world will eventually be the fate of *hers* as well keeps her from leaving:

> And now that my husband is dead, I see no reason not to return home.
> But my husband is of the opinion that when this world dies, it will take every-thing else with it, my own demesne included. So I may as well stay here, and try to help *unknot the mess you men have made of things* [8:11, my emphasis].

Whether "men" Clea refers to in the quoted line is related to the male characters in the story, her interlocutors in this dialogue after all, or whether it refers to mankind in general is unclear. Nevertheless, one could perceive a feminist connotation in that statement when taking into account that in a narrative filled with male-dominated action the key roles played by women such as Clea Strange, Jean Grey, Virginia Dare, and Susan Storm are the ones that ultimately "unknot the mess [...] men have made of things" (8:11).

Stephen Strange's visions, for instance, are evidently fundamental in uncovering the danger behind the disturbing weather and its cause: the pres-ence of the Forerunner in their age. However, Stephen's sacrifice to obtain that knowledge would have been in vain, had it not been for Clea's insight in identifying Rojhaz as the time traveler and not Virginia Dare, as Stephen had suspected. In another example of the importance of her role, during the climactic scene of the series, in a debate between Carlos Javier and Richard Reed about whether or not to sacrifice Fury's life in order to save the world, she is the one that takes charge in the midst of the confusion:

> FURY: Reed! Can you — hear me? I brought you Rojhaz. Make it — happen. What-ever you're — going to do — do it now...

REED: We can't leave Fury out there!
CLEA STRANGE: How *else* are we going to get Rohjaz through the gate? Carry him *ourselves?*
CARLOS JAVIER: But it would mean Fury's *death...*
CLEA STRANGE: Were you not listening? This is what he wants. Enrique. Thor. You heard him. *Make it happen* [8:28, original emphasis].

In the middle of the most powerful men within this already male-dominated reality, it is Clea Strange that "[m]ake[s] it happen." She alone shows the authority to shut down the discussion between Reed and Javier and to make the difficult decision to let Fury die, while issuing orders to Thor and Enrique, who promptly obey. As a former queen, Clea Strange has no trouble taking control or even in imposing her will. Her role can be seen, thus, as emblematic of how postmodern narratives can be critical even while being complicitous with the discourse being criticized, as Hutcheon argues. An example of that kind of subversion could be seen in the scene where Clea presents Stephen's head to the other characters. In a clear castration reference, she carries the severed head across the ocean, so that that she may speak as his medium and warn the other characters about the impending danger to their world. She does fulfill the promise to her husband, being the dutiful wife that she is — thus characterizing the complicitous discourse — visually, however, the narrative conveys a different story, one in which the power is in her hands, quite literally in fact.

Similarly, Susan Storm's role in *1602* deals with the double-codedness, borrowing Hutcheon's term, of invisibility as both a literal and a symbolic referent. As one of the four of the Fantastik, she was endowed with the special power of invisibility after a trip to the New World. In the reality of the series, the only glimpse of Susan as a "visible" woman is in the flashback of a portrait made aboard the Fantastik before the accident that resulted in her powers. Unlike the regular Marvel continuity though, where the character uses this ability to appear and disappear at will, in *1602* Susan is never actually seen, apart from the aforementioned portrait. She can only be perceived by the reader either by the light contours of a hollow figure or simply by the void space of a character below a slightly translucent speech balloon. In other words, in this universe she is always invisible.

Unlike Clea Strange, who is very vocal when it comes to taking charge of a situation, Susan Storm does so almost imperceptibly. If Clea's role is associated with the act of speaking, Susan's is related to the act of listening. Throughout most of the story Susan remains on the sidelines as a sister and a wife, invisible literally as well as metaphorically. By the end of the series, however, while the rest of the main characters try to figure out a way to save their world from the temporal anomaly, it is Susan that steps in and subtlety solves a major dilemma. She is able to convince Donal to become the god Thor again because of her "active" listening:

> DONAL: Do you think ... do you think if I were to become *him* again, that I would ever let myself change back into *this*?
> SUSAN STORM: Donal. Is he wiser than you? [...]
> DONAL: Aye. His mind — it's like a silver fish in a clear brook. Everything is simple for him.
> SUSAN: Then why don't you let *him* decide?
> DONAL: You *were* listening to me, weren't you?
> SUSAN: I told you I was.
> DONAL: Damn you. Damn you all. [transforms into Thor]
> THOR: You are wiser than all of them, Susan Storm.
> SUSAN: No, I just listened when he spoke [8:21].

Susan's special skill besides invisibility is, then, the oxymoron of being an "active" listener. With those two rather "passive" characteristics combined, Susan Storm remains an absent character throughout most of the action. She is never seen and is barely heard throughout the entire series. As such, Susan's role could be seen then as one that underscores the lack of representation, or invisibility, of women characters in action-centered narratives. In the scene of the dialogue quoted earlier, for example, despite the fact that Susan is present is the room from the beginning (one would assume), her presence can only be visually perceived in the panels in which she has lines. In a manner most suited for an invisible woman, it is her absence in the panels that speaks volumes.

Clea Strange and Susan Storm are both emblematic opposites of how "voice" can be a motif used to subvert complicitous discourses within a postmodern historiographic metafiction to underline a feminist critique. Another noteworthy example of this motif is, however, seen in the male role of Werner, the X-man Angel of this reality. If, as Sanders points out, the "retrieval of lost or repressed" voices is a common motif in re-writings, Angel stands out for being one of the very few characters that works as first-person narrator to the story (140). In the original X-Men series, Angel's character, an arrogant multi-billionaire playboy, would probably not have been qualified as a "lost or repressed" voice, but his situation is drastically changed in the reality of *1602*. Within this context he is in a much more vulnerable position. First of all, he does not have any material possessions and is rescued from the Inquisition stake with only the clothes on his body, making him the last to join Javier's pupils in the College for the Sons of Gentlefolk. The most remarkable change of this character in relation to the original version is, however, his homoerotic relationship with Master "John" Grey. Queer characters are not exactly novel in the Marvel universe but their roles have been somewhat minor and their sexuality is often downplayed. A classic example is Northstar.

Despite John Byrne's claim that the hero was conceived in 1979 as a gay character, open references to his sexuality did not appear in the comic until 1992 ("Comic Strips and Books," "Questions"). In this re-writing, however, not only is queerness associated with one of the original X-men, but with one of the very few characters, the only one in Javier's team for example, that acts as a first-person narrator, thus making his role pivotal to the story.

Epistemologically, to say that Angel could be seen as a queer character in the *1602* universe would be much more appropriate than to refer to him as a gay or as a homosexual character. As Michel Foucault argues, homosexuality was not seen as an expression of sexuality until the late nineteenth century, "when it was transposed from the practice of sodomy onto a kind of interior androgyny, a hermaphrodism of the soul" (*History of Sexuality* 43). The sinful act of sodomy had been seen until then as a "temporary aberration;" it was only around the late nineteenth century that the homosexual effectively became a pathological identity or a "species" (43). As such, to view homoeroticism or same-sex desire as manifestations of a "gay" or "homosexual" sexuality in the Renaissance age would incur in an anachronistic and socially inaccurate portrayal. Borrowing Eve Sedgwick's words on the relation between the speaker "Will" and the "Fair Youth" in Shakespeare's sonnets, "within the world sketched [here], there is not an equal opposition or a choice posited between two such institutions as homosexuality (under whatever name) and heterosexuality" (35). Accordingly, thus, the question of identity related to Angel's sexuality does not come up in *1602*. In the final issue of the series, though, Angel explains his feelings for "John" Grey: "I was truly deceived, and thought that Jean Grey was a man. But I do believe I was in love with that young man" (8:11). Not unlike the speaker in Shakespeare's sonnets, Werner does not deny his feelings for the "Fair Youth," John Grey. On the contrary, he owns them throughout.

As a first-person narrator, Angel brings to the surface some of the parallels between mutants and queers, a long withstanding metaphor: "My people—for so I think of them, although we are not united by country or creed, we are joined by our strangeness, made one by our differences—my people are hopeful, I think, but also scared" (6:6). Concurrently, the metaphor of the closet is also embedded in the doubleness of this speech, for the witchbreed are constantly forced to hide themselves in the effort to pass as humans. The ability to appear as human, or at least as non-witchbreed, is essential to their survival much like the closet is for a lot of queers. After spending a whole life in hiding, Angel fully appreciates the freedom of being true to himself, of being out of the closet, as a mutant:

> One gets used to hiding. After a while it becomes second nature ... I am grateful to Sir Javier for so much—for my life, obviously, and all that he is teaching. But

most of all I am grateful that here, I can be myself. At least here, among ourselves, friend John, there is no need, ever, to hide [3:10].

Which of course is not entirely true, since his interlocutor in this scene, Master "John" Grey, is actually a woman forced to disguise as a man to be able to belong to the group and enjoy the liberties that would otherwise be denied her in the time period.

Unlike Angel, who is both literally and metaphorically able to spread his wings at any time, Jean "John" Grey is constantly under the scrutiny of her suitor, Scotius Summerisle, and is kept at a distance from the decision-making process of the group and from contact with outside people. Cross-dressing gives Jean some liberties, but still does not set her free from the gender roles of the time. For instance, at a crucial point in the narrative Javier's group is forced to decide a course of action that could land them in the Tower to be judged as traitors; which prompts a lively debate between the members. Each voices their opinion on the matter — except for Master John Grey, who just stands quietly next to the professor. Visually, Jean's lower status in the group is clear in this scene. As their debate occupies the entire page, four panels are dedicated to close-ups of Scott, Werner, McCoy, and Roberto with their respective opinions on the matter. The final panel is wider and shows Javier addressing the messenger Peter Parquagh, while Jean is positioned in the far left corner, almost out of the page, in a darker space, completely separated from the other characters, silent (4:15).

Grey's role in the group is well summed up in the very first introduction of her character to Angel: "He speaks but little" (1:33). In a world where women are not permitted simple liberties such as walking unaccompanied, the farce of John Grey is a "convenient fiction," as Scotius puts it (7:12). Maybe a more appropriate word to describe Grey's pretense would be "necessary." Looking up the history of women in England in *A Room of One's Own*, Virginia Woolf concludes that, despite being praised and glorified in verse and stage, women of those times were in reality insignificant, as they were "locked up, beaten and flung about the room" (590). This would be the fate expected of Jean Grey if it were not for the recourse of cross-dressing, which enables her, at least partially, to belong to a world outside of the domestic sphere. Perhaps that is why there was much "cultural anxiety about women wearing men's clothes" at the time (Rampone, Jr. 42). King James expressed concern especially about women sporting wide hats, doublets, and short hair, whereas "the popular literature and ballads of the day focused on the pants as the center of male power" (42). Men in power were concerned that women would appropriate known signals of patriarchy (42). In this sense this is exactly what happens in *1602*. Despite Werner's naiveté, there are clear indicators that Grey is female. In the script for the scene where Grey is first introduced to Werner, Gaiman writes to artist Andy Kubert:

> Page 27 panel 6. A shot of Master Grey — in "his" monk's robe, at the back of the boat. He is smiling, and has raised a hand. "His" hair is short, like a girl's, but c'mon, this has got to be a beautiful red-haired girl in male drag. Scott keeps talking...

The script indicates how the visual narrative element can work to subvert the concurrent discourses on the page. In this particular sense, the visual narrative underlines the inherent performative character of gender, borrowing Judith Butler's definition of the term. If, as Butler argues, gender is an assignment that is "never quite carried out according to expectation," the obviousness of Master Grey's female identity only works to expose the regulatory ideals that guide that performance (231).

As a universe that favors stories, *1602*'s heterotopia manages to revisit not only those stories of the classic superhero age but also the fabric of history itself, which, as it turns out, is just another story as well. The self-consciousness of this historiographic metanarrative is seen in several passages where the text gently "nudges" the reader and points to the implicit doubleness of the narrative. Such duplicity carries an inherently political tone, which, as Hutcheon argues, is one of the main aspects of the postmodernist fiction. Recalling Rich's definition: re-vision is "the act of looking back, of seeing with fresh eyes, of entering an old text from a new critical direction," and in a lot of ways Gaiman's heterotopia does exactly that (18). Perhaps a simple re-writing, such as seen in titles like *Elseworlds* or *What If*— in which known heroes of the DC and Marvel worlds are placed in alternative scenarios and realities — would not be seen as being re-visions *per se* in the context of this debate. *1602*, however, is packed with political innuendo and double meanings for the reader, all the while dealing with a host of all-too-familiar characters in not-at-all familiar situations. Gaiman affirms in a press conference that reading *1602*'s narrative simply as an *Elseworlds* or a *What If* does not get the reader very far (Weiland). The author refers to the fact that, unlike these other titles, *1602* is not just an imaginary story outside the universe's continuity; it is set in the actual Marvel universe, only one that saw the rise of the mutant age 400 years too early. *1602*'s novelty *is* its critical edge: it is a re-visionist work.

WORKS CITED

Borradori, Giovanna. *Philosophy in a Time of Terror: Dialogues with Jürgen Habermas and Jacques Derrida*. Chicago: University of Chicago Press, 2003. Print.

Butler, Judith. *Bodies That Matter: On the Discursive Limits of Sex*. New York: Routledge, 1993. Print.

Chute, Hillary L. *Graphic Women: Life Narrative and Contemporary Comics.* New York: Columbia University Press, 2010. Print.

"Comic Strips and Books." *The Encyclopedia of Lesbian and Gay Histories and Cultures.* Vol. 2. New York: Garland, 2000. Print.

Fleming, James. "Incommensurable Ontologies and the Return of the Witness in Neil Gaiman's 1602." *ImageText: Interdisciplinary Comics Studies* 4.1 (2008). Print.

Foucault, Michel. *History of Sexuality— Volume I: An Introduction.* New York: Pantheon Books, 1978. Print.

_____. *The Order of Things: An Archeology of the Human Sciences.* London: Routledge, 2002. Print.

Fraser, Antonia. *The Gunpowder Plot: Terror and Faith in 1605.* London: Orion, 1996. Print.

Gaiman, Neil (w), Andy Kubert (a, i). *Marvel 1602.* #1–8 (Nov. 2003 — June 2004), New York: Marvel. Print.

Hoffer, Peter Charles. *The Brave New World: A History of Early America.* Baltimore: Johns Hopkins University Press, 2006. Print.

Hutcheon, Linda. *The Politics of Postmodernism.* London: Routledge, 1989. Print.

"Questions about Comic Books Projects." *Byrne Robotics.* N.p., 21 Jan. 2012. Web. 30 Jan. 2012.

Rampone, W. Reginald, Jr. *Sexuality in the Age of Shakespeare.* Santa Barbara: Greenwood, 2011. Print.

Rich, Adrienne. "When We Dead Awaken: Writing as Re-Vision." *College English* 34.1 (1972): 18–30. Print.

Robinson, Bruce. "The Gunpowder Plot." BBC History. Web. 26 Jan. 2012.

Sanders, Julia. *Adaptation and Appropriation.* New York: Routledge, 2006. Print.

Sedgwick, Eve Kosofsky. *Between Men: English Literature and Male Homosocial Desire.* New York: Columbia University Press, 1985. Print.

Weiland, Jonah. "Marvel's '1602' Press Conference." 27 June 2003. *Comic Book Resources.* Web. 21 Aug. 2011.

Woolf, Viriginia. *A Room of One's Own.* Selected Works of Virginia Woolf. London: Wordsworth Editions, 2007. Print.

Outfoxed

Feminine Folklore and Agency in The Dream Hunters

BY CORALLINE DUPUY

In 1999, Neil Gaiman was immersed in Japanese folklore while writing the English version of the dialogue for revered Japanese filmmaker Hayao Miyazaki's film *Princess Mononoke*. In order to translate and adapt the story, Gaiman closely studied Japanese folklore and was fascinated by its riveting imagery and nuances. He saw his task as being the mediator between Japanese culture and non–Japanese audiences and aimed "to try and fold in enough background surreptitiously" (cited by McCabe 9). His fascination with Japanese culture soon lead to an artistic collaboration with revered Japanese graphic artist Yoshitaka Amano, who painted Dream for a poster to commemorate the tenth anniversary of *Sandman* #1 (Gaiman "Afterword"). Together, Gaiman and Amano created *The Dream Hunters,* the ill-fated love story about a *kitsune* (fox spirit) and a young monk. The story takes several themes and characters from *The Sandman* series and places them in a Japanese folkloric context. In a fascinating interview with Joseph McCabe, Amano explains that it was his reluctance to collaborate with Gaiman on a comic that motivated the decision to make *The Dream Hunters* a piece of illustrated prose fiction. P. Craig Russell later made his own set of illustrations for the story, resulting in the fully realized "comic adaptation" of the novel. Both the Amano version and the Russell version were recently anthologized in the *Absolute Sandman.*

The story's title alludes to a Japanese folk tale about mythical creatures. In the rich world of Japanese deities, demons, and spirits, the Baku are Dream Eaters, spirits whom humans may invoke to get rid of ominous dreams. While the Baku are the Dream Eaters, the identity of the Dream *Hunters* in the title is hidden until the end of the story.

The Dream Hunters opens with a battle of wits between a badger and a fox to see who can drive a monk from his temple. As the two creatures vie for the temple, in another city, an evil trio of powerful witch-like women also conspire against the monk, but in a much more sinister manner. These women are *The Dream Hunters'* incarnation of *Sandman's* Kindly Ones, *Stardust's* Lilim, or the three Fates. The unnamed creatures of this unholy female trinity give the villainous lord, the *onmyoji*, the means to hurt the innocent young monk.

Initially, the story appears to be centered on its male figure, the monk. This quickly changes, as the female character of the fox gains prominence in the tale. The fox is an independent, self-sacrificing agent of love and healing. She is a strong, determined character who secretly barters access to knowledge and help. Using her magic, she is able to appear in different forms, including a beautiful young woman. In her human guise, she falls for the monk as he falls for her, setting in motion a series of events that can only end in ruin. Initially a playful trickster, the fox emerges as the most complex and fascinating character of the narrative. She represents a female dissenting voice, a protester who fights for self-expression and who endeavors to wrestle control.

The monk, fox, and badger live in an idyllic mountain setting. After introducing these characters, the story shifts to Kyoto, where the Lord of Yin-Yang (ironically named, since he is quite unbalanced) is a powerful wizard and statesman. The *onmyoji's* household contains several minor female characters, including a wife who "treated him in every way as a wife should treat a husband," a "very beautiful" concubine who is "barely seventeen," and servants (40). These details prepare the reader for a man who is used to women being subservient, pretty, and young — details that the clever fox will use against him at the end of the story. Despite his wealth and power, the *onmyoji* knows no rest because his life is overshadowed by fear: "He was frightened. And the fear stole the joy from any moments of pride or happiness, and leeched the pleasure from his life" (42). The course of the two sets of characters (rural and urban, poor and wealthy, honorable and dishonest, good and evil) collide when the *onmyoji* requests help from three mysterious witches who weave a spell to steal the monk's strength and peaceful life-force through three consecutive poisoned dreams.

The witches are knowledgeable and powerful, yet they obey the *onmyoji* and work for him, a relationship that echoes *Macbeth*. They are clearly dangerous and their destructive aspect is reflected in the description of their dwelling:

> On the outskirts of the city, where thieves and the brigands and the unclean lived, the Master of Yin-Yang kept a dilapidated house, and in that house there were three women: one old, one young, and one who was neither young nor old. The women sold herbs and remedies to women who found themselves in unfortunate situations. It was whispered that unwary travellers who stopped in that house for the night were often never seen again [42].

The liminal location of their dwelling on "the outskirts" signifies their isolation from society and by extension their distance from social and moral strictures. Their seclusion is also an indication of their evil nature, according to the paradigms of Japanese fairy tales: "Demons frequent abandoned store-houses or abandoned chapels, the upper stories of city gates, mountain clear-ings, bridges, and other obviously twilight-zone places" (Tyler 48). But the strongest evidence of their power and dark skill is the line that alludes to the ways in which they cater to "women who found themselves in unfortunate situations" (42). This simple sentence does not engage in a debate about whether facilitating an abortion helps an unfortunate woman or destroys a life. Instead, it emphasizes the way they capitalize on the misfortune of others. Their role as abortion facilitators is a common attribute of witches in several cultures. In popular folklore, witches often prey on children. In particular, the Russian *baba-yaga* is a terrifying figure who can travel fast. She has no fixed location, since her house is built on chicken legs. Moreover, the *baba-yaga* can travel through the air in her giant mortar and pestle so that she can swoop down on children and abduct them. The reference, seemingly *in passim* (but this seem-ing nonchalance is an illusion), to the termination of pregnancies purposely emphasizes the three witches' power and aligns them with a certain folktale tra-dition of female predators. Several of the witches' other characteristics fulfill the same function; firmly placing them within this frame of reference. At the end of the tale, after their home burns down, the text reveals: "No one knows if they were in the house when it burned, for the only remains that were found in the ashes were the bones and skulls of babes and of small children" (118).

The three witches in *Dream Hunters* are repeating characters (or a three-in-one character) from Gaiman's work, an element he borrows and expands upon from earlier tales. The fact that the triad is female is particularly impor-tant. As Mary Borsellino notes, "Femininity is very much an elemental force, most commonly seen in triad: maiden, mother, crone" (52). To the reader familiar with Gaiman's universe, the three women echo the Fates as well as specific mem-bers of the Endless. The youngest woman, or the maiden, is a vampire-like *femme fatale* with "cold lips" and "cold fingers" (46). Like the Velvets in *Never-where*, her cold beauty is alluring and lethal: "The *onmyoji* was most afraid of the youngest of the three women, for he suspected that she was not alive" (46). The middle-aged woman, or the mother, is endowed with traditionally female breasts, but they are made grotesque and animal-like: "down her chest curved two rows of breasts, like the breasts of a she-pig or a rat, her many nipples black and hard as so many lumps of charcoal" (46). The old woman, or the crone, has physical attributes similar to Despair: "She was naked, and her breasts hung like empty bags upon her chest, and on her face she had painted the face of a demon" (42).

Amano's luscious two-page spread illustration of the three witches in repose bears a striking resemblance to Gustav Klimt's famous 1905 painting *The Three Ages of Woman* (44–45). This is no coincidence, as Amano acknowledges his admiration for Klimt and the Pre-Raphaelites. *The Three Ages of Woman* is a massive work depicting a young woman at its center, her head bowed down and nestling against the head of a child she cradles against her, while an elderly wrinkled woman covers her eyes and stands on the left. All three are naked. Klimt's palette of colors — charcoal, brown, cream, and black punctuated by bursts of gold leaf, burnished reds and oranges, and deep violet — are also reinterpreted and reimagined in Amano's work. According to Viennese Secession art critic Gottfried Fliedl, Klimt wanted to give a pictorial representation of the never-ending cycle of life and death that would emphasize the fragility of the young child in the center (Fliedl 43). However, one cannot help noticing that the mysterious older woman on the left garners the viewer's attention. Whereas the young woman and the child interact with one other, the older woman is clearly excluded. The picture is far more ambiguous than its straightforward title might indicate. The title creates an illusion of simplicity and direct meaning; the title tells the viewer that this is a representation of youth, maturity, and old age. The complexity of the picture generates several interpretations and shatters this illusion. Amano's depiction of the three witches reflects and distorts Klimt's work. *The Three Ages of Women* evokes youth, fertility, and love (as well as old age and despair), but Amano's work only shows lust, despair, and old age. The three witches are the visual embodiment of the frightening, dark side of the picture, whereas his portraits of the fox emphasize her beauty and sensuality.

The three evil women represent the "uncanny" of female sexuality, the "class of the frightening which leads back to what is known of old and long familiar" (Freud 220). According to Freud, "a particularly favourable condition for awakening uncanny feelings is created when there is an intellectual uncertainty whether an object is alive or not" (233). Thus, the youngest vampire-like witch is repellent because of this crucial hesitation experienced by the observer: is she alive or not? The typical uncanny experience is an uncomfortable blend of the familiar (*heimlich*, literally like something at home) and the unfamiliar (un-*heimlich*). It is the simultaneous experience of resemblance and difference. These states should not coexist, yet they do and the unease experienced by the viewer is created by the incompatible juxtaposition. In Amano's illustration, the third woman's breasts and nipples are familiar; women have breasts. Yet, their aspect and their number make those breasts a symbol of the uncanny. This detail is far from accidental: the uncanny experience is firmly located in a female body.

The analysis of their appearance emphasizes their connection with the

Endless characters Death, Despair, and Desire. The three witches present a distorted reflection of these characters. In fact, the motif of distorted reflections runs throughout the tale. The reflection acts as a reminder of the character it resembles, yet its imperfection points to the fact that it is an illusion, an imitation. The three crones introduce this motif, which later is expanded through the *kitsune*.

The mythological dimension of the three witches is emphasized by the reference to weaving. In Ancient Greek myth, the Fates are the three sisters who respectively spin, weave, and then cut the threads of human lives. In *The Dream Hunters*, they weave a piece of silk. The ageless crone explains to the *omnyoji* that a curse to kill the monk is woven into the silk: "once I have woven, you will have only until the next full moon to cause his death. And he must die without violence, and without pain, or the weaving will fail" (46). The repeated references to weaving are reminders that these witches, though in an unfamiliar Japanese folk tale, are nonetheless familiar types that carry across multiple tales and cultures. Gaiman weaves for the reader several connections between this story, his other works (*The Sandman, Stardust*), and classical fairy tales. *The Dream Hunters* works on its own as a fairy tale for the reader to enjoy, regardless of whether he or she knows the other texts. Yet it also works as a catalyst for a reflection on fairy tales, femininity, feminism, and the Japanese folktale. The two readings of the same text coexist seamlessly, like two threads from different materials woven in the same pattern.

Historically, weaving and the fabric arts have been considered part of the female sphere. At the same time, the weaving of textiles and the weaving of stories is also connected: many fairy tales originated as stories shared by women as they wove. Therefore, on an intertextual level, Gaiman subtly acknowledges his indebtedness to oral tradition by alluding to the origin of fairy tales as stories shared by women as they wove, before the stories were collected by male authors such as Charles Perrault, the Grimm Brothers, and Hans Christian Andersen. Since the re-vision of fairy tales through a feminist lens in the 1970s by writers such as Angela Carter, Robin McGinley and Margaret Atwood, the gender dynamics of fairy tales and folk tales have been critically scrutinized and creatively reimagined. In her analysis of gender and the revision of fairy tales, Cristina Bacchilega uses the metaphor of the fairy tale as a mirror of femininity. According to Bacchilega, the mirror presents to the reader a reflection and a refraction: "The wonder of fairy tales, indeed, relies on the magic mirror which artfully reflects and frames desire. Overtly reproducing the workings of desire, postmodern wonders perform multiple tricks with that mirror to re-envision its images of *story* and *woman*" (146). In *The Dream Hunters*, Gaiman plays with the concept of the magic mirror, both literally (at the end of the tale, the monk finds the fox in a mirror) and figuratively (by offering a mirror image of Japanese folk tales). He warps the reflective surface in order to emphasize the beauty and uniqueness of the *kitsune*.

Both the author and his creation question rules. Gaiman challenges the paradigms of fairy tales and gender roles by writing within the expectations of the genre while simultaneously deviating from its tenets. The *kitsune* challenges power structures and gender politics. On a superficial level *The Dream Hunters* looks like a faithful image of a Japanese folktale, seeming to correspond to Baudrillard's first stage of the sign-order. The readers may initially believe that the reflection in the mirror is accurate and offers a "reflection of a profound reality" (Baudrillard 6). This impression is shattered by the *kitsune*, who deviates and diverges from the normative constraints of gender. The *kitsune* breaks the boundaries and it is through this character that Gaiman moves his story to a superior level: his tale questions storytelling and gender norms.

Although the *kitsune* is a staple figure in Japanese folktales, in Gaiman's hands this character is decidedly different. Gaiman endows the fox-spirit with the most contrasting and nuanced attributes of femininity. Through her, Gaiman introduces a modern feminist concern: the dissenting female voice daring to question masculine authority figures. Gaiman's fox is a blend of modern and traditional. In the foreword to his collection of folktales, Keigo Seki differentiates between the Japanese *mukashi-banashi* ("once-upon-a-time stories") and their European counterparts.[1] He explains that since modern Japan only emerged after 1868 with the Meiji Restoration, folk culture and its beliefs are still very strong. As a result, legends and rituals are still incredibly potent in Japanese culture. The fox, for instance, in the Japanese cultural context, is not a mere animal, but a shape shifter, who once was the special messenger for Inari, the god of abundance (Seki 12). In the genre, the role of trickster is played by either a rabbit or a fox. The rabbit (or hare, depending on the story) often brings revenge. Both the fox and the rabbit are clever and cunning, and excel at outwitting their bigger adversaries. Moreover, the fox is endowed with a flair for shape-shifting and feminine sensuality, as we can see in *The Dream Hunters*.

The fox initially agrees to trick the monk in order to win a bet. Her impulse is playful rather than mean: "And the fox smiled with her sharp teeth, and blinked her green eyes, and she swished her brush and she looked down the hill at the temple and at the monk, then looked at the badger and she said: 'Very well. A wager it is'" (6). *Kitsune*s are the tricksters of Japanese tales.[2] The fox is almost a textbook case of a trickster figure. The psychoanalyst Carl Jung wrote a fascinating study on the Trickster Figure.[3] His analysis of Mercurius delineates the complexity of the trickster. Jung sees Mercurius as a combination of typical trickster motifs: "his fondness for sly jokes and malicious pranks, his powers as a shape-shifter, his dual nature, half-animal half-divine, his exposure to all kinds of tortures, and — last but not least — his approximation to the figure of a saviour" (255). In addition to his shape-shifting powers, the trickster experiences pain, and his suffering helps others: "the wounded wounder is the agent of healing, and that the sufferer takes away suffering" (256). In addition, Jung sees the trickster as a "psychologem: an archetypal psychic structure of extreme antiquity" (260). The fox combines the cheekiness and altruism of the trickster with her feminine wiles. In fairy tales, tricksters are outside the bounds of traditional morality, and use their wits instead of force. For critic J. C. Cooper, the trickster in fairy tales "uses ruses and intelligence to circumvent difficulties and pitfalls," and stands for the triumph of "brain over brawn" (94). The fox is therefore empowered by her gender, audacity, and intelligence. At the beginning of the tale, she turns into an attractive "young woman, soaked by rain" so that she can double her chances of tricking him: either by taking advantage of his kindness and sense of chivalry or by seducing him physically (10). The fox initially is a feminine figure, endowed with strong powers of seduction and intelligence.

As the story progresses, the fox becomes a feminist figure by endeavoring to wrestle control of the plot and by trying to counteract the powerful male authority figure, the *onmyoji*. The fox even confronts the imposing Lord of Dreams and dares to contest his rules. She challenges the patriarchal order and tries to subvert its rules by offering herself as a sacrifice to save the monk. She is a dissenting voice. The story becomes her story, the story of her fight.

The fox does not know how to save the monk, but she intuits that she must make an offering in order to receive the information she needs. She begins by selecting her most precious possession, a jade carving of a dragon that, years ago, she procured with great effort from the base of a tree. The fox carries the dragon "for many miles" and then tosses it off a cliff into the sea, declaring, "all I ask is the knowledge of how to save the life of the monk" (29). The "little statue of the dragon had brought serenity and peace to her den," but she willingly sacrifices it in order to help the monk (29). This is an important point, as it once again connects and delineates the main characters: the monk has peace, the *onmyoji* desperately lacks it and is willing to kill for it, and the fox is willing to sacrifice it in order to save another.

Her sacrifice pays off when she returns to her den, falls asleep, and enters The Dreaming. Her pilgrimage through the realm of dreams and her willing self-sacrifice mark her as the tale's heroine. She clearly follows Joseph Campbell's path of the hero, the road of trials. In *The Hero with a Thousand Faces*, Campbell maps out the path of the hero towards the actualization of his potential as a hero. Leaving home is the beginning: "The adventure is always and everywhere a passage beyond the veil of the known into the unknown"

(Campbell 82). The fox achieves this first by leaving her den for the cliff at the ocean, and then by leaving her world for The Dreaming. According to Campbell, "With the personifications of his destiny to guide and aid him, the hero goes forward in his adventure until he comes to the 'threshold guardian' at the entrance to the zone of magnified power" (Campbell 77). The fox crosses the threshold of The Dreaming (and, we will learn later, her body eventually rests on the threshold of the monk's temple).[4] Finally, she meets the Dream Lord, who assumes the shape of "a huge fox," "bigger than any creature the fox had ever seen" (30).[5] She begs his audience then asks who the other strange animals in the realm are. They are the Baku, the Dream Eaters, and she soon learns that the only way to save the monk is to catch the Baku who have consumed the dream meant for him. In order to protect the monk, the fox needs to deflect the curse on herself. There is no other solution.

Her intelligence and understanding of rules and their consequences mark her as resourceful, smart, and brave. The Dream Lord grants her request and allows her to enter the monk's dreams to save him. She does so discreetly, so much so that the monk almost misses her completely. In the first dream, "he thought he saw the flick of a fox's tail through an open door" (52). In the second dream, he realizes "that he was being watched [...] and he looked around him, but there was nothing in his dream, save for the distant seagulls and a tiny figure on a distant cliff which might, the monk thought, have been a fox" (56). In Japanese folktales, foxes can travel through different spaces and realms. For example, in the folk tale "The White Fox: Four Dreams," a fox is able to travel in the realm of dreams and back (Tyler 304). The dreamer dreams that he holds the fox's tail, and his wish comes true when he wakes up. In folklore, foxes are associated with the god Inari, who grants abundance. Foxes are his messengers.

The fox in Gaiman's tale endeavors to shield the monk from the curse. The monk is unaware of her sacrifice. The fox turns from a playful tormentor into a benevolent guardian for the monk and his temple. In fact, when the dream is over, the monk finds her slumbering body "stretched out across the threshold of the temple" (56). This is in keeping with the paradigms of *kitsune*s in folk tales, in which foxes are agents of protection for those who have earned their respect through kindness or innocence. In the tale "The Fox's Ball" for example, a fox helps a traveler escape from robbers (Tyler 299–300). The fox agrees to protect the traveller after the traveller gives him a ball that the fox is very attached to: "we always repay a debt of gratitude" (299). The traveller realizes the favor that the fox did for him after he sees the terrible bandits who were preparing to ambush him:

> The fox had led him this way — a way no ordinary person would know — just because the bandits would not be looking for a traveller to pass so close. The fox

disappeared once he was safely by, and he reached home without further difficulty. The fox stayed faithfully with him and often rescued him again. More and more touched by its fidelity, he was very glad indeed that he had had the good sense to return the ball [Tyler 300].

This tale deals with the motifs of ethics and justice. The animal is the protecting agent and rewards ethical behavior.

The theme of the grateful animal appears also in the famous tale, "The Good Fortune Kettle."[6] Folklorist Keigo Seki explains that the tale is very popular with children and is taught in schools, with the references to prostitution and animal cruelty omitted. The tale can also be found under the title "The Fox Harlot."[7] In the tale, a poor old farmer rescues a fox from the hands of three boys who are brutalizing it. The old man is a genuinely caring character repelled by the gratuitous cruelty displayed by the youths. He warns the fox, "You must be careful not to be caught by those boys again. Now you'd better hurry back to your den," and he carefully releases the fox in the middle of a thicket. The next day the old man goes again to the mountains. The fox comes up to him and says: "Grandfather, grandfather, you saved my life yesterday when I was in great danger; I am more thankful than I can tell." The fox offers to grant the old man three favors. Each time, the fox turns itself into a valuable that the farmer can then sell. First it turns into a copper kettle that the farmer sells to a priest, then into a beautiful girl that the farmer sells to a brothel, and then into a horse that the farmer sells to a rich foreigner. The farmer becomes rich from the sales, and his kindness to the fox is rewarded by his prosperity. Finally, the farmer honors the fox's last wish; "in his mansion he built a splendid chapel where on the nineteenth day of every month he and the old woman would go and pray for the fox's rebirth in paradise" (Seki 111). The moral beauty of this moving story lies in the mutual affection and respect between the human and the animal. The same theme, and the pattern of three tasks, appears in *The Dream Hunters*.

Foxes protect their benefactors and their homes. "The Fox Wife" is a folk tale that also deals with the theme of transformation and gratefulness. A man rescues a white fox from drowning. The fox swears to repay his kindness, leaves, and then reappears as a maid. Soon she bears him a child. The man does not know of his lover's true nature until the day their son tells him that his mother is sweeping the yard with her tail. In "Enough Is Enough," a fox negotiates with the occupant of a house for the people and the foxes to coexist peacefully, swearing that they will protect the household (Tyler 114–115). The fox promises, "We'll do everything we can to protect you from now on, if you'll forgive us, and we'll be sure to let you know when anything good is going to happen!" *The Dream Hunters* borrows specific motifs of the Japanese folk tale genre while incorporating universal notions found in fairy tales such as the absolute necessity to treat animals with respect.[8] Helpful animals can bring divine aid and an intuitional perspective on the situation, as opposed to the shackles of human logic and rationality. In Japanese fairy tales, spirits are involved to fight for the health of a sick person (Tyler 34). Evil spirits cause the disease, and a protecting spirit invoked by a healer is often the solution. In *The Dream Hunters*, the fox obeys her own desire to protect and save the monk.

After finding the fox in a deep death-like sleep, the monk carries her and leaves his temple to seek help. An old man on the road reveals to the monk what the fox has done. The monk needs guidance (literally beat into him), whereas the fox mostly worked out a way to save him on her own. The old man appears when the monk is in a hopeless and desperate situation from which only profound reflection or a lucky idea can extricate him. The character of the old man can be deciphered as both the Buddhist deity Binzuru Harada and the mentor in fairy tales. According to Jung, the mentor intervenes when the plot has reached a dead end: "Often the old man in fairytales asks questions like who? why? whence? and whither? for the purpose of inducing self-reflection and mobilising the moral forces, and more often still he gives the necessary magical talisman, the unexpected and improbable power to succeed."[9] Apart from his wisdom, the old man tests the monk's moral qualities and makes his gifts dependent on this test. In fairy tales, the mentor's presence is necessitated when the character is in a dead end, helpless and clueless. The intervention of the old man helps the monk but also points to the monk's inability to progress on his own. The presence of a guide for the young man points to his weakness. The fox emerges as the clever and resourceful character of the story, in sharp contract to the monk. She is an autonomous female, independent and clear-sighted; the monk is mostly unaware and passive. He needs a guide, whereas she acts and decides. The dynamics of gender and power are in her favor.

The fox achieves a heroic status by accepting rules knowingly. The Great Fox warns her: "*He is only a human. [...] While you are a fox. These things rarely end happily*" (34). By sacrificing herself willingly, she proves to the King of Dreams that she is a heroine. The King of All Night's Dreaming gives her the help she asks for, as he later explains to the monk: "Your fox also came to me, and asked for a gift, although she was more honest about her love than you. And I gave her my gift. She dreamed your dreams. She dreamed your first two dreams with you, then she dreamed the last dream for you" (100). In this moment, Gaiman plays with the gender paradigms of heroic tales: the heroic rescuer in this story is female and the rescued party is male. Moreover, the rescuer is an animal, whereas animals play an auxiliary role of helper in the traditional tales. The *kitsune* fulfils many exploits: she explores the realm of dreams, meets the King of Dreams, and convincingly pleads her case. While her ultimate wish is not granted (the monk is not saved), the *kitsune* makes the greatest achievements of the story.

Thanks to the fox's irruption in his life and her disruption of his dreams, the monk eventually turns from a passive character to a self-actualized, responsible agent in control of his destiny, however tragic. Before encountering the fox, the young monk is isolated from social interaction and physical pleasures. His diet consists of rice and yams, and his daily life is scheduled according to the prayers and the tasks he needs to perform for the upkeep and maintenance of the isolated temple. His life is only mental and spiritual; there is a clear lack of balance. The fox represents the diametrical opposite to his passivity. By awakening his sensual side, she also addresses the unbalance in his life. In psychological terms, she has an educative and transforming influence on his eros.[10] She helps him to rise out of his helplessness and passivity. The *kitsune* is a heroic agent for change and growth.

Joseph Campbell's influence, such a compelling feature of *The Dream Hunters,* is evident throughout Gaiman's works. Stephen Rauch's captivating monograph analyzes Joseph Campbell's influence on *Sandman.*[11] For Campbell, responsibility and sacrifice are vital concepts. A hero-to-be becomes a hero by facing and accepting the consequences of his actions. Campbell uses "the road of trials" to describe the long pilgrimage from the familiar to the unknown, where the hero-to-be is tested (97). *The Dream Hunters* presents a divergent interpretation of Campbell. The Dream King is clearly "the great figure of the guide, the teacher, the ferryman, the conductor of souls to the afterworld" (Campbell 72). The Dream King represents the link with Gaiman's interpretation of Campbell in *The Sandman.* The *kitsune's* progress through the realm of dreams corresponds to Campbell's "road of trials" (Campbell 97). The testing of the *kitsune's* resolve is essential for her to prove her merits and her understanding of what she is asking: "Once having traversed the threshold, the hero moves in a dream landscape of curiously fluid, ambiguous forms, where he must survive a succession of trials" (Campbell 97). Making sacrifices defines the hero, who "must put aside his pride, his virtue, beauty, and life" (Campbell 108). The *kitsune* closely follows a Campbellian heroic pattern. *The Dream Hunters'* major divergences from Campbell are the hero's animal nature and gender. As a consequence, the *kitsune* becomes an endearing and modern feminist character who articulates desire and who expresses her outrage at male authority figures. This is particularly evident in one of the fox's last scenes with the Dream King, where she realizes that he has allowed the monk to undo all of her work and that, as a consequence, she will live and the monk will die:

> The fox threw herself to the floor at the king's feet. "But you swore to help me!" she said, angrily.

And I helped you.
"It is not *fair,*" said the fox [106].

The *kitsune*'s heroism is clear. But what about the monk? On a psychoana-lytical level, Campbell's notion of heroism could be tied up with Jung's con-cept of individuation, which is essential in reaching the stage of personal development and maturity that makes one a hero. Even though the monk is quite a lackluster character at the beginning, his heroic nature is revealed thanks to the *kitsune*. Indeed, thanks to the information revealed by the Dream King, the monk becomes aware of the willing sacrifice that the fox made for him. The issue of free will and choice is crucial here. In a truly moving and very restrained conversation, the monk demands that the fox stop taking on the curse meant for him. This is the moment in the story when the monk rises to a heroic status; this is his sublime moment of moral nobility and cour-age:

> "My lord," said the monk. "I am a monk. I own nothing but my begging bowl. But the dream that fox dreamed was my dream by rights. I ask for it to be returned to me."
> **But**, said the King, **if I return your dream to you, you must die in her place.**
> "I understand that," said the monk. "But it is my dream. And I will not have the fox die in my place" [106].

Thanks to the fox, the monk is able to tap into his hitherto undiscovered capacity for heroism. By the end of *The Dream Hunters*, the monk becomes aware of his love for the fox, gains knowledge of his moral obligation towards her, and becomes her protector in his turn. This makes quite a sharp contrast when compared to the *onmyoji*'s fate at the end: naked, blind, demented, and shunned by all.

The last facet of the *kitsune* is revealed after the monk's sacrifice. Forced to return to the world by the monk's sacrifice, she cares for his body until he dies and her grief turns to revenge. She vows to avenge the monk, declaring, "The *onmyoji* who did this to you will learn what it means to take something from a fox" (108). In order to seek justice from the *onmyoji,* she turns into a *femme fatale.* This is in keeping with Japanese folk tales, where foxes embody a dangerous sensuality and play on sexual desires. "Foxes are famous in Japan for masquerading as beautiful women — so much so that if a man runs across a pretty girl alone, especially at twilight or in the evening, he is a fool if he does not suspect her of being a fox. In other words, enchantresses are, literally, foxy ladies," notes editor and translator Royal Tyler (49). The *kitsune* appears under the guise of "a maiden of high birth" (112) and bewitches the *onmyoji* with "the way she walked, respectful and seductive at the same time" (112). Her physical attributes match the requirements of the Japanese standards of grace and beauty: "her hair, so long and so very black[12]; her eyes, the shade of green leaves uncurling in the spring sunlight, her feet, which moved like tiny mice; the delicacy of her hand upon her fan; her voice, like a song heard in a dream" (112). Her physical description plays with the dialectics of concealing and revealing: "She bent over to pour him more sake, which caused her robe to fall open a little more" (116). Veils and screens are very important in Japanese daily life. Portable frames are used to make screens to conceal parts of a room. Concealment and "accidental" partial disclosure of her charms only increase her allure.

Once again, Klimt's influences on Amano's style appear in the depictions of the *kitsune*. Hair features strongly as a symbol for sexual vitality in Klimt's luscious portraits and in Pre-Raphaelite paintings. When she masquerades as a woman, the fox repeatedly uses her black hair as an erotic weapon of seduction. She sensuously dries her long black hair by the fire when she poses as a damsel in distress to trick the monk (14). When bewitching the *onmyoji* as a rich maiden, she also uses her hair, "so long, and so very black" to attract him (112). She also insists on wearing her hair down, which is erotic because it is a forbidden pleasure. The erotic power of loose hair is heightened by its transgressive nature. Amano's admiration for the Pre-Raphaelites can be seen in the repeated motif of the fox-woman's loose jet black hair. In the 1860s, the Pre-Raphaelites created quite a controversy by depicting their female sitters with loose hair. The Victorian public did not approve because "loose hair was worn only by children; in womanhood it was braided or pinned up and thereafter visible only when retiring or rising. Its appearance in art has therefore an intimate, erotic significance" (Marsh 48).

The *kitsune* plays the part of the supernatural lover. By using her female charms and her sexuality as a weapon, she refuses passivity and exploitation by male figures. Instead, she turns her body into an instrument in the struggle against the oppressive male figure, the *onmyoji*. He is so mesmerized by her performance, so driven by lust, that he is willing to burn his worldly possessions, kill his family, and destroy his magic implements in order to have her. In old folk tales, as early as eighth-century records indicate, one finds the motifs of the swan maiden, or that of the wife from the upper world.[13] Non-human or enchanted brides represent a strong erotic attraction to the protagonists of these tales ("The Crane Wife," "The Woman Who Came Down from Heaven," "The Snow Wife"). She turns into an agent of retribution:

> The Master of Yin-Yang was found the next morning in the grounds of a house. That had been abandoned twenty years earlier, when the official whose family had owned it was disgraced. Some said it was guilt that had brought him there, for, fifteen years earlier, the onmyoji had been in the service of the lord who had caused the downfall of that family [122].

Earlier in *The Dream Hunters,* we learned that the monk's father had "lost his house and all he owned" due to "powerful enemies" (50). Destitute and shamed, his father committed suicide. With the revelation at the end of the story, we realize that it was the *onmyoji* who destroyed the monk's family. Therefore, the *kitsune* not only avenges the death of the monk, but also his family. This underscores that the *kitsune* is a powerful agent for justice and revenge who refuses passivity. The fox embraces action and empowers herself; she is the only female character with agency in the story.

The intriguing distribution of power in the text makes the fox the real actor in the plot. This link between femininity and power is quite typical of folk tales. Marie-Louise von Franz makes an engaging analysis of gender and power in fairy tales. She sees fairy tales as vectors for the expression of the neglected feminine principle. In particular, folk tales and myths often feature feminine justice and feminine revenge. In Ancient Greek mythology, the goddesses Nemesis and Themis stand for revenge and justice respectively (von Franz 38–39). In *The Dream Hunters,* the *kitsune* combines characteristics of female classical deities. She represents Eros with her sensuality, Athena with her combativeness, and Aphrodite with her beauty. She is multi-faceted and talented.

However resourceful, the fox confronts rules that cannot be changed. The tragic outcome of the story was foreshadowed by the Binzuru Harada, who tells the monk: "the fox will die, or you will, and there is not a thing you can do on this earth or off it that would change this, whether or not your motives are pure" (68). Likewise, the King of Dreams clearly explains to the monk: "If I return your dream to you, you must die in her place" (106). Feminine astuteness and self-sacrifice cannot prevent the tragedy, fate cannot be altered.

The outcome is bleak. The final page of the story announces, "And that is the tale of the fox and the monk" (126). Or is it? Gaiman then adds a small epilogue to his tale:

> For it has been said that those who dream of the distant regions where the Baku graze have sometimes seen two figures, walking in the distance, and that these two figures were a monk and a fox, or it might be, a man and a woman.
>
> Others say no, that even in dreams and in death a monk and a fox are from different worlds, as they were in life, and in different worlds they will forever stay [126].

In this turn at the end, Gaiman plays with the conventions of storytelling and lets the readers decide if this tale ends in a macabre or romantic way. He leaves the interpretation of the ending to the reader, creating an opening for a typical "happy ending" for those who want it. This is also reinforced through Amano's art, since the last illustration in the book shows the monk and the fox (in her human form), heads resting together, walking off into the sunset.

Amano states, "I just hope my images give readers something unique and far reaching, instead of limiting their imagination to one stereotype" (McCabe 240). The same can be said about what Gaiman does with the text and the fairy tale genre. Together, Gaiman and Amano achieve a balanced collaboration in which their individual talents weave something new. In describing collaborative pieces, Gaiman notes, "the whole is not greater than the sum, the whole is different than the sum. The whole is a new person. The whole is a different entity" (McCabe 8).

Together, Gaiman and Amano reimagine a type of story dating back to eighth-century Japan and reimagine it for a twenty-first century audience. They take the sparse simplicity of the folk tale narrative and Campbell's heroic motif to create for an unforgettable, endearing, and original modern female character. The *kitsune* crosses boundaries and fights to express herself, to make her voice heard. She brings to the fore several key themes of feminism; she struggles for self-expression, confronts oppressive masculine figures and their rules, and transcends limitations placed upon her to be heard. The story is hers, rightfully so. All of her qualities and characteristics are threads woven into a tapestry of arresting beauty. The contrasting moral hues contribute to making the overall vision of the *kitsune* motif in this tapestry a rich and complex experience for the viewer.

NOTES

1. *Mukashi* means "long ago" and it is the usual opening phrase of folk tales.

2. Gaiman's novel *American Gods* presents Scandinavian shape-shifter and mischief-maker, Loki. Loki is a trickster *extraordinaire*.

3. Carl Jung, "On the Psychology of the Trickster-Figure" in *The Archetypes and the Collective Unconscious*, 1959. (London: Routledge and Kegan Paul), 1967, 255–272. Print.

4. In retracing her steps, the monk later approaches the threshold as well, this time meeting the *Dream Hunters'* version of familiar guardians and Dreaming characters from *Sandman*: Cain and Abel, the Gates of Horn and Ivory, the gryphon and the dragon, and the raven Matthew.

5. As has been established previously in *The Sandman,* the King of Dreams changes aspects in accordance to his viewer. For example, when a kitten seeks him in "The Dream of a Thousand Cats," he appears as a giant black tomcat. To the *kitsune*, he appears as a giant fox, but when the monk seeks him, Dream appears as a Japanese man clad in flowing black robes.

6. Keigo Seki, ed., "The Good Fortune Kettle," *Folktales of Japan*, 1956–1957. (Chicago: University of Chicago Press, 1963, 107–111, 107). Print.

7. "The Fox Wife" in *The Yanagita Kunio Guide to the Japanese Folk Tale*, 1948, trans. and ed. Fanny Hagin Mayer (Bloomington: Indiana University Press, 1986), 31–32. Print.

8. Marie-Louise Von Franz, *Shadow and Evil in Fairy-Tales*, 1974. (Dallas: Spring, 1983), 119: "one must never hurt the helpful animal in fairy tales."

9. Carl Jung, *Symbols of Transformation*, 1912, trans. R. F. C. Hull (London: Routledge and Kegan Paul, 1967), 220. Print.

10. See Marie-Louise von Franz's discussion of the effect that a real woman has on an

intellectual man's anima in *The Feminine in Fairy Tales*: "A man, especially if very much engaged in mental activities, tends to be a little bit coarse or undifferentiated on the eros side" (2).

11. Stephen Rauch, *Neil Gaiman's "The Sandman" and Joseph Campbell: In Search of the Modern Myth* (Holicong: Wildside Press, 2003). Print.

12. The hair motif is found in the folk tale "The God of Good Fortune" (Tyler, 63–66): Lord Tadazane "dozed off for a moment and saw a woman walk by him with three feet of her magnificent long hair trailing behind her along the floor." Tadazane dreams that he grabs her by the hair, then lets her go. "Then he woke up. His hand was gripping a fox's tail" (Tyler 64).

13. Keigo Seki's collection, *Folktales of Japan* (1956–1957), offers a thematic collection of tales and each section features a well-documented and instructive analysis of the motifs found in these sections. This book is an accessible introduction.

Works Cited

Bacchilega, Cristina. *Postmodern Fairy Tales: Gender and Narrative Strategies*. Philadelphia: University of Philadelphia Press, 1997. Print.

Baudrillard, Jean. *Simulacra and Simulation*. 1981. Trans. Sheila Glaser. Ann Arbor: University of Michigan Press, 1994. Print.

Borsellino, Mary. "Blue and Pink: Gender in Neil Gaiman's Work." *The Neil Gaiman Reader*, Ed. Darrell Schweitzer. Halicong: Wildside Press, 2007, 51–53, 52. Print.

Campbell, Joseph. *The Hero with a Thousand Faces*. 1949. Princeton: Bollingen Series 17, Princeton University Press, 1973. Print.

Cooper, J. C. *Fairy Tales: Allegories of the Inner Life*. 1983. Wellingborough: Aquarian, 1985. Print.

Fliedl, Gottfried. *Gustav Klimt*. Cologne: Taschen, 1992. Print.

Freud, Sigmund. *The Uncanny*. 1919. Trans. James Strachey. London: Hogarth, 1971. Print.

_____, and Joseph Breuer. *The Interpretation of Dreams*. 1900. Trans. James Strachey. 2 vols. London: Hogarth, 1971. Print.

Gaiman, Neil. "Afterword." *The Dream Hunters*. New York: Vertigo DC Comics, 1999. Print.

_____, and Yoshitaka Amano. *The Dream Hunters*. New York: Vertigo DC Comics, 1999. Print.

Guroian, Vigen. *Tending the Heart of Virtue: How Classic Stories Awaken a Child's Moral Imagination*. Oxford: Oxford University Press, 1998. Print.

Haase, Donald, ed. *Fairy Tales and Feminism: New Approaches*. Detroit: Wayne University Press, 2004. Print.

Hagin Mayer, Fanny, ed. and trans. *The Yanagita Kunio Guide to the Japanese Folk Tale*. Bloomington: Indiana University Press, 1948. Print.

Hourigan, Margery. *Deconstructing the Hero: Literary Theory and Children's Literature*. London: Routledge, 1997. Print.

Marsh, Jan. *Pre-Raphaelite Women*. 1987. London: Weidenfeld and Nicolson, 1995. Print.

McCabe, Joseph. *Hanging Out with the Dream King: Conversations with Neil Gaiman and His Collaborators*. Seattle: Fantagraphics, 2004. Print.

Propp, Vladimir. *Morphology of the Folktale*. Trans. Ariadna Y. Martin and Richard P. Martin. Minnesota: Minnesota University Press, 1983. Print.

Rauch, Stephen. *Neil Gaiman's "The Sandman" and Joseph Campbell: In Search of the Modern Myth*. Holicong: Wildside Press, 2003. Print.

Reynolds, Kimberley, ed. *Modern Children's Literature: An Introduction*. London: Palgrave, 2005. Print.

Schweitzer, Darrrell, ed. *The Neil Gaiman Reader*. Holicong: Wildside Press, 2007. Print.

Seki, Keigo, ed. *Folktales of Japan*. 1956–1957. Trans. Robert J. Adams. Chicago: University of Chicago Press, 1963. Print.

Tyler, Royal, ed. and trans. *Japanese Fairy Tales*. New York: Pantheon, 1987. Print.

Von Franz, Marie-Louise. *An Introduction to the Interpretation of Fairy Tales*. 1970. Dallas: Spring, 1982. Print.

_____. *Shadow and Evil in Fairy Tales*. 1974. Dallas: Spring, 1983. Print.

Wilkie-Stibbs, Christine. *The Feminine Subject in Children's Literature*. London: Routledge, 2002. Print.

Zipes, Jack. *Fairy Tale as Myth / Myth as Fairy Tale*. New York: Routledge, 1994. Print.

_____. *Fairy Tales and the Art of Subversion: The Classical Genre for Children and the Process of Civilization*. New York: Wildman Press, 1983. Print.

_____. *Happily Ever After: Fairy Tales, Children, and the Culture Industry*. New York: Routledge, 1997. Print.

ICONOGRAPHY

Klimt, Gustav. *Hostile Forces* (detail of the *Beethoven Friese*), 1902. 2.2m x 6.36m. Vienna, Osterreichische Galerie.

_____. *The Silver Fishes*, 1901–1902. Oil painting, 150 x 46 cm. Soleure, Kunstmuseum.

_____. *The Three Ages of Woman*, 1905. Oil painting, 178 × 198 cm. Rome, Galleria Nazionale d'Arte Moderna.

"A boy and his box, off to see the universe"

Madness, Power and Sex in "The Doctor's Wife"

BY EMILY CAPETTINI

In a review of Neil Gaiman's *Doctor Who* episode, "The Doctor's Wife" (14 May 2011), Matt Risley refers to the Doctor/TARDIS relationship as "the most important, but consistently underappreciated relationship underpinning the entire franchise." The TARDIS (Time And Relative Dimension In Space) is the Doctor's time machine, space ship, and constant companion. He refers to the ship by the acronym "TARDIS" throughout the series. From 1963 to 1973, the TARDIS is referred to as "it," and is a vehicle with little to no personality. During "The Time Warrior" (1973), the third doctor calls the TARDIS "old girl," and this establishes a sex for the TARDIS for the first time. However, the third doctor's decision to call the TARDIS "old girl" is not strictly indicative of the TARDIS having a specific sex, as he also refers to his roadster as "old girl" ("The Time Monster"). Yet, the tradition continues, and future doctors refer to the TARDIS affectionately as "old girl." Whether "old girl" is a nickname for the TARDIS indicating a sex or merely the tradition of referring to a ship as female is not confirmed until Gaiman's 2011 episode, "The Doctor's Wife." In this episode, not only does Gaiman establish the TARDIS as female, but he also codes all TARDISes as female. Furthermore, the way in which the Doctor and TARDIS interact throughout the episode changes and enriches the relationship dynamic between them, easily sidestepping and overturning the all-too-familiar science fiction battle-of-the-sexes stereotypes as well as renegotiating concepts of madness, power, and sex within the relationship dynamic.

To best understand the significance of Gaiman's coding of the TARDIS as female, it is important to examine more closely the evolution of the

TARDIS's presence in the classic and new series of *Doctor Who*. The TARDIS is introduced in the first episode of *Doctor Who*, "An Unearthly Child." Ian, one of the Doctor's first companions, upon encountering the TARDIS, states, "Do you feel it? ... It's alive!" ("An Unearthly Child"). The theme of the living TARDIS reappears throughout the first doctor's tenure. An additional recurring element is the Doctor's lack of control over the TARDIS. As one companion says to another when they land in 1066 England, "As a matter of fact, we never know where we're going to land next" ("The Time Meddler"). Furthermore, the TARDIS keeps its police box form despite a built-in control that is meant to make the ship blend in with its surroundings. In the same episode, another Time Lord asks, "What's the matter, Doctor? Can't you repair your camouflage unit?" ("The Time Meddler"). Though the terminology is modernized in 2005 when the Doctor calls it the "chameleon circuit," the excuse remains: the TARDIS is not in perfect working order. The relationship between the TARDIS and the Doctor hinges on this very fact: the TARDIS does not always run — or behave — the way the Doctor intends. One might even venture to suggest, "it has a mind of its own," for, as audiences eventually come to learn, she does. Though the TARDIS never does run completely correctly for any doctor, its malfunctioning becomes less prevalent in later stories.

Additionally, at first, the TARDIS is called a ship and does not have a specific sex. Once Jon Pertwee takes over as the third doctor, the TARDIS is called "old girl," coding her as female. The adventures in the TARDIS, in addition, become more controlled. The fourth doctor also refers to the TARDIS as "old girl," as well as a "misunderstood, unmanageable old machine" ("The Image of the Fendahl"). However, the TARDIS is not often focused on for longer than these few passing moments. She is not a central character, but rather exists as the plot device by which the Doctor travels, acquires companions, and encounters or solves problems.

Whereas the TARDIS was often a plot device or set in the classic series, she becomes a character in her own right in the new series. In the 2005 episode "Boomtown," the antagonist, Margaret, attempts an escape plan that would destroy the TARDIS, but is foiled in her attempt not by the Doctor, but by the TARDIS herself ("Boomtown"). The Doctor tells Margaret, "[The TARDIS] is not just any old power source. It's the TARDIS. My TARDIS. The best ship in the universe." He further claims that the TARDIS has a heart and is "alive," telling Margaret that she has "opened its soul" ("Boomtown"). In this episode, the TARDIS is given features equivalent to those of sentient beings. Previous episodes established that the TARDIS is alive and conscious of those around her, but prior to "Boomtown," the only features of hers that were mentioned were machine-like: the chameleon circuit and the camouflage unit. Establishing that the TARDIS has a soul and heart lessens the distance between the Doctor and the TARDIS; they are not merely man and machine, but both are living and sentient organisms. Furthermore, the TARDIS becomes more relatable and less like a set piece or plot device; in this episode, the TARDIS displays agency — survival — and takes control of the situation, providing the resolution herself. In the new series, the TARDIS continues developing as a creature and sentient being.

Terminology suggestive of species rather than machinery occurs again in the second season in 2006. When the Doctor and Rose are separated from the TARDIS in "The Impossible Planet," Rose asks the Doctor if he can build a new TARDIS. The Doctor replies: "They were grown, not built. And with my own planet gone ... we're kind of stuck" ("The Impossible Planet"). The fact that the TARDIS was grown, rather than built, is indicative that she is not merely a machine. In addition, this exchange suggests that the TARDIS is indigenous to Gallifrey, the Doctor's planet, not unlike vegetation or species that have their origins in specific environments. Thus the concepts that Gaiman uses to enrich the relationship between the Doctor and the TARDIS have a long history within the canon of *Doctor Who*.

Gaiman's episode, "The Doctor's Wife," plays with these established concepts of the TARDIS as well as drawing inspiration from literature. "The Doctor's Wife" is a story about the relationship between a pair of travelers trying to escape an unsatisfactory environment. This premise echoes several travel narratives in literature, including C.S. Lewis's *The Horse and His Boy*, where the eponymous heroes run away from a cruel master and travel to Narnia. In "The Doctor's Wife," there is a similar impetus to flee: the Doctor is unhappy with the societal norms of his home planet. However, the interesting thing about this comparison is not in how Lewis's and Gaiman's narratives are similar, but in how Gaiman uses the idea of fleeing travellers as a way to investigate a relationship that was, until this episode, one-way in terms of communication.

"The Doctor's Wife" begins when a young woman, Idris, is told that she will be given a new soul ("The Doctor's Wife"). The villain of the episode, House, pulls the "TARDIS matrix herself— a living consciousness" out of the physical structure of the TARDIS, forcing it into Idris's body and turning her into a human version of the TARDIS ("The Doctor's Wife"). As House runs away with the ship part of the TARDIS, the Doctor has to rely on the TARDIS herself to problem-solve. Perhaps most telling of the renegotiation of the Doctor/TARDIS relationship is the way in which the TARDIS and the Doctor communicate after not having spoken for almost their entire time together. In their first encounter in the episode, the TARDIS runs up to the Doctor and kisses him, then, when Uncle (another alien inhabitant of House) apologizes for "the mad person" and cautions, "watch out for this one — she bites," Idris bites the Doctor, commenting: "Biting's excellent. It's like kissing, only there's a winner" ("The Doctor's Wife"). This moment informs a later conversation when the TARDIS tells the Doctor who she is, and the Doctor insists, "No you're not, you're a bitey, mad lady!" ("The Doctor's Wife"). The use of the word "mad" here is worth noting. In "Women and Madness," Shoshana Felman provides an overview of the discourse about women and madness, including Luce Irigaray, observing that madness constitutes a woman acting outside of accepted "behavioral norms," regardless of the norms' social appeal (7). Indeed, the TARDIS is acting outside of several behavioral norms; for one, she is a space ship and time machine transposed into a woman's body and biting her pilot. More importantly, however, the TARDIS is talking to the Doctor, which is not something that she has ever been able to do before and is, by this definition and the opinions of the other characters, mad.

The Doctor's use of the label "mad," however, is most interesting in this context for, as he told companion Amy before they began their travels, "I am definitely a mad man with a box" ("The Eleventh Hour"). Therefore, the Doctor draws a parallel between the TARDIS and himself, uniting them in their supposed madness. The TARDIS is and has been behaving outside of her social expectations — simply to be a ship under the Doctor's control and to go where he directs her. The Doctor, too, behaves outside of his social expectations. He abandons life on Gallifrey — including a high political position — that he finds stifling ("The Five Doctors"). Because the TARDIS and the Doctor are very similar in their rejection of Gallifreyan culture, perhaps it would be more accurate to say that the Doctor is "a mad man with a *mad* box."

Later in the same conversation, the Doctor expresses possessiveness of the TARDIS, which is perhaps unsurprising, as she has been his ship for nearly 700 years. However, what is surprising is the possessiveness that the TARDIS expresses in regards to the Doctor. When the Doctor recognizes that Idris is in fact the TARDIS, the following conversation occurs:

> TARDIS: I was already a museum piece, when you were young, and the first time you touched my console you said...
> DOCTOR: I said you were the most beautiful thing I'd ever known.
> TARDIS: Then you stole me. And I stole you.
> DOCTOR: I borrowed you.
> TARDIS: Borrowing implies the eventual intention to return the thing that was taken. What makes you think I would ever give you back? ["The Doctor's Wife"].

The fact that the Doctor stole the TARDIS and ran away from Gallifrey is not new information to viewers. Previously, it was assumed that the TARDIS was just something stolen, a passive party, rather than an active participant. Such an assumption of passiveness is an evocation of what Simone de Beauvoir states in *The Second Sex*: "Hercules, Prometheus, Parsifal ... woman has only a secondary part to play in the destiny of these heroes" (302). Similarly, the TARDIS was only a secondary player to the Doctor, who in the new series is discussed in mythic language, such as "he's ... the storm in the heart of the sun" ("The Family of Blood") or "The Oncoming Storm" ("The Parting of the Ways"). Certainly, the TARDIS is responsible for where and when he ends up, but for most of the show's history, this is a plot device written off as a TARDIS malfunction, chance, or the Doctor's steering. This conversation, however, rewrites both the concept of the TARDIS as secondary and the moment of the stealing. Because they steal each other, they are equal participants. Furthermore, the TARDIS emphasizes her own agency by stating that it is not "borrowing," because she had no intention to return the Doctor. This implies that she has control over the situation. She is not a passive party, but is active in this relationship and does not have, as Beauvoir says, a secondary part in the Doctor's adventures, but a primary one.

Another renegotiation within this same conversation that is worth examining is the way in which the TARDIS anticipates and finishes what the Doctor is going to say. After explaining who she is and commenting, "House eats TARDISes," the Doctor answers:

DOCTOR: But you can't eat a TARDIS, it would destroy you. Unless —*unless*—
TARDIS: *Unless* you deleted the TARDIS matrix first ... but House can't just delete a TARDIS consciousness, that would blow a hole in the universe, so he pulls that matrix, sticks it into a living receptacle, and then it feeds off the remaining Artron energy. You were about to say all that. I don't suppose you have to now ["The Doctor's Wife"].

By voicing what the Doctor is going to say in the future before he can, the TARDIS establishes herself quite firmly in the conversation. Felman, in her summary of Luce Irigaray's *Speculum of the Other Woman*, states that in Western discourse, there is a "latent design to exclude women from the production of speech" (9). Indeed, the TARDIS has been excluded from the ability to talk and engage in conversation for almost the entire show. However, in this situation, the TARDIS not only speaks quite intelligently about the topic at hand, but she does so before the Doctor can even formulate the thought. Granted, the TARDIS is apparently taking the Doctor's words from the future and saying them before he can, thereby depending on the Doctor's knowledge. However, her claiming the words as her own gives her power within this conversation, for her prompting propels the narrative by causing the Doctor to realize the gravity of their situation. Thus, the TARDIS, after many years of being the silent companion of the Doctor, engages frequently in a discourse with the Doctor, establishing herself firmly in a conversation that, in the end, does not fall completely silent.

In addition to creating a foundation for equality between the Doctor and the TARDIS, Gaiman's episode continually returns to this shifting idea of who stole or was stolen. This is evident in a scene in which the Doctor and the TARDIS are attempting to build a ship to chase House:

TARDIS: Do you ever wonder why I chose you all those years ago?
DOCTOR: I chose you. You were unlocked.
TARDIS: Of course I was. I wanted to see the universe, so I stole a Time Lord and ran away. And you were the only one mad enough ["The Doctor's Wife"].

Once again, this conversation inverts the traditional origin story of the Doctor and the TARDIS. In this reading, the TARDIS chose the Doctor rather than vice versa. The TARDIS has agency of her own — a desire to see the universe — but required a pilot in order to reach that goal. Therefore, she developed and executed a plan. While leaving herself "unlocked" may seem like a passive action or what de Beauvoir calls a secondary role, the TARDIS cancels out any natural passivity that comes with being something that is (sometimes) controlled by another by creating her own itinerary and the frankness with which she addresses the Doctor. The *Telegraph* review of "The Doctor's Wife" calls this conversation "utterly superb," mentioning that because of this episode, viewers "had a greater exploration between the two core elements of the programme than has been achieved before" within the show (Fuller). It seems that for Gaiman, as well as for reviewers, the richness of *Doctor Who* exists in this relationship between the Doctor and the TARDIS, which, as viewers see, is much more complex than previously assumed.

Interestingly, the Doctor does not respond negatively to the TARDIS's possessiveness or her newfound ability to talk back to him. While at first he is frustrated and takes the opportunity to criticize her ability to land in the correct place, her responses, rather than creating lasting anger or frustration, delight the Doctor. The following conversation occurs when the Doctor's frustration with the TARDIS reaches its highest point:

DOCTOR: You know, since we're talking, with mouths, not really an opportunity that comes along very often, I just want to say, you know, *you* have never been very reliable!
TARDIS: And you have?
DOCTOR: You didn't always take me where I wanted to go.
TARDIS: No, but I always took you where you *needed* to go.
DOCTOR: You did. Look at us, talking! Wouldn't it be amazing if we could always talk, even when you're stuck inside the box?
TARDIS: You know I'm not constructed that way. I exist across all space and time, and *you* talk and run around and bring home strays ["The Doctor's Wife"].

Though the TARDIS has frustrated the Doctor by responding to his criticisms with some of her own, the argument never gets more serious than bickering. Such a reaction speaks to the strength of the relationship and the Doctor's own opinion of the TARDIS for, instead of becoming irritated that something that seems not to be his equal — while living, the TARDIS has been somewhat controllable — has been silent for most of their travels is now telling him what to do, he is delighted that they can now communicate. Indeed, at the end of the episode just before the TARDIS becomes silent again, she says that the "big, complicated word" that is "so sad" that she has been looking for is "alive" ("The Doctor's Wife"). She adds, "I'll always be here, but this is when we talked" ("The Doctor's Wife"). These two statements equate being alive with the ability to communicate clearly, once more underlining the importance that verbal communication has to both of them. The Doctor does not attempt to silence the TARDIS but rather welcomes her conversation. This is emphasized by the title of the episode, "The Doctor's Wife." The title comically emphasizes the closeness and mutual reliance between the Doctor and the TARDIS. This moves resists the history in which women were secondary characters to their heroic husbands or lovers, which de Beauvoir recounts, as well as the purposeful silencing that Felman addresses. Quite simply, without the TARDIS, the Doctor is nothing and though he is certainly annoyed with her (vocal and physical) bossiness, once she is able to explain her actions, the Doctor welcomes her judgment.

Just as he welcomed the TARDIS's critiques, the Doctor is also surprisingly receptive to the revelation that the TARDIS has equal power in their relationship. He is excited but this newfound information rather than concerned about the possible repercussions of a struggle between the sexes. This is an interesting aspect to examine, as science fiction has had a long history of a battle of the sexes. As Brian Attebery points out in the introduction to his *Decoding Gender in Science Fiction*, until the 1960s, traditional gender roles were "one of the elements most often transcribed unthinkingly into SF's hypothetical worlds" and that "even if an author was interested in revising the gender code, the conservatism of a primarily male audience ... kept gender exploration to a minimum" (5). Science fiction, until the New Wave in the 1960s, primarily did not address a possible reversal or overturning of gender roles or power. Indeed, as Joanna Russ addresses in "The Image of Women in Science Fiction," the imagined worlds and relationships between men and women in Science Fiction were often "present-day, white, middle-class suburbia" (81). As she continues, when a struggle between the sexes took place, the work was typically populated with "vicious, sadistic" women, "openly contemptuous of the men" who had power over men because they were physically stronger (86–87). Again, this returns to what Felman discusses in regards to the "mad" women who act outside of their prescribed roles. They were depicted as having undesirable traits such as being mad, vicious, or sadistic. Thus, female characters were shallow and static, showing little depth of character and acting as little more than cautionary tales. However, with the advent of the New Wave, writers such as James Tiptree, Jr. and Ursula K. Le Guin began to explore and challenge differences between the sexes and gender roles.

Under the pen name James Tiptree, Jr., Alice Bradley Sheldon made a career out of writing short stories that highlighted the problems and dangers of man-woman relationships and how easily they can tilt into violence. For example, she depicts the mass-murder of women in "The Screwfly Solution" and the complete extinction of men in "Houston, Houston, Do You Read?" One critic comments that Tiptree is "[determined] to follow the implications of gender difference to their grimly logical conclusions; her stories read like darkly parodic representations of the extremes of gender difference" (Hollinger 305). Power dynamics are also often a subject for examination in Le Guin's work. A narrator in Le Guin's *The Left Hand of Darkness* wonders if those responsible for creating the race of androgynous people "[considered] war to be a purely masculine displacement-activity, a vast Rape, and therefore in their experiment eliminate the masculinity that rapes and the femininity that is raped" (Le Guin 96). Here, Le Guin discusses how sex and gender roles play into dominance and violence. Indeed, the entirety of *The Left Hand of Darkness* is focused on this discussion.

Interestingly, "The Doctor's Wife" also references an event similar to Le Guin's "vast Rape." Upon seeing the remnants of other TARDISes that House has eaten, the TARDIS remarks, "All of my sisters are dead, they were devoured, and ... we are looking at their corpses" ("The Doctor's Wife"). Such a line, while overlooking a field of burnt out and dead TARDISes, is reminiscent of the violence in Tiptree's work, such as the multitude of dead female bodies left in rivers or fields in "The Screwfly Solution," as well as the "vast Rape" that Le Guin mentions in *The Left Hand of Darkness* in which the rape is destruction or invasion of land or societies. The "vast Rape" here is the murder and devouring of the TARDISes, leaving their bodies to rot in a field on an asteroid. This is violence against women by men, and like Le Guin, Gaiman works against established techniques in the canon of feminist science fiction. As Hollinger notes, "sf by women writers, and specifically by feminist writers," uses two "'monstrous' figures, the alien and the cyborg" (*Cambridge Companion* 132). The only monstrous character in "The Doctor's Wife" is House, who has lured hundreds of Time Lords to his asteroid and devoured their living TARDISes. While House is an alien, so too are the TARDIS and the Doctor. In this way, Gaiman appears to be rewriting previous canon from feminist science fiction, removing the "otherness" present in the use of a cyborg or alien against a human or humanoid. In addition, the way in which the TARDIS ultimately triumphs over House — by chasing him down and destroying him once she has returned to the console room — speaks to both the strength of her relationship with the Doctor and her own ability to take care of herself. For although the Doctor helps the TARDIS get to where she needs to go (an interesting reversal of the TARDIS taking the Doctor where *he* needs to go), she is the one who ultimately defeats House. Such strength also underlines the "I chose you," claim she makes to the Doctor, for one can assume from this episode that if the TARDIS did not want the Doctor, she would have been able to dispose of him easily. The TARDIS requires clear trust and intimacy with the Doctor.

The intimacy that is brought to the surface in "The Doctor's Wife" draws attention to the ways in which the TARDIS has been given a sexuality. Near the end of the season premiere in 2010, which introduces a regeneration of the Doctor (Matt Smith), a new TARDIS is also revealed. The TARDIS, having crashed at the start of the episode, repairs itself, creating a new look to which the Doctor exclaims, "Look at you. Oh, you sexy thing. Look at you!" ("The Eleventh Hour"). Though the TARDIS has been coded as female since the 1970s, the TARDIS has never been described as sexy. Within "The Doctor's Wife," the most obvious sexualization of the TARDIS is the body the TARDIS ends up in: a woman in her early thirties, wearing a low-cut dress. The TARDIS becomes sexual right away, and furthermore, when she first greets the Doctor, she kisses him ("The Doctor's Wife"). Though there may be concern over the Doctor referring to the TARDIS as "Sexy" when she is in Idris's body, it is important to note that the Doctor initially called the TARDIS sexy after her regeneration in "The Eleventh Hour."

Because the Doctor refers to the TARDIS as sexy while she is still a ship, it negates any interpretation one can make about the Doctor and the TARDIS-as-Idris, for he has already decided that she is sexy prior to seeing her new appearance. In fact, the Doctor is not interested in Idris at all — recoiling from her kiss and dismissing her with, "You're a bitey, mad lady!" — until he realizes that she is actually his TARDIS ("The Doctor's Wife"). Furthermore, when the TARDIS says, "I think you call me ... Sexy," the Doctor becomes embarrassed, stating defensively, "Only when we're alone!" ("The Doctor's Wife"). He does, of course, resume calling the TARDIS "Sexy" when she reminds him, "We are alone" ("The Doctor's Wife"). Later, the Doctor calls her "you sexy thing" and "old girl" easily, though when the TARDIS introduces herself to Amy and Rory as "Sexy," the Doctor again becomes embarrassed ("The Doctor's Wife"). Indeed, the Doctor was alone in "The Eleventh Hour" when he initially called the TARDIS sexy, so perhaps it is something that is supposed to be restricted to a private sphere, further making the argument that the Doctor and TARDIS have an intimate and highly personal relationship.

The affection that the Doctor feels for the TARDIS clearly has not gone unnoticed by his companions. Even Amy asks the Doctor if he "[wished] really, really hard" when he explains the TARDIS is in a human body ("The Doctor's Wife"). But what is most interesting about this is that while the Doctor has consistently referred to the TARDIS as "Sexy" in the new series, he first called her that before she ended up in an attractive human body. Indeed, the use of "sexy" as a nickname seems to underline the closeness of the relationship between the TARDIS and the Doctor. "Old girl," the TARDIS's previous nickname, is certainly affectionate, but carries the connotation of being an impersonal and traditional naval term. "Sexy" is much more personal. Such a nickname suggests that to the Doctor, the TARDIS is not simply a ship. As Hollinger mentions, "sf has often been called 'the literature of change' [but] has for the most part it has been slow to recognize the historical contingency and cultural conventionality of many of our ideas about sexual identity" (*Cambridge Companion* 126). Gaiman certainly challenges this slow recognition by creating a close relationship between the Doctor and the TARDIS that is not overtly sexual but is implied and joked about, as with Amy's comment. Indeed, the entire concept of the TARDIS allowing the Doctor to steal her is rife with intimacy: she left herself "unlocked" or open to the Doctor; she *chose* him to be *her* companion in their travels. Ultimately, the TARDIS chose the Doctor as the one person to spend the rest of her life with, for it is quite possible, given her ability to see future events, that she knew of Gallifrey's destruction. Thus, the TARDIS is not merely a sexual being, but an emotional one as well, further emphasizing her close, highly privatized relationship with the Doctor.

Eventually, the TARDIS must return to the box. Just after this moment in the episode, the Doctor tells Amy and Rory that "being alive" is the "best thing there is" ("The Doctor's Wife"). He then changes the subject to their next destination, including the TARDIS in the conversation, and Amy observes:

> AMY: Look at you pair. It's always you and her, isn't it? Long after the rest of us have gone. A boy and his box, off to see the universe.
> DOCTOR: Well, you say that as if it's a bad thing. But honestly, it's the best thing there is ["The Doctor's Wife"].

Interestingly, the Doctor's repeated "best thing there is" equates being alive with traveling in the TARDIS, implying that both are of equal importance to him. Amy is correct when she comments that it is "you and her ... long after the rest of us have gone" ("The Doctor's Wife"). Even audience members who are only familiar with the new series have already seen eight companions come and go, some in as little time as one episode. The very nature of a companion is transient, and it is only the TARDIS that has been the constant companion to the Doctor. Arguably, this is because the TARDIS has proven that she is equal to the Doctor, something that all other companions could not maintain for an extended period of time without consequences. When the companions have attempted to be equals to the Doctor, it has nearly killed them: Rose almost died after absorbing the time vortex; Martha was hunted for a year; and Donna, after becoming part Time Lord, had to have her memories wiped or else die ("The Parting of the Ways"; "The Last of the Time Lords"; "Journey's End"). Like their time on the TARDIS, these companions' moments of equality with the Doctor are transient.

In speaking about the Doctor's companions one must consider River Song, who the Doctor actually has married and whose life we see out of order, beginning with her death ("The Wedding of River Song"; "The Forest of the Dead"). River Song comes the closest to being an equal to the Doctor, for she is a Time Lord as well, but without any remaining regenerations ("Let's Kill Hitler"). Though technically, River Song is the Doctor's wife, Gaiman infers that the TARDIS is the Doctor's wife. Taking into consideration what has been previously discussed in regards to the intimacy of the Doctor/TARDIS relationship, one can only assume that Gaiman is using "wife" here as an indicator of a constant, loving relationship between equals. As an episode review of IGN.com states:

> It was an audacious and challenging move to attempt to personify and humanise the most important, but consistently underappreciated relationship underpinning the entire franchise, but it was given glorious clarity through Amy's perspective-lending comment — while companions and enemies will always come and go, there's only ever been one irreplaceable partner he could always rely on [Risley].

River, the Doctor's legal wife, is not a constant, which audience members know for almost her entire time on-screen. Thus, Gaiman is using "wife" in this context, not as the legal term, but as a way to communicate this idea of a "constant companion." The TARDIS is the Doctor's wife in the sense that she is the one on which he may always rely and who will always be with him, which is something other companions are unable to do — even River Song.

At the end of the episode, when the TARDIS has returned to her box, it seems she has become silent again. Alone in the control room, the Doctor calls out, "Are you there? Can you hear me? ... The Eye of Orion, or wherever we need to go" ("The Doctor's Wife"). After a moment, a lever next to him flips on its own and the TARDIS takes off; in response, the Doctor cheers and spins around the console ("The Doctor's Wife"). While not a traditional form of speech, the TARDIS still finds a way to still communicate with the Doctor, even while herself. The Doctor echoes the TARDIS's claim "I always took you where you needed to go" when he tells her to take them "wherever we need to go." In this way, the Doctor acknowledges her presence and participation in their relationship, consciously giving her equal choice in their travels. To his credit, Gaiman set up the Doctor/TARDIS relationship in such a way that the major changes of the TARDIS can be contained and examined in one episode, but still allow viewers to assume that the TARDIS continues to play an active role in the Doctor's travels, for audiences know that she will always have control over their destination. She is quite firmly established as no longer a secondary character to the sometimes mythic-hero Doctor. The TARDIS is the Doctor's only equal, and this is why she is referred to indirectly as his constant companion or wife. The episode suggests that the key to creating a lasting, equal, and functional relationship is to create one with interdependency. As seen in previous *Doctor Who* serials, neither the TARDIS nor the Doctor can function completely without the other. It is this reliance that creates a working relationship between the TARDIS and the Doctor that all other companions do not quite manage. Due to the nature of their relationship, the TARDIS is the one companion that can remain with the Doctor.

In *Doctor Who*'s long history, the TARDIS has been changing steadily. When the third doctor called her "old girl" for the first time, it marked the beginning of a move away from just a set piece and a ship to a sentient being that takes an active role in the story. The development of just-ship TARDIS to sentient-being TARDIS only strengthens what Gaiman has done with the Doctor/TARDIS relationship in "The Doctor's Wife." The TARDIS has been given a traditional voice for the episode, allowing her to speak frankly with the Doctor and establish a way for the Doctor and TARDIS to communicate freely, even when she once again becomes voiceless. The episode constructs a relationship in which the TARDIS is a sexual being and an equal to the Doctor within their relationship, which is not something that can be stated by the Doctor's previous companions. Thus, she is the "one irreplaceable partner." In this way, Gaiman confronts and overturns several long-standing tropes that portray violent or disastrous results in response to an attempt to rewrite gender roles or attempts to act outside of socially acceptable behaviors. Perhaps the most compelling feature of "The Doctor's Wife" is not how Gaiman grapples and ultimately succeeds in rearranging these roles in science fiction and within the already established *Doctor Who* canon, but that he makes the changing of them look easy.

Works Cited

Attebery, Brian. *Decoding Gender in Science Fiction*. New York: Routledge, 2002. Print.
"Boomtown." *Doctor Who*. BBC One. BBC, London. 4 June 2005.
de Beauvoir, Simone. "The Second Sex." *Feminist Literary Theory and Criticism: A Norton*

Reader. Eds. Sandra M. Gilbert and Susan Gubar. New York: W. W. Norton, 2007: 291–323. Print.

"Doomsday." *Doctor Who*. BBC One. BBC, London. 8 July 2006.

"The Eleventh Hour." *Doctor Who*. BBC One. BBC, London. 3 April 2010.

"The Family of Blood." *Doctor Who*. BBC One. BBC, London. 2 June 2007.

Felman, Shoshana. "Women and Madness." *Feminisms: an Anthology of Literary Theory and Criticism*. Eds. Robyn R. Warhol and Diane Price Herndl. New Brunswick: Rutgers University Press, 1997: 7–20. Print.

"The Five Doctors." *Doctor Who*. BBC One. BBC, London. 23 November 1983.

"Forest of the Dead." *Doctor Who*. BBC One. BBC, London. 7 June 2008.

Fuller, Gavin. "Doctor Who, episode 4: The Doctor's Wife review." *The Telegraph*. 14 May 2011. Web. 10 August 2011.

Gaiman, Neil, wri. "The Doctor's Wife." *Doctor Who*. BBC One. BBC, London. 14 May 2011.

Hollinger, Veronica. "Feminist Theory and Science Fiction." *The Cambridge Companion to Science Fiction*. 125–136. Print.

_____. "Rereading Queerly: Science Fiction, Feminism, and the Defamiliarization of Gender." *reload: rethinking women + cyberculture*. Eds. Mary Flanagan and Austin Booth. Cambridge: The MIT Press, 2002. 301–320. Print.

"Image of the Fendahl." *Doctor Who*. BBC One. BBC, London. 29 October-19 November 1977.

"The Impossible Planet." *Doctor Who*. BBC One. BBC, London. 3 June 2006.

"Journey's End." *Doctor Who*. BBC One. BBC, London. 5 July 2008.

Larbalestier, Justine. *The Battle of the Sexes in Science Fiction*. Middleton, CT: Wesleyan University Press, 2002. Print.

"The Last of the Time Lords." *Doctor Who*. BBC One. BBC, London. 30 June 2007.

Le Guin, Ursula K. *The Left Hand of Darkness*. New York: Ace, 2000. Print.

"The Parting of the Ways." *Doctor Who*. BBC One. BBC, London. 18 June 2005.

Risley, Matt. "Doctor Who: 'The Doctor's Wife' Review." *IGN.com*. 14 May 2011. Web. 10 August 2011.

Russ, Joanna. "The Image of Women in Science Fiction." *Images of Women in Fiction: Feminist Perspectives*. Ed. Susan Koppelman Cornillon. Bowling Green, OH: Bowling Green University Popular Press, 1972. Print.

"The Time Meddler." *Doctor Who*. BBC One. BBC, London. 3–24 July 1965.

"The Time Monster." *Doctor Who*. BBC One. BBC, London. 20 May-24 June 1972.

"The Time Warrior." *Doctor Who*. BBC One. BBC, London. 15 December 1973–5 January 1974.

Tiptree, James. *Her Smoke Rose Up Forever*. San Francisco: Tachyon, 2004. Print.

"An Unearthly Child." *Doctor Who*. BBC One. BBC, London. 23 November-14 December 1963.

"The Wedding of River Song." *Doctor Who*. BBC One. BBC, London. 1 October 2011.

Unmasking M(other)hood

Third-Wave Mothering in Gaiman's Coraline *and* MirrorMask

BY DANIELLE RUSSELL

> "I swear it," said the other mother. "I swear it on my own mother's grave."
> "Does she have a grave?" asked Coraline.
> "Oh yes," said the other mother. "I put her in there myself. And when I found her trying to crawl out, I put her back."
>
> —*Coraline*, p. 93

Delightfully dark humor aside, the exchange between the other mother and the eponymous heroine of Neil Gaiman's *Coraline* is quite revealing: Coraline's instincts are sharp, and her adversary's desire for control knows no boundaries. Issues of identity, particularly for female characters, often hinge on the experiences of mothering. The mother-daughter motif, so common in Western literature, appears in an extreme form in *Coraline*. The mother as psychological adversary, the obstacle to the daughter's maturation, becomes a literal and potentially lethal adversary. The need to break from the mother seems clear-cut in this narrative. The complication, however, is that Coraline is not battling her real mother; her opponent is the other mother, the dominant force in an alternative world Coraline discovers connected to her home. The other world parallels Coraline's life with eerie differences; it is both familiar and disturbing. On the surface, it offers everything that Coraline desires: "wonderful" food, a "more interesting" bedroom, and very attentive parents who will "just wait here for you to come back" (28, 30, and 33). Coraline is the center of this world. Indeed, it was created for her. It appears to be a case of wish fulfillment, the common childhood desire to find a "better" family. Of course, that wish is tinged with the equally common childhood fear that your parents may have the same desire. In Other Mother's world, Coraline will discover, children are also replaceable.

A similar pattern emerges in Gaiman's film (and adapted graphic novella),

MirrorMask, as the central figure Helena Campbell also enters an alternative realm and encounters a "new" mother. The texts differ in that Helena is the writer and illustrator of what she deems her "weird dream" but insists "this isn't a made-up story" (1). *Coraline* is told from the titular character's perspective, but not by her, and there is no indication that it is a dream. Like Coraline, Helena discovers the dangers of the possessive love of a maternal figure. In the other realm, Helena will have two alternative mothers: the queen of the "city of light" and the queen of the "land of shadows" (22). As their locations suggest, the White Queen will be a positive force (albeit a largely passive one since she is suffering from a curse Helena must break) while the Dark Queen will be a source of suffering and the ostensible antagonist of the adventure. The Dark Queen and other mother pursue their obsessive desires for a daughter with no concern for the damage they are inflicting. *MirrorMask* introduces an additional destructive force: unlike Coraline, Helena encounters another daughter in the alternate world. She sees a "wanted poster with my face on it. It was me, but it wasn't me" (38). This "other Helena" steps into Helena's life in order to escape her own (47). The double wreaks havoc in Helena's life — "she wasn't wearing the kind of clothes I'd wear. And screaming at my dad" and kissing a "dodgy" boy — but she also recognizes that "there was some level on which she was me" (35, 43, and 56). Helena's quest is more complex than Coraline's, in part, because she is older (although Coraline's age is not stated), but also because her conflict with her real mother is more intensive. The narrative opens with her Mum's illness following a heated argument in which her Mum says, "You'll be the death of me" and Helena responds, "I wish I was" (3). It is one of a series of arguments notes Helena, "I don't know what it is with me and Mum. We never mean to fight, but suddenly we're yelling at each other and it's all stupid" (3). The interaction takes a new significance when Joanne Campbell is hospitalized. Helena clearly connects the two events and spends the next nine days saying sorry "for what I said" (7). Guilt is a strong factor in Helena's quest.

Mother/daughter relationships, such as those explored in *Coraline* and *MirrorMask,* are central to many feminist debates. The excerpt which opens this essay can be read as emblematic of the tensions between second and third wave feminist theories. While it may seem to be an odd shift, *Coraline* and *MirrorMask* do embody the struggle to defuse the "trap" of motherhood (common in the second wave's fear of the institution of motherhood and in its tendency to "bury" first wave feminist theories) and instead embrace the potentially empowering aspects of motherhood. The two texts are clearly matrilineal narratives pitting "smother mothers," who would keep their daughters in perpetual childhood, against "genuine" mothers, who would empower them to stand on their own. Coraline Jones and Helena Campbell have mothers who defy traditional expectations. Both of Coraline's parents work at home and share household duties; their relationship seems to be an egalitarian one. Joanne Campbell is also a career woman; Helena describes her as "the brains behind the outfit" (2). Neither mother is described as particularly skilled in domestic affairs, nor are they solely focused on their daughters' needs. Significantly, each woman has a life that extends beyond her role as mother. As Andrea O'Reilly asserts, "only an empowered mother can empower children" (*Mother Outlaws* 13). And yet, at crucial points in the narratives, it is precisely the words of their "genuine" mothers which will enable Coraline and Helena to overcome their "smothering" adversaries. In the case of Coraline, she will hear her mother's voice during her crisis. Helena will be guided by the final page in the *Really Useful Book*: "REMEMBER WHAT YOUR MOTHER TOLD YOU" (58).

In adopting, or more accurately adapting, the genre of the domestic story, Gaiman engages in an examination of gender roles. In foregrounding the mother-daughter dynamic, however, Gaiman's work can be read as explicitly engaging in a debate that continues to challenge feminist theorists: what is the relationship between feminism and motherhood? At first glance, the domestic story may seem like a strange vehicle for a critique of the family—after all, the family is at the heart of the story—but perhaps because of that narrow focus it can afford considerable scope for scrutiny, particularly in the hands of master storytellers like Gaiman. Whether labeled the family story (in Great Britain) or domestic fiction (in North America), these texts have the potential to be very claustrophobic. "Domestic fictions," assert the editors of *The Norton Anthology of Children's Literature*, "are 'inside' stories. Unlike narratives of adventure, fantasy, and school life, in which the child character's maturation often occurs outside the home and away from the familiar, in domestic fiction the home and family remain central to the narrative" (Zipes et al. 2067). In terms of geography *and* ideology there is generally little room for the (typically female) characters to negotiate. Gaiman expands the boundaries of the domestic story by blending it with fantasy, but the home remains the pivotal setting in both *Coraline* and *MirrorMask*. Coraline moves between her actual home, the "other" home, and the grounds around each dwelling. Helena, however, seems to leave her home for a much wider world, but it is a forced relocation to a rapidly shrinking space, and she discovers she must return home to re-establish order.

Coraline's efforts to rescue her parents from her Other Mother is constructed more as an act of bravery than one induced by guilt. It is a continuation of her interest in exploration. Coraline's self-proclaimed role is that of an intrepid explorer. In the first twelve pages alone, "explore/d" is used six times and "exploring" four. A thirst for knowledge lies at the heart of any exploration; Coraline examines her world in order to make sense of it. It is a process supported by her real mother. Mrs. Jones does not obstruct Coraline's activities, but she does place boundaries on them: be home for meals, dress appropriately. She strikes a balance between independence and familial expectations. Coraline's taste of absolute freedom — the initial absence of her parents before she realizes they have been kidnapped — is flavored with chocolate cake and limeade, but it quickly turns sour, leaving her crying herself to sleep in her parents' bed (51, 52). What she needs is freedom with the reassurance that her family is nearby — a kind of contained freedom.

Helena Campbell is also an explorer, but her exploration is through drawing. She has the privacy and creative freedom she needs in the form of a camper. It "wasn't big but it was mine. It had my drawings all over the walls. I love drawing places, imaginary cities with bits of all the towns the circus goes through put in them" (2). Helena's explorations mingle imaginary and real world geographies; her drawings counter the seemingly claustrophobic world of the circus. For each girl, exploration is a means of expanding her own life, a vehicle for self-discovery. The real mothers in the stories offer their daughters more complex lives than those imposed by the Dark Queen and the other mother. The latter pair demands passivity, absolute obedience, mute acceptance, and good manners. The real mothers encourage the girls to use their powers of reasoning, to take initiative, to exert their own agency. They seek to empower their daughters. Female agency is not the problem in *Coraline* or *MirrorMask*. The real problem is the limited and limiting vision of motherhood the other mother and Dark Queen represent and, by extension, the limited and limiting vision of femininity they impose on their "daughters."

Another key aspect of the domestic story that Gaiman retains, but modifies, is the didactic impulse behind many of the original tales. While it is no longer necessary to be overtly didactic, "domestic fiction is especially concerned with communicating life lessons that the child character learns from, or with the assistance of, family members — lessons that will help him or her become a happy and well-adjusted person" (Zipes et al. 2068). Coraline and Helena undergo personal growth and attain a greater understanding of the world around them. The key guides for each girl are mothers — real and fantastic — and — aside from the otherworldly element — Gaiman sticks with tradition, for the "center of the domestic world was acknowledged as female" (Zipes et al. 2070). The twist, however — and it is a big one — is that the traditionally domestic female is not the role model either girl embraces. Both Coraline and Helena refuse to play "Happy Families" (*Coraline* 77), opting instead to remain in their own "real, wonderful, maddening, infuriating, glorious" families with all their "ups and downs" (*Coraline* 134, *MirrorMask* 76).

Gaiman has identified the impetus for Coraline as being his then four-year-old daughter's imaginative narratives. She would "dictate nightmarish stories where her mother would be replaced by an evil witch and tied up in a basement" (Ouzounian E3). Unable to find similar stories for his daughter, Gaiman began writing *Coraline*. A feminist analysis of *Coraline* and *Mirror-Mask* invites the question: has Gaiman left the mother tied up — relegated to the periphery and ultimately powerless? Yes, argue the authors of "The Other Mother: Neil Gaiman's Postfeminist Fairytales": The "too-powerful (phallic) mother's dominance must be overthrown, and, as the happy resolution attests, it is only through a psychoanalytic journey that represses the fantasy of feminine power and agency that the 'normative' position for Gaiman's female protagonists are attained" (Parsons, Sawers, and McInally 371). Because the other mother and Dark Queen are defeated at the end of the narrative — or at least removed as immediate threats — they conclude feminine power is denied leading to the assertion that "Gaiman's recipes for postfeminist power appear as unwholesome as frozen pizza in the final feminist analysis of mothers" (Parsons, Sawers, and McInally 387). A psychoanalytical reading of literature can be fraught with its own traps, as the trio recognizes in their conclusion: "our approach begs questions about how far any earlier or currently fashionable brands of feminism have been able to raise themselves from Freud's couch" (387). Leaving aside the liability/viability of such a reading, I would offer an alternative to their use of "postfeminism" as a theoretical framework and, in the process, bring the mother up from the "basement" where she has been relegated. In point of fact, "feminine power" is not denied in *Coraline* or *MirrorMask*: the power of the real mothers may be muted in comparison with the over-the-top actions of their fantastic counterparts, but it is not negated. The assertion that "in both narratives the girls need to destroy the power of the malevolent mother whose agenda is to encase daughters in an eternal childhood bond that, these stories tell readers, is destructive and dangerous" overlooks the fact that there are examples of benevolent mothering in both narratives (Parsons, Sawers, and McInally 375). The danger lies not in the bond, but in the eternal childhood. Feminine power and agency can be found in both the mothers and the daughters through their connection, not the separation that Freud and subsequent psychoanalytical theorists insist must occur.

In 1976, Adrienne Rich issued a challenge to redefine motherhood in *Of Woman Born: Motherhood as Experience and Institution*; thirty-six years later that definition is still a work in progress. Rich identified "two meanings of motherhood, one superimposed on the other: the potential relationship of any woman to her powers of reproduction and to children; and the institution, which aims at ensuring that that potential — and all women — shall remain under male control" (13). Patriarchy distorts the experience of mothering because it imposes a rigid definition of motherhood, Rich argues. She does not, however, limit her criticism to the proponents of patriarchy, insisting feminists have also been culpable in the denigration of motherhood. "Sisterhood" came at the expense of motherhood insists Rich, "before sisterhood, there was the knowledge — transitory, fragmented, perhaps, but original and crucial — of motherhood-and-daughterhood" (225). For many second-wave feminists of the 1960s and 1970s, the mother (if not their own mothers) became the very symbol of what they were struggling against. Marianne Hirsch asserts that in "the 1970s, the prototypical feminist voice was, to a large degree, the voice of the daughter attempting to separate from an overly connected or rejecting mother, in order to bond with her sisters in a relationship of mutual nurturance and support among women" (164).[1]

Eager to escape the limited lives of their mothers or viewing them simply as agents of patriarchy (and therefore the "enemy") to be evaded, many feminists failed to recognize the importance of mothering. Indeed, Astrid Henry observes that many second-wave critics viewed the movement as "a motherless one," and found "something politically empowering about psychological matricide" (9). It is an exercise in self-delusion on several levels: this "motherless" movement was, as Nadine Muller points out, "built on the substantial political achievements of its forerunners, the first wave feminists and suffragettes" (125). Further, the belief that "psychological matricide" is empowering is a disturbing one; the "act" creates a rupture — a break in one's lineage. Discontinuity distorts: identity built on self-delusion is not empowering.

And yet, for much of the twentieth- and on into the twenty-first- century, the assertion that the daughter must break free of the mother in order to achieve "healthy" maturity has held considerable sway.[2] Drawing on the work of Lacan and Kristeva, David Rudd contends that "in order for a person to take up their place in the world, distinct from the mother figure who once provided all and everything, the maternal must be set apart. In this process, the mother, associated with a time prior to the emergence of individuality, comes to represent a realm of non-being, of all that one is not" (166). Separation not only is crucial to individuation but it results in the inevitable negation of the mother. What could be more natural? A bond based upon mutual love and respect insists Rich: "the psychic interplay between mother and daughter can be destructive, but there is no reason why it is doomed to be" (245). The key is a "strong sense of *self*-nurture in the mother," Rich proposes (245). Rich writes against the patriarchal depiction of mother and daughter and invites other feminists to join in the process of reclaiming motherhood. To do so is, as Andrea O'Reilly (borrowing Toni Morrison's term) observes, to write against "the master narrative ... that this relationship, particularly in the daughter's adolescent years is one of antagonism and animosity" (*Redefining*

Motherhood 70). In this "patriarchal narrative of the mother-daughter relationship" the "daughter must distance and differentiate herself from the mother if she is to assume an autonomous identity as an adult" (70). Critiquing the patriarchal narrative is a vital step in heeding Rich's challenge for a new definition of motherhood. When analyzed from a feminist mothering perspective, *Coraline* and *MirrorMask* can be read as participating in this process.

The distinction Rich made between motherhood (as institution) and mothering (as practice), Andrea O'Reilly insists "was what enabled feminists to recognize that motherhood is not naturally, necessarily, or inevitably oppressive, a view held by many early second wave feminists" (*Mother Outlaws* 2). The potential for mothering, "freed from the institution of motherhood," to be "experienced as a site of empowerment, a location of social change," O'Reilly suggests is the key legacy of *Of Woman Born* (2). The difference in approach is signaled by the preference of mother*ing* with its emphasis on action to mother*hood*. This shift in the concept of mothering is increasingly important for a number of third wave feminists as they explore the possibilities of feminist mothering.[3]

What is feminist mothering? Despite entitling her book *Feminist Mothers*, Tuula Gordon concedes the difficulty of definition. She offers a tentative explanation that suggests feminist mothering is found in

> the way in which [mothers] challenge and criticise myths of motherhood; the way in which they consider it their right to work; the anti-sexist (and anti-racist) way in which they try to bring up their children; the way in which they expect the fathers of the children to participate in joint everyday lives; and the way in which many of them are politically active [149].

Slight modifications to Gordon's model are required to apply it to Gaiman's texts, but *Coraline* and *MirrorMask*, with their pairings of good/evil mothers, clearly "challenge and criticise myths of motherhood." Mrs. Jones and Joanne Campbell work without apology, encourage their daughters to be self-sufficient, and rely on the fathers' involvement in the family dynamic. To borrow Gordon's words, the characters "challenge traditional practices of gender socialization and perform anti-sexist child-rearing practices so as to raise empowered daughters." Gaiman creates examples of feminist mothering in both *Coraline* and *MirrorMask* but we need to look beyond the "false" mother in order to find it (11).

It is easy to recognize the flaws of the other mother and Dark Queen: focused on their own needs and desires they wield power with no concern for the impact of their actions on others. It is tempting to construe these characters as examples of feminine agency gone terribly wrong—the "too-powerful (phallic) mother" that Parsons, Sawers, and McInally identify (371). But a closer examination of the other mother and Dark Queen suggests that the problem is not power itself but its distortion; on several levels, the pair actually represent the ideal patriarchal model of motherhood. Fiona Joy Green offers the following definition of the ideal mother found in "mainstream media, advertising, and entertainment":

> She is a heterosexual woman who stays at home with her children while her husband ... works in the labor force to support them financially. Because of her "innate" ability to parent and her "unconditional love" for her husband and children, the idealized mother selflessly adopts their wants, needs, and happiness as her own [127].

Given that the Dark Queen has no mate and the other father is simply the other mother's tool, they clearly stray from the "ideal" family dynamic. Adding to the discrepancy is the fact that neither of these mothers puts the needs of the daughters before her own. The actions of the Dark Queen and other mother are driven by their own agendas. Nonetheless, I would argue that the core of the ideal — that a mother's love should be all encompassing, that the nurture and protection of the child is her primary mandate — *is* at the center of these two troubling characters. Gaiman's Dark Queen and other mother, in their own ways, love their "daughters." The problem is not the absence of maternal affection but the direction it takes.

Helena's first encounter with the Queen of the Darklands is anticlimactic to say the least. Transported by the Queen's guards in a net like "a web of darkness," Helena tumbles out onto the floor to find the Queen looking down from her throne (*MirrorMask* 47). Cue the dramatic dialogue! Instead, the Gaiman's Dark Queen states: "I don't know what kind of time you call this ... I've been worried sick about you" (48). An unexpected, but highly maternal, response; the kind any mother might make. An extraordinary situation is domesticated but what follows challenges that label. Helena "pleaded with her to let me go, and to stop her clouds and birds from hurting the world ... 'I'm not your daughter,' I told her. She looked me up and down, as if she was coming to a decision. 'You'll do,' was all she said" (48). The Queen has been destroying the world in her quest to recover her lost daughter. It is a willingness on her part to sacrifice everything in the name of maternal love. The quick shift from *the* daughter to *a* daughter suggests that even the child can be sacrificed in the Dark Queen's version of mother-love.

Unlike the Dark Queen, with her willingness to destroy the world in pursuit of her daughter, the other mother builds a world to lure Coraline. As the other father explains, she made "the house, the grounds, and the people in the house. She made it and she waited" (71).[4] In further contrast to the Dark Queen, the other mother does not have a "day" job; her entire being centers on her role as mother. She comes closer to the ideal by offering Coraline what she does not find at home: delicious food (29), a room that "was an

awful lot more interesting than her own bedroom" (30), and undivided attention (33). Coraline's "needs and happiness" seem to be fulfilled by these alternative parents — specifically the mother — in a way that her own parents do
not and indeed cannot. The other mother's domestic skills shine in this first
encounter. She is the epitome of the perfect homemaker. And yet, while Coraline is enticed by this other family, she is also cautious, rejecting the maternal
gesture of the other mother stroking her "hair with her long white fingers"
(44). As appealing as it is to be the center of attention — the center of the
other mother's world — Coraline opts for reality, unwittingly triggering a more
aggressive plan on the part of the other mother.

In her second encounter with the other mother, Coraline discovers she
is not the first child the other mother has pursued. Locked in the mirror until
she is "ready to be a loving daughter," Coraline meets three ghost children
who warn her that the other mother "stole our hearts, and she stole our souls,
and she took our lives away, and she left us here, and she forgot about us in
the dark" (79, 84). Much like the Dark Queen, the other mother has the
ability to shift her focus to a new child when the "old" one no longer fulfills
her needs; however, the other mother takes it a step further and feeds on the
children she professes to love. The concept of the child is more compelling
for these mothers than the reality of the individual child. This point is apparent when the models of behavior imposed by the Dark Queen and other
mother are considered. For Helena, "life as a princess was divided into periods:
I'd wake, I'd eat, I'd play with my toys, I'd study a large book called 17,011
Things a Princess Must Know ... I'd sleep" (53). It is a regimented routine
designed to create the perfect princess: compliant and well-mannered. The
other mother envisions a similarly structured day for Coraline: "this afternoon
we could do a little embroidery together, or some watercolor painting. Then
dinner, and then, if you have been good, you may play with the rats a little
before bed. And I shall read you a story and tuck you in, and kiss you good
night" (78). While Coraline is not being groomed to be royalty, she is being
shaped into a proper young lady who is also compliant and well-mannered.

As controlling as the pair are, their surrogate "daughters" concede that
they are also loving. Helena's new bedroom has "two eyeholes in it, so that
the Queen could watch ... from her throne room" (52). The surveillance by
the Queen is oddly reassuring: "I was pleased she watched me. It made me
feel loved" (52). The line between repression and reassurance is blurred for
Helena. Her parents' attention is also something Coraline craves but she too
discovers that it can be detrimental when taken to the extreme. The other
mother's "voice did not just come from her mouth. It came from the mist and
the fog, and the house, and the sky. She said, 'You know that I love you'"
(106). It is an all-encompassing love, a consuming kind of love — a point the

cat hints at earlier in the book. In response to Coraline's query "why does she want me?" he surmises "she wants something to love.... She might want something to eat as well" (65). And yet, Coraline cannot deny that it is love: "it was true: the other mother loved her. But she loved Coraline as a miser loves money or a dragon loves its gold ... she was a possession, nothing more" (106). The love that these would-be mothers offer is distorted and distorting. It can only be gratified if the daughter relinquishes any claim to autonomy or individuality. Helena drives home this point in her confrontation with the Dark Queen: "you have to let [your daughter] grow up" she asserts. The Dark Queen initially appears to understand: "You mean ... let her choose her own clothes. Her own food. Make her own mistakes. Love her, but don't try to possess her?"—but rejects the idea—"Absolutely out of the question" (66). Relinquishing control of the daughter is not an option that the Dark Queen or other mother is willing to consider. It is this need for absolute control, more so than the ability to spew out darkness or see through button eyes, which makes these characters so unnatural.

The task of deciphering what makes the "bad" mothers bad is quite straightforward but determining what makes the "good" mothers good is a little more challenging. Are Mrs. Jones and Joanne Campbell "good" in their own right or simply by default? Based upon traditional depictions of motherhood, neither woman fits the model of a "good" mother as it is summarized by Elizabeth Podnieks and Andrea O'Reilly: "writers draw on age-old dichotomies to position the mother who is seen to be selfless, sacrificial, and domestic as angel/Madonna ('good'), the mother who is judged to be selfish for seeking autonomy beyond her children as whore/Magdalene ('bad')" (4). Gaiman plays with this dichotomy and, in the process, challenges rather than reinforces it. In effect, he reverses the pattern Adrienne Rich identifies as confronting many young women who "split themselves between two mothers: one, usually the biological one, who represents the culture of domesticity, of male-centeredness, of conventional expectations and another, perhaps a woman artist or teacher, who becomes the countervailing future" (247). The other mother in this paradigm is the engaging and invigorating symbol of a more fulfilled life. Rather than a desire to escape the stifling domestic mother, Coraline (briefly) turns away from the "choice of a vigorous work life" Rich links with the countervailing figure (247). In contrast, both the princess and Helena strive to escape the control of the mother who refuses to allow them to grow up.

For Mrs. Jones and Joanne Campbell the independence of their respective daughters is desirable. As working mothers, they require a degree of self-sufficiency on the part of the girls; Coraline and Helena are encouraged to think and act for themselves at crucial points in the texts. In stark contrast to the other mother and the Dark Queen, the real mothers are relegated to the periphery for much of the narratives but their "presence" is highlighted in pivotal moments. Presented from the perspective of Coraline, her mother is perpetually distracted by her work and unable to comprehend her daughter's desires. The evidence used to indict Mrs. Jones: she fails to entertain a bored Coraline (6); she is distracted by her work, requiring Coraline to remind her to shop for school clothes (17); once on said shopping trip she ignores Coraline's request for "Day-glo green gloves" in favor of the school uniform (23–4); she fails to ensure there is food in the house (24); and, worst of all, she leaves Coraline to tend to her own cut knee (139). It is an open-and-shut case; verdict: Mrs. Jones is a neglectful (ergo, a bad) mother.

Joanne Campbell's "failings" as a mother are nowhere near as extensive: she argues with her daughter, falls ill, and does not reassure Helena who "wanted her to hug me tell me everything was okay and she'd be out of the hospital tomorrow" (7). The mother does not comfort her daughter because she cannot: it is the night before her surgery, Helena will learn. Her absence is not her fault, thought the trauma felt by Helena is nonetheless real, but Mrs. Jones's is by choice. She puts her work before her child. Beyond the knee-jerk reaction, however, Gaiman's depiction of motherhood is more complex; while her work is a key part of Mrs. Jones's character, she is nonetheless maternal. She offers suggestions for Coraline to occupy herself (6); she stops that (contentious) work in order to satisfy Coraline's curiosity about the door (8); she encourages Coraline's explorations but with boundaries (6, 13); and, in a moment of crisis, it is her voice that empowers Coraline (134). Clearly, Mrs. Jones is a non-traditional mother. She is not a domestic figure by any stretch of the imagination, but she is not a truly neglectful mother. Even in Coraline's eyes (or through, since Coraline's perspective dominates), her mother fulfills the expectations of a "good" mother: "Her mother made her come back inside for dinner and for lunch. And Coraline had to make sure she dressed up warm before she went out, for it was a very cold summer that year" (6). The note of complaint — "made," "had to" — is quite revealing. Coraline vacillates between chaffing under her mother's attention and craving more of it. This "ambivalence and anxiety ... existing between mothers and daughters," is fairly typical of matrilineal narratives contends Yi-Lin Yu, author of *Mother She Wrote: Matrilineal Narratives in Contemporary Women's Writing* (25).[5] In fact, it is the "working out of their conflict and dissension that reconnects mothers and daughters" (Yu 25). Gaiman opts for this realistic approach rather than an idealized vision of the mother-daughter relationship. He does, however, "remove" the mother from the picture for a considerable portion of each text.

Literary mothers are often the "casualties" of authors. The missing mother has become a common motif. Given the influences of Gothic and Romantic literature on Gaiman's works, Susan Peck Macdonald's assessment of the absence of mothers in early Victorian novels is applicable to both *MirrorMask* and *Coraline*. She contends that it derives "not from the impotence or unimportance of mothers but from the almost excessive power of motherhood; the good, supportive mother is potentially so powerful a figure as to prevent her daughter's trials from occurring, to shield her form the process of maturation and thus to disrupt the focus and equilibrium of the novel" (58). On a practical level, the plot requires the absence of the "good" mother — too much support and nurturing leaves little room for the character of the daughter to develop or dramatic incidents to unfold. Macdonald concludes, "if she is dead or absent, the good mother can remain ideal without her presence disrupting or preventing the necessary drama of the novel" (58–59). Macdonald does not define this ideal, but she does use the terms "strong" and "supportive" several times. Based upon these criteria, both Joanne Campbell and Mrs. Jones can be read as the "good" mother. The moments when they "re-enter" the narratives are highly significant to their daughters' outcomes.

The real/false mother split is more complicated in *MirrorMask* since the real (ill) mother has a representative figure — the sleeping White Queen — not just a counterpart in the dream world. Despite her illness/state of unconsciousness, Joanne/the White Queen remains a crucial force in Helena's quest. Her physical absence is overcome through symbolism, an encounter in the dream world, and some pragmatic advice recollected in a threatening situation. The Prime Minister is unimpressed by Helena's declaration that she will wake the White Queen. He explains that "finding the Charm (whatever that was) was, as propositions go, completely, utterly, unarguably, quintessentially hopeless" (22). It is discouraging response to put it mildly. When he ends his speech, however, the "white rosebud on the Queen's chest blossomed into a perfect white rose" causing him to concede, "maybe it's not quintessentially hopeless" (23). Unable to speak, the maternal figure encourages Helena through this sign of hope. She will continue to do so as Helena moves through the dreamscape. At one point, the link with Helena's real mother becomes more explicit. The White Queen and her mother merge in Helena's dream: "My mum said, 'Honestly love. What have you lost now?' She didn't look like my mum. She looked more like the White Queen" (44). The advice she offers is clearly in Joanne's practical voice: "It's probably staring you in the face" (44). Vague and yet useful, the words are a catalyst for a more focused search but the wayward princess reaches it first, extending the quest. Once again, Helena must draw upon her mother's "Two Rules for Finding Things That You've Lost" and, in so doing, does indeed find the MirrorMask staring her right in the face (5). Lest we miss the significance of the mother's input, the final page in the *Really Useful Book* insists "REMEMBER WHAT YOUR MOTHER TOLD YOU" (58). The voice of the (real, authentic, feminist) mother is privileged in *MirrorMask*.

Coraline also draws strength from her mother's words. In her desperate bid to close the door between the two worlds, Coraline is aided by the "other people in the corridor — three children, and two adults" (133). With the touch of the ghosts "suddenly she felt strong" but one voice in particular galvanizes her: "a voice that sounded like her mother's — her own mother, her real, wonderful, maddening, infuriating, glorious mother — just said, 'Well done, Coraline,' and that was enough" (134). A simple phrase and yet it is precisely what Coraline needs to hear; she continues to battle and ultimately seals the barrier. Gaiman does not end the book with this victory, requiring Coraline to once again defeat the other mother in a continuation of the maturation begun in the other world. In order to succeed, Coraline must be meticulous in her planning and brave in the execution — traits her real mother models.[6] The "protective coloration" of a tea party with her dolls is a subversive use of the patriarchal model of girlhood the other mother sought to impose (153). This time it is Coraline who fabricates a scene to lure the other mother (or at least her hand — the part that made it through the door between the worlds). Parsons, Sawers, and McInally read the scene in a negative light. They argue that "all of the potential advances ... made by Coraline's real mother seem lost in this climactic moment" (376). Acknowledging that it is a ruse, they still contend that it is "her ability to perform appropriate femininity that saves the day for Coraline" (376). Placing the key over the disguised well is an ingenious move on Coraline's part. The trap is shaped by the predator she wishes to capture. It is a thoughtful performance with one purpose in mind. If Coraline were sincerely enacting "appropriate femininity" she would not be single handily taking on her adversary — even if it is a single hand.

The Dark Queen and other mother are extreme examples of what Adrienne Rich labels "the old, institutionalized, sacrificial, 'mother-love'" (246). Each character puts the daughter before everything else; everything else, that is, except motherhood. In their willingness to sacrifice the individual child in support of the institution of motherhood the Dark Queen and other mother personify sacrificial motherhood gone grotesquely awry. Rich, however, argues it always goes awry and needs to be countered with "courageous mothering" (246). "The most notable fact that culture imprints on women," Rich proposes, "is the sense of our limits" (246). As a result, "the most important thing one woman can do for another is to illuminate and expand her sense of actual possibilities" (246). The example of the mother — the way in which she expands her own life — is a key factor in this process. Empowered children come from empowered mothers insists Andrea O'Reilly (*Mother Outlaws* 13).

Coraline and *MirrorMask* should be read as part of an invigorating debate about mothering and motherhood in the twenty-first century. The complexity of motherhood can only be recognized through "an excavation of the truths of motherhood disguised and distorted beneath the mask," insist Podnieks and O'Reilly (3). Susan Maushaurt calls it an unmasking of motherhood. She advocates an open and honest discussion of motherhood freed from its unattainable ideal. *Coraline* and *MirrorMask* may seem to be unlikely candidates for re-theorizing motherhood, but as Marianne Hirsch points out, fiction is the "optimal genre in which to study the interplay between hegemonic and dissenting voices" (9). Gaiman's voice is powerful in popular culture; his interrogation of motherhood reveals the hopes and fears lurking beneath the surface. There is a danger of the Dark Queen and other mother overshadowing their real world counterparts, but a closer analysis of the texts reveals that Gaiman is engaged in something more subtle than merely reproducing the motif of the good versus bad mother. In his hands, the concept of a "good" mother becomes more complex.

Gaiman's work does not ignore the tension between mothers and daughters — indeed the plots hinge on it — but he does distinguish between the mother who approaches her daughter as a possession and the approachable mother who encourages her daughter's self-possession. The presence of the demonic mother complicates any reading of the feminist aspects of *Coraline* and *MirrorMask* but does not negate them. The encounters with the various mothers answer the "prayer for a blueberry girl" Gaiman offers in another of his works:

> Help her to help
> herself,
> help her to
> stand,
> help her
> to lose
> and
> to find [Gaiman, *Blueberry Girl* 2, 19].

NOTES

1. With the growing awareness that race, class, and sexuality (among other factors) complicate any feminist theory, "sisterhood" has become a "problematic concept for third-wave feminism within their own generation ... as well as across feminist generations" observes Nadine Muller (126).

2. Discussion of the merits of psychoanalytical theories falls outside the boundaries of my paper.

3. Muller provides a useful explanation of third wave feminism: it "can be said to consist of those feminist voices emerging towards the latter half of the 1990s which insist upon their dependency on, as well as their need to move away from, the feminist politics of the

1960s and 1970s. Third wave feminism also opposes the 1980s backlash against feminism and the second wave's focus on white, middle-class, heterosexual women, emphasizing the necessary co-existence of a multiplicity of feminisms and female experiences" (131–2).

4. The cat will cast doubt as to the origins of the other world — "made it, found it — what's the difference?" (Gaiman, *Coraline* 75) — but it is clear that the other mother controls it.

5. A matrilineal narrative, Tess Cosslett explains, "either tells the stories of several generations of women ... or ... shows how the identity of a central character is crucially formed by her female ancestors" (7). The second part of the definition is applicable to *Coraline* and *MirrorMask* in that both central characters look to their mothers to find their own strengths.

6. At this point, Coraline draws courage from her father's song; mothers are clearly privileged in the two texts but the fathers are emotional anchors for Coraline and Helena, albeit from the periphery.

WORKS CITED

Abbey, Sharon, and Andrea O'Reilly. Introduction. *Redefining Motherhood: Changing Identities and Patterns*. Toronto: Second-Story Press, 1998. 13–26. Print.

Cosslett, Tess. "Feminism, Matrilinealism, and the 'House of Women' in Contemporary Women's Fiction." *Journal of Gender Studies* 5.1 (1996): 7–17. Print.

Gaiman, Neil. *Blueberry Girl*. New York: HarperCollins, 2009. Print.

_____. *Coraline*. New York: HarperCollins, 2002. Print.

_____. *MirrorMask*. New York: HarperCollins, 2005. Print.

Gooding, Richard. "'Something Very Old and Very Slow': *Coraline*, Uncanniness, and Narrative." *Children's Literature Association* 33.4 (2008): 390–407. Web. 11 Feb. 2011.

Gordon, Tuula. *Feminist Mothers*. New York: New York University Press, 1990. Print.

Green, Fiona Joy. "Feminist Mothers: Successfully Negotiating the Tension between Motherhood as 'Institution' and 'Experience.'" O'Reilly, *From Motherhood to Mothering* 125–136.

Henry, Astrid. *Not My Mother's Sister: Generational Conflict and Third-Wave Feminism*. Bloomington: Indiana University Press, 2004. Print.

Hirsch, Marianne. *The Mother/Daughter Plot: Narrative, Psychoanalysis, Feminism*. Bloomington: Indiana University Press, 1989. Print.

Jeremiah, Emily. "Murderous Mothers: Adrienne Rich's *Of Woman Born* and Toni Morrison's *Beloved*." O'Reilly, *From Motherhood to Mothering* 59–71.

Macdonald, Susan Peck. "Jane Austen and the Tradition of the Absent Mother." *The Lost Tradition: Mothers and Daughters in Literature*. Eds. Cathy N. Davidson and E. M. Broner. New York: Frederick Ungar, 1980. 58–69. Print.

Mack-Canty, Colleen, and Sue Marie Wright. "Feminist Family Values: Parenting in Third Wave Feminism and Empowering All Family Members." O'Reilly, *Feminist Mothering* 143–159.

Maushart, Susan. *The Mask of Motherhood: How Becoming a Mother Changes Our Lives and Why We Never Talk About It*. New York: Penguin, 1999. Print.

Muller, Nadine. "Not My Mother's Daughter: Matrilinealism, Third-wave Feminism and Neo-Victorian Fiction." *Neo-Victorian Studies* 2:2 (Winter 2009/2010): 109–136. Web. 11 Feb. 2011.

Parsons, Elizabeth, Naarah Sawers, and Kate McInally. "The Other Mother: Neil Gaiman's Postfeminist Fairytales." *Children's Literature Association* 2009: 371–389. Web. 11 Feb. 2011

Podnieks, Elizabeth, and Andrea O'Reilly, eds. "Introduction: Maternal Literatures in Text and tradition: Daughter-Centric, Matrilienal, and Matrifocal Perspectives." *Textual Mothers/Maternal Texts: Motherhood in Contemporary Women's Literatures*. Waterloo, Ontario: Wilfrid Laurier University Press, 2010. 1–27. Print.

O'Reilly, Andrea. "Across the Divide: Contemporary Anglo-American Feminist Theory on the Mother-Daughter Relationship." *Redefining Motherhood*. 69–91.

_____, ed. Introduction. *Feminist Mothering*. Albany: State University of New York Press, 2008. 1–22. Print.

_____, ed. Introduction. *Mother Outlaws: Theories and Practices of Empowered Mothering*. Toronto: Women's Press, 2004. 1–28. Print.

_____, ed. *From Motherhood to Mothering: The Legacy of Adrienne Rich's of Woman Born*. Albany: State of New York Press, 2004. Print.

Ouzounian, Richard. "Close-Up Neil Gaiman: Author returns to 'first girlfriend.'" *Toronto Star*, Saturday, February 7, 2009: E3. Print.

Rich, Adrienne. *Of Woman Born: Motherhood as Experience and Institution*. New York: W. W. Norton, 1976. Print.

Rudd, David. "An Eye for an I: Neil Gaiman's *Coraline* and Questions of Identity." *Children's Literature in Education* 39 (2008): 159–168. Web. 11 Feb. 2011.

Yu, Yi-Lin. *Mother She Wrote: Matrilineal Narratives in Contemporary Women's Writing*. New York: Peter Long, 2005. Print.

Zipes, Jack, Lissa Paul, Lynne Vallone, Peter Hunt, and Gillian Avery, eds. "Essential Elements of Domestic Fiction." *The Norton Anthology of Children's Literature: The Traditions in English*. New York: W. W. Norton, 2005. 2067–2070. Print.

The Fairest of All

Snow White and Gendered Power in "Snow, Glass, Apples"

BY ELIZABETH LAW

"Snow White," as with all folktales and fairy tales, exists in multiple ren-
derings. The tale "Schneewittchen" (Little Snow White) as recorded by the
Brothers Grimm is one among many versions of the tale Jacob and Wilhelm
Grimm encountered as they compiled *Nursery and Household Tales*. In modern
American society however, the Disney film version *Snow White and the Seven
Dwarfs* is the best-known iteration. In the hands of Neil Gaiman, the tale of
"Snow White" becomes "Snow, Glass, Apples." Narrated from the perspective
of the "evil queen," Gaiman's tale interrogates the standard of beauty that
would elevate the deathly pallor of "skin as white as snow," questions the
motives of a prince who is attracted to an unconscious girl in a glass coffin,
and demonstrates how a society driven by fear damns itself when it chooses
a scapegoat over the truth.

The realm of fairy tales, like that of psychoanalysis, is one of symbols.
In the words of Bruno Bettelheim, "fairy stories teach by indirection" (210).
While this may very well be true, what is being taught (however indirectly)
by a fairy tale is not a single, unchanging lesson. Whether "Cinderella" is an
inspiring tale about a young girl who transcends the social sphere to which
she was born or an insipid fable that instructs young girls to wait for their
fairy godmother to improve their lives depends on who is relaying the tale.
The stories we tell end up telling us, for "each age creates its own folklore
through rereadings as well as retellings" (Tatar, *Off with Their Heads* 230). It
is in the realm of fiction, especially folk and fairy tale fiction, that we explore
the dark corners and get lost in the deep forests. Equally important, it is
through fairy tales and their revisions that we are able to see the ways in which
our "truths" change and shift. Fairy tales force us to question our assumptions
and presumptions. Beggar women may be witches or princesses in disguise.

Beasts may be flesh-eating ogres or enchanted princes. One's station in life is never fixed, and the moment you believe you know the truth and operate under that assumption, you will be proven wrong.

Fairy tales remind us, time and again, that few things are as dangerous as certainty. The moment we are sure of something, we close our eyes to other possibilities. We convince ourselves that there is nothing in that dark corner; it's just a shadow–but even shadows shift. "Snow, Glass, Apples" is an exploration of these shadows. Following the tenets of the fairy tale genre, Gaiman's rearticulation reveals that not all princesses are beautiful virgins, not all stepmothers are wicked, and not all princes are charming and handsome. Instead, Gaiman illuminates the valorization of dehumanized women and the gendered nature of power in "Schneewittchen" and Disney's *Snow White*. In place of Snow White's happily ever after, we are left with a frigid vampiric bride, a controlling necrophiliac prince, and a wise woman roasted for dinner.

"Snow White," perhaps more than any other of the Grimms' Tales, has been read as exhibiting anxiety of female virginity (Bettelheim 201). Gaiman's tale interrogates the patriarchal ideal of virginity as presented in Snow White. This virginity, epitomized by an unconscious preteen encased in a glass coffin with "skin as white as snow," is revealed to be a complete absence of passion: not purity but frigidity. Snow White's beauty is tied directly to the contrast of her red, white, and black features, but nearly all written versions of the tale use the title "Snow White" (Bettelheim 199–200). The title and the heroine's name insist that white is the dominant color and the heroine's defining trait. Though her hair is black and her lips are red, it is the paleness of her complexion that is prized above all other features. Her skin presumably reflects her soul, pure and untainted as freshly fallen snow. If, as Bettelheim claims, the "problems the story sets out to solve" relate to "sexual innocence, whiteness, ... [as] contrasted with sexual desire, symbolized by the red blood," then concomitant with the exaltation of Snow White's pale skin over her red lips and black locks, is the praise of sexual innocence over sexual desire in young girls and women (Bettelheim 201).

The words "Snow White" evoke not only unblemished purity but also, as Maria Tatar points out in her annotations to the Grimms' version, "cold and remoteness, along with the notion of the lifeless and inert" (Grimm and Grimm 240). Where Disney and the Brothers Grimm draw attention to Snow White's chastity through their titles, Gaiman's title omits "white" and its associations of innocence. In its place, suggestions of cool glass or the glassy appearance of ice reinforce the connotations of snow as frozen and bitter. Additionally, in Gaiman's title, the whiteness of snow cannot be evoked without also bringing to mind the redness of apples. Gaiman further removes these associations by refusing the moniker "Snow White" for the princess.

She is never named, but referred to simply as the princess, child, and more ominously, merely "she" or "her." Gaiman's use of the pronoun and refusal to name the child, or even identify "what manner of thing she is" ties the female pronoun to an unnamed, unknowable darkness. "She" is some "thing" both unnatural and terrifying.

In both "Schneewittchen" and Disney's *Snow White*, the queen and Snow White are constrained neatly within the virgin/whore dichotomy, that ubiquitous trope found time and again in popular and religious culture and even the American legal system (Fourie 324, Christ 90, Kaye 147). In this over-simplistic view of femininity, female characters are either entirely moral (virgin) or entirely immoral (whore). Neither Snow White nor the queen is restrained to these roles in "Snow, Glass, Apples." Gaiman rejects Snow White, the virginal heroine and replaces her with a vampiric child villainess. The queen, on the other hand, provides an image of companionate marriage. She is strength without dominance, power without the repression of the feminine.

It's important to note that fairy tales generally do not engage in complex character development. The female characters tend to either be helpless princesses and village girls in need of rescue or witches and wicked stepmothers. Their male counterparts are not exactly multifaceted either. Male protagonists tend to be unnamed and are "defined by their parentage (Miller's son), their station in life (the prince), by their relationship to their siblings (the youngest brother), by their level of intelligence (the simpleton), or by physical deformities (Thumbling)" (Tatar, *Hard Facts* 85). Fairy-tale heroes may be clever or stupid but they inevitably succeed by demonstrating compassion and humility (Tatar, *Hard Facts* 89). Fairy-tale heroines must also be humble, but where the heroes demonstrate this through an act of kindness (usually to an animal) the heroines "undergo a process of humiliation and defeat that ends with a rapid rise in social status through marriage but that also signals a loss of pride and abdication of power" (Tatar, *Hard Facts* 94). Even if a fairy-tale heroine is "as good as she is beautiful," she must prove herself through a demeaning ordeal that often involves domestic labor (Tatar, *Hard Facts* 87). Only upon the completion of these tasks is she rescued and given the reward that awaits all good virgins: marriage.

The whore, on the other hand, is "full of artful tricks strung like beads by the hundred on every hair of her head: fraud is her mother, lying her nurse, flattery her tutor, dissimulation her councilor & deceit her companion, so that she twists and turns man to her whim" (Basile, qtd in Tatar, *Off with Their Heads* 112). Gaiman's princess is the duplicitous woman that Basile describes in such florid detail. What Basile misses and Gaiman makes evident is that for a woman to be viewed as the ideal, she must engage in this duplicity and deceit.

There are moments in "Snow, Glass, Apples" when the princess does appear to be the archetypal whore. While in the forest, the twelve-year-old princess approaches the fire of a monk who is traveling through the woods. The monk beckons to her and throws a penny her way. She catches it and he "pull[s] at the rope around his waist," until his robe falls open (Gaiman 332). In the guise of a prostitute, she sinks "her teeth deep into his breast" to feed on him and "a thin blackish liquid began to dribble from between her legs" (Gaiman 332).

Though the princess accepts money from the monk in the forest in exchange for a sexual act, her role as prostitute is as false as her physical appearance of innocence. In a phallocentric economy, the whore exists to be desired and to create desire, but without desire of her own. The princess reveals what patriarchy fears: female desire exists and is not phallocentric; it exceeds male desire. The princess plays at the role of prostitute to entrap the monk, just as she played at the role of the innocent child to overcome the queen in her bedchamber. She steals the monk's life, his strength, for her own survival. She engages in sexual acts for her own end, neither for male pleasure nor for procreation. As she drinks the monk's blood, the patriarchal anxieties of the "the dark continent of woman's sexuality" drip from her abyss (Freud 212).

Gaiman deconstructs the virgin/whore dichotomy through this revelation that the virgin is a whore. The princess exposes that patriarchy does not valorize physical or moral purity, but cold, lifeless chastity. In order to be the "fairest one of all," one is necessarily dehumanized. The ideal woman is nothing more than a pale, submissive body unblemished by desire of its own — a body that ensures the primacy of male potency through an absence of vitality. Whether deified or demonized, the "fairest one of all" is dehumanized. She reveals the consequences of idealizing a kind of virginity based not on purity or chastity of the mind, but instead upon the absence of passion in women. She is a body devoid of substance, the cold, female body that exists only by virtue of complete reliance upon the male. Though the princess is not passive, she and queen are the active drivers of the plot, her vitality is necessarily parasitic. Without the patriarchal phallus — that is, without the power she siphons from her father's body — she would fall "prey" to the Queen (not once, but twice). However, because the princess embodies the ideal virgin of patriarchy, she attracts the quintessential patriarchal male and with him is finally able to overthrow the Queen.

The queen inhabits one of the most pervasive prostitute roles in fairy tales: the stepmother. As a bastardization of the role of mother, the stepmother is always already wicked. Snow White's stepmother is "a beautiful lady, but proud and domineering" (Grimm 244). The Queen's sins are authoritarianism and self-confidence — both traditionally masculine traits. Importantly, these "flaws" are identified in contrast to her physical appearance. The Queen is "a beautiful lady" the text states, but this attribute is then qualified with "but..." While fairy-tale village girls are often humble by nature, the Queen displays the "[a]rrogance, haughtiness, and pride ... runs in the blood of most royal fairy-tale women, and motivates a plot that relentlessly degrades women and declares them to be social misfits until they have positioned themselves as wives in subordinate roles to husbands" (Tatar, *Off with Their Heads* 105). Physical appearance and demeanor are not enough to decide the fate of a woman in a fairy tale. If she is able to be humbled and will submit to her husband by the end of the tale, she will get her happy ending.

Gaiman's queen, however, is damned because she will never be meek. Her death and the ceremony that surrounds it is an exercise in humiliation to punish her for refusing to defer in life. She was not a weakened widow, but instead a wise ruler, both fair and just. Yet, in the end it does not matter how "fair" she is. Justness, wisdom, compassion, and even beauty are not enough to compensate for the grievous sin of female self-sufficiency. While it is her behavior, dangerously close to masculine, that incurs censure, it is her envy of Snow White's beauty that drives her to evil actions in both *Snow White* and "Schneewittchen." In Gaiman's retelling, the idealization of Snow White's appearance is a lie fabricated by the young princess as a cover story for the more sinister tension between the two female characters. It is not the attention or approval of the absent husband/father that the queen and princess struggle for, but the power and authority reserved for the *paterfamilias* and king. The two women are fighting for the right to authority because fairy-tale women have no hope of self-rule unless they are able to rule others.

While Gaiman reveals the limits of patriarchy in the character of the princess, it is the stepmother who offers a view of another structure entirely. The queen, like her stepdaughter, had been a fairy-tale princess, although more in the tradition of Cinderella than Snow White. She was a village girl born to humble origins who, through enchantments, was able to change her status. Though her life followed the upward trajectory of her fairy tale sisters, she was not humbled through humiliation like Cinderella or stolen as a baby like Rapunzel.

The queen was once poor, but beautiful, and skilled in the art of scrying. She had seen the king in her visions for years before he rode through her town, lifted her onto his "high horse," and took her virginity (his "king's right"), then ushered the young beauty to his castle and married her (Gaiman 325). She was her own fairy godmother and her own savior. In Gaiman's telling, she may have been proud, and that inevitably is her downfall, but she had plenty of reasons to be pleased with her accomplishments. The queen advances in the phallocentric economy by enacting expected feminine roles, such as that of the virginal village girl and the dutiful wife. Yet, she goes beyond these roles and maintains her independence. She keeps her own chambers after wedding the king, and it is clear that she considered sex with her husband not a conjugal duty but an act of giving and receiving pleasure. Additionally, she insists that she is as entitled to sexual satisfaction as her partner.

Gaiman's queen is the closest example there is of a woman living honestly in the tale. She is not ashamed of her passion; she has a body and it feels; she has a brain and she uses it. She wields power wisely and truly improves the lives of her subjects, even though to do so requires that she come face to face with what she fears most, the only person (or thing) who could ever make her submit: the princess. Yet, in order to have the freedom to live authentically, the queen had to resort to self-serving, willful deceit earlier in her life. She manipulated the king by casting a "glamour" over herself to gain his attention, and as she offered herself to him hopefully, she let him believe it was his idea in the first place. Real women, like Gaiman's queen, will always fall short of the virgin ideal; therefore, if the binary is valid, every actual woman who masquerades as such is a whore.

Another way Gaiman complicates the "Snow White" tale is by staging the princess, not her stepmother, as an outsider. She is "of a different blood" than her biological mother whose "hair the color of dark wood" and "nut-brown" eyes evoke earthy associations (Gaiman 326). The king, when healthy, is the embodiment of late August with "his beard so red, his hair so gold, his eyes the blue of a summer sky, [and] his skin tanned the gentle brown of ripe wheat" (Gaiman 326). It is during the fall that one prepares to endure the coming winter for "autumn is the time of drying, of preserving, of rendering the goose fat" (Gaiman 326). The king, as the patriarch of the fatherland, embodies both the preparation for and the survival of the frozen season. His warmth and vigor stand in stark contrast to the deathly pallor of his daughter. The princess is the fairest of them all, not because of her beauty, but because of her physical appearance of frailty. She is small, pale, and coldly without passion. Unlike her stepmother, she needs a prince or a king, someone off of whom she can live parasitically. She is the physical embodiment of the patriarchal fantasy of woman: a sexualized girl that simply cannot survive without a man's self-centric potency. The princess' pale skin, when set against the backdrop of her father's visage and her mother's warm complexion, is not beautiful but an indication of unnaturalness.

The convention of staging natural versus unnatural is ingrained within the fairy-tale genre. Traditionally, the stepmother (in opposition to the biological or "natural" mother) occupies the space of the unnatural intruder that invades the domestic sphere of the fairy-tale heroine. This intrusion then results in the expulsion of the heroine from the home, where she finds herself, more often than not, lost in the woods. It is in the forest that the heroine's naturalness becomes apparent. As Tatar points out, "the 'natural' children of fairy tales literally become children of nature, aided by nature and protected by it from the highly unnatural villains of their homelife" (Tatar, *Hard Facts* 80).

When the Grimms' Snow White is abandoned alone in the forest, she is safer than she ever was at home. Though "[w]ild beasts hovered around her at all times, [...] they did her no harm" (Grimm and Grimm 245). Surrounded by predators, Snow White remains untouched. When the day is over and she could go no further, "she discovered a little cottage" seemingly just waiting for her in the midst of the forest (Grimm and Grimm 245). Disney takes further pains to align Snow White with nature. After the queen's huntsman tells Snow White to run for her life, the heroine runs aimlessly through a dark forest where she sees danger at every turn. The trees threaten her with glowering eyes and gaping mouths; branches become long fingers clawing at her clothes; logs transform into terrifying alligators waiting to snap. Eventually, Snow White is surrounded by menacing eyes, and she collapses into a sobbing heap. Lost, alone, likely scraped and bruised, Snow White is saved immediately upon becoming the ideal prey. The terrifying creatures she has been running from are revealed to be gentle rabbits, squirrels, deer, and songbirds. After admonishing herself for being so "silly," Disney's Snow White confides in the forest creatures that she is homeless and they lead her to the cottage of the seven dwarfs.

Disney is equally blunt in showing the unnaturalness of the evil queen. This is most obvious in Disney's portrayal of the queen's death. Rather than having Snow White exact revenge on the queen at her wedding feast (as is the case in the Grimms' version), Disney's queen falls to her death off the side of a mountain. After being chased up the mountain by the dwarfs, the queen is poised to dislodge a boulder and kill her pursuers. At that moment, nature rises against the evil queen. Lightning strikes the precipice on which she stands and down she falls. Through this refiguring of the plot, Disney preserves Snow White's innocence, displays the dwarfs' loyalty to Snow White without forcing them to sully their hands with murder, and solidifies a direct relationship between evilness and unnaturalness.

Gaiman utilizes this dichotomy of natural versus unnatural and its correspondence with good and evil while simultaneously turning the conventional wisdom about fairy-tale good and evil on its head. The reader of fairy tales is always encouraged to align with what is natural. Nature remains aligned with good, but instead of being represented by purity and innocence, Gaiman links naturalness to fecundity and fertility. What is hailed as natural in "Snow, Glass, Apples" is the affirmation of life. It is sterility, stagnation, and frigidity that are unnatural. The princess' pale external features, lacking in warmth and vivacity, are ghoulish and macabre in Gaiman's context. The reader is reminded that though there are certainly many real women and girls with light complexions; only the dead are "white as snow." While it is true that Disney and the Grimm brothers do not necessarily present a child with skin that is literally as white as snow, Gaiman's decision to literalize this metaphor is in keeping with fairy-tale convention.

Fairy tales present a world where ideas not only matter, "ideas become matter" (Tatar, *Hard Facts* 80). Tatar has identified two distinct spheres of action within fairy tales; one of which makes literal what is merely figurative in the other. The first sphere, more closely tied with reality, is the domestic space where fairy tales generally begin. The castle or cottage where the fairy-tale protagonist lives tends to be mundane and recognizable by the reader. Within this sphere, there is family conflict. In the case of Snow White, the discord is a result of the queen's jealousy of her stepdaughter. When the protagonist leaves this sphere and enters the unknown, often a forest or strange land, "the hero escapes the tiresome clichés of reality by entering a world where the figurative or metaphorical dimension of language takes on literal meaning" (Tatar, *Hard Facts* 80). Gaiman's entire tale can be read as a literalization of the metaphors within Snow White. In this way, "Snow, Glass, Apples" serves to question the more conventional retellings of "Snow White." A tale that remains unquestioned and unaltered is unnatural because it, like Gaiman's young princes, is lifeless. As demonstrated with the princess' monstrousness, the "literalizations of metaphors can at times translate into grotesque effects" (Tatar, *Hard Facts* 80). Skin that is literally as white as snow is cold with death. The princess' lips are not red *as* blood, but red *with* the blood of her victims.

Where her father's features evoke the autumn harvest, the young princess personifies winter. As if to prevent mistaking romanticism for truth, Gaiman reminds the reader that "[w]inter is the time of hunger, of snow, and of death" (Gaiman 326). Throughout "Snow, Glass, Apples" the reader is never quite able to escape the chill evoked by the title. The queen sees "frozen moments," scrys into "cold glass," and though the story spans a decade, nearly all the events happen in the winter with each one a bit more harsh and unforgiving than the last (Gaiman 325). The snow in Gaiman's retelling becomes a symbol of disguising and forgetting. After the queen's huntsman removes the princess' heart, "the snow fell, covering the footprints of [the] huntsmen, covering her tiny body in the forest where it lay" (Gaiman 329). A mound of dirt may be indistinguishable from a corpse when covered with snow. Additionally, the queen's side of the story is hidden by "lies and half-truths [that] fall like snow" (Gaiman 328). Her tale, like "a landscape, unrecognizable after a snowfall," becomes lost beneath the stories of Snow White (Gaiman 328). In this wintry tale, the only sign of thaw to be found is the king's visage, and the young princess brings the winter to her father's healthy autumn features.

On his deathbed, the king is reduced to "a shadow of the man" he once was (Gaiman 327). Though the queen is also "frozen ... owned and dominated" by the child, the princess only feeds from the queen once — leaving a scar that looked "ancient" within a day (Gaiman 326). The king's body, however, becomes "covered with a multitude of ancient scars" that were not present when he first remarried (Gaiman 327). His daughter drains him of all vivacity until "his bones showed, blue and white, beneath the skin ... his hands were cold as stone, his eyes milky blue, his hair and beard faded and lusterless and limp" (Gaiman 327–28). The princess murders her father by slowly sapping his strength. Even more terrifying, where the traditional versions of "Snow White," "leave the oedipal entanglements to our imagination," Gaiman's iteration reveals the princess's oedipal desires to be both literal and figurative (Bettelheim 201). The princess instigates carnal relations with her father, and it is clear that her sexual desire is tied directly to a yearning for the power of the patriarchal phallus, the "signifier that is destined to designate meaning" (Lacan 579). All of the king's potency, both literally and metaphorically, is contained and concentrated in his genitalia. The scars on "her father's thighs, and on his ballock-pouch, and on his male member, when he died" reveal that the princess has seized the patriarchal phallus with her teeth (Gaiman 328).

No longer the blameless child, the princess exemplifies the patriarchal anxieties of female sexuality as dangerous and all consuming. Within phallocentrism, feminine desire "is often interpreted, and feared as a sort of insatiable hunger, a voracity that will swallow you whole" (Irigaray 29). The princess, already rhetorically linked to hunger through correlations with winter, now evokes insatiability made especially terrifying by her blood red mouth, full of sharp teeth that render the king impotent in more than just the metaphorical sense. The young princess is castration incarnate.

At first read, this transformation of the innocent child, Little Snow White, into an incestuous, vampiric succubus may appear to reinscribe the limited roles available to women within patriarchy. Where the Grimms and Disney deified Snow White for her purity, it may seem that Gaiman has simply demonized her by relegating her to the other side of the virgin/whore dichotomy. Upon closer inspection however, it becomes clear that this is not the case. This "unnatural thing" is not evidence of the inherently monstrous feminine, but instead the inevitable result of the patriarchal idealization of passive purity epitomized in many fairy-tale heroines.

If Snow White were a fairy-tale hero, instead of a fairy-tale heroine, abandonment in the forest would be the beginning of "the often desperately lonely course to find [her]self" (Bettelheim 201). Instead, the Grimms' Snow White "just stared at all the leaves on the trees and had no idea where to turn" (Grimm and Grimm 245). Eventually, through help of forest critters and the benevolence of nature, Snow White discovers the cottage of the seven dwarfs. When the hero of a fairy tale wanders into the forest he finds himself. Snow White finds a house.

It is in the safety of the domestic sphere that Snow White is expected to find herself. No dragons to slay or giants to outwit. She has just floors to sweep, meals to prepare, and seven "sexually immature" dwarfs to mother until she can be rescued (Bettelheim 200). Everything inside the cottage is "tiny and indescribably dainty and spotless" in the Grimms' version, assuring Snow White that she will be safe here (Grimm and Grimm 245). The residents are immediately identified as non-threatening due to their small stature, indicated by the repetition of the word "little." Not only is there a "little table," there are also "little spoon[s] … little knives … little beds … little plate[s] [and] little cup[s]" (Grimm and Grimm 245–246). Additionally, all of the linens are white. The bed sheets in particular are, like Snow White herself, "white as snow" (Grimm and Grimm 246). This linguistic connection confirms the asexual nature of the cottage's inhabitants; the bed sheets are as unsullied as the virginal princess. She can sleep here safely without fear until the residents return.

The dwarfs in the Grimms' tale, as Tatar points out, are not "differentiated from each other and have no names" (Grimm and Grimm 246). Disney, as indicated by the title that frames the narrative, assigns more importance to the dwarfs than the other versions. They have been considered merely "foils to set off the important developments taking place in Snow White" (Bettelheim 201). Santiago Solis argues however, that the dwarfs are more than just foils. Instead, "the seven dwarfs' supporting role [especially in the Disney version] serves to legitimate physical and sexual normality" (Solis 115). A dwarf, in Disney's telling, is an immature man-child, incapable of proper self-care. Not only does Disney's Snow White discover the cottage in a state of disarray, but the dwarfs are also entirely unfamiliar with personal hygiene. They must learn how to wash their hands and faces if they are to eat the dinner Snow White prepared for them. Where the Grimms' Snow White must be domesticated in the cottage, Disney's Snow White has no such need. She is a natural housekeeper, caregiver, and nurturer.

The dwarfs in the Grimms' tale are aware of Snow White's trespassing not because she has tidied up, but because she has made a mess. They come home from the mine to discover "not everything was as they left it" (Grimm and Grimm 246). In a scene reminiscent of "Goldilocks and the Three Bears," the seven dwarfs realize that someone has eaten out of their dishes, tried their beds, and is finally discovered sleeping across several of their beds at the same time. The condition for residency with them, however, is the same. Snow White "will keep house ... cook, make the beds, wash, sew, knit, and keep everything neat and tidy," and in exchange she can stay with the dwarfs who will "give [her] everything [she] need[s]" (Grimm and Grimm 246). Even though the Grimms' dwarfs are not the inept man-children of Disney, Snow White must demonstrate domestic competency to stay with them. She must perform the household duties in exchange for shelter and the protection provided to her by their masculinity.

In stark contrast, Gaiman's princess and the "ugly, misshapen, hairy little men" she lives with in the forest do not reside in a cottage or other typical domestic space. In fact, "*her* dwelling [is] a high sandstone cliff, laced with deep caves going back a way into the rock wall" (Gaiman 332, emphasis mine). The "forest is a dark place" where the child is not the quarry but "a thing of terror" that "preys on wanderers" (Gaiman 329–330). Rather than become domesticated in the forest, Gaiman's princess turns feral.

The queen in Gaiman's tale also transcends domestic expectations. After the death of her husband, the queen rules the kingdom alone for five years. It is in her role as regent that she exceeds the constraints of patriarchy. She is not wife, mother, or mistress to any man. Instead, the solitary queen is defined in relation to the people she rules. She inhabits the space reserved for the patriarchal phallus but does not engage in the phallocentric economy. Her subjects "claimed that [she] ruled them with wisdom" (Gaiman 330). Not only a wise ruler, she is also known as a "wise woman," in fairy-tale language: a witch. She is wise not because of good judgment but because she "know[s] secrets and [she] can seek out things hidden" (Gaiman 330).

This occult knowledge is revealed to her through her scrying mirror. The queen's mirror, in both the Grimms' and Disney's versions, is traditionally understood as a sign of her pride and obsession with her beauty. The queen's continual return to the mirror in these versions can't help but evoke images of Narcissus. In Ovid's *Metamorphoses*, Narcissus falls in love with his reflection in a pool of water (not realizing it is his own image that he adores) and dies of starvation rather than leave sight of himself. Though the tale is often a warning against excessive obsession with self, it could be read instead as a warning against the dangers of lacking self-awareness. There is no reason to believe that Narcissus would have felt compelled to stay by the water if he knew it was his own reflection that enamored him. The problem is not Narcissus' adoration of himself, but the alienation expressed in his inability to recognize his own image.

Similarly, in "Schneewittchen" the queen does not merely view herself in the mirror, but she uses the art of scrying to determine who is "the fairest one of all." When the specularized vision does not return her own reflection, she is enraged. While this serves as further proof of the queen's narcissism for the Grimms and Disney, Gaiman's take is a bit more complex. When Gaiman's queen gazes into her mirror, she is not seeking validation of self-worth in her own reflection or even inquiring as to how she compares physically with other women. Instead, she looks into the mirror to see the outside world. Yet, as a woman in a patriarchal world, she is the also the mirror upon which the world is projected by the male ego (Whitford 34). She is, therefore, looking to herself for wisdom and for knowledge. When she looks in the mirror she finds the princess and strikingly, the only time she sees her own reflection, it is in the princess' dark eyes. The queen and the princess are not mirror images of each other, but it is only through the other that they are able to see themselves. In their own ways, they are both aspiring to be "the fairest of all."

Though the princess' skin is fair to the point of pastiness, the queen's fairness goes beyond superficial skin pigmentation. She is fair in her dealings with her subjects, including the notably named "Lord of the Fair." But in the end, the people side with the young princess, celebrating the death of the queen and embellishing the lies. For in the realm of fairy tales, it is easier to believe in a cannibalistic evil stepmother than it is to believe in a strong woman, ruling fairly and independently of a man. This is in part because phallocentrism privileges that which can be seen. The queen exceeds a phal-locentric economy because as a "wise woman," she utilizes the non-phallic wisdom of witchcraft, the only way of knowing reserved for women in fairy tales. Additionally, because her subjects valorize her for this ability, the queen represents the possibility of a world outside a phallocentric economy.

But escape from patriarchy isn't easy and the queen's major misstep is an attempt to exert power "safely" within patriarchal structure. She attempts to form an alliance with the prince of a neighboring land through sexual com-merce. This prince needs a frigid body to be aroused. He demands that she "must neither move nor speak" during intercourse and implores her to "[j]ust lie there on the stones, so cold and so fair" (Gaiman 336). The queen is a passionate woman however and she "match[es] him, grind for grind, push for push" and "moan[s]" (Gaiman 336). This vocalization of the queen's passion immediately renders the prince impotent. He requires the trappings of death and absolute submission to maintain an erection. He is aroused only by that which he believes he can control: the inert. He takes but is unwilling to be taken. Pleasure other than his own is terrifying and paralyzing.

The next morning, when he finds Snow White on the side of the road, he believes that he has found his perfect woman, though she is barely more than a child. His ownership is built on belief that the princess is nothing more than a body, a lifeless doll that he can own. What sort of man discovers a comatose fifteen-year old girl encased in glass coffin and buys her, sarcophagus and all, from the seven dwarfs who entombed her? Gaiman's answer is unambiguous: a man with a small penis (Gaiman 336). It's as though the value of the penis is so great that a man with a small sex organ must be reduced to the deviance of necrophilia.

Just as with the princess however, Gaiman uses the character of the prince to undermine patriarchy with its own ideals. The prince is the type of man a phallocentric economy inevitably creates. According to Irigaray, "[t]he more or less exclusive — and highly anxious — attention paid to the erection in Western sexuality ... offers nothing but imperatives dictated by male rivalry: the 'strongest being the one who has the best "hard-on," the longest, the biggest, the stiffest penis'" (Irigaray 24). The prince has bought into the male rivalry of patriarchy but in this, as in every competition, there are those who fall short. The prince's very body betrays and emasculates him. The queen, in rendering him impotent, represents metaphorical castration and for that she must pay.

The recently reanimated princess becomes the enforcer of this punishment as she reinstates the patriarchal hierarchy. She is the fulfillment of the patriarchal structure. She embodies the external traits of virginity, complete with physical submission epitomized in the image of her unconscious body encased in glass. Though the reader knows the princess will control and dominate the prince as she did her father, she has no power of consequence without him. She needs a phallus; any phallus will do. Even the prince's "small, slippery thing" (Gaiman 336) will suffice because the tiniest penis is still more than the woman's "nothing to see" (Irigaray 26). As we learn from Lacan, one need not have a penis to wield the phallus. Gaiman's tale reveals however, that while Lacan may be correct, even when wielding the phallus, a woman is dehumanized in patriarchy. Power is parasitic in a phallocentric economy. One must always be privileged at the cost of all others. The one must constantly be reminded of the others, the not-one, or it is rendered impotent and falls limp.

In the end, the reader realizes the distinctions between the queen and the princess are small but significant. The queen manipulates to gain access to a power structure that she then attempts to restructure. Where the queen attempts to maneuver discreetly within patriarchy, masquerading in the roles assigned to her, the princess fulfills these roles and in doing so reveals the limits of patriarchy. The princess becomes the enforcer of the patriarchal hierarchy. Though the princess literalizes patriarchal fears of feminine sexuality, it is the queen who becomes the scapegoat for those fears.

"Snow, Glass, Apples" is self-consciously aware that it contrasts with other versions of the tale and does not attempt to pass itself off as the original tale. Snow White remains the heroine in the traditional sense because it is she, and not the queen, who "lives happily ever after." Even though, in Gaiman's version, it is the young princess who is evil and unnatural, it is still the queen who dies in the end. Gaiman reminds us that the truth of history is the tale the victor tells. Where Perrault, et al., absolve incestuous fathers, vilify dying mothers, and incriminate victimized daughters from behind the mask of omnipotent narrator and impartial critic, Gaiman's queen pleads her case to the audience directly. This shift in narration reminds the reader that there is another version, told from someone else's perspective, and the queen herself reiterates this by acknowledging "my soul and my story are my own, and will die with me" (Gaiman 339).

Just before she is thrown into the kiln to be cooked for the wedding feast, the queen catches the princess's eye: "She was not laughing, or jeering, or talking. She did not sneer at me or turn away. She looked at me, though; and for a moment I saw myself reflected in her eyes" (Gaiman 339). This moment signifies a changing of the guard. The queen's reflection is both literal and figurative. Metaphorically, the queen sees her own ambitions and striving for power within a phallocentric economy. Both the queen and her stepdaughter are women who attempt to control their fate in a patriarchal world. As the queen roasts to her death, "[l]ies and half-truths fall like snow, covering the things that [she] remembers, the things that [she] saw. A landscape, unrecognizable after a snowfall; that is what [the princess] has made of [the queen's] life" (Gaiman 328). This indistinguishable terrain of earth, dirt, rocks, and vegetation–the tangible, fertile ground the queen and her late husband tended, served, and represented–has been lost and all that remains are stories washed as white as snow.

The modern age is one that is at least partially invested in hearing the other side of the story. The commercial success of Gregory Maguire's *Wicked*, and the Broadway adaptation of the same name, demonstrates a desire to align with, or at least understand, our cultural "villains." Modern readers question those who claim to be "as good as they are beautiful." No longer seeing the audience as blameless victims, readers recognizes and value the flaws and imperfections of our heroes and heroines. There is a cultural distrust of perfection and, on some level, a certain *schadenfreude* in seeing it exposed as false. The catharsis of seeing the villain drawn and quartered or cooked alive is now occasionally replaced by another release: the catharsis of seeing the hero and heroine knocked off their pedestals and revealed to be hypocrites and villains. Interestingly, the endings remain the same. Authors like Gaiman and Maguire don't make everything turn out okay for the misunderstood villain. The ostensible heroine still triumphs over her adversaries, but there is a certain satisfaction in merely knowing that her perfect ending is not so perfect after all. At the end of the tale, even though there is a marriage celebration and a king back on the throne, we have gone too far to believe in the happily ever after.

WORKS CITED

Bettelheim, Bruno. *The Uses of Enchantment: The Meaning and Importance of Fairy Tales.* New York: Alfred A. Knopf, 1976. Print.

Christ, Carol P. "Feminist Theology as Post-Tradition Theology." *The Cambridge Companion to Feminist Theology.* Ed. Susan Frank Parsons. Cambridge: Cambridge University Press, 2002: 79–96. Print.

Fourie, Pieter J. *Media Studies: Media History, Media and Society.* 2d. ed. Vol. 2. Cape Town: Juta, 2008. 4 vols. Print.

Freud, Sigmund. "The Question of Lay Analysis." *The Standard Edition of the Complete Psychological Works of Sigmund Freud.* Ed. James Strachey. Trans. James Strachey. Vol. 20. London: Hogarth, 1953–74: 179–258. 24 vols. Print.

Gaiman, Neil. "Snow, Glass, Apples." *Smoke and Mirrors.* New York: Harper Perennial, 1998: 325–40. Print.

Gilbert, Sandra M., and Susan Gubar. *The Madwoman in the Attic: The Woman Writer and the Nineteenth-Century Literary Imagination.* New Haven: Yale University Press, 1974. Print.

Grimm, Jacob, and Wilhelm Grimm. *The Annotated Brothers Grimm.* Ed. Maria Tatar. Trans. Maria Tatar. New York: W.W. Norton, 2004. Print.

Irigaray, Luce. *This Sex Which Is Not One.* Trans. Catherine Porter. Ithaca: Cornell University Press, 1985. Print.

Kaye, Kerwin. "Sexual Abuse Victims and the Wholesome Family." *Regulating Sex: The Politics of Intimacy and Identity.* Ed. Elizabeth Bernstein and Laurie Schaffner. New York: Routledge, 2005. Print.

Lacan, Jacques. *Écrits.* Trans. Bruce Fink. New York: W.W. Norton & Co., 2006. Print.

Ovid. *Metamorphoses.* Trans. A.D. Melville. Oxford: Oxford UP, 1986. Print.

Snow White and the Seven Dwarfs. Dir. David Hand. Walt Disney Productions. 1938. DVD.

Solis, Santiago. "Snow White and the Seven 'Dwarfs'—Queercripped." *Hypatia* 22.1 (2007): 114–31. Print.

Tatar, Maria. *Off with Their Heads! Fairy Tales and the Culture of Childhood.* Princeton: Princeton University Press, 1992. Print.

_____. *The Hard Facts of the Grimms' Fairy Tales.* Expanded 2d. ed. Princeton: Princeton University Press, 2003. Print.

Whitford, Margaret. *Luce Irigaray: Philosophy in the Feminine.* London: Routledge, 1991. Print.

Inverting the Fairy Tale

The Value of the Complex Female in "Chivalry"

BY JENNIFER MCSTOTTS

chivalrous, adj.
3. Of, belonging to, or characteristic of the ideal knight; possessing all the virtues attributed to the Age of Chivalry; characterized by pure and noble gallantry, honour, courtesy, and disinterested devotion to the cause of the weak or oppressed. Sometimes, "gallant, or disinterestedly devoted in the service of the female sex"; sometimes, in ridicule = "quixotic."
— Oxford English Dictionary

"I'm on a quest," he said.
"That's nice," said Mrs. Whitaker, noncommittally.
— Neil Gaiman, "Chivalry"

In the short story "Chivalry," Neil Gaiman re-imagines an Arthurian Grail quest as a fairy tale set in suburban Britain, casting a traditional Galahad (Galaad) as the hero, a volunteer shopgirl named Marie as the damsel, and a childless widow named Mrs. Whitaker as the Grail's guardian. Gaiman re-interprets the quest from the perspective not of the knight or the damsel but of Galaad's antagonist, Mrs. Whitaker. In a reversal of roles, the hero's antagonist becomes the story's protagonist, a domestic elderly woman passively disinterested in either aiding or thwarting Galaad's quest. The reader follows Mrs. Whitaker through the story and Gaiman focuses his attention on her. By developing Mrs. Whitaker, rather than the hero or damsel, into a three-dimensional character and the heart of the story, Gaiman gives the otherwise traditionally depthless fairy tale an extended feminist layer of meaning.

Gaiman refuses to typecast Mrs. Whitaker as the wicked witch, wise crone, or benevolent godmother. He instead inverts the fairy tale roles and expands the value and role of the older woman. In this particular narrative, he devalues the quest itself, making the winning of the Grail — and I argue the winning of the knight's heart and eternal happiness — of marginal importance. Moreover, Mrs. Whitaker does not behave the way we might expect: she is neither threatening nor overly maternal, despite her regard for the young Marie and Galaad. This shows Gaiman's sophisticated treatment of the childless widow as a character type. He subtly questions the unnatural nature of the immortality offered in fairy tales and myths through the decisions Mrs. Whitaker faces at the climax of the story. Mrs. Whitaker exists outside traditional fairy-tale female roles — villainess, princess, mother, and wife — and Gaiman does not place her in traditional male roles either. She is her own category.

The Story

Gaiman wrote "Chivalry" for inclusion in a collection of Grail stories.[1] The story begins as Mrs. Whitaker explores a local secondhand store where she finds the Holy Grail among stale and musty clothes. With it is "a water-stained copy of Romance and Legend of Chivalry by A. R. Hope Moncrieff," a collection of medieval stories and illustrations of chivalric romance ("Chivalry" 34). Mrs. Whitaker purchases the Grail along with two Mills & Boon romance novels — the British equivalent of American Harlequin or Silhouette novels: category romances produced in short but frequent publishing runs. Mrs. Whitaker's incongruous purchase of an incredibly historic, religious, and mythological object alongside rather pedestrian and popular novels is humorous. Yet it also shows Mrs. Whitaker's desire for romance, both in literature and in life.

Once she returns home with her purchases, Mrs. Whitaker meticulously polishes the Grail and carefully considers where to display it. She finally selects the ideal location between a "small soulful china basset hound and a photograph of her late husband, Henry, on the beach at Frinton in 1953" (35). Mrs. Whitaker's treatment of the sacred object is notable. She does not hoard it, isn't concerned it might be stolen, and doesn't exhibit it as a grand treasure. Instead, she displays it on her mantelpiece as any other middle-class widow might showcase a thrift-store find or similar piece of kitsch; her aesthetic reasoning goes only as far as to say that the grail "looks nice" there.

Whitaker is fully aware of the value of what she has purchased for only 30 pence. She tells her friend, Mrs. Greenberg, about the Grail's Biblical history. However, she discusses the Holy Grail as if it were of equal importance to everyday matters such as who Mrs. Greenberg's son is dating. She employs the same casual attitude even at the next appearance of the fantastic or medieval in the form of a young man at her front door. He appears with "shoulder-length hair so fair it was almost white, wearing gleaming silver armor, with a white surcoat," and introduces himself as Galaad, explaining that he is on a quest for the Grail ("Chivalry" 36). Up until this point in the story, Mrs. Whitaker has been presented as benevolent and polite, very quotidian in her pensioner's ways.

Gaiman subtly plants the seeds of Mrs. Whitaker's neutrality — her disinterest in Galaad's Grail quest — so it is not surprising to the reader when she refuses to yield the Grail to him immediately upon his request. She declines politely, stating, "I rather like it there. It's just right, between the dog and the photograph of my Henry" ("Chivalry" 37). When Galaad offers gold for the Grail, she declines more sharply, emphasizing that her motivations are eccentric but not greedy or unreasonable. This distinction is an important one: Gaiman is careful to convey Mrs. Whitaker as sane and courteous, with her own code of ethics, never grasping or dotty. While Mrs. Whitaker's advanced age is apparent in her physical description and bearing, Gaiman does not depict it as a mental weakness, nor does Galaad regard her as an intellectual inferior. Her reasoning might be irrational — or at least not profit-seeking — but her manner remains polite. Just as Galaad's code of chivalry may seem outdated to us now, Mrs. Whitaker's code too might seem misplaced to the reader, but the knight and the widow recognize in each other strong senses of fair conduct and treat each other well.

Galaad does not regard Mrs. Whitaker as if she must be handled delicately, nor does he treat her as a villain to be defeated, but as a gatekeeper of sorts — one to be appeased. For this reason, he brings an item to exchange for the Grail when he returns a few days later: the mystical sword Balmung. Again, Mrs. Whitaker respectfully declines, though she admits to herself that her late husband Henry would have wanted the sword to hang on the wall and show off to visitors. Before they discuss the exchange, she has Galaad perform gardening chores for her, and afterward, she packs food for him: "Mrs. Whitaker made him some cream cheese and cucumber sandwiches for the journey back and wrapped them in greaseproof paper. She gave him an apple for Grizzel [his horse]. He seemed very pleased with both gifts." The food and hospitality demonstrate Mrs. Whitaker's courtesy and benevolence, despite her disinterest in Galaad's quest. Another person might have taken advantage of Galaad's chivalry and asked for his help in exchange for nothing. Gaiman carefully layers and develops Mrs. Whitaker's character, establishing her need for company without making her appear desperate for human contact. For example, she is happy in her routines when the story begins, not lonely. In addition, she offers a type of hospitality that is independent of maternal care-taking. Like any host or hostess in the Age of Chivalry, Mrs. Whitaker provides for a traveler and his horse.

Denied the Grail, Galaad departs, only to return with another offer. Where Galaad goes between his visits with Mrs. Whitaker isn't clear, though it becomes apparent when Mrs. Whitaker next sees Marie that Galaad has encountered her. Gaiman reveals much in a simple exchange between the two women a few days later, by which time Marie has improved her appearance, dressing in "a rather smart skirt" and wearing lipstick, although "possibly not the best shade for her, nor particularly expertly applied." Mrs. Whitaker opines, "It was a great improvement" ("Chivalry" 41). Marie inquires, none-too-subtly:

> "There was a man in here last week, asking about that thing you bought. The little metal cup thing. I told him where to find you. You don't mind, do you?"
> "No, dear," said Mrs. Whitaker. "He found me."
> "He was really dreamy. Really, really dreamy," sighed Marie, wistfully. "I could of gone for him.
> "And he had a big white horse and all," Marie concluded. She was standing up straighter as well, Mrs. Whitaker noted approvingly [41].

We have no reason to believe, from Marie's observation that Galaad was "dreamy" or from her description of their interaction, that Galaad expressed any interest in Marie. It is not particularly surprising that a seventeen-year-old girl — especially the kind of adolescent who reads fashion magazines like Marie's *Modern Woman* with its "Reveal Your Hidden Personality" questionnaire — would endeavor to improve and feminize her appearance in the hopes of having a second interaction with an attractive young man. If Gaiman's Galaad is following the path of the traditional Galahad, at this point he is still virginal and disinterested in sex. In fact, part of the traditional definition of chivalry, as quoted in the above epigraph from the Oxford English Dictionary, is a disinterested devotion to serving women, meaning a knight of Galaad's virtue would be doubly unlikely to interrupt his quest to romance Marie.

Galaad returns to Mrs. Whitaker's home a third time — a typical number in many fairy tales[2] — after a longer period of days, and offers three gifts to Mrs. Whitaker in exchange for the Grail. First is the Philosopher's Stone, the supreme object of alchemy, "which our forefather Noah hung in the Ark to give light when there was no light" ("Chivalry" 43). Second is an egg from a phoenix, and third is one of the Apples of Life from the garden of the Hesperides, nymphs who guarded the golden fruit with the aid of a dragon. Here too a fairy tale notion of guarded treasure is evoked through a specific example from classical myth. "One bite from it will heal any illness or wound, no matter how deep," promises Galaad, "a second bite restores youth and beauty; and a third bite is said to grant eternal life" (44). Adding to the fairy tale atmosphere in these scenes are the nested threes: this is Galaad's third visit, he has come bearing three gifts, the third of which offers three levels of blessings and was guarded by three nymphs.

Mrs. Whitaker considers the offered treasures, pondering the possibility of eternal youth, and realizes, for the first time in full force, how virile the young Galaad sitting before her is. However, Mrs. Whitaker accepts the Philosopher's Stone and the Phoenix's Egg, not for their mystical or supernatural properties, but for their aesthetics: "They'll look nice on the mantelpiece. And two for one's fair, or I don't know what is" ("Chivalry" 45).

The story could have ended here, the dragon-proxy having yielded the prize to the hero, but instead the undefeated Mrs. Whitaker continues about her business, including another weekly visit to the secondhand store. Marie has abandoned her post as shopgirl to elope with Galaad (a departure from a traditional Grail quest, in which Galahad remains a virgin[3]). If the story is read as a romance, ending with a romantic pairing or wedding is typical and predictable. In turn, if "Chivalry" is read as a fairy tale, one may have expected this tidy resolution.

Finding the Fairy Tale

Pinpointing the fairy tale nature of "Chivalry" and defining it as such requires one to delineate the essential features of the genre. Maria Tatar, chair of the Program in Folklore and Mythology at Harvard University and author of *The Hard Facts of the Grimms' Fairy Tales*, offers several useful definitions for understanding fairy tales. According to Kate Bernheimer, founder and editor of *Fairy Tale Review*, Tatar's definitions are useful, particularly her "description of fairy tales as domestic myths."[4] Bernheimer offers that fairy tales may be recognized by the artistic techniques used in their craft: "abstraction, depthlessness, everyday magic, [and] intuitive logic." While Bernheimer approaches defining fairy tales as an author and an editor — from the perspective of craft — these same elements are present in the more traditionally-framed definition from folklore scholar Stith Thompson. According to Thompson, 'a fairy tale involves "a succession of motifs or episodes. It moves in an unreal world without definite locality or definite characters, and is filled with the marvelous. In this never-never land, humble heroes kill adversaries, succeed to kingdoms and marry princesses" (8).

It is both possible and useful to apply these definitions to "Chivalry" as a contemporary fairy tale. "Chivalry" is a domestic myth, a widow's encounter with an Arthurian knight out of place and time. Gaiman offers a few glimpses of the otherworldly in an otherwise very grounded, middle-class setting. "Chivalry" includes all of the elements of a fairy tale as well as some of its most common tropes. For instance, when Bernheimer describes fairy tale abstraction, she analyzes both the dreaminess of tone and the very specific idea of separation or extraction. Gaiman performs this abstraction by removing Galahad from the Grail stories and relocating him to an unspecified British suburb. Although the story is contemporary, it does not offer a precise time or a "definite locality" where these events unfold, to use Thompson's term.[5] The story seems relatable, and yet unreleal; it is a type of fantasy, "a distorting mirror ... and a concealing mirror, set at forty-five degrees to reality, but ... a mirror nonetheless, which we can use to tell ourselves things which we might not otherwise see" (Gaiman "An Introduction" 2). In the public scenes of "Chivalry," a knight on horseback comes and goes without question, drawing the attention of the town's children and eventually sweeping Marie off her feet, but not drawing any attention from the authorities.[3] Gaiman has stripped this world of the details that would fetter the story, those details that would have given it a dimension of realism and, I argue, would have kept it from being a fairy tale, a discrete form of the fantasy genre. The magic (per Bernheimer) and the marvelous (per Thompson) is treated as mundane by the characters in the story, from the children and passersby to Mrs. Whitaker's friend, Mrs. Greenberg. For example, upon hearing the story of the Grail's role in the Last Supper and Crucifixion, Mrs. Greenberg remarks, "I wouldn't know about that, but it's very nice. Our Myron got one just like that when he won the swimming tournament, only it's got his name on the side."

In many short stories, regardless of genre, secondary and tertiary characters like Mrs. Greenberg receive little development, but in "Chivalry," even Galaad and especially Marie remain two-dimensional in an example of the fairy tale crafting technique Bernheimer refers to as depthlessness. Readers rarely learn the details or motivations behind secondary characters that might explain why a "wicked witch" behave the way she does. This is because offering more background to explain villainy would transform the villain from archetype or trope into character: relatable and too real. This observation holds true of many fairy tale figures: Why does Mother Gothel want the baby who grows to be Rapunzel? Why does the handmaid betray the princess in "The Goose Girl"? Why does almost every stepmother resent her stepchildren, and why does every father bow to his new wife's wishes at the expense of his children? Unexplained greed, senseless jealousy, and other character flaws like cowardice and spite are, like much of the characters' psychology, "just so," without reason. When more backstory is provided, such as when viewers are given a brief hint of Cinderella's stepmother's own trauma in the 1998 adaptation *Ever After*—a glimpse of her abusive childhood and cruel mother's behavior — it detracts from the senseless and shallow vanity the character otherwise exudes by complicating that vanity and giving it depth. The psychology behind a character's motivation in most fairy tales is too simple to be fruitfully interrogated the way it can be in modern fiction.[6]

In this way depthlessness interrelates with the intuitive logic Bernheimer mentions — the idea that events in a fairy tale happen because that is how they are meant to happen — and it is not limited to the negative aspects of character. The fairy tale's structure keeps the reader on the surface of Mrs. Whitaker's character inasmuch as we cannot question why she is neither generous nor selfish with Galaad. Yet, Mrs. Whitaker is the only character who Gaiman develops in any significant way. She has dimension, motivation, and a backstory. As a result of this combination of intuitive logic and the breach of depthlessness, the reader understands Mrs. Whitaker's position (without regard for whether the reader agrees or empathizes with her). Galaad's motivations remain unquestionable. Only late in the story does the reader learn Galaad's history, none of which necessarily explains his quest or his interest in Marie, unless the reader draws literary connections external to the story from the allusions within it. The text states:

> Galaad told Mrs. Whitaker about his mother Elaine, who was flighty and no better than she should have been and something of a witch to boot; and his grandfather King Pelles, who was well-meaning although at best a little vague; and of his youth in the Castle of Bliant on the Joyous Isle; and his father, whom he knew as "Le Chevalier Mal Fet," who was more or less completely mad, and was in reality Lancelot du Lac, greatest of knights, in disguise and bereft of his wits ["Chivalry" 42].

Certainly this is an atypical level of referential complexity for a fairy tale. The narrative stands alone without the references to Galahad and Arthurian lore. Readers might recognize names and places from other Grail stories here, but it is equally possible a reader might only recognize Lancelot's name in the final line. Even avid fantasy readers may have seen more than a few variations of the original Grail stories because there is not a single medieval story from which the others derive: "There are so many medieval versions of the Grail Quest that none can be genuinely said to be definitive, and the tale has been re-written since the Middle Ages so many times that this is also true of modern works" (Young 171). In regard to Galaad's genealogy as Gaiman summarizes it, Helen Young wrote, "The passage relies on knowledge of either Malory or T. H. White for its humour. The tone has a gentle mockery to it that is reminiscent of White, but it is impossible to determine from this passage, or indeed any other, which canonical text of the Arthurian corpus Gaiman might be referencing" (Young 171). The story does not require readers to draw specific connections in order to follow the story; in fact, Gaiman almost certainly didn't intend for "Chivalry" to have a single definitive interpretation. Overall, Galaad's actions are guided by intuitive logic on the one hand and abstractions from literary history on the other, no matter whether a reader is well-read in Grail-lore or recognizes Galahad at all.

Marie, even less developed as a character than Galaad, appears only twice in the text and is mentioned a third and final time in regard to her elopement with the hero-knight. What little the reader knows from Gaiman's description is that she was "seventeen, slightly overweight, and dressed [at first] in a baggy mauve jumper that looked like she had bought it from the shop" (33) before her sartorial transformation (dressing in "a rather smart skirt" and wearing lipstick), presumably inspired by her encounter with Galaad. The reader can extrapolate reasonably from Gaiman's characterization — how she takes quizzes in women's magazines and preens as she hopes for a repeat encounter with Galaad — that Marie is something of a hopeful romantic whose young personality is still forming and dependent on the perceptions of others. However, even more than in the case of Galaad, the reader knows nothing of Marie's past, her thought processes, or her hopes and dreams.

While Galaad and Marie are depthless and stylized archetypes — a fairy-tale prince and a damsel peasant, tropes rather than three-dimensional characters — the widow Whitaker is complexly cast. Gaiman tells the reader about her family, including her late husband whom she misses and her nephew whose family she visits regularly. She has friends whom she is shown interacting with, revealing much about her directly and indirectly; she is the kind of woman who meets with her companions weekly, valuing both the interaction and routine, and the kind of woman who visit friends in the hospital (thoughtfully leaving the walnuts out of the fruitcake for the one whose teeth are growing sensitive with age). She has made a life of gardening and housekeeping and her routines, including these visits and her regular trips to the secondhand store.

Mrs. Whitaker's Third (Feminist) Dimension

What advantage does it give to the story to develop Mrs. Whitaker in so much domestic detail? This is a story that focuses on the surfaces of daily life: ordinary household matters, gardens and fruitcakes, chores and routines — and developing Mrs. Whitaker in this much domestic detail provides a layer of armor for the narrative. A better question to ask is, why choose to re-imagine Galahad's story from this perspective at all? The hero seeks the Grail, which is guarded not by a hoarding dragon or villainous monster but by a sympathetic widow who rightfully acquired the object. Certainly one way to retell the story would have been through Galaad's eyes, exploring the mind of the conquering hero when it would be wrong to vanquish his antagonist, when in fact it would go against the ideas of chivalry, gallantry, and honor to mistreat this elderly woman. Much of the fairy tale atmosphere could have been retained in a story told from this perspective and with the themes of good, evil, and righteousness explored in greater detail — a worthy aim, but obviously not Gaiman's intent.

He also could have written the story from Marie's perspective. A woman winning the virgin Galahad's heart would have been a unique spin on the classic story, and a British shopgirl is no less extrinsic to a Grail quest than a British widow. One would be hard pressed to deny, however, that Mrs. Whitaker is more unexpected and humorous within the Grail quest than Marie, a woman of acceptable age and stature to be a damsel, despite the lack of overt distress. A feminist effort to redeem the damsel as a character type by demonstrating her worth and depth of character would be predictable, even obvious, and increasingly common in young-adult re-imagining of fairy tales.

Gaiman chose a more elaborately feminist path by humanizing and feminizing the treasure-hoarding dragon as a Mills-&-Boon reading, childless widow on a pension. Mrs. Whitaker is not the villain but a morally neutral figure who doesn't aim to thwart the hero; neither altruistic nor selfish, she nonetheless obstructs his goals in the act of affirming her own desires. There is nothing innately feminist about a romance-novel reading widow, and it would not be unreasonable for her to make demands of Galaad. Mrs. Whitaker is not profit-motivated nor dreaming of what possible gains could come from bartering with one such as Galaad, despite some of the treasures he offers her. She is likewise unconcerned with any threat he or other Grail-seekers could pose, or with planning for her future. Instead she is allied with the "revolutionary and antirational forces identified with nature, with imagination, with unconsciousness, and with spontaneity, all qualities historically defined as 'feminine'" (Gilbert and Gubar 75). She exists purely in the moment, deciding what favors to ask of him and whether to accept his offers for the Grail based only on her code of fairness, her instinct, and the immediate variables at hand — that she has gardening chores waiting or heavy objects needing to be moved, or that she does not need gold to spend or a sword that will do nothing more than hang on the wall.

Here is where the feminist consequences of Gaiman's artistic choice become more involved: by crafting Mrs. Whitaker as spontaneous in her decision-making, neutral to others' wishes, and yet committed to this deep code of fairness (her own version of Galaad's chivalry), Gaiman creates an empowered female character walking a fine line between selfishness and selflessness. Mrs. Whitaker neither hands over the Grail against her own desires nor holds Galaad hostage to her needs. She makes the most of his presence without being manipulative and without malice; while there's a gentleman there, one bound to a code of chivalry, why not have him help with heavy tasks she cannot do alone? Yet, when she requires his aid, perhaps taking advantage of his code of honor, she also thanks him with tea and food for the journey, each time engaging in a fair exchange of domestic hospitality for his chivalrous aid, a reflection of her own code of fairness and good conduct. Her code requires courtesy but not generosity, fair dealing with others as much as for herself; in other words, her code is one of balance not victory.

While Mrs. Whitaker's character fills the role of antagonist to the hero, of dragon or villain or mystical gatekeeper, she is not defeated in the course of Galaad's quest. He gains the Grail (and rescues Marie from the fate of a boring life, it seems), but the key to a feminist reading of "Chivalry" is how the widow gains as well, quid pro quo, and balances the scales by requiring labor of Galaad and bartering for the exchange of the Grail. By inverting the perspective of the story, the traditional characters' roles, and the meaning of victory to one of balance, Gaiman valorizes the complexly feminine and thereby crafts a feminist fairy tale.

One counter-argument to this could be that the two-dimensional Marie runs away with Galaad to the wedding that is often the happy ending of a fairy-tale or romance[7]; if Gaiman's re-imagining values the complex female, then why doesn't Mrs. Whitaker choose youth and possibly Galaad instead of (or in addition to) the Philosopher's Stone and Phoenix's Egg? Precisely for the reasons alluded to in the ending of the story, which finds Mrs. Whitaker declining to purchase Aladdin's lamp from the same secondhand store: she "put the lamp back where she had found it, in the back of the shop. After all, Mrs. Whitaker reflected, as she walked home, it wasn't as if she had anywhere to put it" ("Chivalry" 47). The widow's mantelpiece, and her life, are full. After pondering the image of her husband, she declines the apple and thereby eternal life and youth. By valuing Mrs. Whitaker's well-lived life so highly, Gaiman's ending shifts the definition of victory within the fairy tale quest away from happily-ever-after.

But what about Marie? Mrs. Whitaker wins by celebrating the value of her life well-lived and bartering for a good exchange on the Grail without sacrificing her own interests. But Marie's superficial behavior is rewarded with Galaad's heart and a happily-ever-after ending after she changes her behavior and appearance, sitting up straighter and wearing nicer clothing and make-up. The point of "Chivalry," as the title reminds us, is not winning Galaad. By having Mrs. Whitaker choose to continue the natural course of her life, rather than to prolong it or to re-live it with new adventures, making a fairy tale out of herself, Gaiman ironically uses fantasy to value realism and mortality over a wishful Disneyesque storybook ending. Again, Mrs. Whitaker is allied with the forces historically defined as feminine by choosing the natural progression of her life over an artificial albeit magical extension. This is particularly interesting in light of the fact that Mrs. Whitaker is childless, given that she will not live on through her family.

In juxtaposition, Mrs. Whitaker and Marie represent the tension that continues to exist for women between historical ideals of femininity, changing cultural practices and norms, and what Donald Haase calls "the deceptive ideals of the fairy tale," which according to Haase "still exert an 'awesome imaginative power over the female psyche'" (5; quoting Rowe 248). Marie yields to this pull, choosing the skirt, the lipstick, and the knight. However, to read this in a non-feminist, traditional interpretation — that the moral of Gaiman's story is the prettier, younger woman wins the man — requires that the reader assign more depth to the characters than a fairy tale allows.

Galaad and Marie are brought together in the narrative because they are the knight and the damsel; those are the roles they fill, and that is the intuitive logic of the fairy tale. It may even have been Gaiman's intent to foreshadow this pairing by naming the damsel Marie (Mary) after another famous virgin. Had Galaad and Marie never come together, the story might have failed to manifest the fairy tale form fully, detracting from the elegance of the inversion of the main character from villain to neutral obstacle, from dragon to widow-in-a-thrift-store. That Marie apparently wins Galaad's heart is not a reward for her make-up and new clothes or women's magazine reading ways; it is simply the just-so ending of a fairy tale.

Gaiman's introduction to *Smoke and Mirrors* — the second volume in which "Chivalry" is collected — reads:

> I wrote it in a weekend, a gift from the gods, easy and sweet as anything.... Several years ago, on a signing tour, someone gave me a copy of an academic paper on feminist language theory that compared and contrasted "Chivalry," Tennyson's "The Lady of Shalott," and a Madonna song. I hope one day to write a story called "Mrs. Whitaker's Werewolf" and wonder what sort of papers that might provoke [17].

Like many writers, Gaiman admits that often his stories do not end where he expected them to go when he first sat down to write them (16). He may have thought a Grail quest beginning with the discovery of the cup in an unexpected place by an unexpected person was worth exploring on the page and given no thought at all to the fairy tale simplicity of the narrative, the craft techniques Bernheimer attributes to fairy tales, or the relative complexity of Mrs. Whitaker. Nonetheless, by telling the story from the perspective of the neutral guardian of the Grail — the hero's antagonist — and by giving that guardian dimension, by making her a complex female character, Gaiman gave value to the complexly feminine. If the reader is pleased by Galaad and Marie's elopement, that is the fairy tale form at work, and the reader is likely equally pleased, if not more so, by the choices Mrs. Whitaker makes and by her realization, in the closing lines, that her life is too full for even a genie's three wishes.

Facets of Chivalry

What makes Mrs. Whitaker relatable is the chivalry with which she treats Galaad, that she has a code of conduct by which she operates. Although this code is never referred to expressly, it is a form of chivalry, and each main character is chivalrous in their own way: Galaad, most obviously, is a literal knight, but he also possesses those characteristics and virtues of an "ideal knight," such as "pure and noble gallantry, honour, courtesy, and disinterested devotion to the cause of the weak or oppressed," though there are no weak and oppressed characters in this story for him to champion. He seems, as mentioned above "disinterestedly devoted in the service of the female sex" those his elopement with Marie upon the completion of his quest would seem to indicate something more than disinterest. Marie's chivalry is in the semantically rarer sense of "quixotic"; she is idealistic, tilting at the windmills of Prince Charmings riding through town on white horses, because a realistic girl in a realistic world would almost certainly balk at running away with a stranger on horseback dressed in authentic medieval garb.

For Mrs. Whitaker, chivalry takes the form of her strong sense of fairness, of right and wrong, of the balance with which she engages Galaad. She never asks anything of him without making things even, by her reckoning, nor does she accept an offer for the Grail that does not, to her, outweigh the value of having it on her mantel, even if that small aesthetic value might seem trivial to the rest of us. The reader respects Mrs. Whitaker despite her eccentric tastes and jejune attachment to the Grail because she operates under a code of fair conduct rather than using manipulation or expressing any fear that Galaad might treat her unfairly. Moreover, Gaiman sidesteps the potential pitfall of turning Mrs. Whitaker into a matchmaking godmother-type character by keeping her dealings with Marie detached; while she approves of the "smart skirt" and lipstick in the way a woman of an older generation might approve of a teenager taking on the traditional trappings of her gender, she doesn't concern herself with Marie's singlehood or her interest in Galaad, nor does she nose in on Marie's social life.

We want Mrs. Whitaker to be happy at the end of the story for all of these reasons, for her chivalry and fair treatment of others and because she is endearing, or, to use her own language, "nice." Yet a sophisticated reading of the story, a feminist reading, is not about Mrs. Whitaker winning. To want her to choose immortality, to keep the Grail, to win Galaad somehow, to want her to have the fairy tale itself and its "deceptive ideals," would be against Mrs. Whitaker's own code. What Mrs. Whitaker gains from the story is a greater awareness of her own life and the value it has. As Kay Stone notes, "many females find in fairy tales an echo of their own struggles to become human beings" (144). Mrs. Whitaker has critically engaged with the romantic myths, has stood at the threshold of becoming the fairy tale, and has chosen her own life: "If women remember fairy tales, consciously or unconsciously, they can reinterpret them as well. It is the possibility of such reinterpretation that gives hope that women can eventually free themselves of the bonds of fairy tale magic, magic that transforms positively at one age and negatively at another" (143). Marie's choice of Galaad becomes necessary in another way, if we apply this interpretation as a counter-point to Mrs. Whitaker's choice, as a reminder that the allure of the fairy tale when we are young may be strong, but ever-after may not seem so appealing when we have lived a life worth choosing in the balance.

NOTES

1. The collection, edited by Richard Gilliam, Martin H. Greenberg, and Edward E. Kramer is titled *Grails: Quests, Visitations and Other Occurrences* (Atlanta: Unnameable Press, 1992).

2. The number three bears significance, for instance, in "Jack and the Beanstalk," "Snow White," "Rumpelstiltskin," and "Goldilocks and the Three Bears." Vladimir Propp, in his *Morphology of the Folk Tale* (1968), argues that the threefold structure came from the principle that because each element of a folk tale could be negated twice, it had to be repeated a third time in many stories across Western cultures.

3. For an interesting collection of resources on Galahad, as well as other Arthurian elements, see The Camelot Project at the University of Rochester (http://www.lib.rochester.edu/camelot/galmenu.htm).

4. In addition to her credits as an author, Bernheimer has edited three influential fairy tale anthologies: *Mirror, Mirror on the Wall: Women Writers Explore Their Favorite Fairy Tales* (1998); *Brothers and Beasts: An Anthology of Men on Fairy Tales* (2007); and *My Mother She Killed Me, My Father He Ate Me: Forty New Fairy Tales* (2010), which won the 2011 World Fantasy Award for best anthology. I first encountered Bernheimer's definitions directly at a workshop she taught at the University of Arizona Poetry Center in 2010.

5. It is possible to piece together the approximate time of the piece as the time of publication (1992): the picture of Henry on the mantel was taken in 1953. ("Chivalry" 35), which Mrs. Whitaker describes as "almost forty years away" ("Chivalry" 44).

6. It is worthwhile to note that contemporary fairy tales, as one might expect, stretch even the boundaries of Bernheimer's very recent definition. Gaiman's own "Snow, Glass, Apples" re-imagines the Snow White tale, for instance, with much greater depth in the stepmother character. In that instance he maintains the fairy tale form by stripping depth from all other characters and from the world itself, by enhancing the unreality (the everyday magic or marvelousness) of the world, by abstracting the characters within the plot and by abstracting creatures from other myths into the story, and finally by increasing the sense

of intuitive logic in the plot, which marches forward inexorably due to what one might call the deathbed perspective of the narrator.

7. The Romance Writers of America define a romance as a love story between two people than ends in a constructive resolution — industry jargon for a happy ending — though scholar Pamela Regis defines the genre as a courtship leading to a betrothal. There are plenty of fairy tales that do not resolve happily, but those that do, especially those involving a Prince Charming, mostly end in nuptials, especially after the Brothers Grimm.

WORKS CITED

Bernheimer, Kate. Interview. *Room 220: NOLA Book and Literary News.* 23 February 2011. Press Street. 14 August 2011. Web.

_____. *My Mother She Killed Me, My Father He Ate Me: Forty New Fairy Tales.* New York: Penguin, 2010. Print.

Gaiman, Neil. "An Introduction." *Smoke and Mirrors: Short Fictions and Illusions.* New York: Harper Perennial, 1998. 1–32. Print.

_____. "Chivalry." *Smoke and Mirrors: Short Fictions and Illusions.* New York: Harper Perennial, 1998. 33–47. Print.

Gilbert, Sandra M., and Susan Gubar. "'But Oh! That Deep Romantic Chasm': The Engendering of Periodization." *The Kenyon Review,* New Series 13.3 (1991): 74–81. Web.

Haase, Donald. *Fairy Tales and Feminism: New Approaches.* Detroit: Wayne State University Press, 2004. Print.

Propp, Vladimir. *Morphology of the Folk Tale.* 1968. Austin: University of Texas Press, 2003. Print.

Regis, Pamela. *A Natural History of the Romance Novel.* Philadelphia: U of Pennsylvania P, 2003. Print.

Rowe, Karen E. "Feminism and Fairy Tales." *Women's Studies: An Interdisciplinary Journal* 6.3 (1979): 237–257. Web.

Stone, Kay. "The Misuses of Enchantment: Controversies on the Significance of Fairy Tales." *Women's Folklore, Women's Culture.* Eds. Rosan A. Jordan and Susan J. Kalcik. Philadelphia: University of Pennsylvania Press, 1985. 125–45. Web.

Tatar, Maria. *The Hard Facts of the Grimms' Fairy Tales.* Princeton: Princeton University Press, 1987. Print.

Thompson, Stith. The Folktale. 1946. Berkeley: University of California Press, 1977. Print.

Young, Helen. "Approaches to Medievalism: A Consideration of Taxonomy and Methodology through Fantasy Fiction." *x* 27.1 (2010): 163–179. Web.

Feminist Fairy Tales in
Who Killed Amanda Palmer

BY MONICA MILLER

"Like you, I knew exactly where I was and what I was doing when I heard Amanda Palmer had been killed."
— Neil Gaiman, though possibly Amanda Palmer[1]

Evoking shades of Marilyn Monroe, Nancy Spungen, and *Twin Peaks*, the coffee table book *Who Killed Amanda Palmer: A Collection of Photographic Evidence* creates its own delightfully twisted mythology. It invites the reader into the mythic tragedy of the imagined murder of pop singer (and Brechtian Punk cabaret icon) Amanda Palmer. The collection consists of photographs of the singer in various death tableaux, accompanied by her own song lyrics as well as short stories written by Neil Gaiman. In one photograph, a naked Amanda lies dead on a golf course; another shows her as a suicidal fifties house-wife with her head in the oven; another shows a woman, a pre–Raphaelite vision in flowing white translucent cloth, an inch below the water; and so on. What started as a collaboration on liner notes for Palmer's first post–Dresden Dolls solo album evolved and expanded into a book-length collection of photographs, lyrics, and short fiction. The photographs (which run the gamut from amusing to uncanny to disturbing) provide a cultural commentary on the por-trayal of the female body in popular culture. Highlighted by Palmer's lyrics and Gaiman's short fiction, the book addresses provocative subjects, including high school violence, compulsory heterosexuality, teen abortion, and rape. Gaiman's fairy-tale like prose builds on the song lyrics and images to offer a multivalent feminist critique of these issues. His prose brings a mythic dimension to the photographs. Without his words, the collection of photographs and lyrics would remain in the realm of violence, pornography, and black humor. Gaiman's stories provide a mythopoetic dimension that situates the collaboration firmly in the realm of the postmodern fairy tale. Through its use of black humor and parody, *Who Killed Amanda Palmer* acts as a postmodern feminist fairy tale that negotiates the blurry territory between the world of fantasy and the world of reality. Gaiman's evocation of the unique scenarios which are possible in these interstices allows for new understandings of feminist perspectives.

Gaiman and Palmer first met in 2008 at a fundraising event for the Comic Book Legal Defense Fund. Gaiman admits to being a fan of Palmer's work in the Dresden Dolls, the band in which Palmer has performed since 1996 ("The Life and Times of the Dresden Dolls"). When they met, Palmer was finishing *Who Killed Amanda Palmer*, her first solo album. Gaiman agreed to write the liner notes. The album, originally intended to be a "really simple, stripped-down, record-it-in-my-underwear-in-my-apartment-in-boston [*sic*] kinda thing," finally resulted in both a studio album produced by Ben Folds and a coffee table book, both of which share the title *Who Killed Amanda Palmer* ("A Short History of Who Killed Amanda Palmer"). In their correspondence about the project, Palmer told Gaiman that she had been taking photographs of herself dead for about fourteen years and had originally planned to use some of these photographs in the album's liner notes. Gaiman says that the examples she sent him were intriguing, and that he saw the photographs as "small frozen stories" for which he could provide the words. These interactions led to greater collaboration, as Gaiman went to Boston where he worked with Palmer, photographer Kyle Cassidy, Palmer's assistant Beth Hommel, and others in staging, photographing, and imagining various death scenes. While Gaiman claims that most of the time during the photo shoots, he was "off to the side, scribbling in a notebook," he occasionally took a more active role, such as in the scenario titled "The Girl in the Carpet," in which he carries a dead Amanda over his shoulder down a dark alley ("How to order WHO KILLED AMANDA PALMER"). The resulting 119-page coffee table book, whose 10,000 copy, limited first edition run was an instant collector's item for both Palmer and Gaiman fans, is a truly eclectic collection.

Palmer's photographs and lyrics alone pose a (not unproblematic) third-wave feminist cultural critique, through their postmodern parody and interrogation of images of the violated female body in popular culture. Palmer appears naked and in various states of dress and undress throughout. While some of the death scenes involve striking costumes — from ball gowns to dirndls — Palmer is frequently and provocatively naked in the collection. Knowing that his readers, who were not necessarily established Amanda Palmer fans, might be taken by surprise, Gaiman wrote:

> I should probably warn people about the nudity. There are lots of photos where Amanda is fully dressed, but she doesn't seem to have anything resembling a nudity taboo, and is fearless when it comes to getting the photo she wanted, so is fully or partly naked in some of the strangest places.... It's definitely art, not porn, but there, such warnings are useful ["How to Order WHO KILLED AMANDA PALMER"].

Though Gaiman denies comparisons to pornography, *Who Killed Amanda Palmer's* depictions of nudity and violence do situate the book within larger feminist debates surrounding pornography. In contrast to much of the staunch anti-pornography scholarship and activism of many second wave feminists, which posited a direct link between pornographic images of women and the perpetuation of violence against women,[2] many people who identify as third wave feminists also identify as "pro-sex." These feminists defend pornography, recognizing that, as feminist writer Linda Williams explains, "the perverse sexuality of the 'other' can be crucial to the empowerment of women as sexual agents" (234). According to Williams, any differentiation between the perverse and the "normal" in sexuality is troubling. Rather, she advocates for acknowledging the "perverse dynamic" that underlies all sexuality, "of 'diff'rent strokes for diff'rent folks'" to offer a more general "opposition to the dominant representations of pleasure" (262). This opposition can ultimately result in the proliferation of previously-unheard voices within sexual realms (262). Certainly, *Who Killed Amanda Palmer* as both a coffee table book and an album provides media for Palmer's voice and artistic expression. What is troubling about Palmer's work in this collection, however, is its emphasis on violence against the (often scantily clad or naked) female body. Still, such violence might be considered under the rubric of the perverse in Williams' argument. The tableau on the cover is represented three times throughout the book. It shows a woman lying prone on a Victorian couch. Were the body fresh, it would be alluring. However, it's been there a while, strewn with dead leaves on the moldering couch, with "Who Killed Amanda Palmer" scrawled on the wall above the body, a question or a clause is the witness's reading. The book's cover states (and shows) the object and subject of the project: "A Collection of Photographic Evidence (with Stories by Neil Gaiman)." It is shocking, a scene of violation, the subject and object of the photograph is evidence of the violence against this woman and the viewer whose gaze witnesses the grotesque image. The second reproduction (iii) is a full-page bleed opposite an advertisement for the accompanying Amanda Palmer solo album ("The record is available for download, on CD and on vinyl. You should buy it" [ii]). The photograph now rereads as an advertisement, a billboard for the Palmer's commercial project, an album of music and a coffee-table book, the image separated from the mystery it poses and the uncomfortable scene it presents. Finally, Gaiman's original text accompanies a third iteration of the photograph. Reduced in size, no longer a bleed, instead, the photograph is inset with a margin and given a photographic attribution "Gregory Nomoora" (68). The image is recast as a photo of an installation piece by an anonymous artist. The text describing the work reads: "who killed amanda palmer — installation. sofa. leaves. amanda palmer (dead). plasterboard. paint" (69).

The image is now completely removed from the original photograph's authentic violations and is now wholly objectified, literally selling the body as product at auction for Christie's New York ($672,000). Gaiman's text, describing the artist's intent, the work's provenance, and the rationale for its monetary value, completely materializes the object of violence, emphasizing not only the disturbing reality originally photographed, but also parodying the rapid acceptance and commercializing of evidence depicting violence against women. The model's "decay ... [is] able to be viewed in time-lapse photography, now as Quicktime films on the web," Gaiman notes in the brochure text (69).

Palmer's problematic artwork gains an important mythic as well as social dimension from Gaiman's fiction. These stories, like much of Gaiman's work, are in a distinctively mythopoetic register, utilizing fairy tale tropes, themes, and narrative structures to further illuminate the photographs. Gaiman's incorporation of such a mythic dimension into the text forges a connection between the violence in Palmer's work and a larger tradition of violence against women in literature. However, his stories do not simply reproduce stereotypes of female victimhood, such as those in the Brothers Grimm canonical stories. Rather, following in the tradition of (re)visionary feminist writers such as Angela Carter and the work of Palmer herself, Gaiman's fairytale-like stories often subvert reader expectations, defamiliarizing the images of violence against women.

Gaiman's stories clarify Palmer's themes of wresting ownership and control of this kind of imagery, which traditionally has normalized (and some say even perpetuated) the victimization of women. Gaiman's text together with Palmer's photographs and lyrics twist these stereotypes and expectations into subversive foundations for feminist agency and artistic empowerment. The mythopoetic aspects of these stories both strengthen the focus and elaborate on the book's feminist cultural critique. Many of his stories contain traditional fairy tale characteristics, which like the "paradigmatic Grimms' fairy tale," are

> constructed rationally to demonstrate the virtues of an opportunistic protagonist who learns to take advantage of gifts and magic power to succeed in life, which means marriage to a rich person and wealth.... Most of the female protagonists are beautiful, passive, and industrious. Their common feature is cunning: they all know how to take advantage of the rules of their society and the conventions of the fairy tale to profit [Zipes, "Introduction: Towards a Definition of the Literary Fairy Tale," xxvi].

Certainly, the repeated image of a dead Amanda Palmer fits the criteria of having a beautiful and passive female protagonist.[3] Further, the myriad unusual circumstances in which she is shown — including as a singer, dancer, musician, society woman, and housewife — can be interpreted as reflecting a certain kind of variation that resists the easy categorization of female roles.

Gaiman's stories highlight Palmer's natural resistance, often by providing a fuller ground for interpretation or a counterintuitive narrative that nonetheless explicates the photograph. The story which accompanies Palmer's untitled self-portrait as an overdose victim is the oldest photograph in the collection. Palmer originally created it for a self-portrait assignment when she was in art school (*Amanda Palmer and Nervous Cabaret Tour*). In this photograph, we see a close-up of Palmer's face with a pile of pills spilling from her mouth, dead from what at first glance appears to be an overdose. A closer look, however, reveals that what at first appear to be pills are in fact jewels and jewelry, spilling from her mouth as though she had vomited them up and choked on them (35–6). As with much of the photography in the book, the photograph is simultaneously disturbing, confusing, beautiful, and funny. It compels the reader to look closer, to look longer, and to try and untangle the image's story.

The story that accompanies this image has the most overt fairy-tale structure in the collection. It begins, "Once upon the olden times, when the trees walked and the stars danced" (35). In this postmodern fairy tale, however, such stereotypical fairy tale language is grounded in a recognizable (albeit stylized and even stereotypical) urban setting. This is a retelling of the French story titled "*Les fées*" (The Fairies) by seventeenth-century writer Charles Perrault (which also appears in Andrew Lang's nineteenth-century English translation of Perrault, and is included in Lang's *Blue Fairy Book* with the title "Toads and Diamonds"). Gaiman recasts the rural story of a widow and her two daughters to a dangerous cityscape.[4] While the virtuous daughter in Lang's story is sent to fetch water for her evil stepmother, in Gaiman's version the virtuous "Amanda" is sent to buy drugs for her stepmother. Along the way, Amanda encounters various obstacles and temptations, including a mistreated, talking dog to whom she gives water, a prostitute with a swollen face to whom she gives both an apple as well as the drugs intended for her stepmother, and the drug dealer whose filthy apartment she cleans. Not only is her journey itself reminiscent of the mythic quest narrative which so often structures fairy tales, but it also contains several key fairy tale tropes, including kindness to animals, an evil stepmother, an apple, and obstacles which challenge her generosity and unselfishness.

As in the original stories, Amanda's patience and unselfishness are ultimately rewarded. In both "*Les fées*" and "Toads and Diamonds," the virtuous girl is rewarded with flowers and diamonds falling from her mouth when she speaks; meanwhile, her stepsister is punished with snakes and toads crawling from her mouth. In Gaiman's story, jewels fall from Amanda's mouth when her stepmother beats her for failing to procure her drugs, while her stepsister emits frogs and snakes from her mouth after ignoring the needy dog and prostitute and bringing her stepmother drugs. However, unlike the Lang story, in which the selfish daughter dies and the virtuous daughter marries a prince, Gaiman's urban fairy tale has a more ambiguous, less "fairy tale" ending. The story ends with Amanda quoting Keats' "Ode on a Grecian Urn"—"Beauty is truth, truth beauty—that is all ye know on Earth, and all ye need to know"—after which a final sapphire drops from her lips, and she dies (35–36). Ironically, in Gaiman's story, the jewels, which in the photograph appear to be choking Amanda, are instead a product of and a reward for her virtue.

The photograph makes an intriguing statement about fatal femininity. As Amanda seems to be choking to death on an excess of ornamentation—an expected feminine expression—the photograph conveys the idea that feminine expression is fatal. In contrast, Gaiman's overt framing of the narrative in fairy tale terms brings in the gendered expectations of a Cinderella or a Snow White story in which an evil stepmother's punishment of her perfect, selfless stepdaughter becomes the grounds for the heroine's ultimate reward. Though the photograph makes it seem that Amanda has overdosed on ingesting these symbols, in the Gaiman story they fall from her lips. They are emerging from her, not choking her.

Unlike the canonical "*Les fées*" stories, however, Gaiman rejects the princess imagery in the original story for a more ambiguous ending, keeping the story in the register of a mythopoetic quest tale. As Teresa de Lauretis (like many other feminist scholars) observes in her reading of fairy tales, the role of the princess in these stories traditionally is to be a "sought-for person" (79). In the older versions of the story, then, the virtuous girl becomes a princess, the goal of a quest instead of the questing heroine. Her virtue is rewarded by a transformation from subject to object. Gaiman's replacement of the princess plot with a more ambiguous, poetic meditation on silence is a significant, feminist reworking of the fairy tale. In Gaiman's version, the virtuous girl retains her subjecthood.

Also, Gaiman's allusion to Keats' poem here is a deft choice, as the poem celebrates the idea that unheard melodies are sweeter than heard ones. While this theme is most obviously about anticipation, it is also a commentary on silence. The entire story itself is about silence, as it is ultimately words that choke Amanda, finally quieting her. Where the photograph provokes a certain narrative of understanding—a beautiful girl, a fatal overdose, the meaning of the jewelry instead of the expected pills—Gaiman's prose provides a supplementary narrative of agency. By interpreting the photograph through these traditional fairy tale tropes with a feminist revisioning, the photograph is no longer of a suicidal young woman, but is instead the mythopoetic genesis of a fairy tale heroine.

Doubling, like the mirror morals of the jewels, is another fairy tale quality which Gaiman often finds uniquely suited to this (feminist) project. David Rudd points out that Gaiman's use of doubling is often linked to the uncanny (161).[5] While Jack Zipes, in his discussion of the subversive potential of fairy tales, notes that Freud's original analysis specifically excludes fairy tales from the realm of the uncanny, Zipes points out that "the very act of reading a fairy tale is an uncanny experience in that it separates the reader from the restrictions of reality from the onset and makes the repressed unfamiliar familiar again" (*Fairy Tales and the Art of Subversion* 174). Rudd's Freudian reading of the uncanny reads doubling as a form of castration. Specifically, such castration is linked to the cutting out of the eyes, as Freud himself discusses in his analysis of the German Sandman story (162–163).[6]

Though Palmer's eyes remain open (though apparently unseeing) in these photographs, the uncanny sense of doubling is evoked by her frequent appearances as her own twin throughout the collection. Gaiman himself has discussed the significance of mirrors, a trope inextricably linked with doubling, in his work: "Fantasy — and all fiction is fantasy of one kind or another — is a mirror. A distorting mirror, to be sure, and a concealing mirror, set at forty-five degrees to reality, but it's a mirror nonetheless, which we can use to tell ourselves things we might not otherwise see" (*Smoke and Mirrors* 2). In her discussion of the Gothic, writer Angela Carter discusses her fondness for such "Gothic tales, cruel tales, tales of wonder, tales of terror, fabulous narratives that deal directly with the imagery of the unconscious — mirrors; the externalised self; forsaken castles; haunted forests; forbidden sexual objects" (460). Carter's tacit connection here between mirrors and the "externalised self" evinces psychoanalytic theorist Jacques Lacan's theory of the mirror-phase of development as the moment of identity-formation, the individual's entry into the realm of the Symbolic.[7] Doubling, then, is one way in which the fairy tale genre's traditions allows for new perspectives on old problems.

For example, in the photograph which accompanies Gaiman's story "The Sword," there are two Amandas: a dead Amanda in mime makeup and black and white striped tights with blood running from her mouth, over which laughs a victorious living Amanda, in a corset and flamenco skirt, wielding a sword. As the mime costuming is typical of Palmer's stage appearance in the Dresden Dolls, this tableau represents Amanda's Dresden Dolls persona (31–32). The photograph by itself seems primarily a statement about Palmer's solo album, as her new solo stage persona slays her former Dresden Dolls one. Gaiman's story, however, which opens with the line, "You only get to kill yourself once," brings a more explicit element of black humor to the scenario (31). The story also takes the scenario out of the immediate moment of Palmer's career to a larger, more mythic level. For example, Gaiman makes overt references to time travel, as Amanda "materialized in the alley in a crackle of blue sparks and the sharp scent of ozone like all terminators" (32). Further, in Gaiman's narration of the photograph, Amanda is killing her younger self, an act that Gaiman connects to larger themes of "art and compromise" (32). Though the actual sword in the picture is barely visible, by naming the story "The Sword" and ending it with images of Palmer practicing "fight[ing] shadows," Gaiman draws attention to the epic aspect of the scene, to the eternal need to overcome the past in order to survive the present. Further, this image of Amanda fighting shadows posits an empowered femininity through the juxtaposition of her ball gown and the strength of her swordsmanship.

Similar to "The Sword," another instance of doubling occurs in the photograph and story about Amanda Palmer, the "famous dancer" (116–118). Another dreamlike image, in this photograph Palmer (described as a famous actress) appears in her underwear on a lit stage, while her sole audience member is a fully clothed Palmer (described as a famous dancer), slumped over dead in a folding chair. The text begins with a straightforward description of the scene, describing both what the reader sees (Palmer slumped over in the audience) as well as what she doesn't see (the collapsed roof allowing the sunlight in). The story ends ambiguously: "Amanda Palmer is waiting for the sunlight to fall on her face. Then she will close her eyes and let her face stare ecstatically upwards" (116).[8] The photograph alone brings up questions regarding the dynamics of performer and audience as well as performer and self. The text emphasizes and complicates these distinctions by making both of the Amandas in the photographs performing artists, though one is an actress and the other a dancer.

This tension is further complicated by the fact that the more abstract artist, the dancer, is the one who is dead and in the audience. Though the dead Amanda is foregrounded in the photograph, she is in shadow. So, too, in Gaiman's text, it is the living Amanda (who is on the stage) who is alive, sunlit and ecstatic. Gaiman's commentary on performance is ambiguous here. As it is the Amanda in the audience who is dead, Gaiman may be proposing that it is in performance when we are most alive. Even more unclear is the story's claim that the onstage Amanda has ovarian cancer. Is this to be read as real cancer, an attribute of the "character" on the stage, or in some more abstract or metaphorical fashion? As ovarian cancer is a particularly gendered cancer, Gaiman's inclusion of this detail acts as a commentary on the ability of the female artist to create through art. There is a sense in which Amanda's impending death brings her closer to the ineffable and less tied to earthly matters; in this manner, Gaiman invokes both the mythic as well as the feminine in this scene.

The story continues on the next page, where a fully dressed Amanda performs for the dead audience member Amanda. The story ends with the "life-giving energy" of the sunlight shrinking her cancer. The performing Amanda's vision is blurred with afterimages, while the audience member Amanda grows cold. The story ends with the living Amanda sure she is cured of cancer, though the narrator notes that she is wrong. What to make of all of this ambiguity? In one respect, it is a commentary on the power of art. The fairy tale tropes of twins and danger are once again twisted into modern life dangers of ovarian cancer and the cold reality of death. However, the confusion of performer and audience and of performance itself makes it difficult to nail down one static interpretation. Instead, the ambiguity of the story and its images allows for multiple interpretations simultaneously, resulting in further doublings through the potential multiplicity of meanings.

Yet another form of doubling occurs in "The Two of Them," where there are again a dead Amanda and a living one. As the dead Amanda has a plastic bag over her head, however, it is not as clear that they are the same person: in fact, Gaiman's story refers to the two women as the "Palmer twins" (54).[9] These women are less representative of Palmer's stage personae than they are of her playing at being a traditional lady, wearing floral chintz and drinking tea in a drawing room. In the photograph, the living Palmer holds a teacup as she looks nervously behind her, implying that she was at least complicit in (if not responsible for) her sister's murder. Gaiman's text here is less a complete short story and more an evocative scenario, depicting a conversation between twin sisters in which the younger complains of feeling a sense of doom and experiencing omens (including hearing footsteps and seeing shadows) which the older twin dismisses. Once again, the fairy tale trope of doubling — of twins, of sisters — is utilized in the service of black humor, presenting stereotypical characters in a murder tableau. Unlike the overt triumph of "The Sword," however, here the implied guilt undermines Palmer's propriety, and in fact calls into question the very idea of innocence inherently connected to femininity and class. Once more, Gaiman's text plays up the subversiveness in Palmer's crime scene photograph.

The ultimate result of using the fairy tale genre in the modern, urban settings of *Who Killed Amanda Palmer* is a change in the focus of the story. Carter's description of the genre (which she refers to simply as "the tale") is succinct and apt:

> Formally the tale differs from the short story in that it makes few pretenses at the imitation of life. The tale does not log everyday experience, as the short story does; it interprets everyday experience through a system of imagery derived from subterranean areas behind every experience, and therefore the tale cannot betray its readers into a false knowledge of everyday experience [460].

Such a remove from the quotidian that the fairy tale provides allows Gaiman to wrest the focus away from the kind of interpretation of prurient violence which the photographs of naked women (some of them bruised and the victims of outright violence) by themselves might evoke.

Both Gaiman and Palmer have discussed the importance of realizing the true focus of art, particularly in reference to their own work. As much of Palmer's work (particularly in this collection) might be considered to border on the pornographic, their thoughts on the nature of pornography are useful here.[10] Gaiman, who once wrote for the "British 'skin' magazines" *Penthouse* and *Knave* magazines (*Smoke and Mirrors* 24), explains that after his perusal of these magazines, he realized that the types of pictures they publish are often misinterpreted. According to Gaiman, "*Penthouse* and magazines like it had absolutely nothing to do with women and absolutely everything to do with photographs of women" (24). In other words, the photographs of naked women in these magazines are not conveying information about the women themselves; rather, the photographs of naked women convey information about societal stereotypes of how naked women are supposed to be viewed. Problems emerge when these two different meanings — the meaning of the naked body itself, and societal stereotypes of what the naked body means — are confused and conflated.

Many feminist theorists have similarly addressed understandings of and interpretations of the female body. In *Volatile Bodies: Toward a Corporeal Feminism*, Elisabeth Grosz reflects many of these interpretations in her explanation that "the body is literally written on, inscribed, by desire and signification, at the anatomical, physiological, and neurological levels" (60). Each individual body has its own individual, contextual meaning, which is difficult to convey in a photograph: even at a purely physical level, scars, stretch marks, and tattoos are all examples of such physical markers which are inscriptions of very specific meanings on bodies. These meanings are connected to, but should be differentiated from, the body's placement within society. As theorist Judith Butler explains in her discussion of how bodies are understood in terms of the desires of others, "To the extent that desire is implicated in social norms, it is bound up with the question of power" (2). As Gaiman explains, the failure to understand the difference between *women* and *photographs of women* means that we do not see the difference between the stories of real, individual women (nearly unintelligible in unannotated photographs) and the ways in which stereotypical images of women contribute to their interpolation within the larger circulations of power in society.[11]

Palmer has discussed at length (on her blog and elsewhere) the ways·in which many kinds of misinterpretation of her work have been a problem for her. In particular, audiences often miss the dark humor which pervades much of her work. A good example of this is the outcry that erupted after the release of her song "Oasis" (the lyrics of which are included in *Who Killed Amanda Palmer*). Palmer describes "Oasis" as a tongue-in-cheek, ironic up-tempo pop song. a song about a girl who got drunk, was date raped, and had an abortion. she sings about these things lightly and joy-fully and says that she doesn't care that these things have happened to her because oasis, (her favorite band) has sent her an autographed photo in the mail. and to make things even better (!!), her bitchy friend melissa, who told the whole school about the abortion, is really jealous [*sic*] ["On Abortion, Rape, Art, and Humor"].

Some were offended by what they interpreted as Palmer's flippant attitude toward the serious topics of date rape and abortion. Palmer's response, how-ever, is that, "if you cannot sense the irony in this song, you're about two intelligence points above a kumquat" ("On Abortion, Rape, Art, and Humor"). More importantly, Palmer explains that "the song isn't even so much ABOUT those topics, it's about denial, it's about a girl who can't find it in herself to take her situation seriously" ("On Abortion, Rape, Art, and Humor"). What both Gaiman and Palmer emphasize is the question of deter-mining the true focal point of a text. Palmer's song is not about rape in the same way that *Penthouse* magazine is not about naked women. While *Penthouse* encourages the fantasy that the scenarios evoked by pictures are genuinely reflective of individual identities (and the individual narratives inscribed on their bodies), *Who Killed Amanda Palmer* instead highlights the distance between the viewer and the subjects of the photographs, through both the incorporation of Gaiman's narratives as well as the focus on death — an uncom-fortable subject for many readers. The result of this discomfort is to shift the reader's focus to the more fundamental issues from which these images and ideas emerge.

To borrow a term from photography, what these provocative stories and images do is expand the reader's depth of field. Without the text of the "Toads and Diamonds" story, for example, the viewer would simply see an image of a dead Amanda who choked on what at first glance looks like pills. How-ever, the fairy tale quality of the story results in a shift in focus, a willingness in the reader to see things metaphorically or symbolically. The story encour-ages us to look more closely at the picture and realize that it is not pills but jewels we are seeing — and then to question our original assumption that these jewels were choked on and consider other narrative possibilities. The distance created by the narrative formulation of the fairy tale allows us to re-examine our expectations of the stories frozen in these photographs. This dis-tance, this shift in perspective caused by the juxtaposition of the text and the photographs, causes a friction which allows these frozen stories to melt and unfold.

In fact, Angela Carter points to the qualities of both black humor as well as pornography as crucial in the kind of mythic tale that allows for just such a shift. In this genre, Carter explains, characters and events are exaggerated beyond reality, to become symbols, ideas, passions. Its style will tend to be ornate, unnatural — and thus operate against the perennial human desire to believe the word as fact. Its only humour is black humour. It retains a singular moral function — that of provoking unease. The tale has relations with subliterary forms of pornography [460].

Similarly, Gaiman has pointed out that "humor and horror and pornography are incredibly similar — you know immediately whether you've got them right or not because they should provoke a physiological change in the person reading" (Zaleski 56). It is this very fairy tale quality of these stories (as described by Carter and Gaiman) which provides a distinctly feminist dimension to the collection of Palmer's photographs, a dimension which would be much less obvious if the photographs were collected without Gaiman's stories. In the introduction to *Smoke and Mirrors,* a collection of his short fiction and poetry, Gaiman talks about the nature of fantasy and fairy tales: "Fairy tales, as G. K. Chesterton once said, are more than true. Not because they tell us that dragons exist, but because they tell us that dragons can be defeated" (*Smoke and Mirrors* 2). In the face of the violence portrayed in the photographs, the mythic stories Gaiman tells offer just such hope in the face of the bleakness of violent urban reality.

Without the stories, the more overt dark humor in photographs, such as those of Amanda dead on a golf course (21, 79) or of her corpse as part of an art installation (69–70), would be eclipsed by the accumulation of horror at (or worse, desensitization from) the less overtly funny, more disturbing photographs, such as Palmer's bloody body shoved in a shopping cart (63). Page after page of crime scenes and dead bodies, though humorous and at times even quite beautiful,[12] by themselves would easily lead a reader to reach a critical mass of despair, disgust, or even *ennui.* Accompanied by Palmer's lyrics, they would achieve a certain additional dimension of critical distance, which might allow a certain deepening of perspective. However, Palmer's lyrics to songs like "Guitar Hero" (a song about Columbine-like school violence [76]) and "Oasis" (a song about rape [24]) are in a dark register which is quite similar to her photographs. Gaiman's stories, with their fairy tale evocations, elevate the collection by providing a counterpoint with a much needed mythic quality for the darkly humorous and pornographic elements.

For example, "Case of the Besmirched Dirndl" shows a dirndl-clad Palmer, a dropped beer stein at her feet, with a quite phallic clarinet apparently shoved halfway down her throat. The text, a wonderful homage to Sherlock Holmes, is full-on satire:

> "I will advise the police," said the consulting detective, "that they are looking for a man. He is dark-haired, left-handed, and extremely tall, in all probability a basketball player. He has spent time in Bavaria, but his passport is almost definitely

Guatamalan. He was here for the woodwind convention, but will have checked out early" [95].

The use of costume, introduction of death-by-clarinet, and photograph of a dead Amanda deep-throating a woodwind instrument are amusing while also disturbing. Parodying both detective fiction as well as pornography, Gaiman's text once again changes the reader's focus by reframing the photograph as an evidentiary photo in a fictional narrative. In a way, Gaiman more firmly reminds the reader that the collection is making statements about the portrayal of women (and not necessarily about individual women themselves, except for perhaps the role of women in art). Combining these parodies once again demonstrates the brilliance of Gaiman's collaborative powers, as this death scene is straight black comedy.

However, Gaiman's stories are not uniformly optimistic. To the contrary, there are certain stories accompanying photographs which, rather than mediating the violence with a mythic spin, instead drive home the real dangers which women still face. The short text and photograph titled "The Boys Room" is particularly troubling in this respect. It recounts a fight between the unnamed narrator and Amanda, during which "we got kinda stupid," and now "she's not talking" (76). In the accompanying photograph, Palmer's body is not immediately evident — the picture of a cluttered bedroom has at its center a sunny window, which highlights a video game steering wheel. It seems to be a typical boy's bedroom — only a closer look reveals Palmer's shadowed, slumped body in the corner of the room. Something is wrong with her arm — there is blood — and she is wearing a short t-shirt and men's briefs (76). The unexplained violence and matter-of-fact tone in the text are troubling. This is one of the few unmediated displays of violence in the collection, which is ironic, given that its one of the least overt displays of violence. It takes some time and effort to see what has happened, and it is up to the reader to piece together possible hypotheses.

I cannot find even the darkest form of humor in this story and photograph, unless it is the exception of the extremely dark irony implied by the understatement in the dialogue when compared with the violence in the photograph. This in itself may be a commentary on violence against women, at how often it can go overlooked. Here is the flip side of Palmer's "Oasis." If "Oasis" is about denial, then Gaiman's "Boys Room" illustrates the rest of Palmer's commentary on the media controversy over her song:

> i think it makes people uncomfortable to hear the truth about a very real and sick situation: if you don't know — or have never encountered — a teenager who is going through intense heavy experiences (like rape, abortion, eating disorders, abuse, fill-in-the-blank) and is laughing these things off like THEY DON'T MATTER, then you are not ALIVE and AWAKE and living on this planet. IT'S HAPPENING EVERY-

WHERE. i see it all the time. it's called being a confused teenager. it's real. it SUCKS. abortion is serious. rape is serious. lots of things are serious. do they think i'm blind? ["On Abortion, Rape, Art, and Humor"].

Palmer's blog entry ends with a call to arms to not ignore such ugly topics, but instead to bring them into focus: "our COLLECTIVE freedom to approach situations with humor, with irony, with anger, with sadness, with darkness, with an edge, from a different perspective, from within the situation...it's ESSENTIAL" ("On Abortion, Rape, Art, and Humor"). As this story lacks the kind of fairy tale qualities so prevalent in the other stories, its very lack of fantastic elements forces the reader to once again change her focus, bringing a newly heightened form of attention to the issue of violence against women. By once again changing the depth of field, Gaiman is able to bring fresh attention to an important idea.

NOTES

1. In the interests of recognizing the collaborative nature of this project, I will follow the way each of the authors is credited in the book: Neil Gaiman (writer), Amanda Palmer (collaborator), Kyle Cassidy (photographer), and Beth Hommel (photographer). While Gaiman is presumably primarily responsible for the text of the stories in the collection, because of the collaborative nature of the project, I will attribute the stories to both Gaiman and Palmer.

2. See Andrea Dworkin, *Pornography: Men Possessing Women*; *In Harm's Way: The Pornography Civil Rights Hearings*, eds. Andrea Dworkin and Catharine A. Mackinnon.

3. That the passive body is being portrayed by a known living body does, to a certain extent, create an affective tension which underlies these photographs. Further, that this project was conceived of and directed by Palmer herself also gives weight to a reading of empowerment.

4. See Jack Zipes, "Perrault, Charles," *The Oxford Companion to Fairy Tales*, 379–381; "Lang, Andrew," *The Oxford Companion to Fairy Tales*, 288–90; "Toads and Diamonds," *The Blue Fairy Book*.

5. Rudd also notes the irony in the fact that in Freud's discussion of the uncanny, he uses the original German Sandman tale to illustrate his theory (162).

6. Echoes of which can be seen in other works by Gaiman. The Corinthian from *The Sandman* series springs most immediately to mind.

7. See, e.g., Lacan, "The Mirror-phase as formative of the Function of the I." As Lacan's work is foundational to much recent feminist theory, it is particularly appropriate to identify the applicability of his work to a feminist reading of *Who Killed Amanda Palmer*.

8. That this image of Palmer's face upturned in ecstasy is also evocative of saint imagery simply reinforces the mythic undertones of the text.

9. That they are referred to as "older" and "younger" twins, seemingly oxymoronic phrases, only heightens the unreal quality of this vignette.

10. This idea of the distinction between subject and reality is perhaps most eloquently explored in Michel Foucault's seminal text on art and perception, *This Is Not a Pipe* (1968; trans. James Harkness, Los Angeles: University of California Press, 1982]) in the opening chapter, "Two Pipes."

11. Although Gaiman has distinguished this collection specifically as being art and not pornography, because it is a published collection which includes photographs of an attractive, naked woman, I think that comparisons to pornography are fair.

12. See the monochromatic portrait of Palmer in her slip (74), or floating in a lake, surrounded by diaphanous fabric (57).

WORKS CITED

Butler, Judith. *Undoing Gender*. New York: Routledge, 2004. Print.

Carter, Angela. *Burning Your Boats*. New York: Henry Holt and Company, 1995. Print.

De Lauretis, Teresa. *Alice Doesn't: Feminism, Semiotics, Cinema*. Bloomington: Indiana University Press, 1984. Print.

Dworkin, Andrea. *Pornography: Men Possessing Women*. New York: Plume, 1991.

Gaiman, Neil. "How to order WHO KILLED AMANDA PALMER and why outer space tastes of raspberries." *Neil Gaiman's Journal*. April 29, 2009. Web. 19 May 2011.

_____. *Smoke and Mirrors: Short Fictions and Illusions*. New York: Harper, 1998. Print.

_____ (w), Amanda Palmer (c), Kyle Cassidy (p), *Beth Hommel* (p). *Who Killed Amanda Palmer: A Collection of Photographic Evidence*. New York: Eight Foot Books, 2009. Print.

Grosz, Elizabeth. *Volatile Bodies: Toward a Corporeal Feminism*. Bloomington: Indiana University Press, 1994. Print.

Dworkin, Andrea, and Catharine A. Makinnon, eds. *In Harm's Way: The Pornography Civil Rights Hearings*. Cambridge: Harvard University Press, 1998. Print.

Lacan, Jacques. "The Mirror-Phase as Formative of the Function of the I." Trans. Jean Roussel. *New Left Review* 51 (September-October 1968): 71–77. Print.

"The Life and Times of the Dresden Dolls — Chapter 1: So Far..." *The Dresden Dolls*. Web. 14 June 2011.

McCabe, Joseph. "Interview with Neil Gaiman." *Hanging Out with the Dream King: Conversations with Neil Gaiman and His Collaborators*. Seattle: Fantagraphics Books, 2004. 5–14. Print.

Palmer, Amanda. *Amanda Palmer and Nervous Cabaret Tour*. Bijou Theater, Knoxville, Tennessee. 22 November 2009.

_____. "On Abortion, Rape, Art, and Humor." *Amanda Palmer*. February 3, 2009. Web. 19 May 2011.

Rudd, David. "An Eye for an Eye: Neil Gaiman's *Coraline* and Questions of Identity." *Children's Literature in Education* 39 (2008): 159–168. Print.

"A Short History of Who Killed Amanda Palmer." *Who Killed Amanda Palmer*. Web. 19 May 2011.

"Toads and Diamonds." *The Blue Fairy Book*. Ed. Andrew Lang, 1889. *Project Gutenberg*. Web. 29 June 2011.

Williams, Linda. "Pornographies On/Scene: or Diff'rent Strokes for Diff'rent Folks." *Sex Exposed: Sexuality in the Pornography Debate*. Eds. Lynne Segal and Mary McIntosh. New Brunswick: Rutgers University Press. 233–265. Print.

Zaleski, Jeff. "Comics! Books! Films! The Arts and Ambitions of Neil Gaiman." *Publishers Weekly* (July 28, 2003): 46–57. Print.

Zipes, Jack. *Fairy Tales and the Art of Subversion: The Classical Genre for Children and the Process of Civilization*. New York: Wildman Press, 1983. Print.

_____."Introduction: Towards a Definition of the Literary Fairy Tale." *The Oxford Companion to Fairy Tales: The Western Fairy Tale Tradition from Medieval to Modern*. Ed. Jack Zipes. Oxford: Oxford University Press, 2000. xxvi. Print.

_____."Lang, Andrew." *The Oxford Companion to Fairy Tales: The Western Fairy Tale Tradition from Medieval to Modern*. Ed. Jack Zipes. Oxford: Oxford University Press, 2000. 288–90. Print.

_____."Perrault, Charles." *The Oxford Companion to Fairy Tales: The Western Fairy Tale Tradition from Medieval to Modern*. Ed. Jack Zipes. Oxford: Oxford University Press, 2000. 379–38. Print.

Liminality and Empowerment

The Aged Woman in Neil Gaiman's *"Queen of Knives"* and *"Chivalry"*

BY AGATA ZARZYCKA

Older female characters, though present mostly in the background of Neil Gaiman's works, definitely deserve critical interest as not only a prominent motif, but also as politically significant constructs shaped by believable combinations of age, gender, ethnicity, class, and sexuality factors. The theme of aging or aged womanhood has left its imprint on Gaiman's longer narratives such as *The Sandman* series, *American Gods*, *Coraline* and *Anansi Boys*, as well as several short stories, including "The Problem of Susan," "Feeders and Eaters," "Queen of Knives" and "Chivalry." What makes them especially worth considering from the perspective of female aging is both their extraordinary sensitivity to some of the major problems identified by the contemporary gerontology and their cultural self-awareness. These stories handle the questions of aging with an undertone of subversion.

I argue that "Queen of Knives" and "Chivalry" in particular address the problem of marginalization faced by the aged woman in Western society and culture, as well as enable readings which promise a reversal of power relations, yet when juxtaposed with each other, reveal the lack of easy answers to problems at the intersection of gender and age. The subversive potential of "Queen of Knives" and "Chivalry" is partly due to their identification with what Farah Mendlesohn calls "liminal fantasy" (XXIII), which relies on the discrepancy between the characters' and the reader's perception of the supernatural (182). In addition to this effect, which is frequently achieved through "irony" (191), the stories blur the borders between fantastic, figurative, and realistic discourse in the process that can, after Mendlesohn, be defined as the "concretization of metaphor" (195–196). Despite the similar sources of the aging female characters' empowerment, each work differs in terms of scale and type of empowerment. "Queen of Knives" employs "liminal irony" to build a complex picture of power relations, in which the characters' strikingly passive attitude towards the sudden disappearance of an elderly woman draws the reader's attention to the issue of marginalization. The possibility of this woman's empowerment, traceable but unconfirmed throughout the poem, is provided mostly by the potential "concretization of metaphor" suggested in the title.

"Chivalry," in turn, focuses on depicting the elderly heroine in a position of control, founded not so much on a lack of the complexities present in the other text, as the protagonist's attitude towards them. While the "concretization of metaphor" may be seen as the source of her immediate agency, as she becomes a dispenser of powerful items which are simultaneously mythic, symbolic, and material, the "irony" established through the heroine's anticlimactic distance towards her situation provides her with an agency on the narrative level, constituted by both the story and its utilization of the Arthurian myth. By preserving a detached attitude towards the developments of the narrative, the protagonist can impose her own rules on the plot and her function in it. The moderation, or restraint, that allows her to do so, however, may be perceived as empowering in general terms, yet limiting from the perspective of the discourse of aging. As discussed further, in the light of Tillie Olsen's views on aged womanhood, the identity of Pearl from "Queen of Knives" is in a transitional stage[1] marked by disintegration, but signaling a potential turn towards something new. Arguably, Mrs. Whitaker from "Chivalry" has moved beyond that stage and developed an integrity marked by moderation. Still, such an interpretation touches on the problematic concepts of "wisdom" (Woodward, "Against" 187), spiritual sublimation, and isolation (Stuart-Hamilton 13–14) ascribed if not enforced upon the aged identity (Stuart-Hamilton 14; Woodward, "Against" 187).

While the subversive potential in "Queen of Knives" appears inconspicuous, it offers a rather balanced incorporation of age and gender identity aspects. The elderly heroine's empowerment in "Chivalry" is more spectacular, yet its relationship with the age factor may be seen as ambiguous. This claim is intended not to devalue or deny the story's subversive character, but rather to emphasize its entanglement with one of the most difficult challenges in Western culture: a coherent conceptualization of aging, with an additional acknowledgement of the gender perspective.

Aging in Theory and Practice

According to scholarly accounts, the growing preoccupation with aging in the twentieth and twenty-first centuries has paralleled an ongoing marginalization. On the one hand, researchers mention the increasing importance of older persons as a social group and as target consumers (Blaikie 22, Stuart-Hamilton 6), as well as point to the rise of the age-focused research in sociology, cultural studies, and as a separate discipline of gerontology (Blaikie 11–12, 18; Stuart-Hamilton 5–6), whose study fields include "literary gerontology" (Wallace 390). Diana Wallace traces the interest of writers and artists in the theme of aging, as reflected, for example, by the recent development of the "the memoir of a parent" genre (398). This convention has some traces in "Queen of Knives." Though the poem deals with a memory of the narrator's grandparents, its autobiographical quality is signaled in Gaiman's commentary. He writes that "Queen of Knives" is "close enough to the truth that I have had, on occasion, to explain to some of my relatives that it didn't really happen. Well, not like that, anyway" (22).[2] Gerontologists continue to hunt stereotypes about aging, perpetuated by society in general (Stuart-Hamilton 11, Whitbourne and Sneed 247–248), the realm of culture (Blaikie 18, 23, 96) or academia (Whitbourne and Sneed 248–249).

Describing the most traditional depictions of old age in Western culture, Ian Stuart-Hamilton underlines their contradictory character: "On the one hand, [old age] is a reward to be enjoyed [mostly due to the longevity and experience it signifies], but if anything goes wrong, then it is a punishment" (5). Accordingly, psychological approaches to growing old deal with the dilemma by focusing on the internal work the aging subject executes so the process is harmonious and satisfying. Such work involves, first of all, handling the sources of one's past negative experiences, as well as embracing the prospect of death, gradually detaching oneself from the mundane aspects of existence imposed by physicality, egocentricity and social obligations (13).[3] Thus, contradictory depictions of the old age experience might be explained by its presumed link with the respective failure or success in the tasks specified above. The same link is also crucial for the fact that, as Kathleen Woodward puts it, "In the West the time-honored association of wisdom has been with aging, where wisdom is defined in various ways, but almost always understood as a capacity for balanced reflection and judgment that can only accrue with long experience" ("Against" 187). Woodward perceives the seemingly complimentary connection between old age and sapience as a stereotype whose social and political repercussions lead to denying elderly people as a social group the right to effectively voice their objections to the marginalization they face, and pressing them into a position of passive acceptance (205–206). While Woodward's gender focus is noticeable at various points of her essay (e.g., 186–187, 190, 197–200, 204, 207–209), its mission is to "declare a moratorium on wisdom" (205) as a quality ascribed by the Western culture to the old age in general. A number of other stereotypes identified by gerontologists, however, turn out to be women-specific.

The significance of the intersection between age and gender is often emphasized, with the women's experience of old age pointed out as socially dominant (Blaikie 78) yet, paradoxically, insufficiently researched (Blaikie 78; "Woodward," "Tribute" 88, "Performing" 162).[4] Still, the interdisciplinary explorations carried out so far have led to the identification of several problems crucial for the representations of aged womanhood, and revolve mostly around the factors of oppression, transparency and the focus on youth in Western culture. Apart from the already mentioned cultural and theoretical transparency of female aging–e.g. Woodward goes so far as to claim an actual erasure of the older woman from the classical psychoanalysis ("Tribute" 79, 87) and her "invisibility" in the realm of art ("Performing" 162–163)–researchers underline the extraordinary susceptibility of aging women to the social oppression on the grounds of age- and gender-based discrimination combined (Blaikie 83), especially as far as the physical appearance is concerned (Wallace 408, Whitbourne and Sneed 249).

Through Eyes Young and Old

Woodward defines an important problematic feature of cultural approaches to aging in the notion of "the youthful structure of the look" ("Performing" 163–164), which manipulates the receiver into perceiving the aged character from the perspective of someone less advanced in years (164), and thus results in "the culturally induced tendency to degrade and reduce an older person to the prejudicial category of old age" (164). Though Woodward applies this concept to film (164), the concept is also relevant to the construction of the first-person narrator of "Queen of Knives" as he shares with the reader a childhood memory of a time spent with his grandparents. The family's visit to a local theater leads to the grandmother's disappearance as a result of a stage trick during which she is locked in a container and subsequently cut with various blades. After an unsuccessful attempt to obtain some explanation from the performing illusionist, the grandfather and grandson return to their ordinary life. In the final scene, taking place some time after the incident, the boy observes the older man "stab[bing] a knife into a box" (Gaiman 132).

The narrator's unconventional perception of old age is signaled at the very beginning of the poem:

> I knew they [the grandparents] were old–
> chocolates in their house
> remained uneaten until I came to stay,
> this, then, was aging" [123].

Refreshing and innocent as it may be, that view is likely to put some distance between the reader and the focalizing character, exposing the latter's perspective as child-specific. This narratorial position gains a growing significance once he starts relating the events at the theater. Describing an elderly artist, he comments:

> His haplessness, his awkwardness,
> these were what we had come to see.
> Bemused and balding, and bespectacled,
> he reminded me a little of my grandfather [124].

Soon after, he refers to his fellow spectators: "The audience were old people, / like my grandparents, tired and retired, / all of *them* laughing and applauding" (125, my emphasis). These fragments evoke the cultural stereotype of the old person as a funny character (Cuddy and Fiske 3; Woodward, "Performing" 164) and also undermine it through the overt materialization of the young narrator, who, generationally isolated, becomes the ultimate spectator, distanced from the artist and the elderly viewers alike. A disturbing aspect of the sense of detachment granted by the position of an observer is additionally underlined when Pearl, the narrator's grandmother, is invited onstage: "The conjurer applauded her once more —/ A good sport. That was what she was. A sport" (Gaiman 127). Thus, the reader, sharply aware of the narrative's viewpoint is given a choice whether to identify with it or not.

The fashioning of the reader's viewpoint in "Chivalry" is definitely not straightforward, as the story is told in the third-person voice, which, however, represents the perspective of the elderly protagonist rather than the presumably younger receiver as identified by Woodward. The principal differences in the length as well as literary genre notwithstanding, Gaiman's short story reflects, in its own way, characteristics of the *Reifungsroman*, a genre that deals with personal growth in the period directly preceding the end of life (Wallace 394). Barbara Frey Waxman defines the *Reifungsroman* as

> a narrative structure which focuses on a journey or quest for self-knowledge; a narrative voice, either first person or third person omniscient, which draws the reader into the ageing protagonist's world; the use of dreams or flashbacks for life review; a concern with the physical body and illness; and a sense that, even in frail old age, there is the possibility of an opening up of life [394, as cited in Wallace].

All those elements, with the possible exception of "flashbacks," can be traced in Gaiman's story, which might encourage a consideration of "Chivalry" in terms of Waxman's formula, though it would exceed the scope of this essay. For the purpose of the current discussion, it is, therefore, enough to argue that the aspects of the *Reifungsroman* that feature in "Chivalry" establish an "elderly structure of the look," to rephrase Woodward's term.

The short story, set in modern Britain, traces one week in the life of Mrs. Whitaker, an elderly woman who, having purchased the Holy Grail in a local second-hand shop, finds herself visited by Sir Galaad. The mythic hero's attempts to trade other magical items for the artifact and Mrs. Whitaker's reluctance to comply result in three subsequent visits that he pays to her house, each time involving well-mannered socializing and domestic chores. Eventually, the woman accepts two magical objects in exchange for the Grail, though she rejects an item that might make her young and immortal. Galaad leaves, having fulfilled his quest, while Mrs. Whitaker faces an opportunity to buy Aladdin's lamp and decides against it.

Because the aged protagonist is the story focalizer, the predictable and systematic patterns of her daily activities and her focus on details of the everyday routine affect the structure of the narrative. Its regularity is made prominent by the use of subsequent weekdays as a measure of the plot development; while the most important events take place on Thursday (36), Friday (37–39), Monday (40–42) and Tuesday (42–48), all the remaining days are also acknowledged, be it with just one sentence: "On Wednesday Mrs. Whitaker stayed in all day" (48). Descriptions full of seemingly irrelevant details produce both a dense background of the mundane reality into which the mythic is casually incorporated and an aged character's point of view, as exemplified by the following passage:

> At midday Mrs. Greenberg [Mrs. Whitaker's acquaintance] went home, and Mrs. Whitaker made herself cheese on toast for lunch, and after lunch Mrs. Whitaker took her pills; the white and the red and the two little orange ones.
> The doorbell rang [announcing the arrival of Sir Galaad] [37–38].

The older woman's viewpoint becomes even more distinct during her meetings with Marie, a teenage shop assistant. The girl's first description, though not filtered through Mrs. Whitaker's perception directly, underlines awkwardness and lack of self-assurance typical of a young identity in the formative phase:

> The volunteer on duty [as a sales person] this afternoon was Marie, seventeen, slightly overweight, and dressed in a baggy mauve jumper that looked like she had bought it from the [second-hand] shop.
> Marie sat by the till with a copy of *Modern Woman* magazine, filling out a "Reveal Your Hidden Personality" questionnaire. Every now and then she flipped to the back of the magazine and checked the relative points assigned to an A), B) or C) answer before making up her mind how she'd respond to the question [35].

During their second meeting, Mrs. Whitaker's perspective explicitly empowers her to take a supportive, yet evaluative stance: "Mrs. Whitaker stared at her. Marie was wearing lipstick (possibly not the best shade for her, nor particularly expertly applied, but, thought Mrs. Whitaker, *that would come with time*) and a rather smart skirt. It was a great improvement" (43, my emphasis).

Thus, contrary to the construction of the I-speaker in "Queen of Knives," the narrative voice of "Chivalry" adopts a perspective marked by age and approaching youth as an object of an empathizing, but distanced scrutiny.

The defamiliarization of "the youthful structure of the look" becomes even more striking when considered in terms of a broader narrative estrangement which lies at the basis of the short story's retelling of the Arthurian myth. It does not actually challenge the myth's traditional plot development. Galaad mentions his conventionally acknowledged family background (44), pursues his "Right High and Noble Quest" approved by Arthur (38), and eventually moves on with the Grail (48), obtained thanks to his determination, courage, respectful attitude and humble willingness to perform the required tasks. These four qualities reflect the "chivalry" in the title. Instead, what is subverted is the perspective from which the mythic pattern is introduced to the reader.

While the practice of retelling Arthurian tales from various angles in order to make them relevant for changing audiences and socio-cultural contexts, especially those connected with gender relations, can be pointed out as one of the most important forms of the myth ongoing cultivation (Roberts 7, 10–12), Gaiman's perspective reversal may also be expanded onto Joseph Campbell's monomyth, which, though questioned by numerous subsequent scholars (Manganaro 153–154; Miller 68–69), can hardly be denied a widespread impact on the Western popular culture (Day 80–81). As argued by Dean A. Miller, Campbell's crucial contribution is the "set[ting] up [of] stages and categories of the heroic biography" (69), which imposes on the reader the usually young protagonist's perspective by tracing his or her development. When considered in terms of the monomyth, the function of Mrs. Whitaker can be related to those of a helper–associated by Campbell among others with an elderly female character (64–65) and defined as an embodiment of "the benign, protective power of destiny" (66)–or the "goddess" (100), the interaction with whom "is the final test of the talent of the hero to win the boon of love (charity: *amor fati*), which is life itself enjoyed as the encasement of eternity" (109): the quality possible to identify with the Holy Grail (Marino 106). With regard to another influential method of analysis applied to traditional narratives, namely Vladimir Propp's formal morphology, Mrs. Whitaker occupies in Galaad's story the position of a "donor" who faces the heroic character with a task before offering him or her a powerful artifact (24, 27).[5] Thus, the narrator's point of view in "Chivalry" is subversive on at least two levels: it represents not only a female and aged perception of the traditional story and its young hero, but also the perspective of a character whose function in the heroic progress is presumably episodic. In contrast to writers like Marion Zimmer Bradley, who in *The Mists of Avalon* centralizes both the viewpoint and the role of her narrator Morgain, Gaiman does not involve Mrs. Whitaker in Galaad's original story beyond the act of rewarding him with the Grail in exchange for a number of favors. Her stand-alone personal narrative encapsulates the Arthurian myth, making the aged heroine's point of view all the more prominent.

One of the *Reifungsroman* features of "Chivalry" is the aged heroine's perspective, which is elaborately established and incorporates also two other attributes mentioned by Waxman: the "quest for self-knowledge" and the "possibility of opening up of life" (Wallace 394). A direct employment of such a "quest" is offered by the retelling of Galaad's story, yet it also affects Mrs. Whitaker's own identity, as it brings into her existence miraculous possibilities, including that of immortality, thus putting her willpower to a test. Thus, her involvement in the mythic narrative testifies to the potential of an elderly woman's existence.

All in the Family: Power Relations and Empowerment

While the poem as well as the short story denaturalize the "youthful structure of the look" in their own respective ways, the complexity of power relations in both texts becomes even more visible at the intersection of gender and age. In "Queen of Knives," this occurs in dynamics of the grandmother-grandfather and grandmother-grandson relationships, the former reflected in an especially interesting way by the contrast between the vocality of both spouses. "Chivalry," in turn, focuses on the experience of a single character, implicitly suggesting the presence of power relations between Mrs. Whitaker, her family, and the broader community, though it remains in the background. Like most stories of old age, the predominant impression is of the protagonist's independence — or isolation.

In "Queen of Knives," the grandfather is labeled as one who "ha[s] the voice in the family" (Gaiman 131) and though this refers to his musical talent, its broader significance remains clear. While he never talks about himself directly (the majority of his utterances are speculations about the illusionist's show technicalities), the reader gets to learn relatively much about the old man, either from Pearl's recollections (125) or the narrator's own comments (127, 132). The personal information deals mostly with the grandfather's past activities and enterprises.[6] The grandmother, in turn, is said to "ha[ve] no voice, not one to speak of" (124), which seems at odds with her habit of singing while completing domestic chores (123). When she talks, it is about her husband or her own past, but in the context of the anti–Semitic acts in London before World War II and the experiences of her family rather than her own (129–130). What the reader does get to know about Pearl as a person deals not so much with her actions or designs as her physicality:

> My grandmother must have been, what? Sixty, then?
> She had just stopped smoking
> was trying to lose some weight. She was proudest
> of her teeth, which, though tobacco-stained, were all
> her own [126–127].

At this moment in the narrative, the narrator offers a hint of the grandmother's advantage over her husband, but it is based on that physical detail, as the grandfather's daredevil antics while bicycling left him toothless "as a youth" (127). The narration continues to show this slow-burning hint of superiority as she "chewed hard licorice, ... / or sucked hard caramels, perhaps to make him wrong" (127), though the story immediately turns to identify her secondary place in the home. She remains second to the conjurer (127).

Pearl does not talk about herself. However, the borrowed voices of the songs she likes — popular American and British hits from the early decades of the 20th century — may be significant as a part of her unexpressed self-narration. "You Made Me Love You (I Didn't Want to Do It)," written in 1913 by Joe McCarthy and James V. Monaco (Herder 398), suggests her emotional submission is not entirely voluntary, and the selection implicitly depicts her voice as a form of rebellion in her gender relations (Studwell 142). "Daisy Bell (A Bicycle Built for Two)," Harry Dacre's song from 1892, features a young man who refers to cycling as a metaphor of life in order to win a girl's acceptance (Herder 75); as Pearl's husband used to enjoy bicycle rides himself, her attachment to that particular composition may be something more than a coincidence.[7] "If You Were the Only Girl in the World," a 1916 hit co-written by Clifford Grey and Nat D. Ayer (Roshwald and Stites 334), spins an idyllic vision of a romantic relationship (Traditional Music Library n.p.), while Charles Collins and Fred W. Leigh's "Don't Dilly Dally (My Old Man)" produces a slightly sexist image of a wife forced to run after the car with her husband and all household possessions inside (Traditional Music Library n.p.).[8] Thus, the selection of lyrics cited by the grandmother alludes to confining or imperfect relationships, which may reflect her otherwise suppressed frustration.

A more direct indicator of Pearl's possibly underprivileged position in her marriage may be identified in the poem's title. "Queen of Knives" is connected with Will Goldston's *Tricks and Illusions*–the text quoted by Gaiman as a motto–where the phrase serves as the name of a trick similar to the one described in the poem (Goldston 173). While even such a straightforward explanation may suggest an unequal distribution of agency, with the artist as the active, and the woman as the objectified participant of the performance, another interpretation in terms of power relations is invited by the analogy between the phrase and the Queen of Swords Tarot card. In older explications of Tarot symbolism, such as those provided by Samuel MacGregor Mathers in 1888 (20) or A. E. Thierens in 1930 (198–199), the Queen of Swords is often associated with negative aspects of femininity, yet more recent sources emphasize her intellectual potential (Alessi and McMillan 71–72) or "intense personal development" (Paul 168). Thus, among the possible consequences of the card's connection with the poem's title is a suggestion of degradation or reduction — from swords to knives — foreshadowing the theme of the aged woman's marginalization, confinement and inability to grow. The "Queen of Knives" label may be understood as an ironic reinforcement of the woman's traditional role:

> Lunch and dinner,
> those were my grandmother's to make, the kitchen
> was again [after the grandfather's preparation of breakfast] her domain, all the
>   pans and spoons,
> the mincer, all the whisks and knives, her loyal
> subjects [Gaiman 123].

Even though the very attachment to domestic chores is not necessarily oppressive, the further development of events may be read as the "loyal subjects'" rebellion, as it is by means of blades, including the most casual one, that Pearl is stabbed and cut during the show (128–129): "The conjurer took a kitchen knife, / pushed it slowly through the red hatbox. / And then the [grandmother's] singing stopped" (130).[9]

Apart from the identifiable inequalities of power relations in Pearl's marriage, there is no clear suggestion that her husband is abusive; moreover, he has given up some of his own pursuits for the sake of the family, as pointed out in endnote 5. When the label of the "King" appears in the poem, it does not refer to the grandfather, but to "the King's Theatre" (124). It might point to the stage performer as the actual power agent and the woman's eventual destroyer, although her disappearance, catalyzed by the magical trick, can also be seen as a consequence of the overall, decentralized marginalization on several levels suggested above.

A possibly less complicated set of power relations links the grandmother with her grandson, whose juvenile mindset has already been discussed. The "Queen of Knives" narrator may be ascribed yet another attribute involved in the family-specific power distribution: an expectant attitude towards the older generation, and especially the grandmother. Tillie Olsen addresses that kind of relationship in her ground-breaking narrative of aged womanhood, "Tell Me a Riddle." The title of Olsen's story alludes to children's unceasing demands for their grandparents' attention (53–54) and, as pointed out by

Constance Coiner, makes the aspect of enforcement prominent in the intergenerational exchange (294). A similar connection between the narrator of "Queen of Knives" and his grandparents is suggested early in the poem: "It was a hard week for my grandparents / forced to entertain a wide-eyed boy-child" (124). Further on, the kid's unconsciously consumerist attitude towards Pearl is signaled when, after her disappearance, the grandfather reasons: "*She'll come back to us with / flowers, / or with chocolates*" (130, original italics), and the narrator comments, "I hoped for chocolates" (130). The boy does not require pacifying; instead of being anxious about his grandmother's situation, he enjoys the show: "I wanted him [the grandfather] to stop talking: I needed the magic" (129). The narrator's behavior is well explicated and naturalized by his puerile identity, yet at the same time points to the inevitability of the unequal distribution of power between the younger and older generation.

In "Chivalry," Mrs. Whitaker's attitude about her deceased spouse, Henry, is underpinned with a quiet sentiment rather than any kind of obligation, though most situations in which the issue of their marriage is brought up underline its temporal distance from the heroine's current life. The immediate references to the protagonist's husband are triggered by the presence of photograph. The first description specifically locates the picture in space and time, as well as incorporates the framed photo itself into the unique mosaic of mundane and extraordinary items that add to the meaning of Mrs. Whitaker's life: "it [the Grail] sat between a small soulful china basset hound and a photograph of her late husband, Henry, on the beach at Frinton, 1953" (36). In the second direct reference, the photo's content is made almost unreal by its attachment to the past: "her late husband Henry, shirtless, smiling and eating an ice cream in black and white, almost forty years away" (47). The heroine's memories of her partner carry a nostalgic aura when she remembers his fondness of a fishing trophy (42) or tells Galaad the story of their marriage (42). The clear attachment of Henry to a closed and distant chapter of Mrs. Whitaker's life blurs the issue of power relations between them, and though her final rejection of the eternal youth prospect may be seen as at least partly motivated by some kind of commitment binding her to her spouse (46–47), the warmth of her memories suggests that she is driven by love or loyalty rather than some long-lasting sense of submission. What is, however, reflected by the issue of the protagonist's marriage is the gender bias of the aging experience (Wallace 400), with the woman as the one to embrace the solitary life after her partner's death.

The experience of alienation, a significant problem underlined by gerontologists (Stuart-Hamilton 127), becomes even more prominent when located on the background of Mrs. Whitaker's relationship with her living family and broader community. While she keeps in touch with her niece and nephew, the bond with the former, who lives in Australia, is established first of all by means of material objects such as pictures and trinkets (43). The protagonist's contact with the family of her nephew, though direct, is a little one-sided. Mrs. Whitaker is the one to make the effort of traveling to their house and bringing a gift (40). Her alienation is further reinforced when it turns out that there is "no one really to leave them [Mrs. Whitaker's possessions] to, no one but Ronald [the nephew] really and his wife only liked modern things" (44). Thus, the family bonding is depicted as not strikingly different from the protagonist's other social activities, such as the weekly meetings with Mrs. Greenberg (37).

While the heroine's independence and control over her life is an important element of the narrative, it is also clear that the elderly woman might benefit from a more empathic and extensive attention on the part of other people than the one she receives. She does seem dejected when faced with the need of picking up a parcel from the post office because she was not fast enough to answer the doorbell when it was brought to her house (42). It also turns out that, in spite of her general briskness, she is not able to carry out all household activities on her own, and it takes Galaad, driven to Mrs. Whitaker by the Grail search, to provide her with the necessary assistance (44). It may, therefore, be concluded that the aged woman's agency and self-sufficiency, emphasized throughout the story, is not enabled by the absence of marginalizing factors, but rather made prominent against the disturbingly transparent background of social indifference.

To Be Discontinued; To Be Detached

The heroines of both "Queen of Knives" and "Chivalry" are characterized by detachment from their communities, though the scale and impact on the aging woman's identity is different in each case. Pearl's public disappearance is significant not only in terms of the overt power relations, but also another aspect of the transparency affecting aging womanhood, namely, the phenomenon of "discontinuity," identified by Joanne Trautmann Banks in Tillie Olsen's writings as "a pattern imposed on women's lives" (200). Its source is located by both Olsen and Trautmann Banks in the marginalization of the female identity, which prioritizes demands imposed by relationships with other people over its own integrity and needs (Trautmann Banks 200).[10] The disappearance of Pearl may be considered as a culmination of that kind of marginalization combined with other forms of oppression against aging womanhood, though an alternative interpretation will also be proposed later in this paper. One way or another, the grandmother's dematerialization is politically meaningful, as, according to Woodward, the "disappearing female body" ("Performing" 163) constitutes an important factor in cultural approaches to female aging and can be interpreted as a marker of the older woman's irrelevance (163–164).[11] Still, before the heroine disappears entirely, she undergoes a process of fragmentation on multiple levels.

An impression of "discontinuity," though not directly in the context of identity structure, is provided by the very composition of "Queen of Knives." What makes the flow of the poem uneven is its digressive character; the account of the narrator's memory is repeatedly interrupted by references to an even more remote past, which are triggered by various details of the plot development, e.g., when the grandfather's comment on the spectacle provokes an enumeration of facts from his life (125). The retrospective discourse does not blur the borders between timelines and the reader is able to follow the narration shifts, yet the text's structure produces an effect of fragmentation or even a certain incompleteness.[12] The magical performance scene, in turn, offers an overt visualization of the fragmentation process. The performer not only stabs the container with Pearl inside, but also divides it into two in order to "lif[t] the top / half of the box up and off, and put it on the stage, / with half my grandma in" (128). The disintegration continues as the magician separates a yet smaller container, supposedly with the woman's head inside (129). The show ends with all three containers being reconnected and the grandmother disappearing from their interior, having shown her beaming face for one last time (130). Thus, the whole performance relies literally on the woman's dissolution and may be interpreted as reflecting the "discontinuity" ascribed by Olsen and Trautmann Banks to women in general. A more subversive reading of the discussed scene as a turning point in Pearl's personal development is also possible, the identity collapse being a necessary first step towards its redefinition–a process discussed by Trautmann Banks (202).

While it is possible that the poem heroine is about to enter the final phase of her self-development, or perhaps what May Sarton, followed by Waxman, calls the "ripening" of the aging identity (Wallace 394), Mrs. Whitaker seems to have already accomplished the better part of such a process. That presumption is confirmed not only by her quiet independence and self-sufficiency, but also the easiness with which she takes control over the extraordinary development of the story into which she gets involved. Her agency is reinforced by several kinds of detachment, which can be traced back to the psychological postulates of harmonious aging mentioned previously, namely, the distance from troubling issues; functions performed in the society; physical ailments; and egocentric impulses.

"Chivalry," originally written by Gaiman for a Grail-themed collection (17),[3] rests on a detachment from the traditional Authurian Romance, which centralizes Mrs. Whitaker's perspective and offers the quest as secondary to the *raison d'être* of the narrative. This reverses the conventional conflict, resolution, and glory of the successful Grail quest. A similar kind of reversal occurs in the sole relatively extended reference to the protagonist's physical condition. Tasting a sample of the fruit of immortality, she experiences "a moment when it all came back to her — how it was to be young: to have a firm, slim body that would do whatever she wanted it to do; to run down a country lane for the simple unladylike joy of running; to have men smile at her just because she was herself and happy about it" (46). Thus, the insight into Mrs. Whitaker's physicality is made indirectly and any sort of information about its current state or her subjective attitude to it can only be deciphered from the contrast provided by the memory, which also suggests that the topic is not to be elaborated upon. The heroine's distance from her physical as well as emotional self reaches its peak the moment she rejects the enchanted fruit, and the pursuit of moderation can be seen as a part of her motivation to do so (46–47). Mrs. Whitaker's refusal challenges the conventional trope, where immortality-granting artifacts tend to be objects of desire, and thus her refusal becomes a mark of her agency. Moreover, it is mostly through restraint or refusal that she executes other kinds of control over the narrative.

The involvement of the "Chivalry" protagonist in Galaad's Grail-focused mission does not, actually, violate its development, and therefore she effectively carries out her Campbellian helper / "Goddess" or Proppean "donor" function. The form of its fulfillment, however, serves as a spectacular reinforcement of Mrs. Whitaker's empowered individuality. First, it is by an assertive refusal that she accomplishes an important part of her role, turning down Galaad's offerings and thus exposing him to subsequent tests. Second, she spectacularly resists the heroic convention brought into the narrative by its Arthurian underpinning when, on her second visit to the shop, she chooses a Mills & Boon romance over *Romance and Legend of Chivalry* (43–44), previously located close enough to the Grail to look almost like an instruction attached to the artifact (36). Consequently manifesting her detachment from the epic narrative register, the protagonist imposes her own, strikingly anticlimactic and mundane rules of interacting with Galaad. To his voluntarily performed heroic deeds such as the winning of "the sword Balmung" (41), "Philosopher's Stone," "The Egg of the Phoenix" (45) and an "appl[e] of the Hesperides" (46) she answers with non-committal socializing and requests for help with removing snails from her property (41) or cleaning (44). These mundane tasks can be interpreted as effective challenges to the virtues of humbleness, kindheartedness, and respect, so they do not undermine the significance of his mission. She makes no visible effort to adjust to his archaically refined language (39), and having agreed to give him the Grail, interrupts his knightly thanks in order to offer her own mode of celebration by "getting out the very best china, which was only for special occasions" (47). More importantly, perhaps, she confirms her independence from both external authority systems and internal longings. For example, she chooses not to reveal the Holy Grail to the local priest (40) and rejects some of the powerful artifacts that appear within her reach.

The moderation and distance with which Mrs. Whitaker faces her life, from the experience of aging to the involvement in the Arthurian myth, does have empowering qualities, even if they may seem ambivalent from the gerontological perspective. The impact of the protagonist's restraint-based control over the narrative manifests itself, first of all, in a number of ironic effects, some of them developing the "liminal" dimension which, according to Mendlesohn, affects not only the plot and characters, but also the reader.

Empowering Liminality

While "liminal fantasy" elements signaled in the opening of this essay are present in both discussed texts, it is my impression that the explicitly intertextual character of "Chivalry" puts certain restrictions on those attributes, while "Queen of Knives" can be considered as a more representative example of the convention defined by Mendlesohn. A characteristic feature of "liminal fantasy" is the suspension on the verge between a realistic and fantastic reading of the text, a quality which Mendlesohn describes as a "possib[ility of] fantasy" (183). From the "liminal fantasy" perspective, however, a motif even more relevant than the woman's unexplained fate is the surprisingly passive acceptance of her absence by her husband and grandson. After the show they try to contact the performer, but when it proves ineffective (131), they simply move on with their lives. The narrator's emotional reaction is not mentioned at all, while the formulations used with reference to the grandfather resemble those applicable to a mourning person: "He got so old after that night / as if the years took him all in a rush" (131); "He bore it well" (132). The male characters' fatalistic stance results in the "irony" typical of the "liminal fantasy" convention, in which "we are presented with the obviously fantastical, and watch while the protagonists ignore it or respond to it in ways that feel dissonant.... The moment of doubt is triggered by our sense that there should be some reaction to the fantastic" (Mendlesohn 191). Moreover, in some cases (as Mendlesohn comments referring to Joan Aiken's short story), "some participants [of the action] ... are trying desperately to preserve the mundane habits of everyday life in the face of evident chaos" (192). This is something that Pearl's family also seems to be doing. The grandmother's disappearance — no matter if its direct reason is supernatural or rational — is denaturalized in the reader's eyes by the reaction it evokes, and that denaturalization may be extended onto the social and cultural processes of marginalization and erasure as indirect factors potentially contributing to the woman's fate. Still, such a conclusion points to the awareness-raising potential of the poem, but not exactly its subversiveness.

A possibility of the old woman's empowerment, however, is provided by another process which Mendlesohn identifies as crucial for "liminal fantasy." He describes "that moment where metaphor and magic become indistinguishable, where the reader is expected to suspend faith, not in reality, but in metaphor, to allow metaphor to be concrete" (195). The metaphor which undergoes such a "concretization" in "Queen of Knives" is the title phrase itself. The previous sections of this paper have suggested the expression's abstract interpretations referring to the objectified role in the performance, the domestic confinement or the degraded Queen of Swords symbolism. Nevertheless, when considered to be the definition of the heroine's actual identity, the name grants her a position of empowered agency. According to such a reading, Pearl may be said to use the opportunity provided by the blurring of reality borders during the magical show in order to take control over the blades and subvert them from an attribute of her housewife self to a tool of her release.

While the effectiveness of an empowerment which leads to the dissolution of the empowered subject might be questioned, the productivity of that process becomes clearer when referred to the aging woman's identity. Analyzing Olsen's protagonist from "Tell Me a Riddle," Treutmann Banks acknowledges the factor of disintegration as inscribed not only in the dispersal of the heroine's self caused by her lifetime submission to other people, but also in the process of her identity's final emergence, which requires her "to undo, to reverse, in some ways, and to balance the style by which she has lived thus far" (202). Perhaps a similar process is needed by Pearl as she undergoes the onstage de- and reconstruction in order to get rid of the sources of her limitations, all of which — from the body through the family to the public role — are affected by the factors of oppression or marginalization.

In "Chivalry," the already analyzed detachment-based agency of Mrs. Whitaker may confuse the reader as to the status of the protagonist herself, as well as the unrealistic elements of the story, though its strong connection with the Arthurian theme seems to limit the possibility of either a coherent rationalization or estrangement. Still, as concluded in the previous section, the said detachment results in dissonances close to those produced by "liminal irony." One category of such effects, manifested in the story's very first sentence — "Mrs. Whitaker found the Holy Grail; it was under a fur coat" (Gaiman 35) — are the repeated juxtapositions of ordinary and magical items. A medieval parchment appears instead of a "little card with a photograph on it" when the protagonist asks Galaad to confirm his identity (38); various kinds of everyday food are offered to the knight each time he turns up to with a powerful artifact (42, 48); the Grail is packed for the journey in "some old Christmas wrapping paper" (48). Such contrasts may sustain the reader's uncertainty as to the protagonist's judgment, as well as the actual function of the supernatural objects. The ambivalence is further reinforced by the clash between Mrs. Whitaker's calm awareness of their nature and her continuous practice of evaluating the relic, as well as the remaining artifacts, according to the criterion of aesthetics. She keeps referring to them as "nice" (36, 41, 45) even in the climactic moment of making the decision to accept Galaad's offer: "I'll take the other two [Philosopher's Stone and the Egg of the Phoenix].... They'll look nice on the mantlepiece" (47). Whatever reaction might be expected from the heroine when exposed to the magical items, her dominant restraint deprives the reader tangible clues as to the actual scope of her awareness, insight or intentions. Simultaneously, Mrs. Whitaker's aesthetics-oriented treatment of powerful artifacts points, once again, to her independence, marking the distance she keeps from the myth she has become involved in. From that perspective, the ironic dissonances, caused to a large extent by the heroine's narrative agency, testify to her empowerment.

Another type of cognitive ambiguity is generated by the broader inter-action between the mythic and the mundane in the story. While Mrs. Whitaker's impassive acknowledgement of the supernatural events, from dis-covering the Grail in the second-hand shop through meeting Galaad to being offered magical gifts, may partly be connected with her moderation-based integrity, the reception the knight receives from other characters is also worth mentioning. The interest of local kids in the presence of Galaad's stallion on the street (39) shows clearly that they find it extraordinary, yet the only devel-opment of the situation is that the knight encourages them to play with the animal, which they gladly do (39, 44). After Galaad has talked to Marie before visiting Mrs. Whitaker, the only thing that she finds worth commenting on is: "He was really dreamy. Really, really dreamy ... I could of gone for him" (43). While such attitudes towards the mythic disturbance of the mundane reality seem to inscribe in the characteristics of "liminal fantasy," the impact of the characters' unexplained flexibility of judgment seems mitigated by the Arthurian myth working in the background of the story. The intertextual context shifts the polarity framing the plot from the real vs. the unreal or known vs. strange towards Brian Attebery's continuum rather than opposition established by "the familiar" and "the magical" (131); or Jean-François Lyotard's distinction between "scientific knowledge" (23) and "narrative knowledge" (18). Attebery characterizes "mythic discourse" as incorporating the supernatural and mundane elements of a tale into a continuum which is also expanded to contain the worldviews of the persons involved in the narration and reception of the plot, and thus blur boundaries between life and fiction (131). As he underlines in his discussion of modern fantasy literature, such a continuum does not naturally exist in the contemporary Western culture, and the fantasy convention is motivated by an ongoing attempt to reestablish it (131). Lyotard, in turn, associates the "scientific knowledge" with reasoning based on objective evidence (23–24), and "narrative knowledge" with "competence that goes beyond the simple determination and application of the criterion of truth, extending to the determination and application of criteria of efficiency (technical qualification), of justice and/or happiness (ethical wisdom), of the beauty of a sound or color (auditory and visual sensibility), etc." (18). He also points to the crucial role of various kinds of storytelling, including myths, in the latter knowledge category (19–20). Thus, the presence of the commonly recognized mythic narrative in "Chivalry" encourages an explanation of the characters' openness to the extraordinary as an activation of a mode of cognition alternative to the rationalistic one. Such flexibility seems probable in the case of the kids' developing worldviews, while Marie responds to the myth's conventionally romantic potential turned down by Mrs. Whitaker, and, following the rules of a formulaic tale, eventually elopes with Galaad (48). As for the protagonist, her lack of surprise when faced with the young knight, and later with the wonderful items, may be interpreted as a "mythically logical" extension of the preliminary acceptance with which she reacted to the Grail itself — the commonly known story around the artifact has, in a way, made the subsequent events predictable, as suggested by the following exchange:

> "That is the Egg of the Phoenix," said Galaad. "From far Araby it comes. One day it will hatch out into the Phoenix Bird itself; and when its time comes, the bird will build a nest of flame, lay its egg, and die, to be reborn in flame in a later age of the world."
>
> "I thought that was what it was," said Mrs. Whitaker [45–46].

Even though the reader may be confused by both the status of the magical elements in the story or the characters' attitudes towards them, and thus alienated from the protagonist's point of view, the liminality of such an effect is weakened by the possibility of attributing it to the influence of the mythic narrative on the text.

The other attribute of "liminal fantasy" which has demonstrated its empowering potential in the context of "Queen of Knives," namely, the "metaphor concretization" is also possible to trace in "Chivalry." Still, due to the crucial role of objects which, as the Grail itself, are constituted by a combination of material and metaphoric or metaphysical aspects, it may also be seen as a reversed process, which starts with an affirmation of their tangibility — the Grail being introduced as a second-hand item for sale (36), the appearance of the sword being described in detail (41), and the remaining three artifacts entering into physical contact with Mrs. Whitaker's hands (45–46). Only then does the mythic or magical character of each object become clear: the heroine explains to an acquaintance that the newly bought decoration "[is] the cup that Jesus drank out of at the Last Supper. Later, at the Crucifixion, it caught His precious blood when the centurion's spear pierced His side" (37); while Galaad describes his gifts' origins and properties (41–42, 45–46). However, although the nature of the Grail becomes reaffirmed as metaphysical the moment the knight perceives it for the first time and kneels, as "A shaft of light c[omes] through the net curtains and paint[s] his awed face with golden sunlight, and turn[s] his hair into a silver halo" (39), no further specification of its power follows.[14] In the case of the Philosopher's Stone, the Egg of the Phoenix and the immortality fruit, the third and final stage of the "de-substantiation" process — namely the attachment of the actual metaphoric aspect — can be identified as the artifacts are ascribed auras of three specific feelings: "*serenity*" (45, original emphasis), "freedom" (45) and juvenescence (46), respectively. Still, if some kind of hierarchy may be applied to the discussed items' material, magical and metaphoric aspects, it is disrupted by Mrs. Whitaker's continuous practice of treating them, first and foremost, as decorations. The potentially confusing mixture of their physicality, supernatural character, symbolic meanings and aesthetic features may put the reader in a position close to that imposed by "liminal fantasy," yet, similarly as in the case of "liminal irony," such an effect seems mitigated by the presence of specified mythic frameworks to which the artifacts may be related. What is, however, much clearer is the direct as well as indirect empowerment, which they offer to the protagonist.

The Grail's presence not only enables her to demonstrate her narrative agency by triggering the development of the mythically informed plot which Mrs. Whitaker subsequently takes under control in the ways analyzed in previous sections of this essay, but also grants her an immediate power over Galaad, who pursues the item she owns. Her critical consideration of the artifacts he has to offer further underlines her privileged position, while her peculiar focus on their decorative function manifests her independence from literary conventions. Finally, the fact that Mrs. Whitaker rejects the fruit of immortality, and shows no interest in the actual powers of other objects may be read as evidence of that kind of freedom from egocentric impulses that can only come from an accomplished and integrated identity, often pointed out as the ultimate goal in the process of aging. Still, the consideration of the heroine from the latter perspective may also lead to less optimistic conclusions.

Conclusion

The open character of my speculations about the ending of "Queen of Knives" is to some extent connected with the influence exerted on it by the characteristics of "liminal fantasy," whose "ideological determination" (Mendlesohn 240) is called "essentially polysemic" (240), which means that the genre expects "the reader to accept the truth behind multiple and competing narratives while refusing to explain which truth it is we should discover" (240). In Gaiman's poem, the factor of authority is put into question at the very beginning, in the already mentioned motto from Goldston's book: "The reappearance of the lady is a matter of individual taste" (Gaiman 123). Taken out of its original context, the sentence leaves the reader with an open question, whose "taste" it is: the magician's? The lady's? Or maybe that of the audience? A similar confusion is inscribed in the poem's ambiguous final image of the grandfather during a display of some undoubtedly strong, but unspecified emotion, which might be deciphered as a sense of personal or collective guilt, but also as a confusion in the face of the unknown, a simple longing or some entirely different feeling.[15] The discussed scene is closed by two song verses: "You made me love you. / I didn't want to do it" (132), which earlier in the poem are sung by the grandmother (123), but at the end reappear without any markers of either the quotation or the speaker. Perhaps the dangling phrase points to the emotional tumult of the spouse in mourning; perhaps it is the lingering voice of Pearl, which provides the only available explanation of her disappearance — only the poem's reader can decide where the "truth" lies.

The doubts evoked by the poem's ending correspond with those accompanying the whole narrative. It may be laced with the supernatural, but does not have to, while the Queen of Knives herself may be the agent subverting social and cultural mechanisms that affect the aged womanhood, or a victim submitting to them. This analysis, however, has first and foremost been aimed to show that it is exactly Gaiman's skillful employment of liminality as manifested through the blurred borders not only between the real and the fantastic, but also the subject and the object or the active and the passive. This produces a potential for reflection as well as a promise of change.

In the case of "Chivalry," the source of the protagonist's empowerment is not so much liminality *per se*, mostly because its overall impact on the reader is disturbed by the story's overt intertextuality, as the mechanisms of "irony" which underline the control of the heroine over the plot, and "concrete metaphors" in the form of artifacts whose presence reveals the integrity of her identity, manifested through the restraint towards the powers put within her reach. However, as both those forms of empowerment rely on the aged protagonist's detachment, they invite a consideration in terms of the problem of "disengagement," broadly discussed by gerontologists. While Stuart-Hamilton argues that the original "disengagement theory," legitimating older persons' decreasing involvement in the external reality, has been misunderstood as an attempt to erase older persons from the scope of social attention (14), the controversy around it has exerted a strong impact on gerontological explorations of the 20th century (Blaikie 42, 61–62), and the conflict between detachment and empowerment of the aging identity remains unresolved in Western culture. As signaled in at the beginning of this essay, Woodward touches on a specific aspect of the problem, when she depicts the concept of "wisdom" as "carr[ying] the connotation of detachment" (Against 206) and thus depriving aged people of the power of emotion, and especially anger, in the struggle for their agency (205–206). From that perspective, Mrs. Whitaker's refusal to accept both the weapon which makes its user "unconquerable in war, and invincible in battle" (Gaiman 41), as well as the fruit of immortality and the passions it implies can be read as expressing submission rather than empowerment, especially that the artifacts she does keep signify "serenity" and "freedom" (45), which seem conventionally more suitable for an aged person, and especially a woman. Moreover, when the heroine's comment that "[Galaad] shouldn't offer things like that [the rejuvenating fruit] to old ladies. It isn't proper" (47) may refer not only to her internal sense of decorum in the light of which her pursuit of eternal youth might violate the memory of Henry (46–47), but also the externally imposed criteria of what is and is not appropriate for aged womanhood. Such an interpretation is to a large extent speculative, however, the otherwise impressive integrity of Mrs. Whitaker is more explicitly disturbed when, after Galaad's departure, her sole emotional display is revealed to the reader, as she "crie[s] quietly into a Kleenex" and does not leave her house the following day (48). Whether her upset is triggered by an increased feeling of isolation, an unfulfilled longing, resignation or something else, it certainly testifies to the complexity of the female aging experience. Thus, it is to be concluded that even though both texts analyzed in this essay employ the subtle potential of an old woman's empowerment, they remain affected by Western culture's ongoing attempts at grasping the coherence of aging, as in "Queen of Knives" the possibility of Pearl's agency is to be detected among the images of disintegration, while in "Chivalry" the development of such an agency involves an ambivalent treatment of the age factor in Mrs. Whitaker's identity.

Notes

1. The factor of transition was brought to my attention during an in-class discussion, thanks to a comment made by one of the students, Marta Zawieja, to whom I owe credit.

2. An attempt at a broader consideration of "Queen of Knives" in terms of "the memoir of a parent" would be far-fetched, the genre being defined by Wallace specifically as "[texts which] often deal with the issues raised by looking after an ageing and increasingly dependent parent" (398). Still, the poem's autobiographical aspect seems worth underlining.

3. Specifically, Stuart-Hamilton's discussion of psychological approaches to the process of growing old, as summarized in this essay, is based on the "stage theory" of Erik Erikson (Stuart-Hamilton 13) and Robert Peck's concepts of *"ego differentiation versus work-role preoccupation, body transcendence versus body preoccupation* and *ego transcendence versus ego preoccupation"* (Stuart-Hamilton 13, original italics).

4. According to Diana Wallace's essay published in 2011, the first decade of the 21st century has brought a growing contribution of poststructuralist and feminist studies to gerontology's development, as well as feminism's increasing self-awareness in terms of age-connected issues (408–409).

5. While in Propp's model the "donor" usually provides the mission-fulfilling character with some kind of means to reach his or her main goal rather than the goal itself, the ultimate award may also be handed to the character in the form of a present (35).

6. Strikingly, the characterization of the grandfather brings to mind the issue of a wasted potential, which is discussed by Tillie Olsen in the context of gender rather than age. Olsen points, among others, to the requirements of the daily routine as a factor preventing people of both genders from developing their talents (94–95, 98–99, 103). The imprint of such a routine and the burden of the day-after-day caring for the family's well-being permeates "Queen of Knives," from the description of the kitchen duties' division (Gaiman 123) and the monotony experienced by the narrator (124), to the mechanical continuation of the family's previous lifestyle without the grandmother (131). The potential-destroying effect of family life is underlined with reference to the grandfather's musical talent: "they said he could have been a cantor / but there were snapshots to develop, / radios and razors to repair ... / his brothers were a singing duo: the Nightingales, / had been on television in the early days" (132). He is also depicted as an unfulfilled politician and constructor (125).

7. As a very popular song, "Daisy Bell" has triggered the many informal continuations of the original lyrics. Interestingly, such "sequels" are often preoccupied with gender relations, giving voice to Daisy herself and developing into humorous dialogs in which the she turns the suitor down because of his material situation. A collection of such lyrics presented by Chris Komuves on his website includes even a version involving an exchange of emails (n.p.)

8. The last two songs appear in the poem as sung by the grandfather after his wife's disappearance, which may point to his need to fill the gap by taking over Pearl's repertoire.

9. Right after that the woman's living face is revealed to the spectators, so the scene cannot be interpreted as one of an ultimate disintegration.

10. Olsen's remarks can hardly be totalized, as they focus to a large extent on the working-class wife and mother; still they may be applied to the characterization of Pearl, at least on a general level. Both Olsen and Gaiman's protagonists are ageing, married and Jewish by origin; both have grandchildren. The most probable difference between them is Eva's immigration experience connected with her movement from Russia to the U.S. Pearl is only known to have moved from London to some unspecified place — details such as the Silver and Gold Shred marmalade brands mentioned in the poem (123) may suggest an English or perhaps Scottish setting.

11. Woodward talks about American mass culture, but, taking into account its broad influence, her remarks are worth considering also in a broader context.

12. Another consequence of the digressive structure of the poem is an impression that the present, understood as the timeline of the narrator's memory, is strongly conditioned by the past — a conclusion corresponding with the cultural tendency to perceive the old age as past-oriented, offering little at the current moment, and virtually nothing for the future (Caramagno 61, Wallace 390–392, 403). Whether Pearl's surprising and unexplained disappearance is to be read as a confirmation of such an assumption or, on the contrary — a sign that most unexpected things may happen at all times, depends on the reader's own choice.

13. Richard Gilliam, Martin H. Greenberg and Edward E. Kramer, eds., *Grails: Quests of the Dawn* (New York: ROC, 1994).

14. Interestingly, the handling of the Grail's symbolic significance in "Chivalry" goes, up to some extent, against literary and cultural tendencies traced by John Barry Marino, who perceives the gradual movement of the artifact from the realm of spirituality to that of mythology, and next to psychology and secularized metaphor as the reason for the trope's lasting importance in the 20th century (103, 106). Gaiman's tale not only suggests the movement in the opposite direction, from an ordinary object to an artifact, but also attaches the power of the said artifact directly to its Christian background, as confirmed by Mrs. Whitaker's already mentioned description (Gaiman 37) as well as Galaad's religious reverence towards the vessel (38–39, 47).

15. A number of interesting interpretations of the discussed scene can be found in the already mentioned discussion on the Neil Gaiman Message Board, where Cavenagh suggests, for instance, that the grandfather's behavior is an attempt to work out the mechanism of the performance which made Pearl disappear (n.p.).

WORKS CITED

Alessi, Justine A., and M. E. McMillan. *Rebirth of the Oracle: Tarot for the Modern World.* Huntsville: Ozark Mountain, 2005. Print.

Archmage58. Message board entry. 3 March 2005. "'Queen of Knives' Q (spoilers)." Neil Gaiman Message Board. Web. 8 August 2011.

Attebery, Brian. *Strategies of Fantasy.* Bloomington: Indiana University Press, 1992. Print.

Blaikie, Andrew. *Ageing and Popular Culture.* Cambridge: Cambridge University Press, 1999. Print.

Campbell, Joseph. *The Hero with a Thousand Faces.* 3d ed. Princeton: Princeton University Press, 2004. Print.

Caramagno, Thomas C. "Suicide and the Illusion of Closure: Aging, Depression and the Decision to Die." *Aging and Gender in Literature: Studies in Creativity.* Eds. Anne M. Wyatt-Brown and Janice Rossen. Charlottesville: University of Virginia Press, 1993. 61–81. Print.

Cavenagh. Message board entry. 4 March 2005. "'Queen of Knives' Q (spoilers)." Neil Gaiman Message Board. Web. 8 August 2011.

Coiner, Constance. "'No One's Private Ground': A Bakhtinian Reading of Tillie Olsen's *Tell Me a Riddle.*" *Tillie Olsen,* '*Tell Me a Riddle.*' Ed. Deborah Silverton Rosenfelt. New Brunswick: Rutgers University Press, 1995. 271–303. Print.

Collins, Charles. "Don't Dilly Dally (My Old Man)." *Traditional Music Library.* Rod Smith. Web. 10 August 2011.

Cuddy, Amy J.C., and Susan T. Fiske. "Doddering But Dear: Process, Context and Function in Stereotyping of Older Persons." *Ageism: Stereotyping and Prejudice Against Older Persons.* Ed. Todd D. Nelson. Cambridge: The MIT Press, 2004: 3–26. Print.

Dacre, Harry. "Daisy Bell (A Bicycle Built for Two)." *500 Best-Loved Song Lyrics*. Ed. Ronald Herder. Mineola: Dover, 1998. 75. Print.

Day, Mildred Leake. "Joseph Campbell and the Power of Arthurian Myth." *Popular Arthurian Traditions*. Ed. Sally K. Slocum. Bowling Green: Bowling Green State University Popular Press, 1992. 80–84. Print.

Electric Warrior. "Question about Neil Gaiman Short Story 'Queen of Knives.'" 1 March 2010. *The Straight Dope* Message Board. Web. 8 August 2011.

Gaiman, Neil. "Chivalry." *Smoke and Mirrors: Short Fictions and Illusions*. 2d ed. New York: Avon, 2005. 35–49. Print.

_____. "Queen of Knives." *Smoke and Mirrors: Short Fictions and Illusions*. 2d ed. New York: Avon, 2005. 123–132. Print.

Goldston, Will. *Tricks and Illusions for Amateurs and Professional Conjurers*. London: George Routledge and Sons, 1908[?]. Print.

Grey, Clifford "If You Were the Only Girl in the World." *Traditional Music Library*. Rod Smith. Web. 10 August 2011.

Komuves, Chris. "Daisy Bell." Home page. 10 August 2011.

Lyotard, Jean-François. *The Postmodern Condition: A Report on Knowledge*. Trans. Geoff Bennington and Brian Massumi. Theory and History of Literature. Vol. 10. Manchester: Manchester University Press, 1994. Print.

MacGregor Mathers, Samuel Liddel. *The Tarot: Its Occult Significance, Use in Fortune-Telling, and Method of Play, Etc.* 1st ed. 1888. Forgotten Books, 2008. Web. 8 August 2011.

Manganaro, Marc. "Myth as Culture: The Lesson of Anthropology in T. S. Eliot." *Myth and the Making of Modernity: The Problem of Grounding in Early Twentieth-Century Literature*. Eds. Michael Bell and Peter Poellner. Studies in Comparative Literature. Vol. 16. Amsterdam: Rodopi B. V., 1998. 153–166. Print.

Marino, John B. *The Grail Legend in Modern Literature*. Arthurian Studies LIX. Cambridge: D. S. Brewer, 2004. Print.

McCarthy, Joe. "You Made Me Love You (I Didn't Want to Do It)." *500 Best-Loved Song Lyrics*. Ed. Ronald Herder. Mineola: Dover, 1998. 398. Print.

Mendlesohn, Farah. *Rhetorics of Fantasy*. Middletown, CT: Wesleyan University Press, 2008. Print.

Miller, Dean A. *The Epic Hero*. Baltimore: The Johns Hopkins UP, 2000. Print.

Mr. Dibble. Message board post. 1 April 2010. *The Straight Dope* Message Board. Web. 8 August 2011.

_____. Message board post. 1 May 2010. *The Straight Dope* Message Board. Web. 8 August 2011.

Olsen, Tillie. "Silences in Literature." *Tillie Olsen, "Tell Me a Riddle."* Ed. Deborah Silverton Rosenfelt. New Brunswick: Rutgers University Press, 1995. 87–103. Print.

_____. "Tell Me a Riddle." *Tillie Olsen, "Tell Me a Riddle."* Ed. Deborah Silverton Rosenfelt. New Brunswick: Rutgers University Press, 1995. 33–84. Print.

Paul, Sarah. *Mundane Tarot: A Comprehensive Tarot Interpretation Book to be Used with Various Decks*. Bloomington: iUniverse, 2009. Print.

Propp, Vladimir. *Morphology of the Folktale*. 2d ed. Tr. Thomas A. Sebeok. The American Folklore Society and Indiana University, 1968. Print.

Roberts, Adam. *Silk and Potatoes: Contemporary Arthurian Fantasy*. Amsterdam: Rodopi B. V., 1998. Print.

Stuart-Hamilton, Ian. "Introduction." *An Introduction to Gerontology*. Ed. Ian Stuart-Hamilton. Cambridge: Cambridge University Press, 2011. 1–20. Print.

Thierens, A. E. *General Book of the Tarot: Astrology of the Tarot*. 1st ed. 1930. Forgotten Books, 2008. Web. 8 August 2011.

Trautmann Banks, Joanne. "Death Labors." *Tillie Olsen, "Tell Me a Riddle."* Ed. Deborah Silverton Rosenfelt. New Brunswick: Rutgers University Press, 1995. 199–211. Print.

Wallace, Diana. "Literary Portrayals of Ageing." *An Introduction to Gerontology.* Ed. Ian Stuart-Hamilton. Cambridge: Cambridge University Press, 2011. 389–415. Print.

Whitbourne Krauss Susan and Joel R. Sneed. "The Paradox of Well-Being, Identity Processes and Stereotype Threat: Ageism and Its Potential Relationships to the Self in Later Life." *Ageism: Stereotyping and Prejudice Against Older Persons.* Ed. Todd D. Nelson. Cambridge: The MIT Press, 2004. 247–273. Print.

Studwell, William. *The Popular Song Reader: A Sampler of Well-Known Twentieth-Century Songs.* Binghamton: The Haworth Press, 1994. Print.

Winter, Jay. "Popular Culture in Wartime Britain." *European Culture in the Great War: The Arts, Entertainment and Propaganda, 1914–1918.* Ed. Aviel Roshwald and Richard Stites. Cambridge: Cambridge UP, 2002. 330–348. Print.

Woodward, Kathleen. "Against Wisdom: Social Politics of Gender and Aging." *Cultural Critique 51* (2002): 187–218. Print.

_____. "Performing Age, Performing Gender." *NSWA Journal* 18.1 (2006): 162–189. *Muse.* Web. 8 August 2011. Print.

_____. "Tribute to the Older Woman: Psychoanalysis, Feminism and Ageism." *Images of Ageing: Cultural Representation of Later Life.* Eds. Mike Featherstone and Andrew Werrick. London: Routledge, 1995. 79–96. Print.

"Anathema Liked to Read About Herself"

Preserving the Female Line
in Good Omens

BY JESSICA WALKER

The New Testament describes the end of the world as "that day and hour [that] knoweth no man, no, not the angels of heaven, but my Father only" (Matthew 24:36). The title pages that separate the sections of *Good Omens*, written by Neil Gaiman and Terry Pratchett, underscore this context: after "In the beginning," the titles move directly to "Eleven years ago," and then a countdown of days: "Wednesday," "Thursday," "Friday," "Saturday," and "Sunday (The First Day of the Rest of Their Lives)." The book therefore suggests a sort of timelessness, in which the reader is invited to associate events not with a specific past, but with a general type of day. "Saturday" could be any Saturday, including this coming weekend. The story hinges, however, on a fictional text from a specific historical moment. Agnes Nutter, through her *Nice and Accurate Prophecies*, speaks to us from England in the mid-seventeenth century. In this time and place, developing ideas about historiography and gender, intensified by the English Civil War, encouraged autobiography in general and women's family memoir in particular. By examining Agnes's fictional work in context with actual seventeenth-century female-authored family histories, we may better understand her purpose, her idiosyncrasies, and how her connection with Anathema shapes the latter's development as she struggles with her identity as a "professional descendant" (Gaiman and Pratchett 210).

The memoirs I examine here may not seem comparable to Agnes's *Prophecies*. Early modern women's autobiographies document true events; the content is serious, even grim. Agnes's text, on the other hand, is a fiction within a fiction, and a humorous one at that. Memoir recounts the past, while prophecy predicts the future. Nor is there any reason to assume that Gaiman and Pratchett are familiar with, or deliberately invoking, seventeenth-century women's memoir. Examining these texts together, however, underscores important characteristics of *Good Omens*— namely, the importance of the *Prophecies* in helping Anathema establish her identity as a Device, a witch, and a woman. By tracing common threads between Agnes and her real-life counterparts, we can better understand the importance of her writing to the text as a whole.

At first glance, Agnes seems to belong to the tradition of mid-seventeenth-century apocalyptic women prophets like Eleanor Davies and Hester Biddle. Such women, however, framed their prophecies for the public, addressing powerful political and religious figures. Eleanor Davies' 1651 prophecy "The Benediction. From the A:lmighty O:mnipotent," addressed to Oliver Cromwell, references public events such as the Plague and the Thirty Years War. Priscilla Cotton and Mary Cole's 1655 prophecy *To the Priests and People of England* addresses the nation: "Oh apostate England, what shall the God or mercies do for thee? What shall he do unto thee?" (146). Hester Biddle preferred to target particular cities in her *Woe to Thee, City of Oxford* and *Woe to Thee, City of Cambridge*.

Agnes, on the other hand, envisions a specific, private audience for her prophecies; she publishes the book not "for the sales, or the royalties, or even for the fame" but for "the single gratis copy of the book that an author was entitled to" (Gaiman and Pratchett 53). She wants a bound copy of the book not for herself, but as an heirloom for her descendants, whom the predictions seek to guide and protect. It turns out that Agnes's text is not so much a work of prophecy as a collection of "[r]acial memory," a memoir from the future: "Agnes didn't see the future. That's just a metaphor. She *remembered* it.... We think she's best at remembering things that were going to happen to her descendants" (218). In this sense, Agnes's work most closely resembles that of seventeenth-century women autobiographers who recorded their experiences for the edification of their children, immediate community, and descendants.

Throughout the first century of the Renaissance, women's options for writing, circulation, and publication were limited. As the early modern period progressed, "a divide grew up between 'public' and 'private' spheres," and for women, family life was "supposed to map out the limits of their world" (Hobby 3). These limits were often physical as well as cultural, for the "requirement of chastity kept women at home, silenced them, isolated them" (M. King and Rabil xxiii). Any act in the public sphere could threaten a woman's most valuable commodity, her reputation: "for women to be in public affairs was for women to be whores" (Purkiss 67). Only aristocratic, well-educated women, of good families and secure reputations, had access to conventional forms of writing like poetry or drama; others found written expression was more acceptable at a remove, translating male-authored works or commenting on religious texts. These works were circulated among the elite but were rarely performed or printed for the general public.

The Civil War fueled a profound shift in English life writing and family memoir. The tensions and dangers of the Civil War and Interregnum "stimulated the writing of lives in ways that demonstrate how productive of biographies eras of disruption may be.... It would be difficult to exaggerate the impact of the Civil War upon the development of English biography in the seventeenth century" (Pritchard 11–12). Rather than events being recorded after the fact by elite court historians, print culture provided readers with current accounts of battles, sieges, and political developments. Such pamphlets declared themselves authoritative not by the position of the author or his connections, but by the position of the witness. Information was valued according to its novelty, exclusivity, and immediacy, privileging history as a lived experience rather than an abstract intellectual exercise as it had often been for Renaissance humanists: "You may confidently believe this narration; for you receive it not from my ear, but from my eye" ("A Copie of a Letter" A4).

Many of the people involved with the struggles recounted in these pamphlets were women. With a large percentage of the men away at war or exiled, women became "defenders of their homes, pensioners for estates and generally responsible for their families' survival" (Crawford 213). Wartime news pamphlets such as "A Briefe and Exact Relation of the Most Materiall and Remarkeable Passages that hapned in the late well-formed (and as valiently defended) Seige laid before the City of Glocester" report women fetching turf to build fortifications, putting out fires, and dodging explosions. Women "petitioned parliament," "agitated for social reforms," and took part in political debate, which "forced them to refine and sharpen their arguments, and so led to further publications" (Hobby 85, Crawford 213). When censorship of the press ceased in 1641, "they shared with men in the greater freedom to publish," producing political commentaries, prose literature, and personal narratives (Crawford 231). Such involvement in the public world had a profound effect on women's life writing. Much more so than at any previous time in English history, everyday people, aided by increased access to education and freedom of the press, sought to understand their personal lives within the context of staggering public events. When danger and exile drove women from their homes and forced them into the public space in both ideological and physical ways, "many female writers described or analysed their experiences" (Hobby 78). Like most autobiographies of the era, these works were not intended for general publication; but autobiography, "even if not intended for print publication, presupposes an audience beyond the self," and these works usually had intended audiences: one's immediate family, descendants, or religious community (Seelig 73).

The latter half of the seventeenth century provides a wealth of women's accounts, including Lucy Hutchinson's defense of her husband, Anne Halkett's account of her work as a Royalist spy, Margaret Cavendish's tale of exile in the service of Henrietta Maria, and Brilliana, Lady Harley's letters describing her defense of her home against prolonged siege. Two memoirists in particular, Lady Anne Clifford and Lady Ann Fanshawe, demonstrate in their diaries and autobiographies many of the same concerns that we find in Agnes's text. Writing for manuscript circulation within their families and immediate community, both authors recorded their personal and family struggles for the edification of future generations. If the Devices are "professional descendants," then Clifford and Fanshawe were professional ancestors, seeking to guide and protect their families as Agnes does through her prophecies.

By making connections between Agnes's text and the writing projects of seventeenth-century women memoirists like Clifford and Fanshawe, we may ultimately better understand Anathema's position as a reader of and participant in her own life. Like Agnes, Clifford and Fanshawe write to preserve their family line in general and, either overtly or subversively, the female line in particular. To do so, they frequently engage in a nonlinear style that demonstrates the difficulty of recording the past to better understand the present and prepare for the future. Women's writing, Hélène Cixous argues, "unthinks the unifying, regulating history that homogenizes and channels forces, herding contradictions into a single battlefield. In woman, personal history blends together with the history of all women, as well as national and world history" (352). Rather than producing traditional historiography, these women apply the *importance* of historiography to a different way of inhabiting and recording the past.

Clifford's work resists many typical features of early modern historiography: centralization of men's stories, linear narrative, and a binary between public and private events. Her dual-columned diaries enable her to place experiences in a variety of contexts, allowing her to live and write on the border between public and private. She centralizes female figures, rejects linear narrative in favor of drawing temporal and spatial connections based on personal relationships, and creates an inclusionary history that refuses a division between public and private experiences. Fanshawe's text is similarly fractured; beneath the surface narrative, a traditional memoir of a devoted subject and his dutiful wife, lurks a Gothic horror story of a traumatized woman struggling with her maternal role. Clifford and Fanshawe read and write their lives as feminist critics, questioning the usefulness of traditional narratives in forming their senses of self. In the case of Agnes's text, the burden of contextualization and interpretation shifts from the author to the reader — the generations of Devices who bear the responsibility of making sense of her obscure, nonlinear style. Ultimately, Agnes's lessons lead to a resolution of the horrors of the past, through the union of the last of her descendants, Anathema, with Newt Pulsifer, descendant of the Witchfinder General who ordered Agnes's death.

Because Clifford and Fanshawe act as interpreters of their family histories, some background context is necessary to understand their writing. Anne Clifford was born in 1590 to one of England's wealthiest aristocratic families, her parents' only surviving child and therefore "a sole heiress to a great fortune" (Acheson 11). The baronies of Clifford, Westmoreland, and Vescy had belonged to her family for more than three centuries, but "the law was not settled in one way or another" concerning women's rights to inherit such properties (Acheson 18). When Clifford's father died in 1605, he left her a substantial dowry but willed all his estates to his brother. In response, Clifford and her mother Margaret commenced a legal battle that would last for nearly four decades.

To prove that the inheritance of these particular lands was not restricted to male heirs, Clifford and her mother began to collect documents of the Clifford family history going back to the reign of King John. In addition to this family research, Clifford began to keep records of her own life and struggle to gain her inheritance. At the age of 53, she finally claimed the estates for which she had fought for so long by outliving all the male claimants. Once she had possession of the property, "she spent the rest of her life compiling proof that it should have been hers all along," assembling the Clifford family history into a thousand-page tome known as *The Great Books of the Clifford Family*. She also "employed professional scribes to make three almost identical copies of the series which would be preserved for use and edification of her posterity" (Myers 581). In addition to her family history, the work included Clifford's autobiography (starting at conception, no less). She continued to keep a diary until the day before her death in 1676.

"[N]othing," Benedict Anderson writes, "connects us affectively to the dead more than language" (145). Both Clifford and Fanshawe write to connect with deceased family, just as Agnes writes to connect with her family to come. Though Clifford's "desire to document the histories of her family and herself ... [was] stimulated by the need to construct a picture of her lineage and rights that would help her in the legal disputes," she continued to compile the "Chronicles" (a word that she uses to describe both her family histories and her diaries) even after they were no longer needed (Acheson 15). As important as the actual possession of the property was Clifford's sense of identity as "a commentator of the family's past and a guardian of its future" (Myers 588). She intended for the diaries to be preserved and read, and had scribes copy them to that end, later adding further notes in the margins to provide a wider context for her observations. By recording her legal battles "for the future uses of her family members and herself," she inserts herself into her own family history (Acheson 26).

Both Clifford and Fanshawe strive to preserve the female line in the patriarchal world, lamenting the passing of their mothers and expressing anxiety over the futures of their daughters. Just as Agnes guides Anathema across the centuries, Anne Clifford's text records her mother Margaret's support and guidance. Even after her death, Margaret Clifford remains a strong influence on her daughter: when Anne's husband once again tries to convince her to cease her proceedings, she tells him "that my promise was so far passed to my mother and to all the world that I would never do it whatsoever became of me and mine" (16 April 1617 129). Anecdotes about Clifford's young daughter, Margaret's namesake, also appear frequently. The emphasis on female support systems extends beyond her relationship with her mother; the vast majority of her observations in the diaries concern news and scandal among the powerful women of Clifford's community. Motherhood is a significant event in their circle, and Clifford's diaries record a dozen pregnancies and births over the course of the 1616–1619 record. Privileging women's identities and experiences, she identifies men by their connections to women: "my Lady Thomas Howard's son" (3 January 1616 63); "my Lord Chancellor Egerton my Lady Derby's husband" (March 1617m 122). In observations such as "I went to the court, where the Queen sent for me into her own bedchamber and here I spoke to the King" (4 November 1617 149), Clifford's sentence structures give women primacy even over sovereigns.

Like Agnes with her hodgepodge of prophecies, Clifford views public and private events as equally significant. Her diaries are written in a double-columned format; her original entries were copied by a scribe, with a wide margin in which Clifford recorded relevant observations in her own hand. The margins do not reflect a division between public and private, but rather show both kinds of events in close proximity: "Upon the 18th, being Friday, died my Lady Margaret [Clifford's daughter]'s old beagle" (18 October 1616m 98) is followed by "Upon the 4th Prince Charles was created Prince of Wales" (4 November 1616m 98). The dual-columned format helps Clifford contextualize her experiences, interpreting her own text as the Devices interpret their ancestor Agnes's.

The very act of recording the past for the benefit of the future is an act of defying time itself: that which should be behind us is still mentally present; that which has not happened is already being considered. To write a family memoir is to consciously demonstrate the non-linear nature of time. The historian must always place her or himself in multiple moments: the past of the event, the present of the writing, the future of the reading and interpretation. Fanshawe's, Clifford's, and Agnes Nutter's narratives all demonstrate this anxiety about the nonlinear nature of memory. Clifford's writing doubles back on itself, placing events in context with other important times and places rather than telling them in a linear order. Frequently, she emphasizes links between important female figures: "The child was brought down to me in the gallery which was the first time I had seen her after my mother died" (December 1616m 102). She recounts her mother's death thusly:

> Upon the 24th, being Friday, between the hours of six and seven at night died my dear mother at Brougham in the same chamber where my father was born, thirteen years and two months after the death of Queen Elizabeth and ten years and four months after the death of my father, I being then 26 years old and four months and the child two years old wanting a month [24 May 1616m 84].

This description places her mother's death in context with every other significant event of Clifford's life, creating meaning through repetitions and connections.

The same desire to preserve family lines through memoir emerges in Lady Ann Fanshawe's work. Fanshawe was born Ann Harrison to a Royalist family in 1625; she was well-educated, although we know little about her upbringing other than what her autobiography provides. In 1644 she married her second cousin, Richard Fanshawe, Charles II's Secretary of War. During the years of the war and Interregnum, the Fanshawes followed Prince Charles's forces to France, Ireland, Spain, and Portugal. In 1676, a decade after her husband's death and four years before her own, she composed a memoir of their travels for their only surviving son. Unlike Clifford, Fanshawe writes not to connect with her ancestors, but with her immediate descendants. Having only four surviving children out of twenty pregnancies, she categorizes experiences compulsively and is obsessed with sites of erasure: gravesites, unburied bodies, restless ghosts.

Fanshawe's relationship with preserving matrilinearity is more complex and troubled than Clifford's. Her narrative, on the surface, is a patriarchal project: she obeys her father, follows her husband around the world, supports her exiled king, favors her male children (she admits that when "[b]oth my eldest daughters had the small pox att the same time," she "neglected them, and day and night tended my dear son" [139]) and composes the memoir for her only surviving male heir. She is curiously silent about a vital part of her experiences as a woman: the numerous births, deaths, and miscarriages of her children. Constantly on the move throughout the years of the war and Restoration, she endures some twenty pregnancies, fourteen births, and nine childhood mortalities. Although she occasionally recounts pregnancy-related illnesses, we learn little of her feelings about her experiences: the pains of childbirth, the grief at losing children, the lives of her surviving children as they accompanied her on her travels, the terror that must have attended every pregnancy in a time of high mortality both for mothers and children. Mary Beth Rose argues that Fanshawe emphasizes her experiences as a diplomat's wife because she values that role above all others: "in her selection of incidents and her choice of narrative strategies, she assigns of secondary value to those material aspects of her experience that are uniquely female: namely, the capacity to conceive and give birth" (70). Yet there emerges, in the silences and asides of her text, a preoccupation with traumatic, repressed maternal experience.

This obsession emerges in the form of three uncanny tales. In the first, her mother falls ill not long after Ann's birth and appears to have died. Upon waking, she reports having seen "two by me cloathed in long white garments" who had granted her wish to live "15 years to see my daughter a woman" (Fanshawe 109). Her mother's death occurs, Fanshawe reports, "just 15 years from that time" (109). In the second, Fanshawe reports seeing "a woman leaning into the window through the casement, in white, with red hair and pale, gastly complexion"; she learns that this woman "was many ages agoe got with child by the owner of this place, and he in his garden murdered her and flung her into the river under your window" (125). In the third, she recounts the story of a brother and sister who desecrate their parents' tombs and take some of their hair for a "frolick" (151). When the sister dies soon after, her brother "kept her body in a coffin sett up in his buttry, saying it would not be long before he dyed, and then they would be both buried together" (151). These ghost stories contain a recurrent theme of love between mothers and daughters, the wish to preserve the maternal line and the hope for family bonds stronger than death itself. This sense of love echoed in her moving account of her daughter Ann's death: "upon the 20th of July, 1654, at 3 a clock in the afternoon, dyed our most dearly beloved daughter Ann Fanshawe, whose beauty and wit exceeded all that ever I saw of her age. She was ... the dear companion of our travells and sorrows.... We both wished to have gone into the grave with her" (136). At the same time, she is haunted by associations between birth and death, and the ghost stories she recounts reflect an anxiety about desecrated burial sites of mothers and children.

Fanshawe's memoir does not defy chronology as overtly Clifford's does, but its content constantly reflects anxieties over the nonlinear nature of grief. She associates patriarchy with action, forward momentum, movement into the future. After her life is thrown into chaos shortly after her mother's death (her father loses his property due to his Royalism and relocates the family to a series of impoverished dwellings near the King's new wartime court in Oxford), she seeks stability in marriage. Yet the past is literally present at the wedding:

But as in a racke the turbulence of the waves disperses the splinters of the rock, so it was my lot; for having buried my dear brother Will Harrison in Exeter Colledge Chapell, I then married your dear father in [16]44 in Wolvercot Church, 2 miles from Oxford, upon the 18th of May. None was at our wedding but my dear father (who by my mother's desire gave me her wedding ring, with which I was married) [111].

Through the image of the dead brother's burial and the dead mother's ring, the deceased are in attendance metonymically and linguistically. Fanshawe's obsession with hauntings and desecrations that upset the normal linear order of death, burial, and eternal rest continue to resurface in her ghost stories: the resurrection of her own mother, the murdered mother carelessly flung into the river, the violated tomb of the mother and the unburied coffin of her daughter. When her husband dies abroad, she takes their last journey home "with the body of my dear husband dayly in my sight for near 6 months together" (189). Denied resolution, she seeks to give the dead a proper burial through her writing.

In the case of Agnes Nutter, resolution of past trauma comes not through the writing of her text but through the development of its most important reader, Anathema. Agnes's collection of prophecies is "the sole prophetic work in all of human history to consist entirely of completely correct predictions concerning the following three hundred and forty odd years, being a precise and accurate description of the events that would culminate in Armageddon" (Gaiman and Pratchett 52–53). But although "Agnes had a line to the Future ... it was an unusually narrow and specific line" (209). The prophecies rarely concern public events; the prediction for the date of the Kennedy assassination, for instance, is "about a house falling down in King's Lynn" (210). While Agnes's predictions may be "almost totally useless" for the public at large, however, they are "generally very good if her descendants were involved" (209, 210): Anathema's father was visiting King's Lynn on November 22, 1963, so "while he was unlikely to be struck by stray rounds from Dallas, there was a good chance he might be hit by a brick" (210). After more than a century of struggling to interpret Agnes's obscure prophecies, her descendants realize that, like Clifford's and Fanshawe's work, "the *Nice and Accurate Prophecies* was Agnes's idea of a family heirloom. Many of the prophecies relate to her descendants and their well-being. She was sort of trying to look after us after she'd gone" (210).

The nonlinear nature of the texts examined here underscores the paradox of writing memoir: recounting and examining the past (or in Agnes's case, the future) makes it part of our present experiences. The *Prophecies* exist in the same ahistorical space as Clifford's marginalia and Fanshawe's ghost stories. Her descendants are left not knowing in what order the predictions should go: "Agnes was a bit slap-dash about timing. I don't think she always knew what went where ... [W]e've spent ages devising a sort of system for chaining them together" (220). Time itself seems to collapse around the book; Aziraphale is so transfixed by its contents that the cup of cocoa he makes before he begins to read cools and condenses to a "congealed brown sludge" before growing "[g]reen fur ... on the inside of the mug" (160, 170). The title page of the prophecies is comically framed with all the details of a modern-day publication: the assurance that the text is "More complete than ever yet before publifhed" and a blurb from Mother Shipton calling it "Reminifent of Nostradamus at hif beft" (115). Agnes herself is "so far adrift in Time that she was considered pretty mad even by the standards of seventeenth-century Lancashire, where mad prophetesses were a growth industry" (209). Among her pronouncements are characteristically twentieth-century recommendations for penicillin, handwashing, jogging, and eating plenty of fiber — suggestions that strike her neighbors as so nonsensical that finally a "howling mob, reduced to utter fury by her habit of going around being intelligent and curing people," drags her from her cottage to be burned at the stake (194).

It may seem counterintuitive to compare memoirs that record the past with prophecies that predict the future. Memoirists, like all historians, struggle with the inescapable and unchangeable nature of the past. They can frame it, justify it, even ignore it: but they cannot change it. Only the future is open and free, a place of possibility where their offspring may be guided by them even after they are gone. But since Agnes's prophecies are completely accurate, the future she foresees is every bit as unchangeable as the past recorded by typical family historians. While Clifford and Fanshawe record their experiences so that they might better understand them, Agnes makes no such effort; she can only record, never contextualize: "it's not enough to know what the future *is*. You have to know what it *means*. Agnes was like someone looking at a huge picture down a tiny little tube" (210). Since "by the time it'd been filtered through her own understanding it's often a bit confused," here the *readers* rather than the author are left to interpret what cannot be changed (218). The distinction here is vital to understanding the novel: the burden of interpretation is placed not with Agnes but with Anathema, the text's principal reader. Through her developing relationship with the *Prophecies*, Anathema will come to establish her own identity and make peace with her ancestral past.

Since Agnes's predictions only make sense in retrospect, such as the advice for the year 1972: "Do Notte Buye Betamacks," her descendants are left with the task of making sense of her writing (209). Interpreting the prophecies requires the Devices to think like Agnes, a "half-crazed, highly intelligent seventeenth century witch with a mind like a crossword-puzzle dictionary," combining her paranormal insight with their understanding of their own time (93). The cards on which the Devices record their commentary recall Anne Clifford's dual-columned diaries. Newt observes on one of the cards: "It had a ruled line down the middle. On the left-hand side was a short piece of what seemed to be poetry, in black ink. On the right-hand side, in red ink this time, were comments and annotations" (206). Like Clifford's marginalia, the Devices' comments put Agnes's prophecies into perspective so they can be better understood.

The project of organizing the prophecies proves not only advantageous for individual family members who might benefit from Agnes's advice. This act of interpreting the family future also strengthens the bond between the Devices, whose marginalia reveal a conversation across the generations. Unable to interpret a prophecy about Armageddon, one Device comments in 1789, "I feel good Agnes had drunk well this night"; another replies in 1854, "I concur. We are all human, alas" (220). When Newt learns that Agnes foresaw his sexual relationship with Anathema, he is embarrassed to find that "down the ages, various Devices had scrawled encouraging little comments in the margin" (284). The affectionate, familiar tone in the marginalia shows the power of text and supertext to speak across centuries: Clifford and Fanshawe preserve their family identities through their writing, but Agnes actually creates her family identity.

Although the prophecies contain advice for all the Devices, they only mention Anathema by name. She bears special significance in being the last remaining Device when Armageddon comes; the "first sentence she had ever read out loud," a description of the Four Horsemen of the Apocalypse, concludes: "And ye shalle be theyr alfo, Anathema" (38). But she is more than simply the last Device; more than any of her family, she is Agnes's heir, connected to her ancestor through their shared qualities of psychic abilities and good sense. Despite her occult powers, Agnes is practical and down-to-earth. After her death, her mystical possessions, the book and a mysterious box, are found "on the kitchen tale beside a note cancelling the milk" (195); the massacre at her execution is not the result of "any divine or devilish intervention," but of "the contents of Agnes's petticoats, wherein she had with some foresight concealed eighty pounds of gunpowder and forty pounds of roofing nails" (195). Like Clifford and Fanshawe, Agnes guards her family's prosperity (warning against investing in technology that will soon become obsolete) and their safety (the King's Lynn warning). Clifford and Fanshawe offer guidance to their descendants, but their advice is less specific and more abstract: how to persevere in the face of opposition or danger; how to value mothers and children and cope with their loss; how to weather the storms of marriage and survive the loss of a beloved spouse; how to travel to new countries or maintain one's home; how to honor a dead king, or defy a living one. Agnes, on the other hand, teaches her descendants how to avoid falling bricks when a roof caves in.

Anathema's own form of witchcraft is similar: "any prowling maniac would have had more than his work cut out if he had accosted Anathema Device. She was a witch, after all. And precisely because she was a witch, and therefore sensible, she put little faith in protective amulets and spells; she saved it all for a foot-long bread knife which she kept in her belt" (88). She "suspect[s] that she could occasionally think like Agnes" (93) and speaks of her own psychic abilities "as through she was admitting to a *hereditary* disease which she'd much prefer not to have" (221, emphasis mine). Having identified so strongly with Agnes and the prophecies her entire life, Anathema is anachronistic. As a child, her teachers "upbraid her for her spelling, which was not so much appalling as 300 years too late" (39). While identifying strongly with the past, "Anathema ... in the very nature of things always looked to the future"; much of her attention focuses on the inevitable apocalypse that she knows she will see in her lifetime (203).

Like Clifford, Anathema has no sense of self beyond her family identity. Clifford at least has autonomy over that identity, creating and controlling it through the act of writing; Anathema, from earliest childhood, finds that identity and destiny have already been written for her. Like English Civil War memoirists, she realizes that she is living at crucial historical moment and wants to understand her place within it. Rather than situating herself, however, she is situated, literally marginalized in Agnes's history of the world. The prophecies give Anathema a community and a sense of purpose, but they leave no room for surprises or individual choices, even about the most personal matters: when Newt suggests they make love a second time, Anathema replies, "She said we only did it this once" (284).

The relationship between Anathema and Newt is key to the novel's resolution; having struggled with her family's history, Anathema makes peace with it through her union with Newt. While Clifford and Fanshawe emphasize the preservation of female lines, *Good Omens* does not overtly posit a gendered link between Agnes and Anathema. However, Anathema's relationship with Newt Pulsifer suggests a resolution to the gendered oppression her ancestor experienced. About a quarter of the victims of witchcraft persecution in Europe and the New World were male, and men made up as many as half the accused in some continental European countries such as Germany and France. In England, however, "90 per cent or more of known witches were women" (Briggs 261). Women were believed to be more sexually uncontrollable, less reasonable, and, as Eve's descendants, more given to temptation, and therefore more vulnerable to the Devil's influence. In *Good Omens*, however, the serious subject of witchcraft persecution is reduced to absurdity. Anathema's arrival inspires a comic parody of Agnes's own death when Adam, Brian, Wensleydale, and Pepper reenact the Spanish Inquisition by dunking their chosen witch, Pepper's little sister, in a pond until she confesses (135–136). Elsewhere in the story, Shadwell's attempts at witch hunting are similarly undercut by humor. No longer able to draw ninepence for each proven witch, Shadwell bolsters the Witchfinder Army's funds with the invention of "Witchfinder Majors Saucepan, Tin, Milk, and Cupboard," in addition to hundreds of others, to collect additional money from Crowley and Aziraphale (181). If Shadwell is heir to a great tradition, it is also a ridiculous one: "It was a mistake to think of Shadwell ... as a lone nut. It was just that all the others were dead, in most cases for several hundred years" (191).

Just as witchcraft is Anathema's family legacy, Puritanism, misogyny, and witchcraft persecution are Newt's. Certainly not all historical Puritans were misogynists or witchhunters, but Gaiman and Pratchett make use of the way popular culture often associates misogyny and persecution with Puritanism. The Pulsifers, a "very religious family," featured offspring such as Covetousness Pulsifer, False-Witness Pulsifer, and Newt's own ancestor, Thou-shalt-not-commit-adultery Pulsifer, whom Anathema suspects "just didn't like women very much" (207). Adultery Pulsifer, one of "England's most assiduous witchfinders" and the force behind Agnes's victimization, is blown to bits by the explosion at her execution and "might have felt some ancient revenge was at last going to be discharged" when Newt meets Anathema (195, 196). Despite his job as a Witchfinder, however, Newt shows no desire to actually persecute witches; he is not the type to persecute anyone. He embraces history for history's sake: "The way Newt looked at it, it was like being in one of those organizations like the Sealed Knot or those people who kept on refighting the American Civil War. It got you out at weekends, and meant that you were keeping alive fine old traditions that had made Western civilization what it was today" (191–192). His very name is not a witchfinder's moniker, but one traditionally associated with witches themselves (consider *Macbeth*'s "eye of newt," *Monty Python and the Holy Grail*'s temporary enchantment victim who was turned into a newt but "got better," and, more recently, *Harry Potter and the Prisoner of Azkaban*'s Nastily Exhausting Wizarding Test or N.E.W.T.).

Though a Witchfinder, Newt regards Agnes not as an enemy but as a mere annoyance at most, an "elderly female relative" impeding his courtship of Anathema: "He had even been entertaining the idea of inviting her out for a meal, but he hated the idea of some Cromwellian witch sitting in her cottage three centuries earlier and watching him eat" (229). She even predicts their lovemaking "in the most transparent of codes" (284). Her involvement in Anathema's personal life indicates how private "women's matters" like love and sex, rather than patriarchal power, will help unify the forces that the two families represent: female and misogynist, intuition and Puritanism, marginalization and power. Near the novel's conclusion, Shadwell has a dream of which he can remember only one phrase: "*Nothin' wrong with witchfinding. I'd like to be a witchfinder. It's just, well, you've got to take it in turns. Today we'll go out witchfinding, an' tomorrow we could hide, an it'd be the witches' turn to find US...*" (376). Shortly after, Shadwell, the last Witchfinder, finally initiates his relationship with Madame Tracy, the novel's only other surviving witch. This union mirrors Newt and Anathema's, showing that power can be shared rather than abused.

Ironically, by following Agnes's lead and rectifying the injustice done to her ancestor through her union with Newt, Anathema can now let go of her identity as a professional descendant. The past is put to rest, the bad blood between the Pulsifers and the Devices expunged, and they can move into the future together. When the "sequel" to Agnes's prophecies is delivered to Jasmine Cottage post-apocalypse, Newt asks: "Do you want to be a descendant for the rest of your life?" (371). Anathema doesn't answer the question, and the reader never learns whether she continues to devote her life to understanding the prophecies, or leaves the book closed and begins a new life. That the answer lies beyond the scope of *Good Omens* is perhaps the entire point; the issue will always remain ambiguous and undefined, with no text left to guide us.

WORKS CITED

Acheson, Katherine Osler. "Introduction." *The Memoir of 1603 and the Diary of 1616–1619.* Toronto: Broadview Editions, 2007. Print.

Anderson, Benedict. *Imagined Communities: Reflections on the Origin and Spread of Nationalism.* New York: Verso, 1991. Print.

"A Briefe and Exact Relation of the Most Materiall and Remarkeable Passages that hapned in the late well-formed (and as valiently defended) Seige laid before the City of Glocester, collected by John Dorney, Esquire, towne-clarke of the said city, who was there resident the whole siege and appled himselfe wholy to this businesse." London: Thomas Underhill, 1643. Print.

Briggs, Robin. *Witches and Neighbors: The Social and Cultural Context of European Witchcraft.* New York: Penguin, 1996. Print.

Cixous, Hélène. "The Laugh of the Medusa." *Feminisms: An Anthology of Literary Theory and Criticism.* Eds. Robin R. Warhol and Diane Price Herndl. New Brunswick: Rutgers University Press, 1997. 347–362. Print.

Clifford, Anne. *The Memoir of 1603 and the Diary of 1616–1619.* Toronto: Broadview Editions, 2007. Print.

_____. *A Summary of the Records and a True Memorial of the Life of Me the Lady Anne Clifford. The Memoir of 1603 and the Diary of 1616–1619.* Toronto: Broadview Editions, 2007. Print.

Cole, Mary and Priscilla Cotton. *To the Priests and People of England. Early Modern Women's Writing: An Anthology 1560–1700.* Ed. Paul Salzman. Oxford: Oxford University Press, 2000. Print.

"A Copie of a Letter Sent from a Gentleman in his Majesties Army, to an especiall friend in London: Containing a true Relation of his Majesties Army since their removal from Oxford, to an especiall friend in London: containing a true relation of his Majesties army since their removall from Oxford, to the 16. of this present Novemb." London: 1642. Print.

Crawford, Patricia. "Women's Published Writings 1600–1700." *Women in English Society 1500–1800.* Ed. Mary Prior. London: Methuen, 1985. Print.

Fanshawe, Ann. *Memoirs of Anne, Lady Halkett, and Ann, Lady Fanshawe.* Ed. John Loftis. Oxford: Oxford University Press, 1979. Print.

Gaiman, Neil, and Terry Pratchett. *Good Omens.* London: Corgi, 1990. Print.

Hobby, Elaine. *Virtue of Necessity: English Women's Writing, 1646–1688.* London: Virago, 1988. Print.

King, Margaret L., and Albert Rabil, Jr. "The Other Voice in Early Modern Europe: Introduction to the Series." *The Education of a Christian Woman: A Sixteenth- Century Manual.* Ed. and trans. Charles Fantazzi. Chicago: University of Chicago Press, 2000. Print.

Myers, Anne B. "Construction Sites: The Architecture of Anne Clifford's Diaries." *ELH* 73 (2006): 581–600. Web.

Pritchard, Allan. *English Biography in the Seventeenth Century: A Critical Survey.* Toronto: University of Toronto Press, 2005. Print.

Purkiss, *Literature, Gender and Politics During the English Civil War.* Cambridge: Cambridge University Press, 2005. Print.

Rose, Mary Beth. *Gender and Heroism in Early Modern English Literature.* Chicago: University of Chicago Press, 2002. Print.

Seelig, Sharon Cadman. *Autobiography and Gender in Early Modern Literature: Reading Women's Lives, 1600–1680.* Cambridge: Cambridge University Press, 2006. Print.

Doors, Vortices and the In-Between

Quantum Cosmological Goddesses in the Gaiman Multiverse

BY KRISTINE LARSEN

To say that Neil Gaiman's works feature deities as characters is to say the Pacific Ocean has water. Some of these personages are real-world gods and goddesses "rebooted" in modern dress, such as Odin, Bast, and Anansi. Others are his own creation, but very much cast in a classical vein. A third class is the new deities of *American Gods*, personifications of aspects of modern society such as Media and the Internet. But for all their shiny new trappings, these are no better (and in the end no more powerful) than the old gods they seek to replace. Gaiman also creates a new type of idols, whose individuals may or may not have classical names, but more importantly have a truly modern — as in modern *physics* — set of powers. These include a powerful set of new cosmological goddesses, who, rather than merely representing the moon or stars, travel between dimensions and create and/or destroy entire universes. In combining ancient mythological tropes with the modern paradigms of quantum mechanics and general relativity, Gaiman puts a fresh and empowering face on the Great Mother and her reproductive powers. Gone is the Newtonian concept of a singular, linear, mechanistic universe; the universe is now replaced by the chaotic, roll-the-dice multiverse of Einstein, Guth, and Everett. Here "big bangs" occur not just once but a multitude of times, creating innumerable baby universes. Cosmological birth is a continual process, as doors are repeatedly opened to new realities and new possibilities. At the same time centuries-old idea characterizations of the nature as the female victim of the male scientist's domination are challenged, replaced by a powerful new feminine paradigm where dichotomy is replaced by synthesis and symbiosis. On this journey through fiction and physics the reader discovers that he/she is not separate from the universe, but is rather an integral part of it. In a very real sense we are the universe, and the universe is us. Not only does the cosmos affect our actions, but our very actions have the power to shape, create, and even destroy universes. This essay will explore Gaiman's usage of both classical and these new "quantum" cosmological goddesses (henceforth referred to as QCG) in his Secondary Worlds, the former aligning him with J.R.R. Tolkien and C.S. Lewis, and the latter with Philip Pullman.

While Tolkien's works *The Hobbit* and *The Lord of the Rings* feature relatively few female characters, those who are included are strong women who owe much to the medieval Valkyrie tradition (Donovan 109). However, Tolkien's great Elvish cosmology, *The Silmarillion*, features even numbers of male and female "deities," the so-called Valar. While these powers are secondary to the all-powerful creator Ilúvatar, the Valar both personify and direct the workings of specific parts of the world. For example, Varda, the Queen of the Valar, creates the stars and supervises the original motions of the sun and moon. In these traits, Varda is a rather classical goddess figure, and the Valar are in general echoes of the Norse and Greek pantheons. In one of his earliest etymologies of Middle-earth, Tolkien notes that the term Ainur (the generic term for the Valar and similar beings who were created by Ilúvatar but unlike the Valar did not choose to enter the world and are afterwards bound to its fate) derives from *ainu*, "a pagan god" (248–489). While the strong female characters of Lewis's Narnia chronicles (such as the witch Jadis and the Pevensie sisters) do possess the power to travel between worlds, they lack the power to create or destroy those worlds. Instead, they rely on the more traditional powers of enchantment, corruption, and warfare to affect these worlds. Furthermore, in the case of Narnia itself, the world is a flat, medieval cosmology where astrology is as important as astronomy.

In both ancient and medieval cosmologies, and to some extent even in our modern mythology, the moon is, above all other celestial bodies, connected with the feminine principle. Not only is the connection between female and lunar due to the similarity between the 29.5 day cycle of the moon's phases and the menstrual cycle, but also due to the obvious metaphor of birth, growth, and death seen in the waxing and waning of the moon's appearance from new to full and back again. The three major parts of the moon's cycle — waxing, full, and waning back to new — give rise to a three-fold aspect, seen in the common triad of lunar goddesses from classical mythology (maiden, mother, and crone). However, despite the fact that this reproductive/sexual aspect has agency (in a reproductive sense), there is an inherent passivity, as the womb is a passive place of potential until activated by the active male seed. This passivity is inherent in the lunar metaphor, because the moon does not emit any light of its own, but is instead merely a mirror reflecting the light of the sun, a body that is most often seen as male in mythology (Biedermann 224).

The cosmological goddesses of Gaiman's *American Gods* are, on the surface, similar to those of Lewis and Tolkien and classical lunar goddesses, and in fact are manifestations of real-world goddesses trying to survive in the modern world. Their powers appear limited and their roles very traditional. The Egyptian goddess Bast spends most of her time sleeping in cat-form on Shadow's bed; on at least one occasion she satisfies his sexual needs (while he dreams). In the Egyptian pantheon, Bast was seen as a lunar deity, and protected childbirth and healing, respectively, reflecting the stereotypical feminine roles of midwife and nurse (Ann and Imel 79). Therefore her connections to both the night/dreams and sexuality are very much stereotypical in the novel. In a 2001 interview with Rudi Dornemann and Kelly Everding, Gaiman openly acknowledges his interest in the three Slavic cosmological goddesses known as the Zorya, and the frustratingly little that is known of their tradition. Gaiman's Zorya are largely plucked from encyclopedias of mythology unchanged, even down to the tradition of their watching the sky all night, monitoring the evil being chained to the Big Dipper (*American Gods* 89; Ann and Imel 72–73). In this role, the goddesses are again depicted as passive watchers. Their only action in Slavic mythology is to open the gates for their father Dazhbog (the sun god) and his chariot at sunrise and sunset. However, Gaiman takes this mythology one step further in giving the normally nameless third sister, the Midnight Star, a name — Zorya Polunochnaya (Dixon-Kennedy 321). Once again, the reader's introduction to this third Zorya is replete with standard stereotypical language. She complains to Shadow that she never got to see her father in the Old Country because she slept during the day, his time of activity (*American Gods* 89). As the midnight sister who never sees the sun, she is an obvious symbol of the full moon, and it is in this role that she gives Shadow an image of the moon (in the form of a coin) to light his way. However, she admits that this is a "much weaker protection" than the gold solar coin he had previously given away to his dead wife, because it is the protection of the "daughter, not the father" (*American Gods* 90). In other words, once again we are reminded that the moon is seen as inferior and less powerful/active than the male solar deity.

While the cosmological goddesses of *American Gods* are very traditional despite their modern lifestyle, in *Stardust* the female characters take a baby step forward, straddling both the wall between the real world and Faerie, and the transitions in both science and society marked by the Industrial Revolution. Gaiman uses these boundaries to draw attention to the supplanting of the imaginative and romantic by the cold and scientific in our modern world, reminding us that "Few of us now have seen the stars as folk saw them then —

our cities and towns cast too much light into the night — but, from the village of Wall, the stars were laid out like worlds or like ideas..." (41). The cosmological goddesses of this work likewise personify this transition from classical to modern (quantum) realities. Yvaine is a very traditional cosmological divinity, the personification of a fallen star. If she ventures across the boundary between Faerie and Reality she will change into the modern world's most unromantic and scientific notion of a meteorite — a grey lump of rock and metal. On the other hand, the witches called the Lilim exist in, and can pass between, two parallel worlds: Faerie and the reality inside their mirror. However, they are limited in their powers as well, and seek to kidnap Yvaine in order to possess her lifeforce/youth. In their ability to temporarily change from young to old to young again, as well as their threefold nature, they also are reminiscent of the classic lunar triad of goddesses.

But it is not only depictions of the moon as a goddess and the sun as a god that permeate our illustrations and metaphors of the universe, but there is also the much larger engendering of the language used to discuss both aspects of nature and the natural world *in toto*. Central to feminist studies is the concept that language is a social construct, and like many aspects of culture is not gender neutral. Rather, in the patriarchal tradition of Western culture, the gendering of language reflects this role of male power and female passivity and is used to suppress women (Cameron 1985; Lakoff 1975). This is clearly illustrated in the history of scientific writing in the Western tradition. Nature has been depicted as a feminine force since ancient times, and as Evelyn Fox Keller explores in detail in *Reflections on Gender and Science*, ever since the Scientific Revolution the process of scientific discovery has been steeped in sexual metaphor and language. For example, Keller explains that in the early seventeenth-century writings of Francis Bacon, the scientist's role is to master science, to "hound, conquer, and subdue her — only in that way is the true 'nature of things' revealed" (36–37). Three centuries later, physicist and best-selling science writer Brian Greene echoed this sentiment when he noted that "nothing comes easily. Nature does not give up her secrets lightly" (470).

This gendered envisioning of science has increasingly been appropriated by other authors of nontechnical works mass-produced for a general readership, a literary style made popular by astronomer Carl Sagan. For example, in one of his last works, *The Demon-haunted World*, he explains that "science arouses a soaring sense of wonder" and that the book was "a personal statement, reflecting my lifelong love affair with science" (6, 25). In *The Trouble with Physics*, his 2006 book-length argument against the hegemony of string theory, Lee Smolin notes that "the most cherished goal in physics, as in bad romance novels, is unification" (18), and the current king of science popularizations, Stephen Hawking, says of the "Eureka moment" of making a scientific discovery, "I won't compare it to sex, but it lasts longer" (117). String theory is often called "beautiful" or "seductive" by its proponents,[1] and the embarrassment that most scientists consider the "landscape" of string theory (the huge number of possible mathematical realities it predicts) is instead celebrated by the theory's adherents as a "fecundity" that is "part of its appeal" (Pease 987). Roszak points to these "domineering sexual metaphors" as evidence that feminist psychologists are correct in suspecting that there is "a powerful masculine bias not only in science as a profession, but in science as a worldview" (56). Fortunately, in Gaiman's work we shall now see a transition from a passive, oppressed feminine principle in nature to more modern, and far more powerful, "liberated" quantum cosmological goddesses, agents of change who have the ability to traverse, create, and even destroy entire universes.

Noted science fiction writer Harlan Ellison explains in his introduction to Gaiman's *The Sandman: Season of Mists* that "every fantasist builds a new universe each time s/he creates a new story" (9). Ellison notes further that Gaiman's particularly "full-realized cosmology" is "as compelling as it is revisionist." Part of Gaiman's talent lies in this ability to successfully create Secondary Worlds, both singularly and serially, and in multitudes (considering the totality of his published works). But Gaiman flexes his authorial muscles most strongly when he abandons classical fairy-tale worlds (such as that in *Stardust*) and enters the quantum realm, diving headfirst into modern fantasy and science fiction. In his foreword to Paul McAuley's *Doctor Who* novella *Eye of the Tyger*, Gaiman explains that he had "become infected by the idea that there are an infinite number of worlds, only a footstep away" (8). In *InterWorld*, Gaiman and co-author Michael Reaves explore the very quantum idea of an infinite number of alternate universes being created by human decisions — perhaps the most powerful manifestation of free will possible. Here Gaiman refers to an alternative to the standard Copenhagen Interpretation of quantum mechanics, called the Many Worlds Interpretation or MWI (Everett III 1957). In this model, every time an experiment with several possible outcomes is conducted, the universe branches into parallel realities, one for each of the possible outcomes. Therefore, anything that *can* happen, *does* happen. Reality with a capital R is the sum of all possible parallel realities or universes, sometimes called a multiverse. Which one of you is the real you? All of you are just as real, in your own particular universe. What's more, in its original form, the MWI predicts that since there is no effect of one reality on another, there is no way one observer can ever be aware of the splitting process. As Jay explains to Joey Harker, important decisions by an individual "can cause alternate worlds to splinter off into divergent space-time continua.... Of course, the In-Between keeps them apart, so he'll never know" (Gaiman, *InterWorld* 72–73). In the novel, only the Walkers can travel across the hyperspace known as the In-Between, and other characters can only harness the essence of the Walkers in order to travel through the periphery of this hyper-space, a space known as the Static or Nowhere-at-All (considered the long way around in interdimensional travel). Therefore the ability to travel freely between universes is a special skill in the multiverse of *InterWorld*.

But physicist David Deutsch has demonstrated that in a modification of the MWI it *is* possible for the various parallel universes to interact, and in fact it is the existence of this infinite multiplicity of parallel universes, each with its own unique timeline, that physicists now understand theoretically allows for the possibility of time travel into the past without causing paradoxes (such as someone killing their parents before they themselves were conceived). The idea of traveling between parallel realities or universes has been used in numerous works of science fiction. For example, in the TV series *Sliders*, genius physicist Quinn Mallory accidentally creates a machine that opens doorways between alternate realities. Mallory and his friends afterwards "slide" between these different realities, each somehow different from the reality from which they originated. In the 2001 cult movie *Donnie Darko*, an unstable tan-gent universe suddenly opens up in the nick of time to save the title character from certain death when an airplane engine falls on his house. But as Donnie discovers, through reading a mysterious book called *The Philosophy of Time Travel*, he must go back to the primary universe and die in the original accident in order to save the primary world.

Phillip Pullman's *His Dark Materials* trilogy exploits the Many Worlds Interpretation to posit the existence of multiple realities (including an under-world repository for human souls), and begins in the universe of Lyra Belac-qua, a universe that blends science and spirituality in a way that is a clear commentary on the antagonistic relationship between science and spirituality of modern society. Here Lyra's mother, Marisa Coulter, conducts gruesome scientific experiments on children (sanctioned by the Church) in order to try to prevent them from knowing original sin, while Lyra's father, Lord Asriel, uses similar experiments to harness the same psychic power to open a doorway to another universe (with the purpose of gathering an army to declare war on the Deity of the Church). Lyra is able to pass from universe to universe, ini-tially by using the doorway opened by her father, and later through her rela-tionship with Will Parry, who becomes the bearer of the Subtle Knife. With the knife the pair can pass from any universe to any other by creating their own doorway, and their travels are aided by Lyra's masterful use of the alethiometer, a device that gives the answer to specific questions through a series of symbols. In the beginning of the trilogy, Lyra has an uncanny innate ability to read the symbols, but when she symbolically passes into womanhood (symbolized through falling in love with Will) she loses this seemingly magical power and must instead rely on a more scientific approach to relearning how to use the device. Mary Malone (who likewise travels between realities) also bridges the chasm between science and spirituality/magic by relying on her own method of divination, the *I Ching*, a habit which, being a scientist, brings her feelings of anxiety and guilt.

Like Pullman's trilogy, Gaiman and Reaves' *InterWorld* also relies on the Many World Interpretation of quantum mechanics. In this work, the main characters, many of whom are alternate reality versions of Joey Harker, travel between parallel universes. Therefore, QCG can be found in this work as well, but as these characters clearly illustrate another important property of the QCG (namely the relationship between science and spirituality), this work (and its connections with Pullman's work) will be further discussed later in this essay.

In the same vein as Pullman's Mary and Lyra, *Neverwhere*'s Door is also QCG, and like Lyra, realizes her ultimate destiny while working under the impression that she is completely in control of her own free will. Like the bearer of the Subtle Knife, Door can create portals at will, but like *InterWorld*'s Jo, her only technology is her belief that she can do so. Door comes from a family of such "openers," and while her father schooled her in the scientific principles of "Parity, symmetry, topology," the most important lesson was that "all things want to open. You must feel that need, and use it" (215). Thus Door also links together science and the super-natural (experiences outside science) in her unique powers, which is an interesting aspect of these new QCGs. While her own personal mission is to exact revenge for the murder of her family, she becomes entangled in a greater cosmological drama, namely the fate of the jailed fallen angel Islington, who is not only responsible for her family's deaths (and the destruction of Atlantis), but also plans to take over Heaven in revenge for his imprisonment in London Below. Door appears to acquiesce to his demand to save her friend Richard Mayhew, but in actuality she opens a doorway to the most distant location she could reach, "halfway across space and time" (338). Islington is sucked into a chaotic maelstrom through the force of gravity, a tremendous vortex that Richard recognizes as possibly being "the event horizon of a black hole" (329). In this way, Door is more clearly aligned with the general relativity (gravity and warping of space-time) side of modern physics than quantum mechanics, an alignment also seen in another of Gaiman's fascinating and powerful QCG, namely the evil Other Mother of *Coraline*.

The evil Alternative Mother who tries to make Coraline her permanent guest first traps the girl's parents in an alternative dimension behind the hall mirror. She had previously trapped the souls of other kidnapped children behind another mirror. Coraline discovers that the Other Mother has created her own world, one designed specifically to entice and trap children like Coraline. The girl tries to escape, but finds that if she walks too far, she just comes back to the place she started. Coraline is confused, but the black cat likens it to walking around the earth. The Other Mother's "closed universe" is therefore a much smaller example of Einstein's original "spherical" model of our own universe, as described by his general theory of relativity.[2] In such a universe, light rays sent off toward infinity would, after a very long time, return to their starting place. Such a universe is bounded but without an end, since the "end" is just the beginning again. However, as Coraline observes, in this case it is a "small world" (75). Regardless of this world's limited size, the Other Mother is certainly to be included in Gaiman's pantheon of QCG. It should be noted, however, that, as the villain of the tale, the Other Mother has significant limits to her powers (besides only making a small world in which to trap the children). Like other evil characters (such as Tolkien's Melkor), the Other Mother could not "truly make anything.... She could only twist and copy and distort things that already existed," a prime example being the deformed Other Father (118).

The works discussed thus far demonstrate Gaiman's masterful use of parallel worlds. As Gaiman and Reaves playfully remind their audience in the Authors' Note to *InterWorld*, although theirs is a fictional work, "still, given an infinite number of possible worlds, it must be true on one of them. And if a story set in an infinite number of possible universes is true in one of them, then it must be true in all of them. So maybe it's not as fictional as we think" (2). The action in this novel takes place in a subset of the entire multiverse (the sum of all possible universes) termed the "Altiverse," which consists only of those universes that contain Earths (hence the existence of the myriad manifestations of alternate Joey Harkers). Other works of Gaiman in which characters travel between universes include *Neverwhere*, *The Sandman* series, and *MirrorMask*. However, these works pay homage to a different type of multiverse, namely that of the inflationary revision of the Big Bang theory.

The Big Bang theory of the early universe casts reality as the child of an uneasy marriage between quantum mechanics (which describes the rules of the subatomic universe) and Albert Einstein's general theory of relativity, a re-envisioning of gravity as the warping of the four-dimensional fabric termed space-time. According to this model, the infant universe was initially in a very hot, dense state and has expanded and cooled over the past 13.7 or so billion years. Hence when Lucifer bemoans the fact that he's been tending hell for 10 billion years, he's simply rounding the number (Gaiman, *Sandman* 23:14). While the Big Bang has been corroborated by numerous observational tests, it does not actually claim to tell us about the exact origin of the universe, but rather explains the evolution of the universe from that initial hot, dense state. In fact, science can say nothing of certainty about what happened before 10^{43} seconds after a presumed beginning. This is because scientists lack a complete understanding of how the two mathematically disparate legs of modern physics should merge at these high energies and small distances. At current it is a shotgun marriage at best. Be that as it may, this lack of a complete model of quantum gravity has not prevented physicists from developing possible scenarios for the origin of the universe. In 1973, Edward Tryon proposed the rather startling idea that the entire universe began as a random vacuum fluctuation of space-time and grew to its present state long afterwards. As he somewhat flippantly puts it, "our Universe is simply one of those things which happen from time to time" (397).

Tryon's model was initially largely ignored by the scientific community; however, in 1981, particle physicist Alan Guth found that a revision of Tryon's model answered several nagging questions about the nature of the young universe. He found that under certain conditions, there would exist a temporary repulsive force, like an antigravity, which would inflate a small portion of the infant universe exponentially, growing from less than the size of an atom to the size of a grapefruit in the blink of an eye. Eventually this era of "inflation" ends, with the now separate bud of the original universe then resuming the evolution predicted by the usual Big Bang model. Other sections of the original mother universe could have inflated as well, but would never contact its siblings after leaving the quantum mechanical nest.

In 1982, Alexander Vilenkin further extended Tryon's idea by proposing that the entire universe began through the quantum mechanical process known as tunneling, in other words making a sudden change from one state to another. In this instance, the initial state was nothing in its truest sense (no space, no time) and the final state was *something* in its ultimate sense — a universe made of space-time. Further improvements to the inflationary model demonstrate that once inflation begins, it will never end, a concept called eternal inflation. Individual "bubbles" will continue to bud off, each leading to a separate or pocket universe. The collection of all pocket universes that derive from the mother universe is sometimes called the multiverse (not to be confused with the multiverse of the Many Worlds Interpretation). According to eternal inflation, at all moments, some pocket universe is being created by undergoing inflation, and once formed evolves independently of all its sibling universes.

It is these new views of reality as multiple and moldable — in some sense the scientific equivalent of Faerie — that Gaiman draws upon in his writings. For example, in *Neverwhere* "little pockets of old time in London" simultaneously exist as London Below, "like bubbles in amber" (228). In *MirrorMask* multiple realities come into being and are threatened with destruction, as is the case in *The Sandman* series. It is in this latter work that Gaiman's vision of a multiverse is best developed. As Clive Barker explains in his introduction to *The Sandman: The Doll's House*, "There is no solid status quo, only a series of relative realities" which are traversed by "dimension-hopping entities" (6). These myriad worlds include Hell, Asgard, Chaos, The Dreaming (itself a multiverse of individual dreamers and the possibility of dreams), and the other realities created by The Endless Ones. Lucien's library is also a sort of multiverse, as it contains "every story that has ever been dreamed" and "novels their authors never wrote or never finished, except in dreams" (Gaiman, *Sandman* 22:2). Travel between these realities is similar to that in Interworld, in that it takes place in a sort of inhospitable hyperspace. On his way to visit Lucifer in Hell, Morpheus travels through the desolate and cold "NOWHERE" that is "BETWEEN place" (Gaiman, Sandman 23:1). Guth, Farhi, and Guven may theorize about creating an experimental universe in the lab, but in *The Sandman: Season of Mists*, Odin does just that, fashioning a "notional dimension" in which he creates a tiny version of Ragnarok in order to explore the properties of his greatest fear — the inevitable twilight of the Norse gods (26:14).

Is this power of Odin's strictly fiction? If Mother Nature continues to give birth to child universes even today, is it possible to create our own pocket universe in the laboratory? Could physicists follow in the footsteps of biologists and "play God" in manipulating the reproduction not of individuals or species, but entire realities? In a seminal 1987 paper, Alan Guth, Steven Blau and E.I Guendelman described the space-time structure of such "child universes" and found that since this inflation takes place in another space-time, not our own, the gateway to this child universe appears as a black hole in our universe. Like the TARDIS, such a universe would certainly be bigger on the inside than the outside. While a companion paper by Guth and Ed Farhi showed that it may be technically unlikely to be able to create a child universe in a laboratory using classical physics (i.e. general relativity alone), a third paper by Farhi, Guth, and Guven showed that it *might* just be possible to create a pocket universe of one's own using quantum mechanics. In addition, there is no reason to expect that the laws of physics in other pocket universes will echo those of our reality (an integral part of the plotline of *InterWorld*).

The greatest QCG of *The Sandman* series are the Furies, called The Kindly Ones in the eponymous installation of the series. The Furies enforce "the oldest rule" in the multiverse of The Endless, namely the avenging of blood-debts (28:23). In this way The Kindly Ones are also primordial goddesses, having apparently existed since nearly the beginning. As they begin their pursuit of Morpheus (to avenge his mercy killing of his son, Orpheus), all the parallel worlds are affected, as whatever passes for the normal laws of nature in their respective pocket universes break down. Destiny meets a copy of himself, Desire closes off its realm, and Delirium transforms into a school of tiny fish. As the walls between the parallel realities (in both the Guth and Everett senses) begin to break down, Destiny is faced with myriad versions of himself, and multiple Destinies note:

> "As events happen, the conflicting destinies will merge into a whole."
> "As the events take place, the conflicting destinies will cease to exist."
> [...] "Events that never did happen and now never shall, will cast their conclusions and occurrences out into the world."
> "Cause and effect will jostle, unable to tell quite which came first. The event horizon will come closer and closer, wrecks and mirages of time and occasion..." [*Sandman* 67:14–15].

Finally one version finally asks the rhetorical question, "Am I the true Destiny? Are you?" (67:15). When the Furies finally meet up with Morpheus they explain that they are his doom. "We will destroy your dreamworld, Morpheus.... And, in the end, we shall destroy you" (64:18–19). The cosmological powers of The Kindly Ones, and their connections to both classic mythology and modern science, are clear.

There is another QCG in *The Sandman* who deserves our attention. The previously described gravitational vortex that Door condemns Islington to in *Neverwhere* is similar to the vortex in The Dreaming created by Rose Walker in *The Sandman: The Doll's House.* Just as a black hole attracts all matter and energy to it, Morpheus explains to the raven Matthew that Rose will "attract the stray dreams to her — or she'll be drawn to them" (11: 9). Indeed, in her dreams Rose reaches out to all dreamers simultaneously and begins breaking down the walls between their individual dream universes, "loosing them into the flux.... And it would be so **simple** to create one **huge dream**" (14:15, 19). Morpheus explains to Rose that these occasional vortices are humans who have the power to "destroy the ordered chaos of the Dreaming" by gathering the dreams and dreamers together before "the vortex collapses in upon it all.... It leaves behind nothing but darkness" and destroys entire worlds (16:5). Rose Walker is therefore a sort of psychic or supernatural black hole who has the power to destroy worlds — a powerful modern cosmological goddess indeed.[3]

Another QCG who creates — and unwittingly causes the near destruction of — worlds in her dreams is Helena Campbell of *MirrorMask.* She creates a parallel world by drawing it, and is herself drawn into (and temporarily trapped inside) this other universe through the power of the MirrorMask (wielded by the Princess of the Land of Shadows). The Princess (an alternate version of Helena) escapes into Helena's universe, and throws all the parallel universes "out of balance," threatening to destroy them in a selfish attempt to escape from her own unsatisfying existence. After all, she notes in her goodbye letter to her mother, the Dark Queen, "you can't run away from home without destroying somebody's world" (57). The Princess nearly succeeds, crumpling up Helena's drawings and therefore crumpling the parallel world "into blackness and nothing" (69). In order to stop the Princess and return to her own world, Helena desperately seeks the MirrorMask, but when she finds it she initially realizes that "It wouldn't take me to my own world, but it would give me what it had given her. Another world. Another girl like me to displace. It would be a way out. And I couldn't do it" (61).

Helena decides that she can instead use the mask to draw the Princess back, and finds that as she puts it on, "It was like being in the eye of the hurricane; the world swirled and shook around me, but I was fine. I could feel her being pulled towards me, being pulled into the window. For a moment I couldn't remember which one of us I was" (73). Therefore, in Helena's description we see both the black hole meme of Door and Rose Walker's adventures, and the encounter between parallel versions of one's self of *InterWorld* and *The Sandman: The Kindly Ones*.

Thus far in our discussion of cosmological goddesses and their powers of creation and destruction, the language of reproduction has repeatedly cropped up. The usage of reproductive metaphor is also central to the inflationary model, with its "baby" or "child universes" and "mother universes." João Magueijo describes the theory as a "union" between "two enemy gods" (quantum mechanics and general relativity), and the inflationary era itself "a brief affair," a "temporary flirtation," and a "naughty episode in the life of the baby universe" (115). Therefore the very concept of a multiverse draws on our respect for (and awe of) the most fundamental of all feminine powers, that of procreation. In the multiverse of Gaiman's publications, new cosmological goddesses share in this fecundity of the laws of physics, not only by traversing universes, but in creating and destroying them. While science is very much at the core of these characters, they also maintain a very definite mythological, magical, or spiritual element, at the very same time, in keeping with the awe-inspiring power of a Creator (whose presumed powers, despite the recent protestations of physicist Stephen Hawking, cannot be disproven by the laws of physics, but simply rendered superfluous). Seen in this light, Gaiman's QCG bridge the gap between the ancient cosmological mythologies and a new scientific mythology that acknowledges both the importance of the laws of physics and the influence of consciousness on those laws.

Perhaps the primary example of the intricate relationship between science and spirituality in Gaiman's works is *InterWorld*. Here Joey Harker learns that the Walkers are caught in a battle to control the entire Altiverse between the uber-technologists of the Binary and the magic-based empire of HEX. The purpose of InterWorld is to try to instead promote a balance between the two extremes, because "the Altiverse functions best when the forces of magic and science are in balance" (75). Such a respectful balance between the spiritual and the rational — two important aspects of the human psyche — is reminiscent of paleontologist and science writer Stephen Jay Gould's "Principle of NOMA, or Non-Overlapping Magisteria," which he describes as a

> principle of respectful noninterference.... Science covers the empirical realm: what is the universe made of (fact) and why does it work this way (theory). The magisterium of religion extends over questions of ultimate meaning and moral value. These two magisteria do not overlap, nor do they encompass all inquiry (consider, for example, the magisterium of art and the meaning of beauty) [5–6].

But without conflict there is no story, so Joey Harker and his fellow Walkers (male and female "joeys" from other Earths in the Altiverse) are pitted against the Binary and HEX, the latter represented by Lady Indigo and Lord Dogknife.

Among the most powerful of the Walkers is Jo, a winged "joey" who flies not by means of the laws of aerodynamics, but because she has "the conviction that she *can* fly" (95). As a citizen of one of the more magical worlds, she appears on the surface to be more of a throwback to Faerie than a QCG, but the same could also be said of Lady Indigo, who uses spells and enchantments to gain power over others. But such an analysis would be myopic at best, and goes against the central, anti-"black-and-white" message of the novel. After all, according to the often-quoted adage attributed to Arthur C. Clarke, "any sufficiently advanced technology is indistinguishable from magic." For while both Jo and Lady Indigo rely on magic, they also manipulate science/technology, and transcend this cumbersome dichotomy. For example, Lady Indigo's ship, the *Lacrimae Mundi*, is a spaceship, despite the magic that works within it. Jo may come from a magic planet, but her greatest power is being a Walker, with the ability to traverse realities by relying on her own innate power (similar to her innate ability to fly without reliance on either science or magic). Her power is rather her consciousness, the same power which splits universes in the first place in the Many Worlds Interpretation. Therefore Jo comes closer to harnessing the ultimate power of reality as compared to the other characters.

While the Walkers can travel between realities much faster than Lady Indigo, because they can travel from portal to portal directly through the hyperspace of the In-Between rather than relying on the mush longer route through its fringes (the Nowhere-at-All), there are limitations to the Walkers' powers as well. They cannot create portals just anywhere, but instead have to search for "potential portals" where the entrance and exit points in space-time are "congruent" (167–168). Therefore both science and magic have limitations in the Altiverse.

This opening of portals or doorways between universes is reminiscent of both C.S. Lewis's Narnia chronicles and Philip Pullman's *His Dark Materials* trilogy. Gaiman's love for (and frustration with) Lewis's works led him to write the short story "The Problem with Susan" (*Fragile Things*), while Pullman (an agnostic) has said of Lewis: "I realised that what he was up to was propaganda in the cause of the religion he believed in," and called the Chronicles "monumentally disparaging of girls and women.... One girl [Susan] was sent to hell because she was getting interested in clothes and boys." Gaiman himself has described "the things that were so amazing" about Pullman's trilogy as including "the pleasure of being in, and discovering an alternate universe, which is a very specific pleasure" (Bookwitch). While Lewis's multiverse is a clearly an almost entirely magical/spiritual one, Pullman's universe is closer to both *InterWorld* and the NOMA of Gould in its appreciation of both science and spirituality as facets of the world we inhabit. As previously noted, modern science and spirituality are blended in Pullman's works just as they are in Gaiman's, for example in the character Mary Malone, a former nun and physicist who discovers that dark matter is actually conscious (and central to the relationship between angels and humans).

There is yet another fundamental connection between the cosmos and humanity, one hinted at in Pullman's series. Mary Malone discovers that the amount of dust has increased greatly since the time of the first truly modern humans, when our consciousness could interact with the consciousness of the "dust." The so-called anthropic principle likewise connectshuman intelligence and the universe in a very fundamental way. In 1961, physicist Robert Dicke explained that we live in a universe whose fundamental constants seem finely tuned to support human life simply because we could not exist in a universe whose constants were otherwise. Since that time, this "weak" anthropic principle (WAP) has been used by Stephen Hawking and other physicists to cull 'unlivable' universes from theories of the multiverse. But others have taken this idea much further. For example, the strong anthropic principle (SAP), developed by Brandon Carter (1974) suggests that the universe had no choice in its fine-tuning because the eventual existence of intelligent observers was a necessity. Rather than to merely note that the fine-tuning of the universe makes our existence possible (the WAP), the SAP seeks to answer why the universe is fine-tuned by appealing to our very existence. As speculative (and controversial) as the SAP is considered, even more so are the final anthropic principle (FAP) and participatory anthropic principle (PAP). The former claims that not only is the eventual existence of intelligent life a necessity for the universe, but that once it has arisen it will continue to exist indefinitely. The PAP is related to questions of the role of the observer in quantum mechanics. It claims that because of observers are necessary to make decisions, observers are also necessary to bring the universe into full existence (Barrow and Tipler, 22–23). However, the SAP, FAP, and PAP appear unlikely, as the only form of intelligent observers currently known did not arise until the universe was well over 10 billion years old and long after all its basic structures (such as stars, galaxies, and superclusters) came into being.

The possibility that the universe somehow depends on intelligent observers to give it meaning (if not existence) is an interesting one. The same can be said of deities — after all, without someone to worship, what need is there for something *to be* worshipped? This idea is central to the plotline of Gaiman's *American Gods*, and brings this essay (like Einstein's spherical universe) back to the place it began, namely considering Bast and the Zorya. Having originally considered them classical cosmological goddesses, more specifically of the lunar variety, we must re-evaluate our superficial analysis and realize that they form a bridge between the classical and the quantum — a semiclassical approximation in the words of those who are frantically trying to unite quantum mechanics and general relativity into a "theory of everything."

The first clue that these goddesses are more than lunar deities comes in the basic cosmological geography of the novel, where only certain beings can pass freely between the world of humans and the world "behind the curtain," the realm of the gods. Mere mortals are seldom aware of this parallel world, except in places where "Reality was thin," such as Rock City (Gaiman, *American Gods* 535). Zorya Polunochnaya specifically displays her powers over reality by appearing to pluck the moon from the sky for Shadow, yet the moon still remains there at the same time. Shadow himself understood the power and importance of Zorya Polunochnaya much later in the novel, after dying upon the great tree, when he realized she would be there to meet him in the underworld. Indeed, she does, and acts as a spiritual guide, but one of the quantum rather than classical variety. For this is the Gaimanverse, one in which, like in the Many Worlds Interpretation, multiple potentials exist simultaneously, and it is the decision of a single human mind that changes the course of reality. Zorya Polunochnaya receives the moon coin back from Shadow and resets it into the heavens of the underworld to light his way. When Shadow asks which path he should take, specifically "which one is safe," she answers that not only are they mutually exclusive, but "neither path is safe" (*American Gods* 471). Similarly, in the Many Worlds Interpretation, the universe splits when a decision is made, and it cannot be made singular again. What could be more fraught with the potential for danger than creating an entirely new reality? Nevertheless, Zorya Polunochnaya does recommend one path (for the price of Shadow's true name), and he continues on his journey.

Shadow's next guide is the other lunar goddess of *American Gods*, Bast. Seeing her in her humanoid form for the first time, Shadow does not recognize her. Bast reveals that she has been carefully watching over him, as have her people, since the start of his journey. Of the three possible choices set before him, Bast tells Shadow that one path will "make you wise," while another will "make you whole" and the third will kill him (*American Gods* 476). In keeping with the uncertainties of quantum mechanics, Shadow does not know which to choose, and Bast turns the table, playing the role of the human observer in deciding for Shadow, thereby splitting the universe and setting events into motion that will have cosmological consequences. For Shadow's choices shape his new universe, and that of all the characters in the novel. In aiding Shadow in making these choices, Zorya Polunochnaya and Bast are therefore QCG, cleverly disguised as mere lunar deities. As is so often true in the Gaimanverse, little is what it initially seems to be.

Ely, Melzi, Hadge, and McCabe argue that female agency — including "the needs for achievement and power" (261) — has historically been over-looked and suppressed because agency has been seen as the sole province of the dominant male gender. But perhaps it is also the definition of "power" that has been narrowly shaped by the patriarchal hegemony. Certainly the power of reproduction — of giving birth and guaranteeing the continuation of life and the species — can only be mimicked by men, even in science (for example, in the case of cloning). A central aspect of this new female cosmo-logical principle, the ability to give birth to entire realities without the need for a father or male principle, appears to be a connection to, rather than divorced from, another important facet of the human experience, namely the spiritual. In the famous passage from *American Gods*, which he has said "is the most direct expression of his religious beliefs" (Goodyear), Gaiman argues (through the character of Sammi "Sam" Black Crow),

> I can believe things that are true and I can believe things that aren't true and I can believe things where nobody knows if they're true or not ... I can believe that light is a particle and a wave, that there's a cat in a box somewhere that's alive and dead at the same time ... I believe in a personal god who cares about me and worries and oversees everything I do. I believe in an impersonal god who set the universe into motion and went to hang out with her girlfriends and doesn't even know I'm alive. I believe in an empty and godless universe of causal chaos ... [394–395].

The references to quantum mechanics (such as the wave-particle duality and the Schrödinger's Cat thought experiment) are clear and undeniable, as are the references to both science and the spiritual. In creating his modern quan-tum cosmological goddesses, Gaiman does not turn his back on myth and spirituality, but instead aligns his works with one of the most surprising aspects of modern physics, namely the important role of the observer — of human consciousness — in giving the universe not only meaning, but ultimately reality. As Jay explains to Joey Harker, "Consciousness is a factor in *every* aspect of the Multiverse. Quantum math needs a viewpoint, or it doesn't work" (Gaiman, *InterWorld* 72–73). It appears that Gaiman is closer to the truth than one might suspect, for not only does one create entirely new worlds in one's dreams, but these dreams have, at least in theory, the potential to split the universe at the quantum level. Perhaps we truly are all gods and goddesses in disguise.

NOTES

1 For more information on this curious aspect of modern science writing, see Kristine Larsen, "Selling Science: String Theory as 'Science Porn,'" in *Riffing on Strings*, eds. Sean Miller and Shveta Verma (New York: Scriblerus Press, 2008), 15–25.

2. A similar cosmology can be found in the Mr. Tompkins short stories of physicist George Gamow, and the original *Land of the Lost* television series.

3. In Gaiman's episode of *Doctor Who*, "The Doctor's Wife," the TARDIS itself takes her place as a QCG, as the viewers are reminded of her power to travel not only through time and space, and to other parallel realities, but to reboot the universe (in the episode "The Big Bang").

WORKS CITED

Ann, Martha, and Dorothy Myers Imel. *Goddesses in World Mythology*. Santa Barbara: ABC-CLIO, 1993. Print.

Barker, Clive. Introduction. *The Sandman: The Doll's House*. By Neil Gaiman. New York: DC Comics, 1990. 6–7. Print.

Barrow, John D., and Frank J. Tiple. *The Anthropic Principle*. Oxford: Oxford University Press, 1988. Print.

Biedermann, Hans. *Dictionary of Symbolism*. Trans. James Hulbert. New York: Penguin, 1994. Print.

Blau, Steven K., E.I. Guendelman, and Alan H. Guth. "Dynamics of False-vacuum Bubbles." *Physical Review D* 35.6 (1987): 1747–66. Print.

Bookwitch. "Neil Gaiman — 'I worry that I might be respectable.'" 10 Nov. 2008. Web. 12 Aug. 2011.

Cameron, Deborah. *Feminism and Linguistic Theory*. London: Macmillan, 1985. Print.

Carter, Brandon. "Large Number Coincidences and the Anthropic Principle in Cosmology." *Confrontation of Cosmological Theories with Observational Data: Copernicus Symposium 2*. Ed. M. S. Longair. Dordrecht: D. Reidel, 1974. 291–298. Print.

Deutsch, David. *The Fabric of Reality*. New York: Penguin, 1997. Print.

Dicke, Robert. "Dirac's Cosmology and Mach's Principle." *Nature* 192 (1961): 440–441. Print.

Donovan, Leslie A. "The Valkyrie Reflex in J.R.R. Tolkien's The Lord of the Rings." *Tolkien and the Medievalists*. Ed. Jane Chance. New York: Routledge, 2003. 106–32. Print.

Dornemann, Rudi, and Kelly Everdig. "Dreaming American Gods: An Interview with Neil Gaiman." *Rain Taxi*. Summer 2001. Web. 12 Aug. 2011.

Ellison, Harlan. Introduction. *The Sandman: Season of Mists*. By Neil Gaiman. New York: DC Comics, 1992, 2010. 7–11. Print.

Ely, R., G. Melzi, L. Hadge, and A. McCabe. "Being Brave, Being Nice: Themes of Agency and Communion in Children's Narratives." *Journal of Personality* 66.2 (1998): 257–84. Print.

Everett III, Hugh. "'Relative State' Formulation of Quantum Mechanics." *Reviews of Modern Physics* 29.3 (1957): 454–62. Print.

Ezard, John. "Narnia Books Attacked as Racist and Sexist." *Guardian Online.* 3 June 2002. Web. 12 Aug. 2011.

Farhi, Edward, and Alan H. Guth, "An Obstacle to Creating a Universe in the Laboratory." *Physics Letters B* 183 (1987): 149–55. Print.

Farhi, Edward, Alan H. Guth, Jemal Guven. "Is It Possible to Create a Universe in the Laboratory by Quantum Tunneling?" *Nuclear Physics B* 339 (1990): 417–90. Print.

Gaiman, Neil. *American Gods.* New York: HarperTorch, 2002. Print.

_____. *Coraline.* New York: Harper Entertainment, 2008. Print.

_____. "Foreword: The Nature of the Infection." *Doctor Who: Eye of the Tyger.* By Paul McAuley.
Tolworth: Telos, 7–10. Print.

_____. *Fragile Things,* New York: Harper, 2006. Print.

_____. *Neverwhere.* New York: HarperTorch, 2001. Print.

_____. *The Sandman: The Doll's House.* New York: DC Comics, 1990. Print.

_____. *The Sandman: The Kindly Ones.* New York: DC Comics, 1996. Print.

_____. *The Sandman: Season of Mists.* New York: DC Comics, 2010. Print.

_____. *Stardust.* New York: HarperTeen, 1999. Print.

_____ (w), Mike Dringenberg (p), and Malcolm Jones III (i). "Moving In." *The Sandman* #9 (Sept. 1989), New York: DC Comics. Print.

_____ (w), Mike Dringenberg (p), and Malcolm Jones III (i). "Collectors." *The Sandman* #14 (March 1990), New York: DC Comics. Print.

_____ (w), Mike Dringenberg (p), and Malcolm Jones III (i). "Lost Hearts." *The Sandman* #16 (June 1990), New York: DC Comics. Print.

_____ (w), Kelley Jones (p), and Malcolm Jones III (i). "Season of Mists: Part One." *The Sandman* #22 (Jan. 1991), New York: DC Comics. Print.

_____ (w), Kelley Jones (p), and Malcolm Jones III (i). "Season of Mist: Part Two." *The Sandman* #23 (Feb. 1991), New York: DC Comics. Print.

_____ (w), Kelley Jones (p), and George Pratt (i). "Season of Mists: Part Five." *The Sandman* #26 (May 1991), New York: DC Comics. Print.

_____ (w), Mike Dringenberg (p), and George Pratt (i). "Season of Mists: Part Seven." *The Sandman* #28 (July 1991), New York: DC Comics. Print.

_____ (w), Teddy Kristiansen (p, i). "The Kindly Ones: Part Eight." *Sandman* #64 (Nov. 1994), New York: DC Comics. Print.

_____ (w) Marc Hempel (p), Richard Case (i). "The Kindly Ones: Part Eleven" *Sandman* #67 (Feb. 1995), New York: DC Comics. Print.

Gaiman, Neil, and Dave McKean. *MirrorMask.* New York: HarperCollins, 2005. Print.

Gaiman, Neil, and Michael Reaves. *InterWorld.* New York: Eos, 2008. Print.

Goodyear, Dana. "Kid Goth." *The New Yorker Online.* 25 Jan. 2010. Web. 12 Aug. 2011.

Gould, Stephen Jay. *Rocks of Ages.* New York: Ballantine, 1999. Print.

Greene, Brian. *The Fabric of the Universe.* New York: Alfred A. Knopf, 2004. Print.

Guth, Alan H. "Inflationary Universe: A Possible Solution to the Horizon and Flatness Problems." *Physical Review D* 23 (1981): 347 – 56. Print.

Hawking, Stephen. "Sixty Years in a Nutshell." *The Future of Theoretical Physics and Cosmology.* Eds. G.W. Gibbons, E.P.S. Shellard, and S.J. Rankin. Cambridge: Cambridge University Press, 2003. 105–17. Print.

Keller, Evelyn Fox. *Reflections on Gender and Science.* New Haven: Yale University Press, 1985. Print.

Lakoff, Robin Tolmach. *Language and a Woman's Place.* New York: Octagon Books.

Magueijo, João. *Faster Than the Speed of Light.* Cambridge, MA: Perseus 2003. Print.
Pease, Roland. "Brane New World." *Nature* 411 (2001): 986–88. Print.
Pullman, Philip. *His Dark Materials Omnibus.* New York: Knopf, 2007. Print.
Roszak, Theodore. *The Gendered Atom.* Berkeley: Conari Press, 1999. Print.
Sagan, Carl. *The Demon-haunted World.* New York: Ballantine, 1997. Print.
Smolin, Lee. *The Trouble with Physics.* Boston: Houghton Mifflin, 2006. Print.
Tolkien, J.R.R. *The Book of Lost Tales, Part One.* Boston: Houghton Mifflin, 1984. Print.
Tryon, Edward P. "Is the Universe a Vacuum Fluctuation?" *Nature* 246 (1973): 396–97.
   Print
Vilenkin, Alexander. "Creation of Universes From Nothing." *Physics Letters B* 117 (1982):
   25–28. Print.

About the Contributors

Lanette **Cadle** is an associate professor of English at Missouri State University. Her scholarly work includes the articles "Sweet Monsters: Feminism and Blurred Gender in Rose O'Neill's Paris Exhibition" and "Plagiarism and Technophobia: Fighting the Fear." Her poetry has appeared in several literary journals including *Connecticut Review*.

Sarah **Cantrell** is a gender studies scholar and an English instructor at Georgia Perimeter College. She is completing a Ph.D. at Georgia State University in 19th-century British literature. Her dissertation, "Sister Group Novels and the Nineteenth-Century Cult of Family," explores Victorian sororal dynamics.

Emily **Capettini** is pursuing a Ph.D. in English with concentrations in creative writing and science fiction at the University of Louisiana at Lafayette. She is fiction editor for *Rougarou: An Online Literary Journal*, and her creative work has appeared in *The Battered Suitcase*.

Renata **Dalmaso** is a Ph.D. candidate in English at the Universidade Federal de Santa Catarina, Brazil. Her dissertation, which engages authors ranging from Leslie Feinberg to Alison Bechdel, investigates the range of queer and gender studies when dealing with gender-incoherent subjects.

Aaron **Drucker** received his master's degree from Hofstra University and is completing his Ph.D. at Claremont Graduate University. His research centers on the abrupt transitions between humor and horror in revenge tragedy and the fun had by Jacobean audiences. A lifelong comic-book collector, he owns two complete first edition runs of Gaiman's *Sandman*. He is writing a monograph on Pixar's early films.

Coralline **Dupuy** wrote her master's thesis on the evolution of vampire novel paradigms in the late 20th century. Her teaching areas are Victorian detective fiction, 19th-century literature, Young Adult fiction, and translation. The topic of her Ph.D. thesis (NUI Galway, Ireland) is the figure of the mentor in 19th-century Gothic fiction and detective novels.

Kristine **Larsen** is a professor of physics and astronomy at Central Connecticut State University. She is widely published on women in the history of astronomy, astronomy in the works of J.R.R. Tolkien, and the use of math and science in various television series and films, and has worked for years to debunk the December 21, 2012, End of the World scenarios.

Elizabeth **Law** is a feminist, academic and author whose work focuses on the depiction of women in contemporary retellings of folk and fairy tale fiction. She has studied and taught at Rutgers University–Newark, where she earned her master's degree in English with a concentration in women's and gender studies. She discovered the *Sandman* comics as an undergraduate at Westminster College in Salt Lake City.

Rachel R. **Martin** teaches composition and American literature at Northern Virginia Community College. Her teaching interests encompass English, women's, gender, and sexuality studies, cultural studies and identity politics. Her research focuses on moments of revolt and resistance in American postmodern literature and popular culture. She is continually looking for the potential disruption of the patriarchal discourse.

Jennifer **McStotts** is an independent scholar and writer who lectures on speculative fiction and environmental writing at the University of Arizona. She earned an MFA in creative writing, and she has poetry, essays and reviews published in *Re)verb*, *Potomac Review*, and *CutThroat*. In addition, she is a contributor and editor of *Terrain.org: A Journal of the Built & Natural Environments*, and she blogs regularly at *jennifermcstotts.com*.

Justin **Mellette** is a University Graduate Fellow at Pennsylvania State University where he is pursuing his doctorate in 20th century American literature. His research interests also include African American literature, Caribbean literature and, of course, comics and graphic novels.

Monica **Miller** is a Ph.D. student in the English Department at Louisiana State University interested in Southern literature and gender theory. She has a 2010 M.A. from the University of Tennessee–Knoxville. Her work includes "Gothic Revelations of Marriage in *The Witch of Ravensworth* and *The Horrors of Oakendale Abbey*" (*Studies in Gothic Fiction*) and "A Loa in These Hills: Voudou and the Ineffable in Lee Smith's *On Agate Hill*" (*Journal of Appalachian Studies*).

Tara **Prescott** is a lecturer in Writing Programs at UCLA. She received her Ph.D. in English, specializing in 20th-century American literature, from Claremont Graduate University. Her recent publications have been featured in *European Joyce Studies* and *Women's Studies: An Interdisciplinary Journal*.

Danielle **Russell** is an instructor in the English Department at Glendon College specializing in children's, Victorian, and 20th-century American literature. Her publications include *Between the Angle and the Curve: Mapping Gender, Race, Space, and Identity in Cather and Morrison*; "Immeasurable Yearnings: The Legacy of the Landscape in Cather's *The Song of the Lark*" (*Dialogue Literary Studies Series*) and "Familiarity Breeds a Following: Transcending the Formulaic in the Snicket Series" (*Telling Children's Stories*).

Jessica **Walker** completed her Ph.D. at the University of Georgia in 2009 and is an assistant professor of early modern literature at Alabama A&M University. Her research interests include early modern women's autobiography, the Gothic, and film adaptation.

Agata **Zarzycka** is an assistant professor and a member of the Center for Young People's Literature and Culture at the Institute of English Studies of the University of Wrocław, Poland. Her 2007 Ph.D. disertation was titled "World of Darkness: Role-Playing Games as a Multidimensional Space of Interaction between Literary Theory and Practice." She is head of the Council of the Game Research Association of Poland.

Index